STONE COLD GUILTY

The People v. Scott Lee Peterson

Loretta Dillon

*To my mother, Kathleen, who always believed in me;
to the "misfits," without whose constant encouragement,
humor, inspiration and resourcefulness I would still be writing
verse on cocktail napkins;
and to Laci, whose invincible spirit brought us all together.*

INTRODUCTION

Traditionally, true crime books are written in retrospect often years after a trial, and authors have to cull through court documents, trial transcripts, police reports, libraries and archives. They have to track down and interview witnesses, investigators, lawyers, families of the victims and accused, and rely on faulty memories and sketchy information.

With the advent of the Internet, however, numerous crime forums, message boards and Web logs created the opportunity to follow a criminal case live from the earliest news reports through the verdict and aftermath. The age of instant communication has changed the course of crime reporting forever.

Web logs (popularly known as "blogs") are by design personal journals published on the Internet covering the gamut of every subject imaginable. Blogs have become a reliable source for news, political discussion, inside information, and investigative reporting, and often scoop mainstream media because of their real-time, spontaneous format. Popular blogs attract a loyal readership and often include a lively discussion forum, with thousands of daily visitors and regular updates.

This book is comprised of selected entries of my Web log, "Observations of a Misfit" (*www.misfitting.com*) from December 29, 2002, just after Laci Peterson disappeared, to the dramatic verdict and death sentence of Scott Peterson in March 2005. It is a pioneer work that incorporates real-time facts and analysis, law review, editorial, personal insight, commentary on the misinformation of the media coverage, and relevant comparisons to contemporaneous spousal murder cases.

Most viewers interested in the Peterson case relied on television, print media and tabloids for information, which was often unreliable, erroneous, biased or sensationalized to affect ratings. Because of the widespread media attention to Peterson's trial, the court documents (motions, replies, transcripts and evidence) became available to the media through Web sites that Stanislaus and San Mateo Counties posted to accommodate the demand. Nevertheless, based on the reporting and pundit opinion broadcast from May 2003 to the present, it was apparent that most of the media representatives were not reading the transcripts or court documents, or consulting the California criminal code.

This book picks up where cable TV programs, Court TV, magazine features and other books on the case leave off. It is my hope that thoughtful readers, often misled and misinformed throughout the trial, will witness the magnificent story of good triumphing over evil by sharing my journey in *Stone Cold Guilty*.

CHAPTER 1: THE EARLY DAYS

December 29, 2002 – March 24, 2003

DECEMBER 29, 2002
SCOTT PETERSON: MURDERER?

Laci Peterson, a 27-year-old woman who is almost eight months pregnant with her first child, disappeared from Modesto, California on Christmas Eve. It was only yesterday I heard about it, since it's not a local story, and I rarely watch cable TV news networks or read much past the front page of CNN's Web site. I had to search the Internet for information. I found a California newspaper online, the *Modesto Bee*, where I spent some time reading the past few days' reports. I probably wouldn't have heard about Laci Peterson if not for staying late at church for orchestra rehearsal last evening. Shortly after we disassembled, when people request prayers for family illnesses, recent deaths, or other concerns, one of the soloists in the choir mentioned that there was a pregnant woman missing in California since Christmas, and asked that we would keep her in our prayers. She didn't even know the woman's name, but it piqued my curiosity. When I got home, I did some investigating.

Articles detailing the circumstances, and photographs of Laci and Scott Peterson holding wine glasses in front of a Christmas tree aroused my natural cynicism, and from my extensive reading of crime literature and FBI profiling, I tend to believe that the mysterious, sudden "disappearance" of a low-risk individual with a bright future and supportive family is probably a murder victim, and her husband the prime suspect.

While scouring cyberspace for updates, I found many articles that described a massive search effort in Modesto including police, K9 dogs, horses, hundreds of volunteers and a sizable reward. Meanwhile, it appears that Laci's husband, Scott, has wisely retained the services of a local defense attorney.

Who are the usual suspects in a case like this, and what would be their motives? If Scott killed her, maybe it was because he didn't want the baby, or the child support and disenfranchisement of a divorce. Maybe he has a girlfriend and never wanted the pregnancy and has resented it all this time. (Or it isn't his child, speculated on Internet crime boards.) His motives: fear, greed or jealousy.

If the perpetrator is a random psychopath, he hates women and saw the opportunity to abduct Laci in broad daylight on a holiday eve where most people are home. I don't think so.

A baby ring: similar to what happened in nearby Ravenna, Ohio, in 2000, someone could have targeted Laci because she was pregnant and abducted her to take the baby. Although rare, these types of crimes are normally attempted by women who cannot have children and pretend to be pregnant while stalking their victim.

On the other hand, spousal murder is fairly common, and the husband, who is not usually a career criminal, leaves incriminating evidence and often confesses to the crime. If they find Laci's body, the odds are good that the trail will lead right back to Scott Peterson.

JANUARY 18, 2003
ANOTHER GENERATION

Is Scott Peterson the new Jeffrey McDonald? I see some interesting parallels to the McDonald case. In both, we have a "loving" husband and father (or in this case, father-to-be.) Both sides of the family supported the husband until future revelations. If not for his father-in-law's dogged pursuit of the case, McDonald would have remained free. Laci's stepfather, prior to today's news, was fiercely defending Scott's innocence. Today on CNN, he changed his tune and mentioned that he had confronted Scott about a possible affair, which Scott denied.

Nobody could believe that either McDonald or Peterson could commit murder.

While McDonald originally fabricated an outlandish story about the events, Peterson has kept a low profile and refused interviews. McDonald failed his polygraph. Peterson either has already failed one, refused to take one, or will fail one if he does. Neither man had a criminal record or a history of abuse. Both men thought that they were too smart to get caught. While McDonald panicked after killing his wife, and had to kill his children to create the illusion that it was the work of some crazed, cult hippies, Peterson planned the murder and has meticulously covered his tracks.

No biographical information about Peterson's personality has surfaced yet, but I suspect he is a narcissist with control issues, has delusions of grandeur, and a lacks a conscience. I also believe he has been unfaithful to his wife throughout their marriage. Like McDonald, Peterson will attract a group of supporters and women who will proclaim his innocence and invite him to dinner parties. After all, this is California.

A few questions to ponder: where did the police get the pictures of Scott and his female companion taken in mid-December? Did Scott launch the boat on December 24? Could he have come back home after the 10 a.m. phone call (thus establishing an alibi) to pick up Laci, asking her to go out on the boat? That would explain the purse and keys left in the house. Did he dump her body in the Pacific Ocean? Does he consider the life insurance policy a "nest egg" he can collect after Laci is declared dead (years later) if he isn't convicted of her murder? Was "the other woman" in on this?

On other sites, I have read that Scott may have had (or still has) a woman in Los Angeles with whom he has been seen since the year 2000. Other scuttlebutt around cyberspace claims that Scott either refused a polygraph, or failed one. The police are keeping these particular cards close to their chests, since if an arrest is imminent, they need to keep the most damaging evidence to themselves. Another rumor has Scott buying two plane tickets to Paris. This would be relatively easy to check.

If I were investigating this murder (missing person at this point), I would study Scott's cell phone records for the past year, looking for recurring phone numbers, and review his credit card statements. Since he is a salesman, he probably makes most of his purchases on plastic; thus there will be a substantial paper trail.

Peterson's response to the allegations that he took out a recent life insurance policy on Laci and is having an affair were predictably indignant: "In a short phone conversation with CNN affiliate KTVU-TV in Oakland, California, Peterson called the allegations of an affair, originally reported in the *Modesto Bee*, a bunch of lies."

What did you expect him to say? Where there's smoke, there's fire.

JANUARY 24, 2003
INTERESTING DEVELOPMENTS

Tonight on CNN, the Modesto police held a brief press conference that featured Scott Peterson's girlfriend, Amber Frey. Ms. Frey made a statement telling the world that she did, indeed, have a "romantic" relationship with Scott Peterson, but that he had told her he was "unmarried." She could have sold the pictures of her and Scott to the tabloids, but chose, instead, to go directly to the police with her information. She requested that her friends and acquaintances refrain from discussing her with the media for fame or profit. She sent her apologies to Laci's family for any pain she had caused them, and she asked that the public respect her privacy, and that she was a single mom with a two-year-old child. What is the story behind Amber Frey?

My initial reaction when I saw Ms. Frey appear behind the podium and identify herself was, "Are you kidding me?" It's not that Amber isn't attractive, but she looked disheveled, frightened, and unexpectedly plain compared to the stunning Laci Peterson.

What about Scott's saying he was single? In every picture I have seen of him, he is wearing a rather sizeable gold band on his left ring finger. Either she's lying, or he took it off during trysts with his various girlfriends, and remembered to put it back on before he got home. This is relevant. A guy like that has had lots of practice. And why would he go to all that trouble for a mousy single mom with a toddler? How many more of these women are going to surface? Has he been philandering throughout the marriage?

Even if it turns out Scott had nothing to do with Laci's disappearance, he has shown himself to be the complete cad by cheating on his pregnant wife. This won't help his public relations. Snippets from various news sources around the Net include details about a burglary at the Peterson home recently, Scott's public behavior, and some very interesting potential developments in the forensic arena.

On Monday, police revealed that the Peterson home was burglarized while Scott was in Southern California. Peterson reported the break-in Sunday night. Police said burglars entered the home through a window sometime between Thursday and Sunday.

"Detectives don't believe the burglary is connected to the Peterson case," said Detective Doug Ridenour, spokesman for the Modesto Police Department.[1]

---

[1] Giblin, Patrick, "Police Probe Theft at Peterson Home," *Modesto Bee*, January 21, 2003

Perhaps it was a member of Laci's family or one of her friends who broke in to get some of her things, like her jewelry, sentimental items, or even baby items. Whoever it was knew them.

Also on Monday, talking with Mornings on 2, former FBI Profiler Candice Delong said some of the developments have piqued her interest. Particularly, a decision by Scott Peterson to change the focus of the search of his wife from Modesto to Southern California.

Although Delong is not involved directly in the case, she said news reports have led her to draw up some possible scenarios.

"Well, a couple things come to mind," she said. "There doesn't seem to be any sense in going down there (Southern California). He says he's expanding the search, but why L.A.? The most logical place to expand would be the (San Francisco) Bay Area. And he also said next weekend he may go to San Diego. That's pretty close to the Mexican border. I'm wondering if he's thinking of splitting to Mexico."

"Another possibility is that he is trying to draw the search away from the Modesto area. Possibly because he is concerned, if he was involved, that here may be a discovery there."[2]

Some case followers have questioned the reasoning behind his going to San Diego as well. If that is his hometown, he may be going there to get away from the publicity in Modesto and to be on home turf. I don't think he's going to run to Mexico, at least not yet.

Since he began talking with the media last week, Scott mostly has given one- and two-sentence comments, mostly about his plans to keep searching for his wife and child. He has ended most interviews quickly and abruptly.[3]

Mr. Congeniality, he's not.

Some readers think the "closed drapes" the morning of the disappearance is a bigger indication of Scott's guilt than his affair or the insurance policy. It's important to know what his personal life insurance was worth. It would be suspicious if Laci's policy were greater than his, since he is the breadwinner of the family and if something happened to him, he would want to provide for their child.

Other information and unsubstantiated rumors include:

- Scott was planning to sell the house in Modesto and move to San Diego. Scott had more than one affair. Scott has presented a new alibi for his whereabouts on December 24.

---

[2] KTVU staff, "Peterson Search Goes High-Tech," KTVU.com, January 22, 2003
[3] Ibid.

- Scott was casting a concrete anchor prior to the disappearance, presumably for his boat.
- The baby is not Scott's, and the couple had infertility problems for three years prior to the pregnancy.

JANUARY 30
THE MODESTO CONNECTION

Several Modesto residents have e-mailed me and posted comments regarding rumors, gossip, and theories surrounding Laci Peterson's disappearance, and they have passed along suspicious whisperings among locals about Peterson's actions in the early days of the case.

On Christmas Eve, Scott could not quite get his alibi straight. No one knew he had a fishing boat. The Peterson's home smelled like bleach when the doors were open, and people who were in the area mentioned that to the police. Supposedly, a bucket was found with residue of wet cement, and Peterson admitted that he used it as a mold for anchors.

There is a video from a local sporting goods store (Copeland Sports) that shows him buying scuba weights or ankle weights. The police originally thought the files found on his computer were a deliberate attempt to mislead the investigation and had nothing to do with the crime. Insiders claim that cops who interviewed Peterson said he "made their blood run cold," and one of the cops on the scene described him as "the one who's hot is cold as hell."

One item found in the computer search was rumored to have been a site that dealt with body disposal methods. According to early surveillance, the Fresno area, Bakersfield, and the Berkley Marina were places Peterson frequented. The cops in charge of surveillance joked among themselves that Peterson was oblivious of being tailed for some time. After a few days, Scott stopped returning phone calls from friends and began to distance himself from everyone more and more, and locals interpreted it as "disinterested detachment" rather than grief. It was common knowledge that he went golfing instead of participating in the searches. Some saw it as his attempt to stay busy and to take his mind off things, but then it began to unnerve them. His mind obviously wasn't on finding Laci, and the consensus among Modestans was that he wasn't searching because he already knew where she was.

FEBRUARY 2, 2003
THE BERKELEY MARINA

A reader from the Bay Area sent several excellent photographs of the Berkeley Marina today where she went to scout out the site where Scott Peterson claims he launched his 14-foot boat the afternoon of Christmas Eve (the day his wife, Laci, allegedly disappeared) to go fishing.

The first photo is of the automatic pay box where boaters buy a launch ticket they place on the inside of their windshield to show they have paid for the day. There are "missing" posters of Laci Peterson on the pay box and the pole next to it.

The second picture is the berm above the launch. From this view, it is clear that there are many boats docked within view of the launch, and there would have likely been someone on board a boat that morning, either doing maintenance or even preparing for a sail who might have seen Peterson if he really launched his boat that day. The other thing that strikes me in the picture is the lack of privacy in the area, and no way to know if anyone was around. It seems an improbable spot for Scott to bring Laci's body.

Other Web sites discussing the case include descriptions of psychic visions that clairvoyants have had about Laci's disappearance. Some see Laci buried near Yosemite, near an unpainted structure and there is a teddy bear with her. The seers also predict she will be found soon. One psychic researcher claims to have received messages from spirits through a method called "electronic voice phenomena" (EVP) that revealed to her that Laci's body was tethered to the fifth buoy near the Albany Bulb, a landfill between Berkeley and Richmond on the east coast of the bay.

Where did Scott buy bait to go sturgeon fishing? Nobody has reported seeing him at the marina. How did he have time to stop at the office to drop off the umbrellas, make the 88-mile trip to the marina, launch the boat, fish, take the boat out, drive back to Modesto and arrive home by 4:30? Has anyone timed this trip? This story is full of holes.

The launch ticket is useless as an alibi without an eyewitness, because it doesn't prove he was at the marina. According to locals, you can drive or walk up to the launch ticket dispenser, put in a $5 bill, take the ticket and drive off. There is nobody there to validate it, and since it's time-stamped and good through 11:59 pm of any given day, Peterson could have bought a ticket to provide an alibi, never launched the boat, and drove somewhere else to dispose of the body or come back and launched the boat later. I am not convinced that he launched the boat or went fishing at all. He used the launch ticket to prove he was in Berkeley and not Modesto at the time and never actually went fishing, or he had gotten rid of the body before he got there and went out for a very short time.

The picture of the boat ramp shows how a boat would be backed into the water from a trailer, and then how a boat would navigate around the breakwater of the marina to enter the Bay. We have to ask ourselves: is this Laci's grave?

FEBRUARY 14, 2003
THE EVIDENCE (SO FAR)

Modesto police aren't talking, but everybody else is.

Tonight I watched a CNN rebroadcast of an earlier *Larry King Live* with Laci Peterson's family represented by her step-dad, Ron Grantski, her brother, Brent, and her sister, Amy. They provided some answers to a few questions we had about Laci, Scott's boat, forensic evidence, Scott's truck, events of the evening of the 24th, and other compelling information that leads one to believe that an arrest may be only weeks away, or sooner if a body is found.

The latest facts:

What the police took on December 26: Scott's truck, the boat and trailer, a vacuum cleaner, the mop Scott used to clean the kitchen floor, a blue tarp, the computer(s), possibly clothing out of the dryer, personal effects, the Berkeley launch ticket, phone records, probably bank records, medical information from the obstetrician, photographs, and samples from the swimming pool.

Originally, there was a rumor that there was no evidence of salt water on the boat, but the police later refuted this; however, the Modesto police are not exactly forthcoming.

The fact that the police continue to hold Scott's truck made most of the legal panel on *Larry King Live* (Nancy Grace, Wendy Murphy, and Mark Klaas) believe that it contains some blood evidence, maybe even Laci's. Wendy Murphy and Nancy Grace discussed that perhaps the blood is being analyzed for the hormone levels to determine if it came from a pregnant woman. Scott's blood was found in the truck, and he as much as admitted to this in his interview with Diane Sawyer.

Scott was cleaning the house when the police arrived. He had changed his clothes and was washing his "fishing" outfit. The lingering rumor that he used bleach in his housekeeping came from several sources.

The Peterson family (Scott's) is insisting this is a kidnapping motivated by Laci's pregnancy. The Rocha family is organizing searches for Laci's body in local waterways upon advice and guidance from the MPD.

Inferences:

Scott weighted Laci's body down with concrete or other weights. The police must have some evidence or assumption about this, or why else focus on the water? The outfit Laci was said to have been wearing on December 23 (by her sister, Amy) was a black blouse with cream dotted pattern and cream-colored pants. This may be very important to keep in mind.

I believe Scott planned the murder and has been stewing over this for many months. As the youngest in his family, he was used to people either letting him get his way, overlooking a lot of the details, and spoiling him to some extent. He definitely demonstrates some narcissistic personality traits, as in his blatant disregard for what people think about his behavior, and his remarkable skills at self-preservation and immediate gratification superseding his duty, along with his peculiar lack of grief and empathy, and his apparent belief that he is above consequence.

Laci, a very real, very loved, beautiful, vivacious, emotionally deep woman, eclipsed vacant Scott on a daily basis. He felt emasculated by her superiority, which is why he was unfaithful to her. His infidelity was a passive-aggressive form of undermining her power over him. The sale of her car, the attempt to sell the house, the removal of his wedding ring, and (probably) the disposal of her body were all attempts to eliminate her power over him. He wanted to delete all traces of her from his life. No doubt, the pregnancy was yet another usurpation of his ego, keeping the spotlight on her, and the threat of another person (the baby) taking attention and focus off him for years to come. Perhaps this was unbearable for him, and he cracked. Considering Scott is not a career criminal, he has probably made a number of mistakes; assuming, also, his myopic, self-absorbed concept of reality, he cannot see what others see and doesn't understand the relevance of his behavior. We can also hope that he sabotages himself.

FEBRUARY 18, 2003
THE SECOND SEARCH

Today the Modesto police obtained a "sealed" search warrant for Scott and Laci Peterson's home in the La Loma section of Modesto. The search was allegedly prompted by "witnesses" who may have seen Scott on December 24 or other dates where his whereabouts were in question. The police seized his new Dodge Ram Truck, which he has only owned for a couple of weeks. Reporting indicates that fresh probable cause would be required to obtain a second, broader search warrant; however, the affidavits for the warrants are sealed from the public.

Reporting also suggests that land searches (presumably for the body or other evidence) are under way rather than the continued focus on fresh waterways (lakes, reservoirs and rivers around Stanislaus County).

9

According to sources, Scott's work-related documents were seized, which might include call reports, inventory, sales reports, receipts, expense reports, and other documentation that would account for Scott's whereabouts or familiar territory during the time frame. Laci's sister, Amy, was on the scene at the search, and her presence there suggests that there was clothing or other intimate items being sought that she may recognize. She may also only have been there as a representative of Laci's family to observe or note if anything in the house was missing or out of place. The police are downplaying the search, and with the warrant sealed, it makes it impossible for the press to know what the search was designed to uncover, or what specific items they were seeking. A camera shot showed an investigator under a crawl space with a flashlight, inspecting the floorboards above.

Scott Peterson has not been officially named a "suspect," but he is considered a "person of interest" at this time. (No kidding.) Scott showed up for the second search sporting a new goatee, which lent him a sinister cast compared to his clean-cut, chubby look in December. Now he resembles a junior version of David Westerfield. Nevertheless, his change in appearance is completely in character for a narcissist who constantly morphs his image as part of his chameleon nature. Scott did not look pleased, in spite of his protestations to Ted Rowlands that he "wasn't upset" about the search and that the police are only helping him find his wife.

The searching ended for today but will reconvene tomorrow morning, according to the Modesto police. They plan to conclude the search tomorrow. It was suggested on *Larry King Live* that the police planted a GPS sensor on Scott's new truck, which may have led them to new evidence or fresh probable cause. I agree with Nancy Grace in the caution of naming Scott a "suspect," since that would legally confer an entirely new status upon him, which may be premature at this juncture. Once they officially name him a suspect, they may taint the case if the evidence is faulty, thus predisposing to a mistrial or a preponderance of reasonable doubt. Trying a murder without a body is not without precedence. Forensic science is credible and accurate enough to contribute significant damning evidence, and if motive, means and opportunity are solid, there have been cases presented and won without a *corpus delecti*.

Where is the clothing Laci was wearing on December 23? Those clothes (black blouse with cream polka dots or flowers and cream pants) and also the clothing she was allegedly wearing on the 24th (white top, black pants) and the black coat.

Does Scott have an alibi for the evening of the 23rd, and verification of his whereabouts all day the 24th? There may be conflicting witness testimony to both, including possible gasoline purchases via credit card, cell phone calls, or evidence in the boat trailer or truck tires of debris, gravel, mud, sand or water.

Concerning the concrete, Scott has changed this story so many times nobody knows the truth. First, he said the empty concrete bags belonged to the pool maintenance people (who denied it). Then he said he uses concrete for projects around the home. From photographs of the exterior of the house and the patio, there doesn't appear to be any recent concrete patches, which are fairly obvious.

Laci's due date was February 10, no matter what Scott said or why. There was never any doubt that this baby was his. Speculation otherwise is totally without merit and borders on defamation.

Were pool chemicals used for clean up, or did he douse the pool to have the neighbors notice the smell of bleach?

Scott raced home this morning (from where?) at 7 am to arrive before the cops, which means he was tipped off. Unfortunately for him, they beat him there.

Is there evidence in the new Dodge truck, possible movement of weapons, chemicals, or clothing used in the crime? Was there any evidence in the Ford truck seized in the first search of flora and fauna of different locations, gravel in the tires, salt or algae from water sources, plant material, blood, hair, nails, body fluid, paint, tools, rags, hand prints on the windows, other residue in the truck bed or tool box? Has anyone yet come forward that saw Peterson at the Berkeley Marina on Christmas Eve or on any other date? Among the boat, the extended cab and the Greenlee toolbox on Peterson's Ford truck, there were several places to easily obscure a body.

FEBRUARY 19, 2003
UNANSWERED QUESTIONS

Tonight on *Larry King Live*, Janey Peterson, Scott's sister-in-law, was a featured guest along with a legal panel, including Nancy Grace, a former prosecutor from Atlanta; Ted Rowlands, a reporter from San Francisco's KTVU; Dr. Henry Lee, a forensic and crime scene investigator; Mark Klaas, father of child murder victim Polly Klaas; and a useful idiot, "high-profile" defense attorney, Mark Geragos.

When Larry asked Janey, "What is Scott's theory?" Janey avoided answering the questions. Instead, she talked about how "we" (she and the mouse in her pocket) were still looking for Laci and that "we" were still keeping all the options open and considering all theories. Not once did she mention what Scott thinks. When she was offended by Ted Rowlands using the word "bizarre" to describe Scott's behavior, Larry asked her if Scott was normally an "emotionally detached" person. She replied he was not and claims that the media have misrepresented him. She described the situation as "unreal," and that there is no textbook to define normal behavior for everyone; but she slipped up with "He's Scott," as if that should explain everything.

Janey is sticking to the Peterson party line that Laci's "abduction" had to do with her pregnancy. She defended the second Laci tip line by noting that it is toll-free and anonymous and that "all information is forwarded to the Modesto Police," which some of us have read otherwise on the official Laci Peterson Web site and other sites. She defended Scott's trading in Laci's Land Rover because "he needed a truck for work," and that the couple had discussed replacing the Rover to get something "more suitable for a baby." She thought it was entirely possible and in character for Laci to keep the knowledge of Scott's affair to herself, but then she backpedaled a little and said she could see Laci going "either way." To most of us, this seems ridiculous.

Janey trotted out the old "sturgeon fishing" story as a viable recreational pursuit on Christmas Eve, 90 miles from home. After she found out about Scott's affair with Amber Frey, she said she told him she was going to "slug him and hug him." Slug him I can understand, but hug him?

She also insisted that Scott and Laci had a "wonderful relationship" and implied that the affair would not have damaged it. With regard to the police requiring a warrant to search the house, everyone had his own opinion about that, but both Mark Klaas and Nancy Grace think that a "consented search" would have been entirely reasonable if Scott were not hiding something. Janey defended the warrant and even suggested that Scott was not notified to give his consent to search before it was issued. I assume that the police would obtain a warrant, regardless of Scott's cooperation.

When asked about cement found, once again Janey did not answer the question, and instead said something about his fertilizer samples being liquid and his doing projects around the house. There was mention of the rumor that there were 55-gallon drums ordered and were they accounted for? Dr. Lee assured the panel that the police would know if they existed and verify their origin. Scott's refusal to take a polygraph was defended by Geragos and Janey, but deemed suspicious and uncooperative to Nancy and Mark Klaas.

It is curious that none of Scott's direct relatives (brothers, sister, parents, or even he) appear on these widely viewed shows in his defense. Why did Janey Peterson embrace this onerous responsibility? Doug Ridenour, spokesperson for the Modesto Police Department (shown between breaks on a tape feed) stated that the investigation is going well and that they are looking to either eliminate Scott as a suspect or "move in a different direction.

FEBRUARY 20, 2003
"I CAN'T THINK OF A BETTER TIME TO HAVE A LAWYER!"

...*thus spake* Mark Geragos, a frequent (and somewhat self-aggrandizing) commentator on the Peterson case on cable television news shows. He defended some famous people (unsuccessfully) lately, including Winona Ryder and Robert Downey, Jr. If Geragos is right, and Scott Peterson needs a lawyer, what would be the first advice competent counsel would offer Peterson regarding his behavior, his cooperation with law enforcement, his activities involving the search for Laci, his inconsistent statements, and any future remarks to the media?

Personally, I would advise Scott to at least fake being a bereaved husband. I would recommend he carry pepper spray and give himself a quick shot in the eyes any time he sees a television camera or reporters lurking. I would suggest he practice looking sad in the mirror, and take a crash course in acting. Then I would have him appear in his own defense on Larry King Live and shed some crocodile tears in front of Nancy Grace and continually refer to his "baby boy." Every third sentence out of his mouth should include, "Laci, I miss you, I love you, I'll never stop looking for you," and hang his head in shame when he is asked about Amber Frey. I would give him a script to memorize that would include telling everyone how stupid he was to go fishing that day, how Laci was the greatest thing that ever happened to him, and that he won't rest until her return.

I would have him call or visit the Modesto Police Department daily to inquire on new leads or the status of the investigation. If I suspected he was guilty, I would advise him to refuse a polygraph "at this time," and leave it at that. I would caution him never to deviate from our script or conduct any more interviews. If I thought he was innocent, I would arrange a private polygraph, and if the results were advantageous to his defense, I would let the police conduct one as well. I don't expect him to confess or to reveal the whereabouts of Laci's body, but rather will deny any involvement in her disappearance until the bitter end; and I mean *the bitter end.*

FEBRUARY 25, 2003
STALEMATE OR STEALTH?

On CNN's *Larry King Live* tonight, the Rocha family (Ron Grantski, Sharon, Brent and Amy) were briefly interviewed and took a few viewers' phone calls. The Rocha family gave me the impression that although they were subdued and tight-lipped about the investigation, they seemed more positive and less distraught than in previous appearances.

Both Ron and Sharon in separate comments said that "someone knows something," and that "somebody should come forward" and tell the police where Laci is and what happened to her. I suspect they were referring to Scott. I found it curious that Ron described Scott's anticipation of pending fatherhood as "noncommittal." I also noticed that Brent Rocha seemed pleased tonight, as if he knows quite a bit more than he is letting on about the direction the investigation is taking. He announced that there were no more organized searches planned, and that they are contemplating a "different strategy."

Amy Rocha could not comment on the role she played in last week's search of the Peterson house, but reiterated that Scott's behavior was "disturbing." Ron praised the Modesto police as doing a "heck of a job," and that the family has been well informed, but that there were "some things they [the family] won't talk about."

When questioned by a caller, nobody knew who introduced Scott to Amber Frey. Scott's excuse for attempting to sell the couple's house was "basically ridiculous," according to Brent. In response to another call, the family commented that they had not considered using a psychic at this time.

When the panel came on (Nancy Grace, Mark Geragos, Mark Klaas, Dr. Henry Lee and Ted Rowlands) the main issue was whether this investigation was at a "standstill" or a "dead end." Dr. Lee reminded the panel that forensic investigation is time-consuming and painstaking, and that many items that were taken from the home would require microscopic examination.

Ted Rowlands stated that Scott was currently not in Modesto, but that he was confident that the police were "keeping tabs on him." He tried to inject some hope by restating that the police were working methodically, continuing their searches of the vast areas, and have a game plan. Nancy Grace was optimistic that the second search of the house, and the subsequent search of the storage facility implied that the investigation was "honing in" on Scott.

Mark Geragos seems to be subtly promoting the "Let's Frame Poor Scott" theory and minimized the issue of whether Peterson took a lie detector test or not. Nancy Grace called him on his insistence that a lie detector test "means nothing," in spite of his having used successful polygraph test results with clients like Gary Condit when it suited him. Geragos, like other defense attorney pundits, talks out of both sides of his mouth.

Mark Klaas said that if Scott Peterson took and passed a polygraph, it would go "a long way in the right direction," presumably to relieve him from further intense scrutiny. The panel agreed that Laci's family is probably guarded with their opinions because of their relationship with law enforcement, and that the family knows much more than they are permitted to discuss.

FEBRUARY 27, 2003
DRAWING THE LINE

It is clear from recent news stories that the line between the Peterson family and the Rocha family has been drawn in the sand.

On the Rocha side, we have confidence and praise for the police, reserved comments about evidence and speculation, and palpable grieving and angst. Laci's family has conducted organized searches, hosted a widely read and well written Web site, appeared on numerous cable, national and local news programs, and has cooperated in every facet of the investigation.

On the Peterson side, we have distrust; accusations of harassment, illogical explanations, contradictions, a notable lack of grief, and more recently, an attempt to undermine the police investigation. The Petersons host a toll-free hotline that has been accused by sources close to the investigation of deliberately discounting tips that would indicate Scott's involvement. They have conducted no searches of which I am aware; their only spokesperson has been a sister-in-law, Janey, who isn't even an immediate family member, and recently, Scott's mother and father have spoken out, reiterating the *inconvenience* this case has become to their son.

The Petersons are building a public defense designed to establish reasonable doubt, regardless of logic, timeline, opportunity, probability or facts. Tonight on *Larry King Live*, Janey Peterson practically accused the Modesto police of being negligent in their duties and planting evidence, with her remark about the cement dust found in Scott's boat, implying that since the police have had the boat in custody all this time, they could have left the dust. She also misquoted Vivian Mitchell's statement regarding seeing a woman walking her dog that she thought was Laci. Instead of the actual quote, "There's that lady with the golden retriever," Janey quoted her as stating, "There's that pregnant lady with her dog." Janey also managed to forget the name of the former owner of the boat Scott bought (whose name, oddly enough, happens to be Peterson) by referring to him as "this guy."

By employing misquotes, misstatements, selective truths, and innuendo, the Petersons appear to be implementing an insidious campaign to damage the case against Scott, cast aspersions upon the investigators, and create a scenario unsupported by facts. The schism between the families is official.

FEBRUARY 28, 2003
THE MITCHELL SIGHTING

Thanks to a source in Modesto who sent me a detailed map of Dry Creek Park and the La Loma neighborhood where Laci walked the dog, it is obvious from the geography and topography that Laci, in her condition, did not walk the dog down the steep, muddy embankment a half block north of her home to the park, or the 15 blocks to pass the Mitchell's house by 10:00 the morning of December 24. According to the reports, octogenarian Vivian Mitchell saw a woman walking a golden retriever past her house while her husband was searching for a football game on television. Mr. Mitchell claims only to have seen the woman turning the corner when he looked out the window.

In order to pass the Mitchells' home on La Sombra heading south, Laci would have had to walk west along the edge of the park on an unpaved, marshy path past Kewin Park, a densely foliated, dangerous area known for a transient population, vandalism, and drug dealing. To approach the Mitchells' home from the north, Laci would have had to cross a very busy street (Maze) and walk the dog on streets without sidewalks.

When MSNBC's Dan Abrams asked Mr. Mitchell if he was aware that there were no football games broadcast on Christmas Eve, and that perhaps he and his wife had seen a different woman or had the dates confused, the Mitchells became more adamant that they had seen Laci and complained that the police were deliberately ignoring their calls.

MARCH 3, 2003
DEBUNKING THE MYTHS

The lack of recent real news regarding the Laci Peterson case has resulted in the invention and perpetuation of several fallacies. We can eliminate them with logic, evidence (or lack thereof) and sound reasoning.

- **Myth 1:** Laci was seen walking the dog on the morning of Christmas Eve.

- **Myth 2:** Laci is still alive, pregnant, and was abducted for her baby.

- **Myth 3:** The Modesto police are conspiring to frame Scott Peterson for his wife's murder.

- **Myth 4:** Scott Peterson's arrest is imminent.

Myth #1 has been addressed previously and does not require substantial rehashing. The alleged sightings of Laci on the morning of December 24 have been refuted by police investigation. The bloodhounds, incapable of any agenda, would have tracked Laci to the path she walked along the neighborhood or to Dry Creek Park. The current hullabaloo over the Mitchell sighting has already been

15

discredited. A story that began as a sighting of "that woman with the golden retriever" evolved to "that pregnant woman with the dog," and then to accounts that Bill Mitchell actually knew Laci personally. Pretty soon, we'll hear that Laci stopped in with a coffee cake and watched the first quarter of the (nonexistent) football game with the elderly Mitchells. To impugn incompetence on the Modesto police by accusing them of deliberately ignoring eyewitness accounts defies logic, reason and fact.

Myth #2: Unless Laci were a whale, elephant, or other large mammal, she cannot still be pregnant. Her mother-in-law's continual insistence of this is beyond biological reality. Theories that Laci was abducted for the baby have not one scintilla of evidence to support them. Assume someone took Laci for the baby: she was not due for another six weeks, which means that the baby would require special perinatal equipment to sustain life. We are supposed to suspend our disbelief that a kidnapper would possess such equipment. Keeping Laci alive for the duration of the pregnancy poses grave risks to the perpetrator(s), including the possibility of her escaping, getting ill and requiring medical treatment, contacting someone, or injuring herself to thwart their mission.

Myth #3: Based on common sense, local sources, and the national attention on this case, there has been no evidence to suggest that the Modesto police are conspiring to frame Scott Peterson. If such a conspiracy existed, it would be impossible to maintain due to the number of people involved required to keep a secret, and the dearth of leads that steer the investigation in a different direction from the primary person of interest: the husband.

Myth #4: Unless the general public has been completely kept in the dark, I don't see how an arrest is imminent at this time. I would prefer that this myth were true, but there is no substantiation from any reliable source from the investigation or behavior by police or Scott Peterson to support this recent media claim.

MARCH 5, 2003
UPGRADED TO HOMICIDE

At a press conference today, Doug Ridenour of the Modesto Police Department announced that law enforcement are now categorizing the Laci Peterson case as a homicide, and that $50,000 of the $500,000 reward money posted for Laci's safe return will be allocated to her location and recovery.

Kim Petersen (from the Sund-Carrington Foundation) read a statement from the Rocha family that emphasized that finding Laci is their first priority. The Rochas and the police believe that the reward may lead to information that will disclose what happened to Laci and where she is, which will end the "horrific nightmare" they have been experiencing since her disappearance. The Rochas stated they will never stop searching far Laci, and beg the person or persons who took her to "dig deep and show compassion" for the family. They encouraged anonymous letters or phone calls to expedite the discovery of her whereabouts. The family also thanked the media and public for their support throughout this ordeal.

Investigators must have reason to believe this is a homicide investigation and no longer a missing persons case. Doug Ridenour described it as a "violent homicide," which implies there is evidence to suggest foul play. The Laci Peterson Web site has changed its main page to read "$50,000 reward for her location and recovery." Will $50,000 provide enough incentive for someone who knows something to come forward?

MARCH 8, 2003
ANATOMY OF MOTIVE

The following excerpt is from John Douglas's book, *The Anatomy of Motive*. John Douglas is a former chief of the FBI's Investigative Support Unit and pioneered modern behavioral profiling of criminals.

We found that the men we studied seemed to realize early on, sometimes even as very young children, that the power to manipulate others gave them a sense of control that they felt was so lacking in their lives...after this power recognition is fantasy...of overcoming the problems of his life...eventually they do what they want because it makes them feel better.

What motivates many, if not most, of these guys is a desire for power and control that comes from a background where they felt powerless and out of control. Being able to manipulate, dominate and control a victim, to decide whether that victim lives or dies, or how that victim dies, makes them feel grandiose and superior, as they believe they are entitled to feel.[4]

How does Douglas's research apply to our current case?

Scott grew up in a big family, the youngest of seven, in a blended environment, with an older dad than his peers and may have felt powerless and learned to manipulate very early on. He may have been concurrently rejected and overprotected by his parents, which would create the perfect foundation for a narcissistic personality to emerge that compensated for his paradoxical feelings of entitlement and inadequacy.

We know very little about his adolescence, except from reports by his parents that he was competitive, a good student, and helpful. It is difficult to know when the point of no return occurred for Scott. Apparently, it may have evolved during his relationship with Laci. At some passage, if he committed the act in question, he became completely overwhelmed by his responsibilities as husband, father, and provider. He felt trapped, frustrated, resentful of his lack of freedom, and desired emancipation from this heavy yoke. It's possible his ego was continually bruised by Laci (and eventually, the baby), upstaging him at every turn.

I am presenting this analysis as a vehicle for trying to understand Scott's behavior, if in fact he is responsible for Laci's disappearance. We would like to comprehend why he would murder his pregnant wife when he appeared to have the world in the palm of his hand. According to John Douglas, emancipation is a very common motive for murdering one's wife or family.

---

[4] Douglas, John, *The Anatomy of Motive*, Scribner, 1999.

MARCH 16, 2003
READING BETWEEN THE LINES

Due to the scarcity of proffered information from Modesto police regarding the Laci Peterson investigation, we are left with analyzing their actions and what few scraps of salient detail it lets slip. From the chronology of the case, I believe it is safe to surmise the following:

- Police suspected the husband's behavior from the outset, thus obtained search warrants, utilized bloodhounds, and attempted to rule out his involvement. They determined from the initial search that Laci had not taken a walk with the dog on December 24.
- Scott's alibis for the timeline of 8:30 pm December 23 through 6:00 pm December 24 is being thoroughly researched, and may include witnesses and information thus far undisclosed.
- The boat, the auxiliary wheels from the boat, the Ford F150, all of the concrete-related items including anchors, residue and empty bags, are considered vital clues in the case, which is why those items either remain in custody or are being sought.
- Police have only publicly cleared from involvement Amber Frey and the Rocha's immediate family (Laci's mother, father, step-father, brother, and sister.) This leads us to believe there may be other persons of interest in the investigation that have been neither named nor cleared.
- Searches, of which we are aware, conducted and financed by the Modesto police, have exclusively focused on the San Francisco Bay. There must be a compelling reason that suggests the disposal of a body or incriminating evidence, and that Scott's boat was, in fact, launched in salt water during the timeline in question. To speculate that these searches are some kind of bluff or distraction is unrealistic. There is reason to believe that other searches above ground are undergoing, but have not been publicized.
- Material obtained during the second search of the Peterson home, the warehouse, the storage unit, personal data from computers, and any forensic evidence (however minimal) have brought the investigation to its present stage: classification as a homicide, and an ongoing search for remains in the Bay.

MARCH 24, 2003
DOUBLE HOMICIDE

The Modesto Bee published an article today declaring that, of the various charges assigned in the investigation and prosecution of Laci Peterson's assumed demise, double homicide would be among them.

In recent years, lawmakers in 15 states debated "unborn victim" bills during legislative sessions, and over 20 states, including California, already have laws on the books that treat unborn children as independent victims. California Law is harsher than many other states that define killing an unborn child as merely "manslaughter."

In 2001, a House Bill was introduced in Congress called "The Unborn Victims of Violence Act" that would elevate the status of a fetus to a "person," as far as federal law is concerned. This bill failed passage in the Senate, and has been denounced by abortion-rights advocates and women's groups as a ploy by the current conservative administration to undermine reproductive rights. If nothing else, it would open a Pandora's box of potential litigation. State legislatures, on the other hand, have raised penalties and assessed special circumstances to murders that include an unborn child. Acknowledging the alarming statistics on murders of pregnant women and raising the stakes on criminals who harm unborn children seem much more sensible than a blanket declaration of a fetus's rights, insofar as deterring crime is concerned.

The outrage we feel regarding the victimization of the most vulnerable members of society is not lessened by the declaration that Laci's murderer will face a double homicide charge. In fact, it makes us even more impatient to see justice.

CHAPTER 2: ARREST AND ARRAIGNMENT

APRIL 4, 2003
LACI'S AGENDA

Many case followers have wondered if Laci had an inkling that Scott was unfaithful to her, if she ever noticed his narcissistic tendencies, or if she was "an agreeable woman," as her mother-in-law described her, and blind to his faults. Why did she stay with him for so long, if not due to naiveté or co-dependence? I would like to propose an answer to the mystery of how Laci, a dynamic, strong-willed, charismatic, talented, popular, and determined woman, could be with a man like Scott Peterson, and what her personal agenda was in this partnership.

Their courtship began in college where many activities, friends, academic demands, and the freedom of youth kept much of the pressure off the relationship. No doubt Scott said things that Laci wanted to hear, he came on very strong when he knew he wanted her, and overwhelmed her with romantic intensity, typical behavior of the narcissist. She, in turn, was a driven individual, and when she saw something she wanted, she went after it with a passion. Early in the marriage, they ran a business together (the restaurant), which required long hours, hard work, and frequent distractions from focusing on each other. They were together quite a lot, but not alone. Scott probably considered "The Shack" a constant source of attention and girl-watching, while Laci applied her talent to making a success of the enterprise. I believe it was during this time that Scott's true colors began to surface. I theorize that Laci noticed that Scott was flirtatious, if not potentially unfaithful, and eventually presented him with an ultimatum: sell the restaurant and move to Modesto, or the marriage was over. Scott complied perhaps out of a necessity to save face and because he was using the marriage to camouflage his secrets.

At this point, I believe Laci wanted to preserve her marriage, and felt a geographical cure, where she had more power, friends, and family, would solve the problem. She also initiated starting a family, partly because this was her agenda to have children, and partly perhaps because she felt that a child would reel in her wandering spouse. When she became pregnant, she expected Scott to settle down, embrace the responsibilities and joyful expectation of fatherhood, and become more serious about the marriage. During the pregnancy she may have become more demanding, more critical, less tolerant of his absences and more focused on the future. There may have been conflict in the marriage over money, sex, and priorities which, in a healthy marriage, would have resolved themselves out of mutual care and love, but in an unhealthy one, created a rift. Since I believe Scott's lifetime motivation was seeking admiration, he began to become disillusioned with his marriage, and considered it a sentence. He felt trapped, powerless, emasculated and betrayed.

Thus, we have the chronology of the relationship: the first years spent in the carefree world of college, the middle years involved in a business that imposed a constant focus and routine, recent years getting pregnant and developing a safe, domestic environment to raise a family. This could account for why Laci was with Scott for as long as she was: she had a personal agenda. I believe, also, that if

Scott had not dedicated himself to fatherhood and his marriage, Laci would have left him within a year. She was an intelligent, proud, stubborn girl with a dream she would not forfeit, not for anyone, not even Scott.

APRIL 5, 2003
THE GRIEVING HUSBAND

From both media and witness reports, I have gathered the following information about Scott Peterson, "the grieving husband," regarding his activities and whereabouts since his pregnant wife "disappeared" over 100 days ago:

- Scott has been seen in Modesto infrequently, and the house he shared with his wife has gone unattended, to the dismay of neighbors and Laci's family.
- He has been spotted recently in San Diego, with the tips of his hair bleached, enjoying dining out, swimming and working out at a private beach club, partying with friends, and reveling in his new freedom.
- His family, still in denial over his involvement with his wife's disappearance, treats him as if he is the victim.
- He spoke to people about selling the house *within a week* of Laci's disappearance.
- His excuse for selling Laci's Land Rover was that the police had broken the locks, and he needed a vehicle he could secure.
- Scott has a wealthy sponsor: his half-sister Anne Bird, who is enabling him both financially and socially at the present time. He has been staying at her home in Berkeley (on and off) since possibly as early as February.

It appears that reports of his "being paralyzed and unable to work, eat, or sleep" have been greatly exaggerated. I predict that unless he is arrested, Scott will continue to live his life as if none of the events involving Laci ever transpired. He will almost always find a willing woman or family member to protect, defend, and finance his pretenses of innocence. We can only hope that this farce plays out its last act in the courtroom, before any more naïve and well intentioned women are victimized and devastated by his unconscionable selfishness.

APRIL 14, 2003
THE BODIES SURFACE

A body of an infant boy with the umbilical cord still attached was discovered yesterday washed ashore in a marshy area near Richmond by a local resident walking a dog. Today, another partial body, that of a female, was discovered about two miles from the fetus at Pt. Isabel, an area of the East Bay Regional Park System by, oddly enough, another dog walker. From a report in the *Contra Costa Times,*

"The head and legs of the body were missing and it was apparent that the corpse had been pregnant. The body was identified, according to the newspaper source, to be a petite female that apparently was clothed in maternity wear."

Are these the bodies of Laci Peterson and her unborn son, Connor? We can only speculate at this time, since DNA testing could take several weeks, but it is beyond coincidence that these remains could be anyone else. One of our readers has seen Scott's truck parked at his parents' home in San Diego, and another reader has informed me that Scott was planning to housesit for Anne's adopted parents after Easter. Currently, his whereabouts are unconfirmed, but I believe his activities and behavior since these bodies have surfaced may be very telling. Will he act nonchalant, or panic? If he is innocent, he should be in touch with the Modesto police immediately and heading to Modesto at this time to verify the find. If he is guilty he may act indifferent, avoid the media and the police, and possibly plan an escape. I wouldn't put anything past him at this point.

Much consternation and speculation has been expressed about the missing body parts, and we cannot jump to conclusions about how this transpired. I believe it is possible aquatic predators made off with limbs, and that the skull possibly became embedded in the silt; or if she were weighted down, it caused the disarticulation. It is also possible that these parts were removed prior to sinking the torso. In either event, it is only a matter of time before it is confirmed what we have dreaded for the last four months.

Good Friday: a solemn day for many; a day of fasting, reflection, and commemorating the unjust, barbaric torture and crucifixion of a man who was blameless; and in that mockery of a trial, and the wickedness of the system that persecuted and executed him, we are mindful of our own weakness, unworthiness, and failings.

This week, Holy Week, has been a blurred series of long days awaiting the results of the DNA identification testing of the bodies that washed ashore on Sunday and Monday, and late nights corresponding with friends and contributors who have become a community in vigil for Laci Peterson and her unborn son, Connor.

Our wait, though at times tortuous, interspersed with humor, anecdotes, speculation, research and opinions, has finally been rewarded. This afternoon, an arrest warrant was issued for Scott Peterson, who, unlike the son of man, is not blameless, innocent, or unjustly accused. In fact, Mr. Peterson will receive the best trial modern western society can grant him. He will be treated infinitely better than were his beautiful wife and baby and her grieving family, for whom these past four months have been nothing short of hell.

There will be a press conference at 9 pm EST that will reveal the latest developments, including the positive identification of the baby as Scott and Laci's, and the probable cause for which Scott Peterson was arrested.

* * * * *

From reports of local readers, quite a large crowd gathered on the grounds of the Modesto County Jail awaiting the arrival of Peterson, reminiscent of the old horror movies where the mob, armed with torches, dogs and pitchforks, surround the castle of the vampire. Unfortunately for them, and for the media, Peterson was not shown to the world in shackles.

I was surprised that people could still demonstrate this level of outrage, considering we have been inundated with violence, war, terrorism and wife murders on a daily basis. It is good to see people still care, grieve, mourn and rally in fury over the murder of this young woman, a stranger to most of us, yet inextricably part of some of our lives, forever.

From today's mug shot showing his recently bleached hair and goatee, it is obvious that Scott has made yet another metamorphosis in his strategy to exit this gruesome scenario as though it were a mere theatrical event. There are many things Scott didn't plan on, not least of which was the attention his missing wife would attract by both the media and the public. He surely didn't plan on the bodies resurfacing as he presented a defiant face to the world, challenging us to "get something on him!"

It is apparent from the decor of your new surroundings, Mr. Peterson, that your best laid plans to dispose of your wife like a rusty bicycle, liquidate her property, erase her existence, and deny her legacy have utterly failed. Perhaps a bit of divine intervention along with the vigorous efforts of the Modesto Police

Department expedited the resolution of the mystery of this case, and we can only hope that justice for the Rocha family will be swift.

APRIL 21, 2003
THE ARRAIGNMENT

Scott Peterson was arraigned today for the murder of his wife Laci, "with malice aforethought," which resulted also in the death of their unborn child, Connor. He arrived in court in a state-issued red jumpsuit, *sans* the David Westerfield-style goatee, with his spiky, punk hair a color not found in nature. He resembled more the Scott we saw early in the case, forlorn and shaken, reverting to his original (and best) act: that of a victim.

His attorney, Kirk McAllister, has resigned from his position supposedly due to Peterson's financial limitations, and Peterson has been appointed a public defender. This came as a surprise to me at first, because I was under the impression that the Peterson family would pool their liquid assets to underwrite a competent defense for their "innocent" son, who has been so maligned, smeared, vilified, and shamelessly tried and convicted by the media. I realized, however, that the Petersons are possibly the kind of people who initially operate under the presumption of entitlement: they are more than happy to let the State pay for their son's defense, however inadequate, and will no doubt complain about and criticize the results throughout the trial.

It will be interesting to see whether the Petersons hire a private investigator to follow up on the alleged leads and witness reports that place Laci or Scott in different circumstances during the days of December 23rd and 24th, or take some action on behalf of their son, besides accusing the Modesto police of "bungling" the investigation. Perhaps that would be too "inconvenient" for them, since it would certainly require a commitment of time and resources that were notably unavailable for finding their daughter-in-law.

Scott's booking report indicates his marital status as "single." This reminds me of the adage, "Be careful of what you wish for, because you will get it." Perhaps Scott has wished for singlehood for some time, even presenting himself as such this past November, while his wife of five years, almost seven months pregnant at the time, happily decorated a nursery, attended Lamaze classes, and prepared a nest for her eagerly anticipated baby.

We are amazed at the staggering price Scott has paid for his newfound marital status and wonder what ultimate penalty he will incur for the monstrous crime of which he has been accused and now arraigned for committing. To some, it will never be high enough.

APRIL 25, 2003
THE LOVE SPIN

Lately there has been an avalanche of media coverage highlighting Scott Peterson's relationship with Amber Frey. Phrases like "lovestruck," "love birds," "desperate romantic phone calls," and other insipid descriptions are being spread like Tradecorp manure.

There is no doubt that Amber Frey had genuine feelings for Scott. She was swept off her feet, fed insidious, honey-coated fables doled out like luscious confection to a starving sugar addict. Scott's pursuit of Amber was predatory; void any sincere romantic intentions, merely a sport to him to fondle his ego as he reveled in the victory of his deception.

To depict Scott as "lovestruck," or to imply that his fling with Amber was anything more than a convenient conquest, is imposing sentiment on him that he simply does not possess. Perhaps focusing on the affair lends credence to a motive for Scott to murder his wife; however, it humanizes him, presents him as somehow sympathetic to people who cannot grasp the reality that he is a cold-blooded, calculating, unrepentant, opportunistic, amoral fiend. Amber was duped, as was Laci, and countless intelligent, proud, vivacious, loving women who are vulnerable, by their very integrity and good nature, to the sinister charade of a seemingly perfect partner. Let us not be hoodwinked by the hype or deluded by a gossip-seeking media who want to put a "love spin" on this horrific crime.

CHAPTER 3: GERAGOS AT THE HELM

FACTS, HEARSAY, RUMORS

From the transcript of last night's *Larry King Live*, Mr. King stated: "Oh, that's different. Facts, an actual fact; it's not a fact until it's in evidence, right?"

Wrong! We do have some salient facts in this case. We also have hearsay, speculation, unconfirmed rumors, and conflicting witness statements. Let us review these items to distinguish among them.

Facts:

- The last contact Laci had with someone other than Scott was with her mother on December 23, in a phone call at approximately 8:30 pm. The timeline begins there.
- Scott was having an adulterous relationship while his wife was pregnant, traveling a considerable distance, and misrepresented himself to Ms. Frey as an "unmarried" man.
- The blinds were closed on the 24th, later confirmed by Scott, who said it was because it was a cold day. In fact, the temperature was in the 40s.
- Scott was seen loading something into his truck on the morning of the 24th, as witnessed by a neighbor, and corroborated by his explanation that they were "market umbrellas" in several media interviews.
- Scott has a marina launch ticket date and time-stamped for December 24th.
- Scott purchased the 14-foot aluminum boat on December 9, with $1,400 cash.
- Laci and Connor's bodies washed up within three miles of the Berkeley Marina, where Scott claims to have been fishing on the 24th.
- Scott attended Arizona State, where he did not play on the golf team. He dropped out of the college within six months.
- A blue tarp was found in the Berkeley Marina area during an early search, and a black plastic sheet, commonly used in flowerbeds, was discovered washed up shortly after the bodies surfaced.
- Scott traded in Laci's Land Rover and consulted with a real estate agent about listing their property on Covena Avenue within a few weeks of her "disappearance."
- Scott visited Mexico in early February, ostensibly to attend a trade conference in which he did not participate.
- Scott had obtained another storage unit besides the warehouse for Tradecorp.
- Police confiscated Scott's truck, boat, and 95 bags of evidence from his home.
- Scott states he told Laci of his affair with Amber early in December, and the police on the 24th; however, the police affirmed they were not aware of the affair until Ms. Frey stepped forward in late December.

- Scott said he used concrete around the yard for projects and then admitted to making anchors for his boat.
- Scott did not participate in any of the searches organized by the Rochas.
- Scott changed his appearance and dyed his hair shortly before his arrest. He was also carrying a substantial amount of cash and driving a recently purchased vehicle.
- The bloodhounds tracked Laci's scent in the opposite direction of the park and did not lead their handlers anywhere near Kewin Park, or the Mitchells' house.
- There was another pregnant woman in the neighborhood that walked a dog regularly.
- There were no football games televised on December 24.
- Several witnesses have claimed that they saw Laci walking the dog the morning of the 24th.
- The Petersons were insisting that Laci was taken for the baby until the bodies surfaced, and were recently quoted saying that Laci was "snatched off the street" in an "impulsive act."
-

Unconfirmed rumors, hearsay, conflicting statements:

- Scott received a partial golf scholarship to Arizona State.
- Scott was continuing to contact Amber Frey long after his wife's disappearance.
- Amber sent Scott a book with a note inside warning him not to call her because her phones were tapped.
- Scott went to the Super Bowl.
- Scott has had other affairs.
- Another Peterson family member is under suspicion.
- A 55-gallon drum Scott purchased is unaccounted for, as are scuba weights he purchased shortly before the incident.
- Scott bought the boat without anyone's knowledge.
- Scott was researching tidal and current data for the area around Richmond.
- Scott went to the office before going to the Marina.
- Scott's fishing gear appeared unused.
- Scott was spotted at a convenience store buying a Red Bull the morning of the 24th, dressed neatly with a pristine truck and boat.
- A staff member of the grounds saw Scott at the Berkeley Marina between noon and 1 pm of the 24th.
- Police discovered blood or other body fluid evidence on a mop taken from the Peterson home.
- Laci's remains were discovered in maternity pajamas.
- Scott told Amber he lost his wife in December 2001 and that he did not want children.
- Searchers using side scan sonar may have detected a body in mid-March, in the shipping channels near Richmond Harbor, that was dislodged by the storm, a propeller, or other disturbance in the area.

HIGH FIDELITY

fi·del·i·ty
1. Faithfulness to obligations, duties, or observances.
2. Exact correspondence with fact or with a given quality, condition, or event; accuracy.
3. The degree to which an electronic system accurately reproduces the sound or image of its input signal.

High fidelity is a term to describe the quality of sound reproduction of an audio recording. The higher the fidelity, the more it imitates live music, with its dynamics, resonance, vibration and dimension. As audio systems became more sophisticated, listeners preferred distorting the original sound with subwoofers, buffers, loudspeakers, and equalizers. Eventually, the reproduced tracks scarcely resembled the original recording. I find myself adjusting the bass on other people's car stereos to restore the midrange; I believe the bass should be the accompaniment, not the lead; however, our dance clubs, rock concerts, and stereo salesmen have trained generations of ears to crave the bass line, like rancid oil in fried food.

Fidelity to music means that you play the piece as closely to the composer's intent as you can, following the original instrumentation whenever possible, the tempo, dynamics and nature of the work. Playing a Sousa march as a dirge, or arranging Debussy to a polka beat violates the fidelity of both music and artist, except where humor or satire is the rationale. As somewhat of a purist, I insist that art, sport, and love be played true to form.

At most weddings I witness, the couples exchange the traditional vows: "to have and to hold from this day forward, for better, for worse, for richer, for poorer...forsaking all others, I pledge my troth." Fidelity is the iron ore from which a relationship is forged. Without faithfulness, you have fissure, fretting corrosion, and fraction. Commitment to one's obligations begins at home. If you can't honor your vows to your spouse, or consider your obligations to your family as essential, how have you integrity in any other realm?

When I discover infidelity in people's primary relationships, I tend to believe they are dishonest in most areas of their lives. How can we trust a person like Scott Peterson, who has routinely breached his vows and carelessly lied to his friends, family, and the media without any apparent demonstration of regret? I suspect he also padded his expense accounts, fictionalized his call reports, cheated on his tests, and displayed chronic dishonesty throughout his career. How can his attorney expect us to believe anything he says at this point? Those of us who embrace fidelity as a core value, regardless of its attendant sacrifices, inconvenience, deferral of selfish pleasures, or heartache, consider the actions of Scott Peterson a defilement of all we hold dear.

Fidelity in reporting is not a commodity to be bargained with, and the adherence to accuracy, truth, and the facts in this case has been fragile at best, and blatantly ignored at worst. Reporters who tweak the bass line and mute the midrange would have the public hear a soundtrack that has been processed beyond recognition. The simple, sad melody of the original song contains the pure tones of greed, envy, and betrayal.

MAY 12, 2003
"KARNEVIL"

It appears that Mark Geragos is incapable of expressing himself in public without employing outrageous hyperbole. His grandiose garrulousness is geared to arouse his audience, shake them out of their Peterson-loathing lull, and cast the shadow of suspicion upon the investigative tactics of the Modesto police. His throaty battle cry to exonerate his maligned and misunderstood client, and flush out the real killer, would be laughable if it were not so reprehensible. Recently, he has alluded to mysterious witnesses and some deliberately disregarded deviants who may have had access to Laci during the time of her disappearance.

Welcome back, my friends, to the show that never ends[5]. Has Geragos recently received irrefutable, compelling evidence that the murder occurred in the Peterson home? The former party line that Laci was "snatched off the street" has to be hastily revised to reflect the newly discovered evidence. Now, the defense has to focus its distraction and sleight of hand on an opportunistic perpetrator who attacked Laci in or near her home on Covena Avenue the morning of the 24th, and whisked away her badly wounded or dead body in his vehicle at the edge of the driveway. This theory neatly includes the evidence found in the home, the bloodhound behavior, and the defendant's timeline.

Unfortunately, it does not include a large, buttered popcorn, Milk Duds, Raisinettes, and a soda. Geragos's gullible audience is expected to suspend reason, logic, and common sense and swallow, like sturgeon, the following defense bait:

* A woman saw something suspicious in regard to a "walking Laci" and a strange van on the street, and who did not report this to the police, to the news media, to Laci's family, to the Peterson hotline, or to anyone who would listen, when at stake was a $500,000 reward and a pregnant woman's life.

* That the real killer would murder Laci in her home without taking anything of value, including her purse, vehicle, or jewelry. In fact, not only was his crime purely non-mercenary, he was amazingly considerate by cleaning all visible traces of his existence and of any obvious altercation.

* Scott Peterson, upon returning from his fishing trip, oblivious to anything askew in his own home, for some unexplained reason gave a few swipes to the floor with a wet mop, inadvertently assisting the killer as well.

* The "real" killer would have the motive, means, and opportunity to not only murder Laci in her home (prescient of Petersons' absence), but also dump her body in the Bay, cognizant of Peterson's alibi. This killer is amazingly resourceful. He is also clairvoyant. He should be at the racetrack, making buckets of money rather than murdering pregnant woman, which last time I checked didn't pay too well. The very least this mystery killer could have done was lead the investigators to the body, considering the obvious focus on Scott, perhaps collecting some of the $50,000 reward for the remains. But, no, our villain hasn't a materialistic bone in his body.

---

[5] Emerson, Lake and Palmer, "Karn Evil 9," 1973

MAY 15, 2003
THE PETERSON FILE: THE SYSTEM ON TRIAL

When the State of California v. Scott Peterson goes to court, Scott Peterson won't be the only one on trial.

I believe our entire criminal justice system will be judged, as well as the Peterson family, the Modesto police, the epidemic of misogyny and spousal murders in our culture, prosecutors and defense lawyers who make court a sport and, by extension, the media tradition of glamorizing criminals whose egos are only exceeded by their depravity.

Let us not lose sight of the fact that a vulnerable woman and her defenseless infant were cruelly slaughtered and then discarded in the filthy, frigid waters of the San Francisco Bay. It is for the victims we ensure justice, not the perpetrators. So much of our judicial system has been distorted to protect the innumerable "rights" of the accused, that jurors and the public are confused by the definitions of "reasonable doubt," "burden of proof," and "presumption of innocence." The defense in the Peterson case is likely to resemble a variation on the W.C. Field's adage: "If you can't dazzle them with brilliance, baffle them with bull."

In cases where a husband murders his wife, every facet of their marriage, personal histories, family dynamics and behavior is microscopically examined for public discourse. Who among us could endure such scrutiny? The jury pool will be inundated with facts, conjecture, logic, fantasy, wishful thinking, distraction, DNA science, forensics, nebulous motives, and faced with the daily presence of Scott Peterson: clean-cut, athletic, boyish, defying by all appearances the portrait of a killer.

This case has not received the wide range of attention it has by accident. The Peterson trial may well become a turning point in restoring our faith in a justice system that we fight wars to protect, yet with which we have become disillusioned and cynical.

MAY 24, 2003
THE MCDONALD PARALLELS

In January, I introduced the Peterson case by drawing comparisons between Scott Peterson and Jeff McDonald, the Green Beret who was convicted of murdering his pregnant wife and two children in 1979. The parallels I drew were somewhat peripheral, since it remained to be seen what had actually become of Laci, and how Peterson would behave in the days ahead. I called the "disappearance" a murder immediately, not because I was presumptuous or accusatory, but rather because statistically that was the probable scenario, and after reading the news articles detailing the events immediately following Christmas, there remained little doubt in my mind that Scott was responsible.

Although Joe McGinnis's book, *Fatal Vision*, was published almost 20 years ago, I had only read it recently, so the details of the murder and subsequent McDonald trial were fresh in my mind. Jeff McDonald contributed diary entries and personal correspondence to the book to portray himself as a victim of a mishandled investigation and his father-in-law's personal vendetta. I recognized

Dr. McDonald as a textbook narcissist within two paragraphs of his disturbing first diary entry, which was in the first half dozen pages of the book. My January essay about the Peterson case became eerily prophetic not only in its prediction of the fate of Laci Peterson, but, as it turns out, in the McDonaldesque defense of employing implausible, outlandish theories of the "real perpetrators."

Early in the case, McDonald fabricated a fantastic fable that crazed, acid-dropping hippies, members of a Manson-type cult, broke into his home and savagely butchered his wife and two small children in a drug-induced rage, leaving him comparatively unharmed, unconscious, and unaware. It wasn't until his father-in-law noticed McDonald's lack of grief, careless self-indulgence after his family was murdered, and suspicious, arrogant behavior, that he decided to relentlessly pursue justice for his daughter and grandchildren. His labors were rewarded when McDonald was convicted and sentenced to substantial prison time. Prior to his trial, McDonald had managed to relocate, find a patroness, and hobnob with the wealthy and glamorous aristocracy in Southern California.

The parallels between McDonald and Peterson are now inescapable. Like McDonald, Peterson's wife's family initially supported him, adamantly denied the possibility that he could be involved in Laci's disappearance, and backed him to the hilt. It wasn't until they discovered his deception about his affair with Amber Frey, his mission to sell his wife's property, and his avoidance of complete cooperation with law enforcement that the Rochas distanced themselves, became wary of his statements, and finally had to accept the devastating, mind-paralyzing possibility that he murdered their precious Laci and her unborn son.

Like McDonald, Peterson exhibited peculiar, self-serving, and callous behavior after an event that, for most of us, would be fraught with anguish, terrifying imaginings, insomnia, and desperation. Like McDonald, Peterson acquired a patroness of sorts, frequented country clubs, golf courses, and parties, seemingly immune to the normal grief process, and was vigilantly protected by self-styled elitists in Southern California.

Apparently, the Peterson defense has taken a page from the McDonald case, if not the entire book, because it was a successful defense at first. Unlike the McDonald case, however, Peterson has received exponentially greater public exposure. Fooling a small, conflicted group of military officers on a North Carolina army base is a far cry from duping a nation of millions. Nevertheless, Geragos and his unnamed mouthpiece are presenting the "crazed cult members" theory, as well as accusing the State of California of unconstitutional wiretapping, inept investigation, arresting their client without probable cause, and possessing absolutely no evidence that connects Scott Peterson to the murder of his wife. Never mind Peterson's alibi, which places him within a couple of miles of where the bodies surfaced; pay no attention to his inconsistencies, lies, avoidance of questioning, his constant metamorphoses, or his blatant cavorting and carousing during the Rochas's unremitting search efforts. Forget about his secret boat, the concrete anchors, the pliers found with Laci's hair attached, the suspicious blood in his truck likely the result of an injury sustained that fateful night. Disregard his complete lack of character in his infidelity to his pregnant wife, and recently reported numerous affairs prior to her pregnancy. The defense would have you overlook these issues, in favor of your accepting the impossible: that Laci was abducted and murdered by a nonexistent cult, in broad daylight on Christmas Eve,

31

when she was not walking the dog, and that her remains were transported 90 miles away to an area heavily populated by law enforcement searching for the body.

My description of Geragos's tactics as a carnival has become a perfect analogy for the antics we are witnessing: Geragos, speaking through his unnamed source, is the masked wizard behind the curtain, churning the calliope music, drawing the unsuspecting patrons to his rigged wheel of fortune, cashing in on their gullibility before the carnival moves to another venue, where he resumes his ridiculous role of illusionist anew. He, like Peterson, would presume collective amnesia, naiveté, and sympathy for a young man with no history of violence or lawbreaking, and who is well educated, attractive, and affluent. Funny, that sounds exactly like Jeff McDonald.

MAY 27, 2003
FREEDOM OF THE PRESS

How free is our press, really? Does the seemingly large quantity of information available to us in the media indicate its reliability, accuracy or absence of censorship? What is the original intent of the First Amendment of the Constitution, which states that Congress "shall make no law...abridging the freedom of speech, or of the press"; the word, "abridge" in this context means to "cut short or curtail." I interpret that to mean the press is entitled to unencumbered access; however, that is obviously not the practice. There is no law, evidently, against buying the press.

Before the advent of the Internet, where the "underground" relocated to publish its fringe opinions online, most mainstream media, including the major city newspapers, news magazines (*Time, Newsweek, U.S. News World Report*) and broadcasting networks dictated our information. It is no secret that only a handful of individuals own most of the media in this country, namely Disney, Turner, Warner, Murdock, Scripps-Howard, and The New York Times Company, (which publishes *The New York Times, The International Herald Tribune, The Boston Globe* and 16 other newspapers; owns eight network-affiliated television stations and two New York radio stations.) How "free" is our press if monopolized by a few elite moguls? Not very. Anyone who thinks otherwise is kidding himself.

At today's hearing in the case of California vs. Scott Peterson, access by the press (and therefore the public) to the search warrants, affidavits, autopsy reports, and other documents, sealed since their inception, was the main issue debated in court. The State argued that the media was "generalizing" the warrants, affidavits and autopsy reports as presumed to be public. I, too, would presume that based on the First Amendment but that, in fact, they are different in "type, scope and security." It appears to be "abridgment" to me. I don't see how this argument or interpretation of the law merited acceptance. Geragos's response to media: we (the defense) don't have all the documents, we don't have the entire autopsy report, and just because there is a complaint doesn't mean the real perpetrator isn't still at large. Again, I don't see how this argument precludes the public's right to know. If anything, the public could assist the defense in its mission to find the "real killer" with more information about where the police investigation ended and Geragos's began. Does the defense have more rights than the public? What makes these documents so sensitive that the letter and spirit of the Free Press justifies repeated violation?

Today's hearing resulted in the following actions: the aforementioned documents will remain sealed until at least the preliminary hearing, which was scheduled for July 16. On July 9, a hearing will be held to determine whether television cameras will be permitted in the courtroom (assumed to be our right), and on June 6, the defense will decide whether intercepted phone calls between Scott Peterson and his then released attorney of record, Kirk McAllister, contained any privileged information that may subject any evidence or information acquired from those conversations as inadmissible or illegal. All tapes of these and other phone conversations were to be turned over to the defense for its audit.

Scott Peterson appeared in court today resembling his former self, his blond tresses cropped down to its natural dark brown, and his face clean-shaven and dispassionate, as he sat dressed in a smart gray suit and brown and tan patterned tie. His parents, sister, and sister-in-law were there. Notably absent, as usual, were any of his brothers. Laci's family (Sharon, Ron, and a few friends) was allowed to leave the courtroom first, to prevent their having to be in the aisle with their accused son-in-law. Their demeanor was calm, confident, and noble. Geragos gave a brief press conference indicating he expected his client to be released from custody after the preliminary hearing, and that it was his "fervent hope" to find the real culprits of this despicable crime. He, naturally, would not discuss the evidence or witnesses that lead him to this expectation, because he would just as soon dictate to the American press and public what they have a right to know, and only reveal to them information that portrays his client as innocent.

Has everyone in this case: the State, the Court, and the defense, conveniently forgotten the First Amendment? Perhaps we deserve this, since we, the People, have allowed the media to censor, corrupt, shape, spin, misinterpret, mislead and manufacture our news for so long, our present demand for freedom of the press proves futile, if not farcical.

MAY 28, 2003
CELL-O IT'S ME

The latest news and rumors are that Scott Peterson may have owned up to *five* cell phones from which he was calling Amber Frey, as well as a separate bank account. Back in the beginning of the case, I noted that if I were investigating this crime, I would have combed through his phone records (land line and cell) as well as his bank records, to determine if he had any separate accounts, or if he were attempting any real estate transactions, out of town employment searches, or other activities that indicated he was planning a life without Laci. Any evidence of this would lend to premeditation.

There was a rumor of a cell phone missing from the first search on December 26, which this news supports. Many of us theorized that Scott had more than one affair, and had reason to believe there was a local woman among them. The news that there were other women besides Amber Frey who had a "romantic" relationship with Peterson came as no surprise. Whether the women in question will serve as witnesses for the prosecution or the defense remains to be seen. My theory maintains that Scott's illusive motive was simply the desire to be

33

unburdened of his marriage and child, regardless of its incredulity to most people who would get a divorce and move away rather than resort to murder. Although Peterson is alleged to have told Frey he wanted to spend the rest of his life with her, that was simply his way of placating his new source, allaying her fears and doubts, and seducing her into a false sense of security. He failed to realize that those statements would return to haunt him, providing even more ammunition to the punishing press, which is having a field day with the daily dirt shoveled on top of his already considerably tall pile of loam, topsoil and peat moss.

Scott's parents currently hold power of attorney and have exercised that right recently by forbidding Laci's family from entering the couple's home on Covena Avenue, ignoring Sharon Rocha's continual requests to gain entrance. Since all evidence of a possible crime has already been removed by law enforcement, and the police have not prohibited the family (or anyone else) from using the house, I see no reason, except spite, for these actions. I believe the Petersons are punishing Sharon and her family for recanting their support of the Peterson's "innocent" son, and for allowing themselves to be "brainwashed" by the police and the media. I only hope that the revelation of this atrocious behavior will affect a change of heart. Their obsessive image consciousness, if not their questionable consciences, may suffer intolerable injury. For those who have viewed the Petersons thus far with sympathy and tolerance, this recent demonstration should give you pause.

CHAPTER 5: THE SURREAL SUMMER

June 1 – August 22, 2003

THE SINS OF THE FATHER

Nothing that the Peterson family does, or their representatives do, comes as any surprise to me, because I expect them to behave badly. No, let me restate that: I expect them to behave horridly, vindictively, and reprehensibly. I expect Mr. and Mrs. Peterson to maintain their son's innocence, to distract, deny, disavow and disregard any evidence to the contrary. I expect the Petersons to keep a ledger of every penny they or their son spent on Laci, Connor, and the house on Covena Avenue. I am not dismayed by the Petersons' use of the couple's house while in Modesto, nor do I begrudge them that right; however, to then label it a *crime scene*, after the following facts, is simply absurd:

- Except for December 26, the house was accessible to Scott from before Laci went "missing," until it was searched on February 18 and 19; ample time to remove any incriminating items, journals, broken objects, and restore or sanitize previously unexplored areas.
- The police turned the place upside down in two separate searches and hauled off what they deemed relevant.
- Scott had full access to the house again from February 19 until he was arrested April 18.
- Scott permitted the media entrance, along with anyone else he cared to, in the interim.
- There was a burglary at the house when Scott was in Los Angeles for a one-day alleged search effort where he handed out flyers. Police identified a suspect as someone known by the Petersons, and said he or she was one of many people with access to the home.
- The Petersons themselves had unfettered access to the interior of the house, the pool, and any of Scott's new vehicles or other property for the duration of the case.
- Curious visitors could enter the yard, place or remove gifts, cards, or signs; trample the flowerbeds, remove bricks (as was recently reported) or anything else that wasn't nailed down. Not to mention the tabloid photographers, or anyone with a camera, who wanted to film or take shots of the interior of the house through the windows. Laci's house on Covena Avenue has become a national landmark, as recognizable as the White House. The fact that it still stands and hasn't being burned down or vandalized is a testimony to Laci, not to the Petersons' security or, even less likely, any sympathy toward Scott.

After the defense leaks of the autopsy began to trickle into mainstream media, and the conflicting reports of the condition of the bodies of Laci and the baby became hourly fodder to the ghoulish press, I believe the Rochas's tolerance cup runneth over. Up to this point, they were handling the Petersons with caution, deference, and distance. When the animosity progressed and their requests were stonewalled, the Rochas felt compelled to act, perhaps to some extent regardless of the consequences. Their stance of dignified silence, focus on justice, and refusal to comment on the case was forced to change to one of swift action and retaliation, to protect what was left of their memories of Laci and Connor, and as a public defiance of the Peterson's petulant, perverse position with regard to Laci's property.

I would personally send Mrs. Peterson a check for the value she has assessed for the items removed from Laci's home on Friday, if I thought for a minute this would appease her. But it won't, because it's not about money; it's not about property or sentiment or any other pathetic, petty principle here. It's actually about vanity, power, and revenge. It's about their twisted notions of justice, entitlement, and the relentless perpetuation of their obfuscation, and that of Geragos, may not only damage an already dismal public opinion of Scott Peterson, but also reveal the origin of his maladaptive mindset.

JUNE 13, 2003
A SMALL VICTORY

Yesterday, June 12, Judge Al Girolami issued a Protective Order covering the attorneys, agents, staff, experts, law enforcement, court employees, and all witnesses and potential witnesses in the case of The People of the State of California vs. Scott Lee Peterson. Since an attorney for the media and Gloria Allred (representing potential witness, Amber Frey), the prosecution and the defense all filed opposition points or memorandum to the gag order, I consider Judge Girolami's decision to be a victory, albeit a small one, for the *victims* in this case.

Judge Girolami reads the newspapers, hears the whispers and scuttlebutt in the courtrooms and coffee shops. He cannot avoid the ubiquitous talking heads, self-proclaimed experts, or media saturation of this case, and it concerns him. He observes dispassionately as both sides vie for attention, relevancy and superiority. He shakes his head with dismay as each news program attempts to trump the last in spectacle and sensationalism, bordering on surreal.

Most important, Judge Girolami can't help noticing the devastating effects on the victim's (and to some extent the defendant's) family of the constant exposition of partial, inaccurate, or horrifying details. Girolami has not lost sight of his responsibility to maintain order and control, and to impose some dignity upon these areas of his jurisdiction. His judgment reminds all of us that this trial is about justice for the murder of Laci Peterson and her unborn baby, and not about competition for ratings, aggrandizement of either legal team, or selling newspapers.

Specifically enumerated in the order are the strict prohibitions to the attorneys involved in this case from releasing any information regarding evidence, photographs, testimony, or witnesses. Considering the vehement denials by the defense of its culpability for recent stories regarding the autopsy reports, alternative perpetrators, and irrational theories involving satanic cults, brown vans and Laci sightings, it will be interesting to see if the imposition of the gag order will cork these leaks once and for all. I believe that, in spite of commentaries to the contrary, a thoughtful public will indeed have the discernment to distinguish between fact and fiction as the predicted torrent of information disseminated by "sources close to the case" continues to be reported by the media.

JUNE 20, 2003
THE WEEK IN REVIEW

It was a busy week in Stanislaus County Superior Court, with 12 separate documents filed between Monday, June 16, and Friday, June 20, by attorneys for the defense, attorneys for the media, the county District Attorney, Gloria Allred (counsel for a potential witness on her own behalf), and the City Attorney of San Francisco. A summarization of a selection of these filings, interesting and amusing citations, and my analysis follows:

June 16:

Geragos & Geragos, lawyers for the defense, filed a "Consolidated Motion for 1) Reconsideration of the Court's June 12 Protective Order, and 2) Setting of a Hearing on OSC (Order to show cause) re Contempt of Court by Gloria Allred."

Geragos objects to the protective (gag) order on the grounds that it is unconstitutional, is prejudicial to his client, and that Ms. Allred:

> By mocking the court's authority, an attorney in effect sends a message to the jurors that they, too, may disregard the court's directives and ignore its authority...Here, the Court's protective order is being flouted on national television in front of millions of people and countless potential jurors...the protective order has done no more than further exacerbate the misinformation campaign and prejudice any semblance of a fair trial for Mr. Peterson.[6]

I find the use of the words "mocking" and "misinformation" ironic, considering Geragos and his team have "mocked" the intelligence and sensibilities of the jury pool with their unsubstantiated and ridiculous satanic cult theories, their indecent leaks of the autopsy report, the dead-end tan van, demands for DNA testing on body parts found in Davis, California, and the recent rumor of an Aryan Nation revenge murder upon the "wrong" Scott Peterson's wife.

James C. Brazelton's office of the DA filed a "Return on Search Warrant" which enumerated 11 individual packages returned by various telecommunication companies, including AT&T, Nextel, Cingular, Sprint, and SBC, which contained wireless phone records, surveillance video, toll calls, legal documents, and retail information regarding cell phones purportedly owned by the defendant.

Much ado was made about the fact that Scott Peterson possessed so many cell phones and logged nearly 4,000 inbound and outbound calls in little over a month's time. We recall seeing Scott with a phone connected to his head on most occasions and are quite willing to believe he had numerous phones for business and pleasure, perhaps one for each girlfriend, which might explain the account with a San Francisco area code.

---

[6] June 16, 2003, Defense Consolidated Motion for Reconsideration, p. 8

June 18:

The DA's office filed a "Request of Review of Wiretap Recordings Recovered from Audio Buffer" submitting the 176 new audio recordings of additional intercepted phone calls from Peterson's multiple cell phones during the period of time the wiretaps were in place. These recordings have not been heard by either the prosecution or the defense, and are subject to review by Judge Girolami to determine their relevancy and admissibility in court.

Talking heads in the media proceeded to make issue of these "lost calls" to bolster their continuous criticism of the State's case against Peterson and its alleged misconduct or incompetence, because of the potential loss of valuable evidence, or the possibility that more client-attorney phone conversations were captured. In either case, if there is evidence damaging or exculpatory to the defense, both sides will have access to it, and if law enforcement agents failed to detect or hear the calls, no violation of Peterson's rights was committed.

Gloria Allred filed a "Preliminary Opposition of Defendant's Motion to set OSC Re: Contempt of Court" in response to Geragos's motion, which refutes his accusation that she has violated the gag order and jeopardized Peterson's chances for a fair trial. In her brief, she turns the allegation around on Geragos:

> The pending motion by defense counsel, who is certainly no stranger to the media, is so utterly without legal or factual merit as to give rise to serious questions regarding his good faith. Indeed, when the facts of the matter are examined, it would appear that it is defense counsel who has violated the spirit of the protective order by filing a hopeless motion which itself has drummed up massive media attention.[7]

Ms. Allred proceeds on page 7, footnote 4, to reveal her interpretation of Mr. Geragos's true intentions:

> Mr. Geragos has taken issue with Judge Beauchesne's order...as highly prejudicial to Mr. Peterson and that the judge's recitation is mistaken. Thus, it appears that the real motive behind Mr. Geragos' motion regarding purported contempt is to point out what he believes to be the unfairness of the gag order.[8]

In television appearance throughout the week, Ms. Allred has maintained that Geragos is using frivolous motions to keep his interests in the media spotlight by objecting to the judges, the rulings, and Ms. Allred's freedom of speech, and undermining in the process the very order he claims she is scoffing.

---

[7] June 18, 2003 Opposition of Gloria Allred, p. 3.
[8] Ibid, p. 7.

June 19:

Geragos filed a "Stipulation and Order to Continue Briefing Schedule," which basically requests a continuance of a scheduled June hearing on the wiretaps obtained from conversations between the media and his client, transcripts of which he only just received on June 17, and for which he requires more time to review, as well as the newly discovered calls submitted the previous day.

The City of San Francisco filed a "Motion to Quash Subpoena" they received from Geragos on May 30, regarding the ongoing investigation into the death of Evelyn Hernandez, another pregnant woman whose partially dismembered body was found in the Bay near the Embarcadero in September, 2002.

Geragos will likely be unsuccessful in obtaining the murder file on Evelyn Hernandez because it is protected by various privacy laws and is an active case. His purpose for requesting it is ostensibly to show a connection between the Hernandez murder and Laci's, perhaps to prove Scott killed both women, Ms. Hernandez's boyfriend killed both women, or some madman killed both women. Like most of the desperate and delusional tactics waged by the defense, this, too, shall fade into obscurity long before the trial, forgotten by all but the most avid followers of this case.

Recent reports on the status of the preliminary hearing indicate the likelihood of postponement due to vacation conflicts with key witnesses or staff, and the good chance that the autopsy report, search warrants, and probable cause affidavits will finally be unsealed by early July, which will provide a plethora of material for news programs to carry us through the summer. Then there are, of course, the dependable and predictable weekly filings by both sides of the case and hearings on the extant motions, creating additional public record readily available to any interested parties.

June 20:

Lawyers representing various local newspapers and television stations filed a "News Media's Request for Reconsideration of Protective 'Gag' Order" late Friday afternoon, presenting four points of argument addressing "specific defects" of the order:

1. No evidence supports the clear and present danger finding.
2. The gag order is unconstitutionally broad and vague.
3. The Court's order is overbroad and vague, especially as applied to individuals other than the prosecution.
4. The proscribed speech is overbroad and vague.

The news media cannot, in any event, be restrained from reporting in detail on the ongoing litigation, including by "rehashing" prior reports. The narrower, constitutionally appropriate alternative to the court's current overbroad and vague order is to admonish counsel and their agents to observe the requirements of rule 5-120." [Professional Code of Conduct][9]

Basically what the media point out is that we (the public) don't know what evidence will be admissible; we don't know who the potential witnesses may be or what experts will ultimately testify, which essentially prohibits discussing the case at all. The defendant should be permitted to reply publicly to the government's conduct and to any misinformation, leaks or gossip that damage his right to a fair trial. By including employees of the agencies, law firms, and numerous individuals peripheral to the case, many of whom may have no idea they are covered by the prohibition, it increases the possibility of widespread violation and impossible enforcement.

Geragos filed a "Motion for Setting of a Hearing on OCS re Contempt of Court by Stanislaus County District Attorney James Brazelton" in response to Mr. Brazelton's remarks to the *Modesto Bee*, published this morning, June 20. The statements the defense found most alarming included the pointed assertion that "The longer this drags on, the more stories get bandied about out there, and about 95 percent is pure fiction and fabrication. By putting on a prelim, they're going to see some stuff that might open some eyes." Brazelton's other quotations cited in the motion did not, in my opinion, merit Geragos's wrath.

> *Brazelton...appears to have hit the trifecta of prosecutorial misconduct, violation of the protective order, and at the same time transgressing the Rules of Professional Conduct...In fact, one would be hard pressed to imagine how much more disdain one could express for the order of this court when Brazelton utters "we spend all our time running down this phony baloney stuff they throw up."*[10]

One would be hard pressed to imagine how much more vitriolic Geragos would become if someone from the prosecution actually described something *damaging* to his client, as in the real evidence and testimony in the case, or began addressing the complete, shameless disregard for professional conduct the defense has displayed with its ongoing farcical scenarios. However, Brazelton may have erred in describing the preliminary hearing as "eye opening," and some sanction may result. No stranger to the ponies, Geragos employs the noun "trifecta," an exotic bet where you choose the win, place and show horses in a given race, which pays off rather handsomely, is statistically improbable and played only by amateurs.

---

[9] June 20, 2003 News Media's Request for Reconsideration, pp. 8-9.
[10] June 20 Defense Motion for Setting of a Hearing on OCS re Brazelton, p. 5.

JULY 13, 2003
THE PETERSON FAMILY DYNAMIC

Even in the most "functional" families there exist elements of rivalry, favoritism, scapegoating, addiction, unresolved conflicts, alienation and reconciliation; those unique dynamics that naturally occur among blood relatives. The Peterson family presents a veritable smorgasbord of relationship drama: full siblings, half siblings, step-children, adopted children, remarriage, age gaps, and a myriad of ambiguous and obscure issues of which the family is undoubtedly fiercely protective. Were there no murder case, most of us would probably respond to the unorthodox Peterson family with, at worst, mild disapproval; however, under the glaring scrutiny of publicity, and their blatant pageant of "Brady Bunch" perfection, we are compelled to analyze the primary environment in which a callous, self-absorbed, amoral individual such as Scott Peterson was nurtured.

The eldest Peterson siblings, Susan, Mark, and Joe, are the progeny of Lee Peterson and his previous wife, but we are not certain of when or how Lee's marriage ended. The former Mrs. Peterson has been conspicuously absent from the scene. We don't know if that was Lee's first marriage, or if he exercised custody or visitation with his older children after the separation. Based on the fact that his sons are involved in the family crate and packing business, it is safe to assume that he has maintained a close relationship with them.

How did Lee's first children feel about Scott? Did they resent him? What involvement, if any, did they have in his upbringing? Did they participate in the pampering, enabling and permissiveness, or was there abuse, ill will and envy? We have seen Susan recently in court and early in the case giving interviews in support of her half-brother. Joe's wife, Janey, made regular appearances on cable TV news shows adamantly defending Scott, with her typical rationalization for his behavior as "That's just Scott!" Curiously silent were Mark and Joe, whose personal financial futures and inheritance are intrinsically interwoven with Lee's solvency. I would imagine they are terribly conflicted, if not outright enraged, by the immense resources expended towards Scott's defense.

With the recent public appearance of Scott's half-sister, Anne, it is now accepted fact that Jackie Peterson gave up two babies for adoption while in her 20s: Don Chapman and Anne Grady. Don was raised out of state, and now resides in Pennsylvania. His daughter, Melody, presumably knew Laci well enough to declare her a "favorite aunt." Don made a brief appearance early in the case doing some of his own investigation at the Berkeley Marina to seek out potential witnesses who could corroborate Scott's alibi. When that alibi proved Scott's undoing, Mr. Chapman gracefully faded once more into obscurity.

A couple in San Diego adopted Anne Grady, and her adopted brother, Steve, actually worked in a restaurant along side John Peterson, both oblivious to John's biological relationship to Anne. Aside from the interesting coincidences, what was Don and Anne's reaction when they discovered their birth mother kept her other two children, one born less than two years after they were given up? This had to elicit a confusing, complex, and profound array of emotions; Anne's professed adoration of Scott and her financial and emotional assistance to him in the last two months before the bodies of his wife and unborn son washed ashore are somewhat bewildering.

Why did Jackie give up Don and Anne but keep John? How does John, the apparent "lost child" in the typical family roles, feel about his younger brother, Scott, the professed favored son, beloved and wanted, born in wedlock and security, stealing the spotlight, currently commanding all the attention, sympathy, and sacrifices of his parents? Is John well adjusted and content with his position, or is there unresolved rivalry and resentment? The insanity, uncertainty, stress, and shame created by this case has left an already disturbed and complicated family dynamic in complete chaos, the outcome of which becomes the unmitigated legacy of Lee Peterson.

JULY 25, 2003
DEFENSE MOTION TO CLOSE THE PRELIMINARY HEARING

In a brief filed July 22, Mark Geragos moved the Court for an order to close the September 9 preliminary hearing in the case of California v Scott Peterson.

> *The Motion will be based upon the grounds that said closure is necessary to protect Mr. Peterson's right to a fair and impartial trial and that no less restrictive means exist for protecting said right.*[11]

One must assume, from this opening argument, that there *will* be a trial. Given that the defense is conceding the probability that their client will be bound over, what justifies their request for a closed preliminary hearing? The vaguely worded reasoning to protect their client's "right to a fair trial" would apply to all preliminary hearings that involve any suspect who has suffered negative publicity, or low presumption of innocence in the court of public opinion. The entire criminal justice system would require a complete overhaul to accommodate this level of protection of a defendant.

> *This Court has already found that the unique circumstances surrounding the prosecution of Mr. Peterson require the imposition of a protective order...[because of] the intense media attention that plagues this case.*[12]

Geragos goes on to use the arguments in Judge Girolami's gag order to likewise apply to his request for a closed hearing. He reminds the Court of Brazelton's alleged violation of said order and reiterates his inability to "publicly respond to any false media reports stemming from the preliminary hearing." This is a valid point; however, it assumes that there is a future in this defense and that the evidence presented at the preliminary hearing will, in fact, be substantive enough to keep Peterson behind bars until trial.

> *The defense is particularly concerned with the danger that this prosecution team will attempt to utilize the preliminary hearing as a*

---

[11] July 22, 2003 Defense Motion to Close Preliminary Hearing, p. 1.
[12] July 22, 2003 Defense Motion to Close Preliminary Hearing, p. 4.

vehicle to disseminate bogus "evidence" and theories that will not be admissible at trial and that the prosecution has no intention of introducing at trial... With discovery still proceeding at best a glacial pace there is no way to predict what evidence the prosecution might seek to introduce and the defense is unable six weeks away to predict what possible affirmative defenses will be presented.[13]

This is where the arguments become absurd, contradictory and illogical. Geragos implies that the evidence against his client is bogus, inadmissible, or that he doesn't know what it will be, since he hasn't had time to review the discovery. From all previous reports, it is my understanding that over 30,000 pages of discovery were given to the defense months ago, and one would think that it would have a pretty good idea by now of the salient evidence against its client, particularly enumerated in the probable cause affidavits for the searches, the wiretaps, and the arrest. If it doesn't know what the prosecution has on its client by now, I would recommend its immediate removal, and competent counsel retained in its stead.

However, in terms of the ongoing discovery and investigation, significant developments have occurred - developments further necessitating the closure of the preliminary hearing. Specifically, within the past week, the defense is in receipt of discovery that is not only exculpatory, but which the defense contends totally exonerates Mr. Peterson...the evidence, which demonstrates Mr. Peterson's innocence, also provides evidence of the true killer...therefore, if the evidence is made public the ability of both the prosecution and defense to ascertain the identity of the actual perpetrator(s) will be irreparably prejudiced. This is clearly prejudicial to Mr. Peterson's right to a fair and impartial trial and requires that the preliminary hearing be closed...so that Mr. Peterson (and the prosecution) can continue to pursue leads as to the identity of the killer or killers.[14]

If Geragos were in receipt of information that exculpates his client (which is ironic, considering he is unaware of what evidence the prosecution has to *indict* his client, yet he found something in the voluminous discovery that *exonerates* his client), why would he be concerned with a trial at all? Why would he not take that evidence to the appropriate authorities and have the charges against his client dismissed? Presumably, this exonerating evidence is information the prosecution itself supplied to the defense, and therefore of which they are cognizant; unless Geragos is suggesting that the prosecution is so dense that, in one of the most cautiously handled cases in recent history, the Modesto police and the Stanislaus County District Attorney are ignorant of, oblivious to, or deliberately discounting evidence that points to a different perpetrator. If this were true, Geragos, the Peterson family, and his client would be crying, "foul" so loud, it would be heard

---

[13] Ibid, p. 5.

[14] July 22, 2003 Defense Motion to Close Preliminary Hearing, p. 7.

in Boston. The defense would certainly risk contempt, violate the gag order, call every newsperson in the Rolodex, and demand Scott's release. Remember with whom we are dealing, here.

> *The recent discovery provided by the prosecution negates any possibility that Mr. Peterson committed this horrific crime. Consequently, in order to safeguard the ability of the defense (and prosecution) to identify the actual perpetrator(s), thereby exonerating Mr. Peterson, the preliminary hearing must be closed.*[15]

Since when is it the defense's responsibility to identify the actual perpetrators? Isn't that the investigator's job? Not only has Geragos blatantly accused the prosecution of having no factual case against Scott Peterson, in effect, falsely arresting and incarcerating him; along with willfully ignoring evidence that points to another perpetrator, leaking prejudicial information that taints the jury pool, and violating attorney-client privilege through illegal wiretaps, but now he is saying they can't do their job of investigating the murder, either, and he intends to take that upon himself. He's SUPER LAWYER!

If this nonsense were true, there would be a motion to dismiss, a dramatic, tearful press conference with Scott and his family expressing their righteous indignation, and with Geragos center stage, strutting around, flaunting his peacock feathers, declaring his client's innocence, and spewing, "I told you so!" Do we believe for a second he wouldn't do that if there were any merit to his claims?

Geragos belies his belief in the exculpatory evidence by continuing to hedge his bet with repeated references to a trial. His strategy is tantamount to betting on every horse in a race: one of them will cross the finish line first, but do the winnings cover your wager? It's no way to make money at the track, and it's no way to defend a man whose life is on the line.

AUGUST 1, 2003
MEDIA OPPOSITION

If you can imagine deriving pleasure from digesting and analyzing court briefs, the *News Media's Opposition to Motion to Close Preliminary Hearing*, filed recently in the case of California v Peterson, presented organized, logical, and convincing arguments against the defense's legally unsupported and desperate tactics that included relevant legal citations and was actually a rather satisfying read. Here are some of the highlights of the document, and my interpretation of its bearing on the landscape of the case.

> *This court's rulings in delaying access to sealed records and in issuing a protective "gag" order have anticipated that, at the time of the preliminary hearing, the public would have access to this presumptively public information.*[16]

---

[15] Ibid, p. 9.

[16] July 31, 2003, News Media's Opposition to Motion to Close Preliminary Hearing, p. 2.

45

The media has argued all along that the public has a right of access to the probable cause affidavits and other documents that have continued to remain sealed throughout the investigation and pre-trial, and expects that the preliminary hearing, and any subsequent hearings, would reveal the evidence with which the State holds the defendant in custody. If the evidence falls short of meeting the standard for either proceeding or a trial, or if it is strong enough for a potential conviction, the people need to know this. The intent of public disclosure and an open judicial system demand public oversight.

If the defense plans to produce "exculpatory evidence" or methods and circumstances of the "real perpetrators," all the more reason to hold the State accountable to its evidence, and present its case to the public, which will vindicate its client and change the course of the investigation and future trial. Neither side wants a mistrial; the expense of prosecuting and defending this case a second time would be astronomical. Why not end Peterson's nightmare and have the case dismissed at the preliminary, if indeed there exists such exculpatory evidence?

> *The very absence of a jury in these proceedings makes access even more important as "an inestimable safeguard against corrupt or overzealous prosecutor[s]...and compliant, biased, or eccentric judge[s]." In other words, public scrutiny is a primary safeguard of the defendant's rights.[17]*

The media go on to describe alternatives to a closed hearing, including changing the venue, thorough *voir dire*, and jury sequestration (should the trial take place), and demonstrates the reference to the Sheppard case by the defense as irrelevant to the current issues:

> *Defendant's reliance on Sheppard v Maxwell...is also misplaced. Sheppard addresses the failure of the court to control the trial itself...nothing was done to control jury access to publicity during trial...the jurors were themselves the subjects of ongoing news coverage...the jurors were not sequestered and they were subject to [media] coverage of the trial while not taking part in the proceedings.[18]*

It was a shame that the Cleveland newspapers and television reporters tried the Sheppard case on the front pages every day, and even though Dr. Sheppard was probably guilty of the deliberate staging and commission of his wife's murder, the trial was definitely harmed by the sensational publicity and the appalling behavior of the media at the time. However, in the Peterson case, the defense would have us believe that the popularity of this case is somehow unique, and selecting a fair and impartial jury in a county of over half a million people is impossible. The defense implies also that the judge will not impose controlling measures to prevent jury contamination, privacy, or proper instruction.

---

[17] Ibid, p. 2.
[18] July 31, 2003, News Media's Opposition to Motion to Close Preliminary Hearing, p. 6.

I find it amusing that the defendant, an accused, unknown, unimaginative, unimpressive, unlikable wife murderer, considers himself such a celebrity, so notorious and dreadful, that every citizen of Stanislaus County and the state of California, if not the entire country, has weighed in on his guilt or innocence. Talk about delusions of grandeur!

> The United States Supreme Court recently stated again that empirical research shows that jurors can disregard pretrial publicity...in the few instances when jurors have been exposed to extensive and prejudicial publicity, they are able to disregard it and base their verdict upon the evidence presented in court.[19]

For all intents and purposes, the pretrial publicity regarding the Peterson case has been largely speculation, theory, hearsay, rumors, armchair sleuthing, and projection. If the State has a compelling case against Peterson, the pretrial publicity won't have any impact on the verdict. Conversely, if its case is weak, the preconceptions of a condemning public will be reevaluated and dismissed as ratings-generating hype. Most of us have learned to view the media with a certain cynical cast, and certainly a jury would be open to examining the facts with objectivity and within the context of the law. A wide disparity exists between assumed guilt and guilt beyond a reasonable doubt.

> An open hearing would be consistent with the court's prior orders protecting the defendant from extra-judicial statements and premature exposure to evidence that may or may not be presented in court, subject to the court's rulings on its admissibility. At stake is public confidence in a judicial system that abhors taking evidence in secret...an open preliminary is a primary safeguard of both the public's and the defendant's rights.[20]

Geragos's motion to close the preliminary is an affront to the judge, the Court, the People, and fails to clear the "substantial, substantive and procedural hurdles" required to merit serious consideration. If this were a poker game, it's time to call: People v Peterson, show your hands.

AUGUST 4, 2003
ANATOMY OF A VICTIM

Some of the blanks of the unfortunate but unremarkable history of "mystery woman" Amber Frey have been filled in by a recent article that appeared in the *Fresno Bee*, written with the flavor and presentation of tabloid fare, and a dismal lack of imagination that permeates most of the editorial found in articles about Kobe Bryant's accuser. In both cases, neither victim can speak for herself due to protective orders imposed upon them by the Court, thus their motives, mentality,

---

[19] Ibid, p. 8.
[20] July 31, 2003, News Media's Opposition to Motion to Close Preliminary Hearing, pp. 10-11.

associations, and sexual history are open season to scurrilous and subjective dissection, while their victimizers enjoy extensive defenses.

"I would appreciate my friends and acquaintances to refrain from talking about me to the media for profit or recognition," requested Amber Frey, in her nationally broadcast January 24 press conference when her "romantic" relationship with Scott Peterson was revealed to the world. Bryant's victim's parents made a similar plea to their daughter's classmates, who were placing themselves in front of microphones discussing the personal details of the accuser. Neither Amber nor the Colorado girl was treated with any discretion by their so-called friends, and were assaulted with character assassination by the media.

We have learned that Amber's parents were divorced when she was five, and that she has a half-brother close in age to her natural sister, which presents a curious portrait of her father as a model for overlapping (unfaithful?) relationships. Therapy couches and recovery rooms are filled with women who attempted to find unconditional love from unavailable men in a subconscious effort to gain acceptance from their fathers. In Amber's case, she replayed a common pattern of attracting unavailable partners, either because they were married or emotionally incapable of commitment. Underachievers, liars, players, and abandoners populate her romantic history. When she met Scott Peterson, he must have looked pretty good to her in comparison.

Here was Amber: a single mother determined to make a good life for herself and her child, having worked her way through college and trade school to carve a little niche in her comfort zone involving fitness, perhaps still smarting from abuses sustained by poor relationship choices, eager to put her life on a successful track. The void in her heart led her to organized religion, and she may have initially considered Peterson an answer to a prayer. From Amber's perspective, Scott represented the perfect package: a handsome, well-groomed, charming, gainfully employed guy, with a nice vehicle, all the accoutrements of success, and most attractive of all: wanted her! Compared to the inarticulate, buff, amoral stripper-boy, and the party-hearty rock star wannabe, and the notably absent deadbeat daddy, after the first few dates with Scott, she was pinching herself to make sure she wasn't dreaming. And Scott, in his talented, predatory way, honed in on her weakness, loneliness, hunger for approval and security, and accommodated her with unctuous assurances of his exclusivity and enduring desires, while basking in the glow of her admiration and affection.

Amber was low hanging fruit for Peterson, easy pickings. From news reports, we learned there was trouble in Paradise in late December, perhaps after Scott's alleged tearful admission of having been married but "losing" his wife a year before, which was undoubtedly designed to elicit sympathy and distract Amber from his misrepresentation; but dark doubts began to dwell, activating the lie meter (which pinged like a tuning fork at boyfriends of yore) instigating a personal investigation of Peterson's integrity. I believe that Amber would have soon discovered Scott's domestic reality rather easily without the publicity surrounding the case, and the consequences of her folly would have been entirely manageable.

Had Scott been just another married cad out for a little extramarital activity, perhaps the experience may have been chalked up to another ill-fated attraction; however, because of the murder and subsequent suspicions surrounding his involvement, Amber's life, as she knew it, was over, replaced by routine reporter tails, glaring flashes of strobe lights, insidious innuendo of her profession, opportunistic peddling of her photos and private possessions, and the stage-struck simpering of her family members. What could have been a navigable stone in her rocky road of romance became an unforeseeable nightmare of regret and recrimination. Let's not be too quick to judge Amber for falling for Scott. She was an unwitting victim of tragic timing.

AUGUST 5, 2003
THE LOST BOY

This morning, my three-year-old son gave me a spontaneous hug and kiss, and said, "I yuv you, Mom!" after I helped him dress in his favorite outfit: the orange Spiderman shirt with blue trim and matching blue shorts. He ran to the door and put on his Spiderman sneakers by himself, zipping them up and proudly announcing, "I have a Spiderman shirt, Spiderman shoes, and Spiderman toys! I have a lot of Spiderman!" The moment crystallized for me the joy of having a son in that wonderful age group between toddler and kindergarten, when the child's experiences are magnified by his delight in discovery, uninhibited affection, growing vocabulary, and enthusiastic participation. The moment also brought forth the poignant reminder that Laci Peterson will never dress her son, feel his small arms around her neck or his wet winsome kisses on her face, or hear him tell her he "yuvs" her. She was denied watching him splash in the swimming pool and squirt her with toys, his smooth skin golden in the bright California sun, asking for snacks and juice, and falling asleep before sunset after a day of vigorous play and passionate childhood purpose.

This has been a difficult, surreal summer for the other victims in the Peterson case: Laci's family, and friends. It has probably been the worst summer of their lives; the first without Laci and her never-born son, imagining her baby now six months old, sitting up by himself, creeping, pulling things to his mouth, laughing, babbling, laying his small, fuzzy head on their shoulders with his fist clenched around grandma's finger, enjoying scenic strolls in the park to watch the dogs frolic in the long, light evenings, every precious development discussed with intense interest. There will be no first tooth, first awkward, wobbly steps, first Christmas, or first birthday. The upcoming trial portends a torturous reenactment of their irreparable loss, eradicated futures, and shattered spirits. Perhaps they find some small consolation in believing that Laci and her baby are in a better place, without sorrow or pain, but know that, given the choice, Laci would have preferred to deliver her baby, experience motherhood, and hear the soft, sweet rhythm of her son's breath as she rocked him to sleep.

This has been a distressing summer for Scott Peterson, as well. Confined to a cramped, grim jail cell without access to golf courses, swimming pools, fishing trips, wireless phones, secret mailboxes or women, he must long to wake up in a bedroom with open windows and the smell of freshly brewed coffee, and would by now gladly exchange the sound of a cell door clanging shut with that of a baby crying. I pity him if he realizes he misses his wife in the dark lonely hours of restless sleep; I pity him even more if he doesn't. Unlike Laci, her family, and her baby, however, Scott's pathetic predicament is of his own devices, and his losses mere inconveniences compared to those of his victims.

As the lazy August days burn late into humid twilights, children beg to stay outside to ride their trikes through the sprinklers, or linger on the playground, seemingly immune to heat and fatigue. When they reluctantly submit to having their sticky faces scrubbed, finally collapsing into a coil of sleep, secure in their crisp sheets, cooled by the whirr of a window fan, and the silent shadows move over their innocent forms, we mourn the little boy who never was.

AUGUST 7, 2003
MOTION TO SUPPRESS WIRETAP EVIDENCE

On August 5, the defendant, Scott Lee Peterson, through his attorneys, filed a *Redacted Motion to Suppress Illegally Obtained Wiretap Evidence*, in the Superior Court of California in the case of California v Peterson, which we have been expecting, and which should bolster our confidence that the State has, in fact, a very strong case against Peterson for the murder of his wife and unborn child. Although the motion presents numerous contradictory arguments, generic case law, and specious logic, it nonetheless includes some heartening revelations: the investigation of Peterson, prior to the wiretaps, ostensibly as a result of the seized vehicle(s) and boat, and the original search of the house, produced DNA evidence and information that would lead to the location of Laci's body, referred to on page 16:

> *Although Jacobson claims that the wiretaps are necessary, he entirely neglects two key facts. First, Jacobson acknowledges (redacted portion)...Second, Jacobsen admits that on January 9, 2003, the day before the wiretap applications: (redacted portion)...In light of the prosecution's possession of DNA samples as well as the possible recovery of Laci Peterson's body, there was no necessity at the time of the wiretap application.* [21]

I interpret this argument to mean that "traditional" investigative methods were progressing toward a solution of the case, and the defense relies heavily on the issue (reiterated throughout the motion) that the affidavits for the wiretaps prepared by Mr. Jacobson failed to establish their necessity. This argument contradicts the defense's allegations that the police were solely focused on its client as the perpetrator, that there was "no physical evidence (let alone forensic evidence) that a crime had occurred," and that "since wiretaps are only permitted in connection with certain enumerated crimes, including murder," they had no probable cause to suspect a murder had taken place. You can't have it both ways! You can't have them looking at the wrong guy for a crime that does not exist and also demonstrate that less intrusive investigative techniques were sufficient to expose the crime. This is tantamount to saying, "They obtained, through standard procedure, DNA material and incriminating information on the [alleged] suspect,

---

[21] August 5, 2003 Defense Redacted Motion to Suppress Illegally Obtained Wiretap Evidence, p. 12

and were progressing in their investigation without the need for wiretaps; but their investigation was biased against the husband, they weren't looking at other leads, and there was *no crime*!" Is this deliberately confusing, or just pretzel logic?

Let us examine the six factors enumerated in support of wiretaps, from the *Zepeda* case law cited in the motion, of which the defense claims the surveillance against Peterson fails to support numbers 2, 4, 5 and 6, and only applies to 1 because he is "factually innocent [and] there can be no direct evidence."

1. The case against defendant was entirely circumstantial. Defense concedes this point, yet it is another contradiction to their rejection of the Jacobsen Affidavit, which they claim (and most of it is redacted, but you can glean the gist of it) omitted "material information" that would have disqualified their request. What material facts could the DA have excluded from their affidavit except proof that their investigation was successful in uncovering evidence, thus, discounting the need for wiretaps?

2. It appeared that witnesses were reluctant to come forward other than in an anonymous manner. The defense argues that "numerous witnesses [were] coming forward." I assume it is referring to the discovery information that indicates thousands of tips were submitted to the police, many of which were bogus, including the several reported sightings of Laci walking the dog on Christmas Eve, which we have already shown to be physically and logistically impossible. On its face, this argument seems feasible; however, it is based primarily on false information, not material witnesses. If, for example, there were witnesses who could place Scott Peterson at the Berkeley marina any time before 9:30 a.m. Christmas Eve, this would constitute direct evidence against its client, thus refuting its protestation that "Mr. Peterson did not know the location of his wife," since, as we all know, her body was found in that exact vicinity.

3. Questioning the defendant...was unlikely to produce any additional evidence. Why, if Peterson were innocent, would not questioning him help to eliminate him as a suspect? If he had participated more fully, perhaps the investigation would have moved in a different direction, away from his curious behavior and reluctance to cooperate.

4 and 5. The defendant was unaware that he was the focus of the murder investigation; the defendant was unaware the police had seized evidence from his room and vehicle. Was Peterson aware that he was the focus of the investigation? In several interviews, he denies any involvement in his wife's "disappearance," and shrugs off any concern that the police will arrest him. He claims on camera that "they have to have something on me," and watches dispassionately as they search his home a second time. If he realized he was a suspect, albeit unnamed at that point, he certainly didn't try to alter their opinion of him, by actively searching for his wife or demonstrating any grief or dismay at her absence. Instead, he calls his girlfriend, sells his wife's car, abandons his house, hides out at his half-sister's home in Berkeley, parties in San Diego, plays golf, dyes his hair, and doesn't return to town when the bodies surface.

6. The defendant was likely to alert others and ask them to destroy other evidence. We don't know if Peterson had any accomplices after the fact to the murder, but we can be certain that if he were tipped off to where the police were searching, or what evidence they had procured up to the time the wiretaps were approved, he would have gone to great lengths to destroy it or create reasonable explanations for it. Meanwhile, he made numerous trips to Berkeley early on (not including the time he stayed there in March and April) to the area where the bodies were submerged, keeping tabs on the police search, playing his little game of cat and mouse.

The motion goes on to claim that the prosecution failed to make the surveillance application to the presiding judge (which was Girolami) and rather "shopped" the affidavit to find a judge who would authorize it. It insists that Peterson was offered a plea in January to avoid the death penalty, and that by making that offer the prosecution defined the case as a capital one, which mandated court reporters at the meetings with Judge Ladine regarding the wiretaps. This is another example of skewed logic, and will unlikely merit relief; however, it will be interesting to see how Girolami rules on this motion on September 9, when the issues of what evidence, if any, obtained by the wiretaps will be suppressed, and what evidence will be included that was derived from the "eavesdropping." Even in the worst case scenario, if Girolami throws out all the wiretap evidence, he can't rule on the constitutionality of the penal code (which is fodder for appeal), and it appears, through the defense's own arguments, that the State may have a "slam dunk" case against Scott Peterson after all.

AUGUST 18, 2003
IN DEFENSE OF ART AND DISCOVERY

From the stories about the strange art found at the Albany Bulb:

Some of the artwork features decapitation and devil figures. Many of the paintings portray sexual activity, and several show pregnant women.

One shows a man with an ax beheading a man in a rowboat on a body of water; a topless woman kneels next to the beheaded man.

On the inside of a concrete structure on the peninsula, Rayburn's group painted a goat-headed figure spearing a caged man as a demonic image lurks.
"We called the inside of that place hell, because that's what it was to paint," he said. "You had to lay on a board in a foot of water to paint it."[22]

Based on images described above, let us examine several famous works of art that contain some of the very same alarming iconography purported to be of a satanic nature:
- Michelangelo's Last Judgment: From the Sistine Chapel, circa 1534
- Gustav Klimt's "Hope," painted in 1903
- Picasso's "Guernica," 1937
- Marc Chagall's "Goat" series, 1927

---

[22] Cote, John and Stapely, Garth, "Defense Outlines Cult Theory," Modesto Bee, August 14, 2003

- Francisco de Goya's "Saturn," 1873

Are we to conclude that Michelangelo, Klimt, Picasso, Chagall and Goya were each members of a devil-worshipping cult because their works depict pregnant women, death symbols, goats, the damned being sent to Hell in boats, dead infants, bulls, decapitation, murder, cannibalism and imprisonment? You be the judge.

People's Response to Defense Motion for Discovery

According to the Response filed today, The People:

> *...have fully complied with the discovery requirements...over 23,700 pages of documents, 18 videotapes, 100 audio tapes, 5 DVDs, 3 wiretap CDs, all search warrant material, and all wiretap documentary evidence has been provided.*
>
> *The People formally request reciprocal discovery...specifically any real evidence that the defendant intends to offer at trial...including any reports or statements of experts made in connection with the case, and including the results of physical or mental examinations, scientific tests...or comparisons which the defendant intends to offer in evidence at the trial...or at the preliminary hearing.*[23]

To wit, the People have provided names of witnesses, statements the defendant [Peterson] made (including those made to the media), all real evidence seized including that which has come back from scientific testing, most of the police notes, wiretap information, subpoenas, and one interesting tidbit: transcripts of a statement from a hypnotized witness, Kristin Dempewolf. I wonder what part she has to play?

Of particular value to the defense is the information about the bloodhounds, since items 18 through 24 deal exclusively with the dogs, their handlers, training methods, credentials, and veterinary records. Why is the defense so interested in the bloodhounds? Is it because of the fact that the dogs, by tracking Laci's scent in the opposite direction of the park, and nowhere near the Mitchells' house, refute two out of the three sightings of Laci on the 24th out of hand?

Without a credible, logical sighting of Laci on the morning of December 24, and if the clothing found on her remains does not match that which was described by Mr. Maldonado, the defense theory that Laci was kidnapped is completely shattered. Never mind their feeble attempt to connect the artists from the Albany Bulb with any incidents of ritualistic murder.

Not only do the bloodhounds dissemble Scott's statements about Laci's plans that morning, but the weather, her condition, and her plans for the holiday rule out dog walking, early morning or otherwise. She would have taken the time that day to bake for the family gathering that evening, and prepare for her brunch the next day. More likely, McKenzie would have had to trot outside in the backyard when necessary.

---

[23] August 18, 2003 People's Response to Defense Motion for Discovery, p. 1.

Despite the defense's provocative alluding to the contrary, according to the People's response, the existence of "exculpatory evidence" is nil. It appears the People are ready for trial. If the defense requests a continuance, I hope the judge considers the adage, "Justice delayed is justice denied." This case should be focused on justice for Laci and her baby, not Scott Peterson.

AUGUST 22, 2003
AUGUST 13 DOCUMENTS

On August 13, five documents were filed in the Stanislaus County Supreme Court in California v Peterson, which included:

- *From the Defense*: Notice of Motion and Motion for Discovery, Declaration of Adam Talaat, and Opposition to Motion to Conduct Venue Survey.
- *From the People*: Opposition to Motion to Suppress Wiretap Audio Recordings
- *From the Court*: Further Stipulation and Order Authorizing additional limited examination of remains [of Laci and baby Peterson], which were to be x-rayed today and returned to the next of kin, presumably Laci's family.

A summary of the salient points from these documents follows, along with my editorial analysis and observations wherever relevant.

Motion for Discovery: *filed by Kirk McAllister, counsel for the defense*

Among the 26 items listed in McAllister's request for discovery, several items reveal deeper layers of the case of which we (the public) were not aware, and validate our belief that a substantial amount of evidence has been gathered against Peterson. Item 14 includes "all wiretaps, state or federal, including all applications for wiretaps, orders authorizing wiretaps..." which implies a federal interest in Mr. Peterson, recently mentioned in media reports that suggest Peterson's fertilizer business may have intersected with methamphetamine laboratories. The feds' interest and collaboration with the wiretaps is intriguing; nevertheless I find it implausible that Peterson possessed the street smarts, wherewithal, underworld connections or nerve to fraternize with dangerous and unscrupulous drug manufacturers. Not that he is a moral, upstanding citizen, but because his self-preservation instincts superseded any short-term financial gain. I imagine that Peterson was planning a long, happy, unfettered future once his wife and baby were conveniently out of the way, with a tidy nest egg of her life insurance benefits (when she was declared dead after a few years), boundless sympathy and enabling from both families, and a world of adoring, devoted sources for the making. I don't see him complicating this delicious fantasy with drug-related enterprises.

Item 24 enumerates "color-accurate reproductions of all writings generated by any and all trackers showing or attempting to show the whereabouts of Scott

Peterson and/or a vehicle operated by him." And Item 25: "All notes, memoranda and logs relating to law enforcement surveillance of Scott Peterson."

We concluded early on that the police had a GPS device on the Land Rover, (which was traded in) and then the new Dodge truck (which was abandoned in San Diego and replaced by either a family vehicle, a friend's vehicle, or the new maroon Mercedes purchased in April), and had employed other surveillance methods that Peterson was evidently attempting to thwart. I don't know how the defense intends to use this information, except perhaps try to argue that the Modesto Police Department solely focused on Peterson at the exclusion of any other potential suspects, bolstering its "rush to judgment" theory and its accusation of professional misconduct of the investigators. Unfortunately, it will have a difficult time justifying Mr. Innocent's behavior in abandoning any active search for his wife, and especially after her remains and those of their son washed ashore in mid-April.

Declaration of Adam Talaat

Adam Talaat, Vice President of Technology for WashingtonLive, Inc., performed a search of articles mentioning "Scott or Laci Peterson" on August 12 and 13, 2003. From his search (of sources he does not specify), over 5,000 articles were available online. For the majority of people interested in this case who are not residents of California or who do not have cable access, the Internet was the only source of updated information. I can attest that most of my readers found my Web site from a search on Laci Peterson. Local TV stations rarely, if ever, broadcast anything on the case, and stories about the Petersons appeared only in tabloids and the occasional national news clip. The Internet is the last bastion of a market-driven press, providing information in a free, uncensored format, with loyalties only to the truth, the readers or in some cases, personal agendas. The defense may use the volume of Internet articles to show cause for a closed hearing; however, it may be argued that unless you purposely seek out information on the Net, it is hardly automatic or unsolicited.

Opposition to Motion to Conduct Venue Survey: *Filed by Mark Geragos, counsel for the defense:*

> *Mr. Peterson has not had a preliminary hearing in this matter. Discovery is nowhere near complete in this matter...Yet, unbelievably the prosecution proposes to have this Court expend taxpayer funds to conduct a survey before a preliminary hearing...a type of survey designed to not only tamper with prospective jurors in this case but in any other criminal cases in which those prospective jurors would sit...Not only is this procedure illegal and ethical [sic] - its mere suggestion would almost be amusing if it was not proposed in a capital case.[24]*

---

[24] August 13, 2003 Defense Opposition to Motion to Conduct Venue Survey, p. 3.

Notice that Mark Geragos mentions his lack of "discovery" in the first sentence of his motion, which is the dead horse *du jour* he now beats, replacing the "exculpatory evidence" and "witnesses to the real perpetrators," and innuendo and references *ad nauseum* to the satanic cult theory perpetrated for the last two months. Incidentally, why should Geragos concern himself with "taxpayer funds," since none of those funds are coming out of his pocket? Is he trying to ingratiate himself with the public as a protector of Stanislaus County tax dollars? How ironic, considering every document he submits, every hearing he continues, every extraneous use of court personnel, resources and time he squanders with his frivolous motions and delays wastes exponentially more tax dollars than a venue survey. The hypocrisy is denser than the August humidity.

> *No motion for a change of venue has been filed in this case...it is somewhat insulting to the Court (and defense counsel) for the prosecution to assume a month before the preliminary hearing that Mr. Peterson will be bound over - particularly prior to the prosecution's having even seen all the evidence.*[25]

Does the request for a venue survey merit this level of righteous indignation? Geragos's earsplitting opposition is tantamount to playing every measure of a sonata *fortissimo*. Where can the dynamics go from there? One cannot stay at this volume without rendering its impact completely impotent. With regard to the People's confidence that Peterson will be bound over for trial, if this were not the case, the defense would have expedited the hearing long ago, and Mr. Innocent would be enjoying the dog days of summer on the putting green, rather than puttering around the tiny floor of his oppressive jail cell.

> *...the prosecution never addresses the fact that every defense lawyer who has a case with one of the jurors who is surveyed will have a built-in motion to excuse that entire jury venire panel...any juror in the courthouse can disqualify himself from this case merely by seeking out an agent of the prosecution and volunteering to take the survey. Given that a trial in this matter (should one ever occur) would undoubtedly last many, many months, it is not difficult to imagine hordes of prospective jurors clamoring to surveyors in order to avoid serving on the jury.*[26]

I hope the Honorable Judge Girolami got a good laugh from this motion, because I certainly did. The leaps into an illogical abyss, misinterpretation, histrionic language, and theatrical projections of improbable scenarios are worthy of a comic book! It is even more ridiculous knowing that there will certainly be a motion to change venue, after the predictable (drafted yet as we speak) moves to continue, based on the defense's dead horse discovery complaints and wiretap suppression, that I hope are denied, and the preliminary hearing finally takes place, at which point a venue survey will be moot.

---

[25] Ibid, p. 4.
[26] Ibid, p. 6.

Opposition to Motion to Suppress Wiretap Audio Recordings: *filed by the People, represented by Rick Distaso, Stanislaus County District Attorney*
        ...the defense contention that Congress intended to limit wiretapping to organized criminal enterprises is not correct.[27]

In fact, the defense's entire premise, comprising several pages with selective citations, interprets the laws governing wiretaps incorrectly. Regardless of whether the police had publicly declared Laci's disappearance a homicide is irrelevant in their application to obtain wiretaps. As many of us did, from early on in the case, they determined that a homicide had taken place. We are not privy to their reasoning, but certainly Judge Ladine was.

> *...The defense team having over a century of collective criminal defense experience is unaware of any alleged case of domestic violence in which the prosecution has sought a wiretap, much less been granted one.' While the prosecution questions the authority of the defense experience with domestic violent homicide, the fact that no member of the defense team has previously dealt with wiretap evidence certainly doesn't mean that the wiretap authorization was improper.*[28]

I am not sure if Mark Geragos has even tried a capital case, although I know McAllister has. The defense team appears to have collective experience with plea-bargaining, contempt of court, probation violators, drug addicts, and shoplifters.

> *The defense also states that Inv. Jacobson neglected two 'key facts' from his claim that the wiretap was necessary...that the prosecution possessed DNA samples [from other investigative techniques] and second, that there was a possible recovery of Laci Peterson's body...these contentions are without merit...*[29]

DNA evidence and the searching not for a missing person, but a body, again indicate that the investigators had reason to believe Laci was dead. The defense maintains at this time, it was a missing persons case, and contradicts itself with its assertions that the wiretaps were not required because of the impending discovery of Laci's body. They can't have the case classified a capital crime, thus requiring court reporters at the meetings, while concurrently declaring there was no evidence to suspect a murder, and therefore have no probable cause to acquire court approved wiretaps.

> *The defense does not state which 'proceedings' should have been recorded. Since all proceedings regarding both wiretaps took place during the investigation of Laci and Connor's murder, and none after the*

---

[27] August 13, 2003 People's Opposition to Motion to Suppress Wiretap Audio Recordings, p. 3.
[28] Ibid, p. 3.
[29] August 13, 2003 People's Opposition to Motion to Suppress Wiretap Audio Recordings, p. 7.

criminal case was filed, the People are unsure as to how far back in the investigation the defense alleges that a court reporter should have been present...every time a search warrant was authorized in a capital murder investigation, a court reporter would have to be present.[30]

The Affidavit for Wiretap No. 3 contained a large amount of information gained from Wiretap No. 2. It was also written months later, after significant developments had taken place in the investigation. The most notable development was the discovery of Laci and Connor's remains in the exact location where the defendant said he went fishing on Dec. 24, 2002.[31]

..because the defendant was aware that certain traditional investigative techniques were taking place (thereby limiting their effectiveness) no necessity was shown for Wiretap No. 3. That is the exact opposite conclusion that the court should draw from these facts. Such facts actually show the limitations of traditional law enforcement techniques, and further demonstrated the need for Wiretap No. 3.[32]

The defense...desires to turn the Dustin decision into a vehicle for inflammatory and personal attacks...in an attempt to improperly influence this court..[and] the People will not respond in kind to such provocation, preferring instead to let the record itself reflect the absurdity of the defense remarks.[33]

"Absurdity" seems to define the defense's entire case.

---

[30] Ibid, p. 14.
[31] Ibid, p. 10
[32] Ibid, p. 11.
[33] Ibid, p. 13.

CHAPTER 5: DELAYS, DELAYS

SEPTEMBER 1, 2003
OUTLINE OF THE PRELIMINARY HEARING

At a preliminary hearing in California all that is required for the People to establish is A) a crime was committed, and B) the defendant was the probable perpetrator. Whatever evidence presented tends to be simply an outline of the case, and because California law allows hearsay testimony in a preliminary, law enforcement representation is permitted to reiterate events from statements of witnesses. The defense will introduce no witnesses, but is expected to cross-examine the People's.

Because of the nature of the crime and the inexperience (and anxiety) of the key players, I predict that most of the testimony at the preliminary will be given by law enforcement rather than members of Laci's family or necessarily Amber Frey. This serves two purposes: it protects them from antagonizing and confusing cross-examination from the defense, and gives them more time to prepare for trial, where their testimony will have much more impact in front of a jury. However, Lee Peterson may have to testify to the phone calls and other conversations with his son regarding the events of December 23 and 24; I wouldn't be surprised if the prosecution deliberately called him up to show him just who's running the show, and to justify the subpoenas served as a little payback for his defamation of the Modesto police.

Possibly, Amy and Sharon Rocha, and police officers at the scene will testify to the last known contact with Laci. They will describe her as being happy and excited about the baby, and in no way depressed, much less suicidal. They will nip in the bud any speculation that Laci went to the Bay on her own, or was involved with anyone else who could take her there. They might ask about Laci's habits, including her routine to walk the dog, and they may say they were not aware that she walked the dog, or doubt she walked the dog that morning, or that she ordinarily walked the dog in the afternoon. They may question Laci's known habits about carrying her cell phone with her, keys from her house, what she wore outside to walk, and the path she normally took. They will try to establish that she probably didn't take a walk that day, and that she was never seen or heard from after 8:30 pm on the night of December 23.

Members of law enforcement will testify to the 9-1-1 calls that Ron Grantski and Peterson made, and the officers who responded will review what they did that night, to the condition of the house, Peterson's behavior, any injuries they observed on his hands, neck or face, any reluctance on his part to cooperate, the smell of bleach and other oddities about the scene, and any search of the house. Scott's phone calls to friends and family about Laci "missing," and using the word, "missing" over and over, which was particularly peculiar to Laci's family, will intimate his foreknowledge of her fate.

Officers will testify to the ways in which they tried to eliminate Peterson as a suspect in their investigation, yet how all paths led back to his involvement. They will show that the sightings of Laci were false leads, or they may skip that until trial. They will show how the bloodhounds tracked Laci's scent to the end of the driveway, and then south to Maze, rather than to the park where Scott said she was headed. They may indicate they have witnesses that saw Scott near the marina in the early hours of the 24th, and to his admission to being there later in the day based on his launch ticket, witnesses who saw him at the boat launch, and forensic evidence that shows the boat was in the Bay, including possibly the paint marks (which may match buoy paint), the computer researches (from files obtained), salt water in the motor, and other botanical evidence.

Peterson placed himself at the site where the bodies surfaced, thus establishing a link to her murder, and witnesses may report (through surveillance) that he revisited the site frequently in the early months of the investigation. They will show that there were concrete anchors mixed in a bucket, impressions of several left on the surface in the warehouse, and which are still unaccounted for. They may discuss his lack of fishing gear, bait, and the logistics of his alibi that, based on phone records and travel time, precluded Peterson from being in the Bay longer than an hour in the afternoon of December 24.

They will show that from her autopsy, Laci's death was determined to be a homicide (they don't have to show manner of death), and that there was no reasonable way for her to be in that condition or in that vicinity by her own volition. They will conclude that the baby's death was a direct result of the mother's death, and by law constitutes a double homicide with special circumstances; thus the defendant was held without bail.

They will defer information derived from wiretaps until that issue is resolved after the hearing, and because they don't need it at the preliminary, anyway. If they introduce the affair with Amber Frey, it will be to show the defendant's state of mind: he was cavalier about his wife gone missing; he continued to pursue Ms. Frey while everyone was looking for Laci, and that he did not participate in any of the family's organized searches. They will bring up his selling of her vehicle, inquiries into selling the house, his change of appearance, deliberate avoidance of Modesto, and his refusal to submit to a routine polygraph and his lack of cooperation.

Other evidence about which we have speculated may come out in the hearing, such as Laci's DNA found on the boat, fresh blood from Peterson in his truck, DNA retrieved from the blue tarp found in the water near Berkeley, possibly other physical evidence obtained from the second tarp in which Peterson claimed he was transporting umbrellas, which were actually never moved. If they have enhanced photographs of him in the Bay, they will definitely produce those. They will bring out everything that connects him to the Bay, the area in which the body was dumped, and to the murder.

They will establish that a murder took place, and Peterson is the only person who could have committed it. That's really all they need to hold him over for trial, and I would be surprised if they use as much as I have presented. If most of the testimony (if not all) comes from police, investigators, and professionals, I doubt Geragos will have much to do on cross, except propose that they focused mainly on Peterson because of laziness, "tunnel vision" (as in the reports that state the police were taking this case "personally"), and to redeem themselves after the Stayner/Yosemite debacle with quick closure of this widely publicized case. In the Stayner case, along with other reported events of mishandling the investigation, the Modesto Police stopped Roary Larwick, a suspect in the Carol and Julie Sund murders, based on information from an anonymous tip. Larwick ran from the scene and holed up in a Modesto residence near where Carol Sund's wallet was found. After a 14-hour standoff during which he opened fire on the police, Larwick was arrested. Four months later, Sund's confessed murderer, Cary Stayner, killed a fourth woman, Joie Armstrong near Yosemite National Park where he worked as a handyman for a lodge.

In his questioning, Geragos might jump up and down about the surveillance, the rush to judgment, the violation of Peterson's rights, the lack of a definitive "manner of death," and suggest other possible explanations for the evidence that do not implicate his client. He may argue that there is no explicit nexus linking Peterson to the murder, and that the circumstantial evidence is not strong enough to hold his client; that, in fact, the defense is conducting an ongoing investigation to uncover other potential perpetrators. Undoubtedly, the preliminary will result in setting a trial date, which will be subjected to numerous continuances and delays and an immediate motion by the defense for a venue change. That's what I expect, and we will see what actually occurs on September 9, or when the hearing finally takes place.

SEPTEMBER 21, 2003
THE FRESNO CONNECTION

What is so special about Fresno that the city and some of its residents (new ones appearing recently) are playing a key part in the Laci Peterson murder case? Why not the more cosmopolitan city of San Francisco, or the eclectic, college town, Berkeley; or even Peterson's old stomping grounds, San Luis Obispo or San Diego? Let us examine the particular attraction and significance of Fresno for Peterson, its connection to the murder, and why its fertile farmland may yield much more than grapes and garbanzo beans.

Peterson's employment as a fertilizer salesman naturally led him to Fresno: a large, heavily populated agricultural area with what the natives boast as a "small town mentality." Fresno is centrally located and quite possibly a common overnight stop during Peterson's sales call routine. He quickly became familiar with the local nightspots, particularly those that would cater to his appetites. Perhaps Scott was drawn to the slimy underbelly of society, enjoyed surrounding himself with inferiors, and felt comfortable and superior among the polo shirts in tony sports bars or the polyester shirts in sleazy strip joints. Peterson could be anonymous in Fresno, portraying himself as an affluent, well-employed, single man with a room key and an expense account. Much of his entertainment was a potential write off, and he was seen often dining in style, accompanied by women; or slinking, unfettered, into a dark, disco thumping dance bar, without being recognized or accountable.

Our first introduction to Fresno was through Amber Frey, Peterson's most recent conquest just prior to the murder. It was reported that they saw each other regularly between November 20 and December 14, which would account for Peterson's regular presence in Fresno. He often stayed downtown in a hotel called "La Quinta," which is, ironically, right across the street from the courthouse and jail in which his new accuser, Cory Carroll, resides. Amber Frey, however, was not only oblivious of Peterson's marriage, but also of his other rumored Fresno girlfriends, of whose acquaintance we have yet to have the pleasure of making. Fresno had it all for Peterson: a discreet locale for business, action and women.

The latest startling development in the case involves events that allegedly occurred in Fresno between Peterson and a relapsing petty criminal, Cory Carroll. From Carroll's statements, Peterson met him at City Lights, a popular strip club, and their conversation turned to car theft and kidnapping. I suspect Peterson had several of these types of conversations with Fresno barflies, chatting them up about his developing scheme in an innocuous way, couched in hypothetical scenarios or in context with ambient events such as television shows like "The Sopranos" or local news. It is evident from Carroll that Peterson was planning his wife's murder at least as far back as November, if not earlier. The subsequent secret purchase of the boat, another post office box, and the materials he acquired for the anchors and disposal fall neatly into place in the complex confluence of premeditation.

Peterson's family insists he could not have been in Fresno the night of November 29 for the alleged meeting with the Nazi low rider members, but I disagree. I think it not only possible, but probable that Peterson returned from San Diego early that Friday evening, had his bags already packed with plans to meet a client on Saturday to make up for the two days off. He ventured to Fresno and arrived before 9 pm with the intent to explore his kidnapping-for-hire options, and spend the night with his new girlfriend whose arms were guaranteed open at any hour. Only Amber Frey can tell us for sure, because I am certain she will recall if she spent any part of Thanksgiving weekend with Peterson. Her memory, etched by emotions of horror and grief, is quite reliable; in contrast to that of Carroll, whose professed ignorance of the most publicized murder case in recent local history reveals an acute lack of awareness.

One may now wonder why Peterson didn't dispose of Laci's body on a remote farm or along the many winding rural miles of his frequently traveled path. Early speculation about Peterson's alibi promoted the idea that he intentionally misled the authorities, and that he hadn't gone fishing on December 24 at all. With this new information, I surmise that Peterson was, in fact, deliberately focusing the investigation away from the scene of his other crimes: the fruitful and furtive facets of his counterfeit life in Fresno.

SEPTEMBER 26, 2003
THE WEEK IN REVIEW: FACTS AND RUMORS

After several weeks of rehash and relative lull in activity, suddenly we're buried in an avalanche of information about Scott Peterson's behavior prior to, and shortly after, the events of December 24. In separating the facts from unconfirmed rumors and speculation, some of the blurry outlines of the implications of Peterson's activities gain a much sharper focus on premeditation, predisposition, and culpability for his wife's murder.

On Monday, September 22, we learned that Laci's autopsy indicated she had caffeine in her system, but none was found in the baby. This essentially refuted the myth that the baby lived beyond the time of her murder, as if he would grow outside the womb like an unripe tomato. Toxicology tests returned negative for any other substances, including the illusive GHB (in reference to leaks that information about the drug was found on Peterson's computer), which even if used, would have dissipated quickly, months before their bodies were discovered.

Rumors of the Petersons' dissatisfaction with Geragos circulated early in the week, culminating in the factual report that Matt Dalton had been removed from the defense team and was no longer affiliated with Geragos's firm. Whether this was due to professional differences, scapegoating, or misconduct remains to be revealed, but Dalton's indecorous photo opportunities regarding the missing sandals, the Rocha's retrieval of Laci's property from her home, and his dog and pony show for Drs Lee and Wecht on the satanic cult theory were imprudent at best, and a public relations disaster at worst.

Last weekend we heard from the now infamous Cory Carroll, an alleged acquaintance of Scott Peterson, who allegedly arranged (for $300) a meeting between Peterson and the innocuously nicknamed Skeeter and Dirty, members of the nefarious Nazi low rider gang, ostensibly to discuss stealing Laci's car for insurance fraud, or kidnapping her for ransom. Few facts are known at this time about the meeting, including the actual date, what was discussed, or any subsequent meetings between Peterson and the low riders. We know for a fact that Carroll passed a lie detector test, conducted by Melvin King, a legitimate former law enforcement agent in Fresno, but Carroll's story reeks with inconsistency and suspension of disbelief. Are we to accept Carroll's insistence that he was unaware of Laci Peterson's murder (or her missing status) for six months? It strains the benefit of any doubt.

Resumed searches on the Bay were also reported this past weekend, followed by a story in a weekly tabloid that claimed one of the four missing concrete anchors was found in the area between Brooks Island and Richmond. If the find is true, I expect more searches for the rest of the weights and remains, pending available resources and cooperative weather conditions. As long as the preliminary and trial are delayed, it stands to reason that the prosecution and defense will continue their investigations. There is no such thing as too much evidence, and the discovery of more physical material that could have been used to submerge a body can only further the cause of justice.

Amber Frey was front and center most of the week, among stories of her security issues, the pornographic Web site that is now selling downloads of her pictures without her consent (or financial interest), and the once speculated but now verified fact of her alarmingly frequent phone contacts with Peterson just before and after the murder. The most curious of all the statistics: 14 calls to Peterson on December 26, when she was still under the impression that he was an unmarried man traveling to Maine and later to Paris for "up to a month," according to her father. What prompted this frantic calling is left to our imaginations, but I suspect most, if not all of those calls went unanswered. It is clear from the published phone log graph that she was alerted to something extremely disturbing in late December when she felt compelled to call the Modesto Police at 1:30 in the morning. Either she saw a news break on television regarding the case and recognized Peterson, or received conclusive proof that he was, in fact, the husband of the missing woman in Modesto. In any event, it appears she was emotionally distraught and eager to cooperate.

From this plethora of intriguing innuendo, there emerges an unmistakable and insidious framework of premeditation in Peterson's underground inquiries, the fictitious travel itinerary he gave to Amber, and the secret cash purchase of the boat in early December. Combined with the tidal searches mined from his computer cache, and his abysmal fishing trip alibi that lamentably places him at the scene of the disposal, leaves little doubt that Peterson implemented a pernicious, preconceived plan to not only murder, but to *eradicate* his wife and baby.

OCTOBER 8, 2003
SEE NO EVIL, HEAR NO EVIL, SPEAK NO EVIL

Desperate times call for desperate measures, and in the hopeless case of California v Peterson, counsel for the defense, Mark Geragos's frantic filing of motions to exclude as much salient evidence against his client as possible is heartwarming proof that he is clamoring for a credible defense.

The five motions filed October 7 include:

1. Motion to Conduct Franks Hearing
2. Notice of Motion and Motion in Limine to Exclude GPS Tracking Evidence
3. Notice of Motion and Motion to Exclude Dog Trailing Evidence
4. Notice of Motion and Motion to Exclude Testimony of Hypnotized Witness
5. Notice of Motion and Motion in Limine to Exclude Mitochondrial DNA Evidence

Of these, let us "fisk" the inane arguments presented to exclude the GPS tracking evidence, the dog trailing evidence, and the mitochondrial DNA evidence for the worthless rubbish they are, and conclude that Geragos's pathetic hitting slump to date in achieving Court approval for his shameless claptrap will remain unbroken.

The GPS Evidence

> *In the case at hand, the Court has the opportunity to make good law and precedent case law on an issue of first impression...The GPS technology has not been generally accepted by the scientific community for several reasons. GPS has inherent inaccuracies. Furthermore, the government, at times unknown to the pubic and users of GPS based technology, will intentionally reduce the accuracy of GPS.*[34]

Here we have Geragos in effect asking the Court to create law (which is not its function), as it did with earlier motions striking the wiretap evidence based on its arguable unconstitutionality. Then, there is the deliberately false statement that the technology is not accepted by the "scientific community," and the suggestion right out of a spy novel that the "government" secretly undermines GPS satellite receivers. Let us remind Geragos of two devices currently used for our national

---

[34] October 7, 2003 Defense Motion to Exclude GPS Tracking Evidence, p. 7.

security and defense: "Smart Bombs" and "Predator" unmanned aircraft, which rely on GPS technology and have proven phenomenally accurate and singularly successful. Geragos goes on to explain the technology in several tedious and unnecessary pages, and if it were not for deriving consolation that Peterson is paying dearly for each superfluous paragraph, the tome would be unbearable to navigate in order to find the most ridiculous statement of all:

> *GPS technology is a fairly new technology. The system was first launched in 1978 when the first 11 experimental satellites were placed in orbit.*[35]

How does a technology devised in 1978 qualify as "fairly new?" The Hubbell Telescope wasn't introduced until 1990; does that mean we should disregard its results? Using "geralogic," we should also disqualify people who have had corneal surgery from driving an automobile, and those who have had arthroscopic surgery from resuming careers in professional sports, and all data obtained from MRIs. Never mind the billions of bits of information deciphered from Pentium processors, which were not introduced until the late 90s. Geragos cites an article entitled, "GPS Explained: How the Global Positioning System Lets You Know Where You Stand," by Alan Zeichick, which I found online. His careful and selective quotations conveniently omit the author's conclusion, which reads:

> *New uses for the Navstar system appear every day. Businesses use GPS signals to calibrate their computer clocks and transmit the position of mobile radios. When used in conjunction with special differential GPS transmitters, often found near harbors and airports, the system's accuracy can be within 10 feet. Surveyors use DGPS to map large plots of land. Considering that the Navstar system was built by the military, you can't get much more civilian than that.*[36]

In reality, GPS systems are so widely used, so widely accepted (if not taken for granted) in their reliability and validity, that virtually every aspect of modern life, from driving to defense, implements its tested and continuously improving technology. Even Mark Geragos has a Navstar system in his Porsche.

The "Dawgs"

> *The foundation for dog scent evidence must include evidence that the circumstances of the tracking itself make it probable that the person tracked was the guilty party...Every California case, and indeed every out-of-state case disclosed by our research, deals with dogs tracking the scent of suspects. In the case at the bar, however, the prosecution*

---

[35] Ibid, p. 8.

[36] Zeichick, Alan, "GPS Explained: How the Global Positioning System Lets You Know Where You Stand," published on various Web Sites.

proposes evidence of dogs tracking the scent not of a suspect but of Laci Peterson.[37]

Mr. Geragos, I suggest you fire your "research" team, because in less than 10 minutes, I was able to find the following California (and one Nevada) cases where dogs were used to track the victim, and this was just the first page of "hits":

In 1996, Earl Rhoney, 20, was convicted of murdering an Irvine, California woman during a burglary -- based on a bloodhound identifying scent extracted from the victim's sweatshirt, preserved for nine months in an evidence freezer.[38]

(From the obituary of a dog named "Friday") Friday worked details for 40 different law enforcement agencies in the greater San Francisco Bay Area during his 8 plus years as a working Bloodhound. He had a well-rounded track record that included two underwater drowning victim finds, treeing a bad guy and working countless crime scene investigations. One crime scene trail Friday worked successfully turned out to be 15 days old. Friday had the distinction of working a great number of Northern California kidnapping cases.[39]

At 12:30 p.m., a full Search and Rescue team callout was initiated including about 15 SAR officers and volunteers, Air 3, 2 bloodhound teams, and 2 Metro K-9 teams. The search focused on the point last seen with the two bloodhound and k-9 teams. One bloodhound team was able to pick-up the scent of the two missing children and proceeded to follow the tracks while ground search teams were flown by helicopter to various locations to contain the search area. As the afternoon and evening progressed, the two children could not be located within the initial search area. A second Search and Rescue callout was made to bring in more searchers to relieve others in the field and prepare for night operations. Air 4, which is equipped with night vision, was also brought in to search at night.[40]

In the Richard Trenton Chase case: (California)

Police officers continued the search for the baby, using a bloodhound. They even went to Chase's mother's home and she was uncooperative,

---

[37] October 7, 2003 Defense Motion to Exclude Dog Tracking Evidence at the Preliminary Hearing, p. 3.

[38] Johnson, Eric, "Man Found Guilty of '94 Murder is Dead," *Irvine World News*, December 31, 2001.

[39] Contra Costa Sheriff's Search and Rescue Web Site (www.contracostasar.org.)

[40] Las Vegas Metropolitan Police Department (LVMPD) Search and Rescue Missions, May 29, 2000.

insisting that despite what they had found, it did not prove that her son had done anything. (He was convicted.) [41]

Mitochondrial DNA

Geragos, dancing the "Time Warp" like a demented Rocky Horror Show cultist, presumes to attack the legitimacy of mtDNA testing, based on its ambiguity, questionable procedures, and "novel scientific technique." If that argument doesn't fly, Geragos's Plan B is to exclude the hair evidence "on the grounds that there was a complete break in the chain of custody based on the handling of the evidence items and the search conducted."

> *The fact that counsel sought only mitochondrial DNA testing is significant because mitochondrial testing is not a unique identifier because it is shared by individual with a given maternal line...Furthermore, the analysis set forth below clearly establishes that mtDNA evidence lacks the reliability and exactitude required to be admissible in court.* [42]

The "given maternal line" severely reduces the pool of remotely potential candidates for the hair sample in question: Sharon Rocha, Brent Rocha, and Laci, and that none of them knew about the boat or had reason for their hair to be in that boat. If the hair has a root and follicle, that implies forcible removal. If it is a stray hair, it may have been "transfer" from the house, and therefore insignificant. Geragos's obvious concern about the hair evidence indicates the former, and despite his ham-fisted clinging to nincompoop notions borrowed from the Flat Earth Society, will nonetheless be forced to surrender to modern forensic science.

OCTOBER 14, 2003
THE PEOPLE'S RESPONSE TO EVIDENCE SUPPRESSION

Today the People of California filed their "Points and Authorities in support of the Admissibility of [State's] Evidence" in the Superior Court in response to the five defense motions filed last week to suppress evidence. In the Points and Authorities, the prosecution addressed the mtDNA evidence and the dog tracking results.

In support of the hair sample evidence using mtDNA testing, the People argue that:

1. Mitochondrial DNA testing has been used for over 20 years, which refutes the defense's classifying it as a "novelty." (I suggest we send the defense team a microscope. The magnifying glass it is using has been obsolete for decades.)

2. Mitochondrial DNA testing is "scientifically valid, admissible, relevant, reliable and generally accepted."

---

[41] Ramsland, Katherine, "The Making of a Vampire," Court TV Crime Library.

[42] October 7, 2003 Defense Motion to Exclude Mitochondrial DNA Evidence, p. 6.

3. An FBI laboratory conducted the analysis; therefore specific, documented procedures were followed using "appropriate technology." (We hope.)

4. *California case law has resolved the admissibility of PCR-type testing,* so there is obviously legal precedent, and the procedure itself has already passed the Kelly-Frye standard for inclusion in trials and should no longer be deemed controversial.

5. As blood group evidence was widely accepted in countless trials in the past, so has mtDNA counting become a reliable indicator of eliminating groups of populations to a substantially narrower profile, and the process is generally understood, if not expected, by today's juries.

6. The supporting documents and citations used by the defense in their argument that mtDNA can be carelessly extracted were either unscientific publications (such as various Web sites unrelated to the scientific community, or articles from *The Wall Street Journal* and commercial business sites), or, upon further reading, actually supported the use of mtDNA! I thought the defense's reference to *The Croatian Medical Journal* was rather interesting. Considering Geragos & Co. resides in the most advanced country in the world, why would they cite an obscure journal from a second world nation for support?

7. Recent California trials that used mtDNA as evidence include the Westerfield and Johnson cases. As some of us know, in the Westerfield trial, mtDNA testing determined that the victim's hair was found in the defendant's bedroom and dryer lint.

8. The question of tampering with the hair evidence was explained: the piece of hair, originally approximately six inches long, may have broken after being packaged as evidence. Even if a stray hair from the defendant's clothing had somehow been gathered from the boat, the original hair(s) retrieved from the pliers would still be significant if attached, thus establishing it as forcefully removed rather than as natural cast off.

With regard to the dog trailing evidence, the People argue that the handlers are competent; the dog in question has already been deemed reliable in California courts. As a response to the ridiculous defense position that the dogs didn't follow the "suspect," the People remind the Court that the dogs followed the scent of the "missing person" to the body of water where Laci was taken. Assuming the dogs followed a relatively fresh trail, this information would serve to preempt any defense notion that Laci and Connor were kept alive for any length of time, as the dogs honed in on the Bay and the washed-up tarp within days of December 24.

Finally, since the 402 evidentiary hearing can be held concurrently with the preliminary hearing, because there is no jury present to hear potential inadmissible evidence, the People conclude that two separate hearings would waste resources and time, and should be combined into one. From this argument, we can conclude that the People are ready and eager to go forward with their case.

OCTOBER 19, 2003
"A BUNCH OF LIES"

"A bunch of lies" is what Scott Peterson called the report on his affair and the life insurance policy on Laci when confronted by Ted Rowlands back in mid-January. Peterson is now delivering his new bunches of lies through his defense counsel, on steaming platters in the form of motions and press conferences where his "factual innocence" is touted. In the wake of the long awaited and oft postponed preliminary, it is time for us to review the blatant mendacity, half-truths, omissions, and various levels of fetid fraud that Peterson conveyed from the beginning of the case to the present.

Fishing for sturgeon on Christmas Eve: We know he did not bring gear or bait, or have adequate time to fish for anything in the Bay. We surmise he returned to the scene of the crime out of an impulse to check if everything was still submerged. His frequent visit to the area (logged by GPS and surveillance) further reinforces the fact that he was insatiably curious and concerned. Placing himself at the Bay and repeatedly returning to the scene are two of the top three things that to me are compelling evidence of his guilt.

Denying the affair: Peterson vehemently denied having an affair to Laci's stepfather, her brother, and to the media, while all along maintaining constant contact with Amber Frey, based on telephone records showing hundreds of calls between them. Eventually, when he was "pinned and wriggling on the wall," he admitted the affair on national television and showed no qualms about continuing to see Amber after telling his pregnant wife about the relationship (which most of us believe was another lie, but will never be able to prove).

"They were those market umbrellas, you know, eight-foot umbrellas. I was taking them to the warehouse because it had started to rain." The market umbrellas were not found in the warehouse. In fact, police found them on the patio at the Covena Avenue residence during the first search on December 26. The question remains, why was he loading them on the truck that morning?

"Last saw his wife at 9:30 in the morning preparing to take the dog for a walk." This nonsense, and his recall of her wearing black pants and a white top, were both fabrications conceived during his travels on the 24th, possibly because he saw Ms. Dempewolf (another pregnant brunette woman who resembled Laci) walking her dog that morning, and due to his dismal lack of imagination. I have it on good authority that Laci's remains were found in light-colored pants.

"I needed a truck for work." When Scott traded in Laci's Land Rover, this was his excuse for what appeared shocking and insensitive behavior. Another excuse I heard was that he told his sister that the locks were broken (presumably by police) when the vehicles were seized. I postulate that there were several reasons why he traded in the vehicle, none of them involving a job to which I am convinced he never returned after Christmas. One theory is that he wanted to dispose of everything that reminded him of Laci, as a way to erase all traces of her existence. Another possibility is that he suspected they planted a GPS on the Land Rover (which they had), and he wanted to avoid being tracked. This was just one of many callous and contemptible decisions he would make for the next four months.

"I bought the boat as a surprise Christmas present," and, *"I got her a Louis Vuitton wallet."* To purchase a $1,400 fishing boat two months before your first child was due in a one-income family before the holidays is certainly odd. However, to then claim it was a gift for a pregnant woman who previously experienced seasickness and was about as likely to get in a boat as get into the basket of a hot air balloon was simply ridiculous. And by the way, where is that wallet?

"My name is Jacqueline Peterson. It's a family name." When Scott bought the maroon Mercedes in San Diego shortly before the bodies of his wife and baby surfaced on the rocky beaches of the San Francisco Bay, he used a fraudulent driver's license with his mother's name to transfer the title. Once again, Peterson shows that he thinks everyone else is stupid, and believed himself to be above suspicion.

"They'd have to have something to arrest me for!" Peterson was quoted as saying when asked if he was afraid of being arrested after the second search of his home, warehouse and storage facility in February. He may have been deluding himself, in deep denial and confident that his wife's body would stay beneath the cold waters of the Bay indefinitely. Nevertheless, he was terrified of being arrested, which is why he abandoned the house, hid at his half-sister Anne's in Berkeley, and took refuge in San Diego among his remaining enablers and supporters, where he bleached his hair and prepared to flee with camping gear, a new vehicle, and cash. When he failed to return to Modesto after the remains of his wife and baby were found, the proverbial death bell was tolling in the distance.

Among the many lies he told Amber Frey include that he was unmarried, then saying he lost his wife the previous December; telling her he was going to Maine and Paris and would be gone for up to a month; along with pretty much everything else from his mythical "Handbook of Romance" he uttered to seduce and sway her. I am sure we will hear many more lies he spewed once we are privy to the recorded phone calls and Amber's testimony.

Needless to say, every time he walked out the door of the house he shared with Laci and into the arms of another woman, he was perpetuating a life of lies, secrets and faithlessness. To those that protest that a liar and philanderer do not a murderer make, I remind them that there is a murdered woman now who trusted and loved a man who committed the ultimate act of betrayal, while mercilessly manipulating everyone he encountered in his cavalier career of duality and deceit.

70

CHAPTER 6: THE PRELIMINARY HEARING

OCTOBER 26, 2003
THE LATEST CAST OF CHARACTERS

FOR THE DEFENSE:

Dr. Henry Lee

Renowned celebrity forensic has-been who testifies so often in court, he loses track of his whereabouts. His greatest claim to fame is the infamous "Wood Chipper Murder" in Connecticut, where he pieced together bone fragments, roller chain links, and other bits of evidence to help convict another wife murderer. A stickler for preserving the crime scene, Lee carries yellow tape and an oversized magnifying glass to every call. Dr. Lee is notorious for his oft-quoted, "Sumting wrong," in regard to blood evidence in the Simpson trial. Lee is best known for his work in forensic serology, and among his specialties are characterizing blood spatter and trace evidence. His credibility has been recently besmirched due to his rather bizarre testimony for the defense in the Michael Peterson trial, where on the witness stand he spit watered-down ketchup onto a white piece of cardboard to demonstrate aspirated blood spatter. Michael Peterson was convicted.

Dr. Cyril Wecht

A native of Pittsburgh and loyal Steelers fan, Dr. Wecht's most famous autopsy involved the Kennedy assassination, where he testified in front of the Warren Commission. He has written a book about the Ramsey case, where he basically accuses the parents out of "a process of elimination." Dr. Wecht has never missed a photo or panel opportunity to opine on an issue, regardless of his knowledge or experience. His favorite term is "disarticulation," the cause of which in the Laci Peterson case he changed his mind on a weekly basis. Chances are, unless he can come up with a viable theory that Laci was not in the Bay for four months, or that she was murdered by a cult, he will likely not appear at the trial.

Bill Pavelic

Another Simpson alumnus, he promised to help O.J. find the "real killers" nearly a decade ago, with no word on the progress of that investigation since. With a track record like that, we are delighted that Geragos has hired him to hit the streets of San Francisco (where he was allegedly following up on leads for Simpson), and the seamy red light district of Fresno to find the evil villains who actually murdered Laci Peterson and planted her body in the Bay to frame another innocent, grieving husband. A former LAPD officer (yet another sterling reference), Pavelic is no stranger to creating reasonable doubt from paper mache and the pre-chewed gum from his shoes.

Gary Ermoian

According to his Web site, Ermoian, a private investigator from Modesto, "will customize his investigation efforts to fit your specific needs! Just because you don't see it listed here, doesn't mean it can't be done." However, it appears that exculpating Peterson may be too daunting a task for the versatile and resourceful

Ermoian. Peterson informed Frey that Ermoian had been tempted by the deep pockets of the *National Enquirer*. Perhaps he actually cashed in on the publicity and acted as a secret source for them for some of their early (and accurate) stories. One of Peterson's phone calls to Ermoian was captured among the hundreds of "lost" calls, which became an issue of contention in defense accusations that the wiretaps were illegal.

FOR THE PROSECUTION:

Steve Jacobson

Steve Jacobson is a sportswriter for *Newsday* who moonlights as an affidavit writer for the Modesto Police Department. Actually, a Stanislaus County investigator, Steve Jacobson's name has appeared almost as often as Peterson's in the voluminous pages of motions to suppress evidence, and has been accused by the defense of deliberately misleading Judge Ladine and others in regard to probable cause in the warrants for the phone taps and searches. Jacobson's testimony should be very revealing as to what the Modesto police knew in the early weeks of the case, and the methods and means of their strategy.

Jon Buehler

Jon Buehler has the dubious distinction of receiving more phone calls from Amber Frey in one week than from telemarketers, his bookie, or his entire family in a year. Besides being Frey's reluctant confidant, Buehler was among the four arresting officers who traveled to San Diego on April 17 to arrest Scott Peterson on Good Friday. He referred to Peterson as "the package," which shows what level of esteem he felt Peterson merited.

Craig Grogan

Detective Craig Grogan reportedly has an excellent reputation and has been described by people who worked with him in this case as a man of impeccable character and professionalism. Grogan was an occasional spokesperson for the department (chief spokesperson being Doug Ridenour) and was quoted often by the press. He was one of the officers (along with Buehler, Brocchini, and Al Carter) who went to San Diego to arrest Peterson. Grogan will prove to be one of the key people from the Modesto Police Department testifying to much of what we have questioned and speculated throughout the many months of silence imposed by the gag order.

Al Brocchini

A target of the defense, the so-called, "Mark Fuhrman" of the Peterson case, Modesto police Detective Al Brocchini made solving Laci's murder a mission and personally escorted Peterson to jail in April. Unlike Fuhrman, however, Brocchini will not be found to have an agenda any more questionable than a fierce dedication to truth and justice. There is no race card, no inherent prejudice against Caucasian golfers or fertilizer salesmen. He and Detective Hendee were accused of "spontaneously deciding to review the hair" back in February, that the defense contended qualified as a break in the chain of evidence or misconduct. I suspect Geragos is attempting a peremptory strike against Brocchini because of his

72

passion and perspicacity regarding Scott Peterson, whose guilt was blatantly obvious to Brocchini within moments of their encounter.

James Brazelton
Stanislaus County District Attorney James Brazelton's main function in the trial will be to monitor the activities of Distaso and Harris, and see that the case is handled within the parameters of the law to ensure a flawless presentation. I believe Mr. Brazelton was influential in convincing Laci's family that the special circumstances for a death penalty were warranted in this case.

OCTOBER 29, 2003
DAY 1 – THE PRELIMINARY

Most of us were introduced to Laci Peterson by her striking photographs displayed on dozens of news sites, thousands of flyers, and countless exposures throughout the nearly year since she disappeared on Christmas Eve. Even now, I still look upon her image with a mixture of pain and pleasure: we mourn the tragic loss of her vibrant, tangible magnetism; yet we also sense her whimsy and amusement. Of the brief glimpses of Laci's personality we were privileged to observe, the most notable to me was her gift of humor, apparent in the videos of her mock commercials, her spontaneous giggles, and her irrepressible wit. Her mother, Sharon, when reminiscing through what must seem unbearable grief, cannot restrain her laughter when she describes Laci.

Laci's murder resonates for many women on so many levels, it's impossible to separate their interrelationships: as sisters in betrayal, as mothers, as a victims of narcissists, and as grandmothers. At some point early on, I had a choice to either completely detach myself from this case or ensconce myself in it; there was no middle ground. Once I invested my emotional energy into her brilliant but abbreviated life, my arsenal to avenge the senseless cruelty of her death is perhaps most appropriate to her personality: pragmatism and parody. My means are comical, conscious and instructive; my intended ends are friendship, inclusion, and justice.

Today the long awaited preliminary hearing is under way, predicted to last up to five days, covering Peterson's activities from the weeks prior to the murder until his arrest in April. The hearing represents a new chapter in an already lengthy volume of speculation, piecemeal facts, theories, dysfunctional dynamics, secrecy, layers of lies, incomprehensible motives, and closely guarded material evidence that we appreciate the opportunity to examine.

OCTOBER 30, 2003
DAY 2 PRELIMINARY HEARING

I have theorized in the past that Peterson was jealous and threatened by his vivacious and much loved wife; similarly, he was jealous and displaced by the baby on the way. It is very likely he had been fantasizing about his freedom for months, perhaps as soon as he found out Laci was pregnant, and concocted the most beneficial and permanent solution to achieve it: staging a "kidnapping" to obscure a murder. I disagree with those who think the murder was the result of a confrontation or sudden explosion of rage. I am convinced this murder began in Peterson's imagination as a fantasy, while he was involved in his adulterous parallel life, as eventually those passive-aggressive forms of betrayal and defiance failed to allay his feelings of seething resentment of his perceived confinement. Procuring the boat when he did, and without anyone's knowledge, hiding Laci's body in the depths of a body of water he studied and mapped out; selling her car, the attempt to sell the house, the removal of his wedding ring, changing his appearance, and abandoning their home were all the actions of a man who wanted to reinvent himself and erase all traces of his former life.

It is entirely possible that Laci confronted Scott about something the evening of the 23rd; perhaps suspicious phones calls, a discrepancy in his purported whereabouts, or a money issue. We now know that Scott was living a duplicitous existence that required constant lying to perpetuate, so it is very reasonable to assume he left a trail of some kind that Laci noticed. If Laci was as feisty and proud as her friends and family describe, she may have instigated an argument that led to some physical aggression. This would result in Scott's easily overpowering her, and then carrying the violence to its terrible finality. That would explain why the incident occurred on the holiday rather than closer to her due date. Whatever way it transpired, it was planned to some extent, and the actual "D-day" may have been premature based on unforeseen circumstances. He did not extemporaneously decide to take her to the Bay in the middle of the night with a boat nobody knew about, hidden in a warehouse that was supposed to contain chemicals and samples for his trade, using freshly poured concrete anchors and recently purchased weights, after informing his out-of-town lover that he would be away for up to a month during the holidays. No, this murder was no accident.

Today we hope to hear from the cleaning woman and Amy Rocha, both of whom may flesh out some of our ideas about the Petersons' marriage behind closed doors, Laci's health and mobility with regard to dog walking, her plans for the holiday, and her routine. We may also learn about what, if any, interior cleaning Peterson did the evening of the 24th when he returned from the Bay.

OCTOBER 31, 2003
GRIEVING THE UNBORN

How do we grieve for an unborn child, who never took a breath, felt his mother's tender cheek, or saw her loving smile? He knew her voice, of course; he rocked in the rhythms of her heartbeat, and the serenity and music of her womb, but was deprived the warmth of her touch and the radiance of her joy. Perhaps he now experiences her presence and eternal love.

Connor will never be a little boy. He will never play ball, trick or treat, sit on Santa's lap, ride a bike, win a spelling bee, fall in love, or have a child of his own. His loved ones were denied not only his wonderful life, but also those of his legacy and potential progeny, snipped from the family tree as a bud, never to blossom or bless the world with his flourish.

Some of her friends and family may be consoled by the idea that Laci and Connor are together in a kind of paradise, free from fear, sorrow, and pain. It is for the family we grieve, for their unfathomable and irreplaceable loss, who must face each day for the rest of their lives with the aching void created by Laci and Connor's absence, which can never be filled, and the cruelty of which can never be comprehended. It must, at times, make them feel helpless and crazy with despair, looking to the sky in anguish and confusion asking, "Why did this happen to them? How could we have prevented this horrible event?" Nothing anyone can say or do will ever suffice to restore their shattered lives or mend their hearts. We are, all of us, broken. The splendid innocence of Connor is lost to the world, and our only hope is to believe in a perfect love and peace *that is beyond our understanding, wherein dwell Laci and Connor's spirits.*

Peterson's complaints of unpalatable green soup and his austere living conditions pale in comparison to the excruciating suffering he has caused his wife's family. Forgive me if I find sympathy difficult to muster on his behalf.

NOVEMBER 1, 2003
PRELIMINARY DAY 3 TESTIMONY ANALYSIS

From the cleaning woman, Ms. Nava:

- She used bleach to clean only in the bathrooms (a bath and a half, small floors.)
- The dog barked when she arrived. McKenzie was a barker, so the chance that someone could kidnap Laci and he wouldn't bark like crazy is nil.
- Laci did not walk the dog on the 23rd, and was moving rather slowly. She brought the alleged five bags of groceries in one or two at a time, which indicates she was not very strong.
- Her routine was to put the rags she used to clean in a bucket on the washing machine, that were ordinarily laundered before the next scheduled cleaning. We know Peterson was doing a load of wash when the police arrived the next day, through his own admission.
- Nava did notice jewelry on the dresser in the bedroom. Geragos may be trying to establish that she had access to it, because rumors abound that Laci's jewelry is missing or was given to Amber Frey.
- The prosecution asked if Nava ever cleaned the outside windowsills, to which she replied, no. Geragos, on cross, asked her about cleaning the windowsills (presumably inside) couched in a question about rags. Clearly, something is suspicious about the outside windowsills, and maybe other areas that were cleaned recently, besides the kitchen that neighbors said smelled like bleach.
- Nava confused the issue about the blinds (fabric blinds) being drawn open in the living room that a neighbor claimed occurred daily. Perhaps because it was "cleaning day," the blinds were left down to be cleaned the morning, but that Laci normally opened them mid-morning. In either event, it will not be provable, and the issue of the blinds won't be introduced at trial.

From Amy Rocha:

- She never colored Scott's hair throughout their relationship of hairdresser-client.
- She confirmed that Scott told her he was going golfing on Christmas Eve and would pick up a gift basket before 3 pm.
- She tried to call him at around 3:45, on both his cell phone and at the house, and got no answer. She did not leave a message (although those calls will be on the phone records). Scott must have been on his way back from Berkeley by then, based on when he got home, and therefore was in his truck. Why didn't he answer the cell phone? When did he call his friends about the New Year's Eve party? All of his outbound calls will be documented.
- Amy established that Laci was looking tired and mentioning fatigue those later weeks of December.
- She did not know about Scott's boat or Amber Frey.
- Both Rocha girls inherited some jewelry from their grandmother.

From Sharon Rocha:

- She was very close to her daughter and would be considered a confidant.
- She had warned Laci not to walk the dog in the park after learning that Laci had been feeling dizzy and sick in recent walks.
- She did not know about Scott's boat or Amber Frey.
- She had dinner at Laci's on December 15, the night after Scott was at the Christmas party with Amber. They never discussed his boat, which he had recently purchased December 9, that she found odd, since Ron is an avid fisherman and would have enjoyed learning about the boat.
- Scott called her at 5:17 pm and used the word, "missing" immediately to describe the situation, which she found alarming and strange. When she went to the park to look for Laci, she called for Scott, who was standing about 40 feet away and he never acknowledged her. We also learned that Scott had brought McKenzie to the park. Whether you find that behavior suspicious depends on your level of paranoia; I happen to find it very peculiar. I believe Sharon is convinced Scott murdered Laci, and that she knows much more than any of us regarding evidence. Her calm demeanor in court reinforces that notion; she believes in the State's case and seems utterly confident.

From Officer Jon Evers:

- Most of Evers's early information came from the defendant, and he was initially acting on the scene with the idea that it was a missing persons case.

- Something he saw in the house alerted his suspicion, and he called for detectives. He does not describe what that was in direct, but that may come up in McAllister's cross.
- He describes two wet mops in a bucket outside, underneath where it was still damp. He does not mention the smell of bleach.
- He clarifies that Peterson told them that he was fishing in the Bay, then that he was at Berkeley (and produced a "parking receipt," that may in fact be the launch ticket, since parking at the marina is free) and also asks him what he was fishing for, and Peterson does not answer. Similarly, Peterson does not respond to Ron Grantski's comment that going out at 9:30 is late. We also learn that Peterson told his father-in-law that he changed his golf plans because it was too cold. Most people would expect it to be even colder out on the Bay, so this excuse isn't terribly logical.
- When the officers went to Peterson's warehouse at around 11 pm, Peterson claimed the power was off, and did not offer any assistance to the police when they attempted to light the area.
- Peterson told Evers he came home, ate some leftover pizza, took a shower and changed his clothes before calling Laci's mother. We also know he was doing a load of wash. This is not the behavior of a man who was worried about his missing spouse, or one who was expecting to have a big dinner that evening.

McAllister, in his cross of Evers, seems very interested in the timeline of activities of the police that evening. This may be calculated to demonstrate the police department's focus on Peterson from the beginning, thus skewing its investigation and ignoring any other leads or theories. More details of that first night and the onset of the investigation will probably be described on Monday, when we can deduce by McAllister's cross-examination the implications of his line of questioning.

NOVEMBER 3, 2003
DAY 4: BIRDS OF A FEATHER

In day four of the preliminary hearing, Dr. William Shields, the first of several Simpson trial alumnus, took the stand to impeach the method and validity of mtDNA testing in regard to the hair sample found on Peterson's boat. Shields, a professor of Biology and a zoologist by training, wrote his dissertation on the inbreeding and *evolution of sex in* birds. His area of expertise prior to being on the court circuit was ornithology.

Dr. Shields joins some of his mangy flock, Henry Lee, Cyril Wecht, and private investigator and former LAPD officer Bill Pavelic, to preen his feathers in a scaled-down "dream team" for Peterson. From his own beak, Dr. Shields acknowledged he had never "personally extracted a mitochondrial DNA sample in a lab, and garnered his expertise from reading reports done by others, viewing work in other labs and some of his own lab work." This is akin to being a self-proclaimed expert on childbirth without ever having delivered a baby.

The following are some of Dr. Shields' statements regarding mtDNA:

"Burned bone can produce enough undamaged tissue from within to allow for successful mtDNA analysis. Such tests have been successfully done on actual cremated remains, so one will not know until the extraction is performed and the amplification attempted whether good DNA can be had from such samples. The smaller the remain, the less likely the success." [43]

"The FBI is bringing mitochondrial DNA into the courtroom and painting it with the same reliability as other DNA typing. It isn't as unique to an individual as nuclear DNA." [44]

Shields said Melton's form of DNA testing is more susceptible to lab contamination than others and that current methods of lab verification are not sufficient. He also suggested that using just 1,657 samples does not give an accurate enough estimate of the likelihood that the DNA found in the hair samples could have come from someone other than the suspect or victim.

If burned bone can be used to extract viable mtDNA samples, how much more accurate are undamaged, relatively fresh hair samples? I have not seen anyone in the Peterson case likening mtDNA with the statistical probability of nuclear DNA, and considering the narrow sample of potential donors of the hair found in the boat (possibly two), leaves little doubt as to whom the hair belongs.

A decade ago, when mtDNA testing was still rarely used for criminal forensics, microscopic comparisons of similarity between the hair on the boat and Laci's hair would have been sufficient to satisfy most juries. I predict that the mtDNA procedure and findings will be allowed, perhaps requiring another molting appearance from Dr. Shields, but where the outcome will likely be a study in contrast to the mishandled miscarriage in Simpson.

NOVEMBER 5, 2003
THE HAIR MYSTIQUE

The mystique of hair, particularly women's hair, precedes historical record. A woman's hair is attributed with sensual power, and in many diverse cultural myths, a life force itself, from which emerge energies that sustain or control the orbit of celestial bodies. There exist today cultures that forbid a woman from publicly displaying her hair, or require the covering of hair for religious services. The traditional wedding veil is a variation of the convention of concealing the hair to express virginal modesty and purity, exclusively reserving the pleasure of its exposure for the groom.

---

[43] National Alliance of Families Web Site, Korea Update, (www.nationalalliance.org/korea/mutta.htm).

[44] Cohen, Laurie P, "Accuracy of new DNA test is called into question," The McDonald Case website, (www.themacdonaldcase.org).

It is mystically poetic, therefore, that a barely visible sample of woman's hair carries such magnitude in the case of California v Peterson. Despite Peterson's ferocious efforts to extinguish all traces of Laci's essence, her physical being, and her earthly possessions, he is yet haunted by the traces of her indomitable spirit, manifested in a simple strand of hair, its delicacy and fragility belied by its power to defeat him.

In retrospect, we can chronicle Laci's life, much like our own, through her hair: from the silky fuzz as an infant to the sophisticated, low-maintenance bob of a mother-to-be. The transformation of her hairstyles represent another connection to women everywhere, as we identify with her experiences. In photographs, we see Laci as a child in braids, resting a baseball bat on her shoulder. We remember perhaps our own braids, or plaiting our daughters' hair, brushing through fidgeting and tangles in their impatience to run and play. Later pictures show Laci in a cheerleading uniform, with a bountiful head of curls, and we may laugh recalling our own experiments with perms, either sensational or disastrous.

Laci in her wedding gown, with the traditional veil artfully obscuring her raven locks, is as lovely and classic as a budding rose. We regard the radiant bride, reminiscent of our private moments of keen anticipation of the promise of happily ever after; or for some of us, giving away our own precious daughters in matrimony, filled with hope and tearful pride. More recent photographs narrate her mid-20s, showing her long, free flowing hair, reflecting the ebullience of her nature, and encapsulating what has become her most endearing and indelible character trait.

NOVEMBER 6, 2003
THE TABULA RASA MOTIVE

The term "tabula rasa" was introduced in a theory proposed by 17th-century British philosopher, John Locke, to define the human mind at birth as a blank slate upon which experience imprints all knowledge, without ancestral memory, moral precepts or innate understanding. Locke maintained, "Good and evil, reward and punishment, are the only motives to a rational creature: these are the spur and reins whereby all mankind are set on work, and guided."

For a narcissist, a "tabula rasa" describes an entirely different objective: he seeks to reinvent himself after every adversity as a means to avoid consequences for his behavior, reinforce his false self-image, and eliminate any responsibility for his shortcomings. This motivation drives much of a narcissist's *modus operandi*: he pursues frequent physical, geographical, employment, and relationship changes, and seeks forgiveness and the promise of a "clean slate" from those he has offended. It's not enough for you to forgive a narcissist, in his mind; you must also be willing to forget. If you cannot accommodate his perpetual pretenses, he is often compelled to leave and start "fresh" elsewhere. His ego cannot tolerate an environment that constantly reminds him of his fallibility.

With regard to motive in Scott Peterson's case, the desire for domestic emancipation alone lacks the gravity and substance to commit murder and disguise it as a kidnapping. Seeking simply a divorce, for Peterson, would impose an unacceptable social stigma, represent personal defeat, and require financial and paternal obligations that were untenable to him. He recoiled at the thought of having not only to support a child he did not want, but also a permanent connection to a woman with whom he repeatedly failed as a husband and provider.

Therefore, the perfect solution to achieving a "tabula rasa" was to become a widower. Laci's "disappearance" (and the eventual declaration of her death after a certain number of years) would have allowed Peterson to have his cake and eat it, too. He would have been granted a fresh start without the messy ramifications of divorce and visitation issues; his family and friends would rally around to support and console him through the transition, and he walks away free, unencumbered, and financially secure, once the life insurance pays off.

Yesterday, the self-implicated "Green River" serial killer, Gary Ridgeway, was sentenced to life without parole. His motive for killing over 40 women he assumed were prostitutes was that he despised them for charging him for sex. The State of Washington accepted this motive and offered it to the Court as an explanation for two decades of random and senseless murders. If this man can rationalize such incomprehensible and heinous actions with that pathetic a motive, why should anyone insist on imparting a more complex and erudite motive to Peterson?

Today, we expect to hear testimony from Modesto Police Detective Al Brocchini, and another detective at the scene of the Peterson home on December 24, in day six of the preliminary hearing.

NOVEMBER 7, 2003
NO EXIT

As I occasionally search for literary metaphors to illuminate the Peterson case, I realize that the French play, "No Exit" (*Huis Clos*) by Jean-Paul Sartre, provides some interesting parallels. For those not familiar with the play, it is a one-act drama set in an ugly, somewhat sparsely decorated, constantly lighted room from which none of the three characters can escape (a type of hell). The three characters, a man and two women, represent conflicting social and ideological archetypes, and are doomed to torture each other eternally without hope of reprieve. Some of the more famous lines from the play (translated) include, "Hell is other people," "It's amazing what the human spirit can endure," and "One always dies too soon, or too late." There are no mirrors in the room, so the characters depend on each other to validate their existence, rather than depend on their own senses of self.

Scott Peterson is confined to a spartan jail cell, similar to the room in "No Exit," tormented (we hope) by the memory of the woman he murdered, and the dreaded future testimony of a woman who betrayed him. His behavior has defined him far more realistically than the deluded impressions and reflections of others in his life; his austere circumstances a harsh contrast to his former materialistic lifestyle. He, like the character Garcin in "No Exit," failed to accept the responsibility of his freedom, lived his life in reckless and ignoble bad faith, and was the architect of his own prison.

Peterson is nothing but what he made of himself, although he and his defense team will attempt to deflect the blame onto the phantoms of police incompetence, mysterious kidnappers, or reasonable doubt. His consequences, however, are not a quirk of fate. Free will is a condition of making choices, accepting the results, and learning from mistakes. It is doubtful that Peterson will experience any existential enlightenment regarding his actions, since that would require self-analysis and awareness of a conscience he obviously lacks. From the depths of his lost soul, and the interminably lit room in which he languishes, there will be no exit.

It was a short week for testimony in the preliminary hearing of California v Scott Peterson, which commenced Wednesday with more scientific support for the FBI's mtDNA procedures and results, and it was determined that hair found attached to a pair of pliers in Peterson's boat statistically belonged to Laci. The hair may be the strongest (if not only) piece of actual physical evidence linking her to the boat Scott used to embark on his "fishing trip" on December 24. Judging by the Herculean efforts expended by the defense to exclude this evidence, either by refuting its forensic validity, the means of testing, or questioning the chain of custody, the ruling on its admissibility will prove a huge victory for either side. No crystal ball is required to predict that the hair evidence will be allowed and the case will be bound over for trial.

From the transcripts of testimony, let us review some essential and interesting facts that were either glossed over or ignored by the media legal analysts' discussion:

Al Brocchini

In direct and cross-examination, Detective Al Brocchini admitted to procuring recording equipment for Amber Frey to tape her phone conversations with the defendant after December 30, while Peterson was telling her he was in Europe as she watched him on television news updates hanging posters for his missing wife. Through the questioning, it was apparent that the defense was trying to prove that Frey recorded phone conversations prior to contacting the police. Even if those tapes existed (which I highly doubt), they would not be admissible in trial, and her future sworn testimony from the stand will be more than sufficient to describe their relationship, Peterson's promises, his fictionalized history, and his state of mind. Therefore, the reasoning escapes me as to why the defense would make an issue of the alleged tapes, except to try to portray Frey as somehow duplicitous and scheming in an attempt to besmirch her character to the potential jury pool. This scurrilous tactic was used recently with the (false) report that the defense has subpoenaed Frey (or documents related to her).

Brocchini explained the mysterious surveillance camera installed across the street from Peterson's house on or around January 3, the equipment possibly obtained from the DEA or FBI, and its purpose as a substitute for personnel stakeouts that were deemed too obvious for success. The detective also spoke to Peterson's friends, whom he insisted were Laci's friends, not Scott's, in order to procure information (and for "other" curiously unexplained reasons) and his exploratory methods that most people would consider standard operating procedure in missing persons/homicide investigations. McAllister would have us believe that these were the actions of a "rogue" and sinister nemesis.

Brocchini publicly confirmed our suspicions of the fraudulent and self-serving "Laci-Info" tip line established by the defendant's family, designed to censor and quash any tips that pointed to Peterson's involvement in his wife's disappearance. Perhaps there could be charges brought against the Petersons for their deliberate obstruction of justice.

Brocchini interviewed the woman who introduced Frey to Peterson in November, and who, after some lingering suspicions, asked him about his marital status, to which Peterson tearfully requested discretion and permission to explain the "lost" wife to Frey himself, adding another hash mark to the column of defrauded women in Peterson's cavalier career.

Not surprisingly, Peterson is something of a pack rat, since it was revealed in testimony that he kept several expired fishing licenses in various places, including his tackle box, glove box, and desk drawers. Strangely enough, he obtained a two-day license for December 23, 2002, yet another piece of the premeditation puzzle.

Karen Servas and Amy Kringbaum

Two of Laci's neighbors testified to their familiarity with the Petersons, some of their routines, and most important, neither one saw Laci walking the dog alone on any regular basis. In fact, Kringbaum indicated she never saw Laci walking the dog, but remembered seeing Scott "run" the dog frequently, especially in the weeks after the disappearance. That dog got a lot of exercise in January for the sake of the media. The "muddy" leash was demoted to "encrusted with dry dirt and leaf debris," and the impact of the open/closed blind issue was somewhat deflated when Kringbaum revealed her erratic work hours. According to these neighbors, Peterson gave each a different explanation for his whereabouts on the 24th, and appeared distraught and preoccupied that night. What probably struck both women as odd (though not specifically verbalized or elicited in questioning) was their expectation of Peterson's behavior to be more frantic, devastated, and consistently upset. Peterson's demeanor, to most reasonable people, was underwhelming if not inappropriately calm.

Phil Owen

Detective Owen confirmed what we have known for some time: Laci's remains were found in tan pants rather than the black pants Peterson reported seeing her in when he left the house, as well as the witnesses who claim they saw a pregnant woman wearing black pants walking a dog the morning of the 24th. We learned that Peterson did not try to contact Laci's OB after discovering her "missing," and that Laci had been complaining of dizzy spells in early November, for which she was advised to walk later in the day and after eating. If these facts do not eliminate the possibility once and for all that Laci walked the dog that morning, I don't know what more it will take.

Additional Observations

- Counsel for the defense, Kirk McAllister, displays a peculiar paranoia, a circuitous, unfocused, and disorganized interrogatory style, and a very volatile temper.
- Geragos continues to testify for everyone instead of asking questions.

- Geragos referred to his million-dollar client by saying, "I don't want you to have to drag him back in here," during a break in the proceedings. Drag him back in here? For that payroll, I would expect him to refer to his client in a more respectable fashion, such as "Please escort Mr. Peterson back to the court room."
- Geragos presumes that his client subscribed to or had access to the morning newspaper (*The Modesto Bee*), which dictated his daily itinerary. If Peterson were so concerned with the search efforts, why didn't he participate in the locally organized searches, or make his presence known to law enforcement, or use his wife's vehicle? Why drive three hours round trip to stay only a few minutes? Why, indeed.

NOVEMBER 15, 2003
MORE QUESTIONS THAN ANSWERS

For those of us who have followed the Laci Peterson case from the beginning, the preliminary hearing has failed to provide answers to some of our speculation, or explain many of the things we know to be important issues, but which have yet to be addressed. The following is food for thought with quite a few more questions than answers:

* Launch ticket: why haven't they told us what time the ticket was stamped? A good source early in the case told me it was stamped at 1:00 pm, but nothing official has confirmed that.

* Bleach: If there was no bleach smell reported by anyone at the scene, why bring it up with the cleaning woman and Officers Evers and Brocchini?

* Why would Scott call the report on the insurance policy back in mid-January "a bunch of lies"? Why not just admit to a legitimate insurance policy on both of them? Are we convinced there was not another secret policy taken out more recently, just on Laci?

* Scott's Tradecorp records were not subpoenaed just to see if he was skimming from the till, but rather to verify his customer base and see where he made sales calls. There was certainly the possibility that he dumped the body on some remote farm or in a lagoon, and narrowing down the vast Central Valley agricultural area by customers with whom he might be familiar would have been a starting point for the investigation.

* What is the real story with Kim McGregor? Why would she break a window to climb into a home to which she allegedly had a key, if the story that she walked the dog is true? Considering how hot that house was at the time, what person in their right mind would do that?

* Why did they keep Scott's truck, as Brocchini emphasized this week in court with, "He can't have it." We know why they kept the boat, but what did they find in that truck?

* Where is the testimony regarding his computer files revealing the tidal calendar, GHB research, and other reading material he perused prior to the murder?

* How could Laci have been kidnapped in the park (wearing black pants) while walking the dog without a single person's seeing this? With all the people hanging out hospital windows, jogging, looking out their kitchen window at the

84

street, pumping gas, jumping out of bushes, and swearing at dogs, how is it that nobody witnessed this abduction in broad daylight on a day where most people are off work?

* Why didn't the State show the video from Salon Salon to verify the tan (beige) pants Laci was wearing as being similar (if not exact) to the ones in which her remains were found?

* Why have the affidavits for the search warrants and wiretaps remained sealed?

* If trying a murder case without a body has been successfully won (e.g., Koklich) in California, why is the media making a big deal about "cause of death"?

* Back in February, Janey Peterson defended their "Laci-Info" tip line, by noting that it is "toll free" and "anonymous," and that "all information is forwarded to the Modesto police," which was a big, fat lie. What did the police find when they subpoenaed those records?

* Peterson's family defended his trading in the Land Rover because "he needed a truck for work." When did Peterson go to work between his trips to the marina, dodging police, staying overnight in Bakersfield, lurking around Fresno, and renting cars? If he needed a truck for work, why did he rent and borrow cars?

* Where are the rumored 55-gallon drums we heard about back in February?

* What happened, or what evidence was collected in the second search that came back from forensics, to make the police publicly reclassify the case as a homicide on March 5?

* What happened to the auxiliary wheels for launching the boat, and why did Peterson have a flat spare tire for his trailer?

* Did McAllister actually resign as Peterson's attorney in February, or was that a rumor?

* Why did Scott go to Mexico in early February and not attend the trade show? Was he followed there by undercover cops and decided to cut his trip short?

* Since the dog evidence doesn't require a Kelly Hearing, why hasn't the prosecution used the bloodhound data (tracking her to the driveway instead of the park, opposite direction of park, tracking to the marina, cadaver dog hits in Bay and on tarp, etc.) to contradict these so-called witnesses who saw some woman walking in the park?

* Where in the world are Dirty, Skeeter and Corey?

NOVEMBER 16, 2003
THE SEVEN HABITS OF HIGHLY OFFENSIVE DEFENSE ATTORNEYS

Habit 1 -- Be Proactive

Plead your case in front of any camera, microphone, journalist, webmaster, editor of the school paper, cocktail napkin artist, or anyone with a pulse to advocate the defendant's innocence, knowing full well your client is a murdering, thieving, lying cretin. Wave a copy of the Constitution and vociferously declare his inalienable rights to effective counsel and the presumption of innocence.

Forfeit any remaining semblance of self-respect to obtain a high-profile case where your smarmy, reptilian mug can be broadcast on the greatest number of television programs and newspapers. This will ensure your continued notoriety, impressing a cadre of impressionable, well-heeled deviants who will consider hiring you for their future defense.

Habit 2 -- Begin with Acquittal in Mind.

Reject any consideration of a plea bargain for your client, regardless of the titanic magnitude of time, resources, agony for the victims, or trees this would save. Insist not only will you prevail at proving your client's innocence, but in spectacular fashion, vindicate him by delivering the actual perpetrators, upstaging the investigators and forensic experts with your own hired guns. This strategy is most effective early in the case, before the actual trial forces your hand. By then, be confident that most people have forgotten your grandiose (albeit empty) promises.

Habit 3 -- Put First things Last and Last things First

Your priorities should always be to obfuscate, confuse, distract, and make irrational motions and objections to derail the focus of the prosecution. Continue to make unreasonable demands on the judge to test his patience. In court, appear disorganized, incoherent, enraged, obnoxious, and indignant to postpone as long as possible the presentation of substantive issues of the case. Delay, delay, delay! File motions of no fewer than 200 pages, written by your menial clerks, composed of excessive, redundant, irrelevant citations, poor research, and non sequiturs, which both the Court and your opposition will have to read, guaranteeing frustrated ennui, diminished eyesight, sleep deprivation and other infirmities that will dull their senses. Strive for quantity, not quality, substituting volume for merit.

Habit 4 -- Think Win, Win, Win At Any Cost!

Your personal victory is more important than truth, justice, or professional behavior. Self-aggrandizement, promotion, fame and fortune must remain at the forefront of your strategy at all times!

Habit 5 -- Seek First to Convolute, Then to Misrepresent the Facts

When presented with irrefutable evidence of your client's suspicious activities, counter this information with fictitious scenarios, impossible explanations, and accusations of law enforcement tampering with or planting evidence, tunnel vision, conspiracies, incompetence, and other shenanigans. Be prepared to produce dusty, rusty, or cobwebbed tools, dog hairs, amateur art, prostitutes, nebulous drug connections, alleged innocent research outlines, deluded witnesses, unrelated (but similar) criminal cases, military records, Boy Bcout merit badges, and SAT scores. Remember, the truth is relative.

Habit 6 - Master Principles of Creative Communication

Good lying is an art form, as is eliciting mistakes and contradictions from witnesses. Manipulate your questions on cross-examination to confound the witness, badgering him to make unreasonable assumptions, agree to human fallibility, refute scientific laws, consider outrageous alternative scenarios, and contradict incriminating facts.

Habit 7 - Successfully Bankrupt Your Client

Justify your astronomical fees with your consistent entertainment value, your savvy public relations skills, and by making your client a household word. Remind him that celebrity doesn't come cheap. Besides, he won't need any money when he's locked up for the rest of his natural life, anyway.

NOVEMBER 19, 2003
AMBER'S EPIPHANY

January 6 is commonly referred to on many western calendars as the "Epiphany," a historical day on which the Magi reached the stable in Bethlehem to acknowledge and bestow precious gifts upon the baby, Jesus. In modern usage, an "epiphany" is an experience of immediate, intuitive understanding or insight. From an analysis of excerpts from the January 6 phone call transcript[45] between Scott Peterson and Amber Frey, a terrible epiphany unfolds.

SP: I am so sorry I hurt you in this way. I don't want to do this over the phone. I want to tell you this; I want to be there in person to tell you this...

Although narcissists often employ the telephone as a preferred weapon of manipulation, they are much more convincing in person, especially when they feel the need to plead their case when they're in a fix. They will go to great lengths to get you to see them face-to-face, where they believe their irresistible, boyish charms will win you over.

SP: It's the worst thing. I'm sorry, Amber.

Peterson's use of "it's" and other vague, undefined references throughout the conversation show his detachment to events and denial of his responsibility, as if things just happen "to" him, rather than as a consequence of his behavior.

SP: The girl I'm married to ... her name is Laci.

Peterson remembers to use present tense here, although calling Laci, his wife of over five years and the mother of his unborn child, a "girl" is a casual, diminutive expression under the circumstances.

---

[45] www.courttv.com, Scott Peterson's Phone Log, January 6, 2003, 11:02 pm.

SP: *She disappeared, just before Christmas...For the past two weeks I've been in Modesto with her family and mine ... searching for her.*

This, I presume, is to clarify his actual whereabouts, while pretending to be in Maine or Europe in previous conversations between Christmas and January 6.

SP: *She just disappeared, and no one knows ...where she's been.*

Finishing that thought with, "where she's been," I found a perplexing use of the verb, and its connotation. "Where she's been," is not the same as saying, "Where she is." It implies past tense and that she is back. I believe this is a deliberate attempt to suggest a new scenario where Laci has returned from her mysterious disappearance (as if she left on her own, perhaps because of their problematic marriage) and Scott can try to diffuse the situation with Amber as long as she believes him, and doesn't watch the news, of course. Little does he know that the police are sitting in Amber's living room during this conversation.

SP: *Okay, they are amazing.*

I believe he is referring to the media as "amazing," because he is amazed, floored, and nonplussed that such a big fuss is being made over his wife's disappearance. It lends credence to our speculation that he never expected this kind of attention, and it radically altered his game plan.

AF: *You came to me earlier in December and told me you had lost your wife. What was that about?*
SP: *She (unintelligible). She's alive.*
AF: *Where? She's alive? Where?*
SP: *In Modesto. Now, I...This is the hardest ... I ... I wanted to tell you in person.*

There you have it. He now wants her to believe Laci is alive and has returned, and the whole thing was just some misunderstanding. He reiterates his desire to see Amber "in person," so that he can cast his little spell on her again, as he did in the beginning, believing he has some kind of Svengali powers of persuasion, bolstered by years of successfully duping nearly everyone he met.

SP: *... the media has been telling everyone that I had something to do with her disappearance. So the past two weeks I've been hunted by the media. And I just ... I don't want you to be involved ... in this, to protect yourself. I know that I've, you know, I've destroyed. And I, God I hope ... I hope so much that ... this doesn't hurt you.*

The media has [sic] been telling everyone? He really means that the police are suspicious of him, which is much more disturbing than the media. He doesn't want to mention the police to Amber, as if he can shield her from that reality. The police are hunting him, and as an extension of that, the media are interested in the case. He is starting to feel like a cornered rat, and has no one but Amber to turn to for sympathy. When he says, "I've destroyed," and doesn't say what he has destroyed, are we to think he means he has destroyed the trust between him and Amber, or that he has destroyed everyone close to him by his behavior? Either one is true; however, he (and his defense) would interpret it as the lesser of two evils.

SP: I have just been torn up the last two weeks wanting to, tell you and I'm so weak that I haven't.

This statement bothers me a lot. He is torn up because he wanted to tell Amber? Why isn't he torn up because his pregnant wife has been missing for two weeks, and he is in the spotlight? The notable lack of concern for his wife is inconceivable, and a major indicator of his pathology.

SP: You deserve so much better. There's no question you deserve so much better.

This is yet another attempt to elicit pity, a variation on the narcissist's parlance of ingenuous lines such as, "I'm not good enough for you," and "You're the best thing that ever happened to me."

AF: Yeah, and I deserve to understand an explanation of why you told me you lost your wife and this was the first holidays you'd spend without her? That was December 9th ... you told me this, and now all of a sudden your wife's missing? Are you kidding me?

SP: Yeah, she...I did ...I don't know what to say...

He's scrambling, now. He can't decide whether to perpetuate the lie that Laci is in Modesto, or to admit he did something, or how to explain his dilemma. He can't come up with anything remotely convincing, so he plays dumb, which comes naturally.

AF: I think an explanation would be a start.
SP: I know you absolutely deserve an explanation, sweetie... And I want to give you one.

He wants to give her one that will curry favor with her and exculpate him. Unfortunately, his lack of imagination and poor planning (not to mention guilt) have left him without a good cover story, so instead he falls back on the old cop-out: "you don't understand."

SP: It's ... to protect all of us.
AF: To protect all of who?
SP: Everyone involved.

I don't read any underworld connections or accomplices in this statement. I interpret it as his trying to protect himself and his future with all of the people involved. As long as they can't prove he had anything to do with Laci's disappearance, he fantasizes everyone's enabling, good will, sympathy and the opportunity to walk away with a clean slate.

AF: ...you told me you lost your wife. You sat there in front of me and cried and broke down. I sat there and held your hand, Scott and comforted you, and you were lying to me.
SP: Yeah.
AF: Again, lying to me about lying.
SP: I lied to you about traveling, yeah.

He is willing to say he lied about his trip to Maine and Europe. What a guy.

AF: How is that just not such a coincidence?
SP: If you think I had something to do with her disappearance ... or it ... that is so wrong.
AF: Really? And you still have the audacity to call me sweetie right now?

Oh, he still has the audacity to call her, dozens of times, period. And what is "or it"? Or her murder, you mean? I think he almost said that, but caught himself just in time.

AF: [What] Role did I play? How long were you looking for me, Scott?

Bingo. The epiphany. It has just dawned on Amber that he set her up. Not only did he take advantage of her vulnerability and her history of betrayal and heartbreak, but she now believes he may have set her up to be implicated in Laci's disappearance, and she is furious.

AF: Weren't you looking for me? Isn't that what you told Shawn you were looking for me ... or someone like me...How is..I am just such at a loss right now. You say you can't tell me, you want to tell me in person. At what point are you gonna tell me in person. At what point are you gonna tell me in person, Scott?
SP: Once we find her...And that will be, I mean resolution and I will be ... I will be able to explain everything to you ..

Resolution? What sort of resolution does he expect? He doesn't want them to find her; he is counting on them not finding her. He tells the media that finding a "body" is not an acceptable resolution. What possible resolution does he mean? One in which he is no longer under suspicion, the poor, grieving husband, and when he is off the hook?

SP: I've never said anything to you that I didn't mean.
AF: You never told me anything you didn't mean?
SP: I lied to you about ... things I did.

As opposed to lying about his marital status, his lost wife, his holiday plans, and conveniently forgetting about the baby on the way. The correct response here by Amber would be, "What haven't you lied about?" It's a very short list.
SP: You don't deserve to do the things that, I've done to you but ...

This makes no sense. I cannot help thinking that he means she did not deserve for him to involve her in the murder, but she was a convenient scapegoat, and she succumbed to his charms, thus made herself another victim of his malignant modus operandi.

SP: I never cheated on you.
AF: You're married. How do you figure you never cheated on me?

Are we to believe that Scott considers sexual exclusivity (if true) in an extramarital relationship a form of fidelity? This is the most irrational and deranged statement of the entire conversation.

AF: Of course you couldn't tell me the whole story about your wife because it hadn't happened yet. And you were hoping to resolve, in January, that it would be resolved and you'd have a story to tell me.
SP: Sweetie, you think I had something to do with her disappearance? Amber do you believe that? I am not ... evil like that. I am ... oh my God!

Since we cannot hear the inflection of his voice, or the phrasing of these statements, it is difficult to decipher what he means by "I am..." Is he admitting he is, in fact, evil like that, or is he merely spitting out fragments of thought like seed hulls?

SP: Amber, I ... I had to tell you. I've been wanting to tell you. I hope in the future, I can tell you everything ... if you'll let me...

As Henry Higgins from Shaw's *Pygmalion* would say, "Sentimental rhetoric! That's the Welsh strain in him."

To his credit, here are some partial truths Scott uttered in this conversation, where I have taken the liberty of finishing his thoughts:

- I lied to you. (So what? It's as normal as breathing.)
- There are entirely too many repercussions, and they're not all for me. (But the ones about me are the most important.)
- I can understand that you could never believe what I'm saying. (Because I am not sure what the truth is, and never have been.)
- I wanted to tell you about this (but I can't trust anyone).
- I destroyed ...(everything).
- I'm sorry ...(for not getting away with it).
- Sweetie, you don't know everything. (Not by a long shot.)
- I think I know I hurt you. (But it's not very important, and I don't care.)
- I just hope that I mean you don't get hurt more by this than I'm doing. (And you will never forget me for it. I have changed your life forever, and nothing else compares to me.)
- I was a coward...(of deplorable caliber).
- You know I could make excuses now to justify it to myself about...(everything. And I will).

NOVEMBER 22, 2003
PROBABLE CAUSE

"In determining what is probable cause, we are concerned only with the question whether the affiant had reasonable grounds at the time of his affidavit for the belief that the law was being violated on the premises to be searched; and if the apparent facts set out in the affidavit are such that a reasonably discreet and prudent man would be led to believe that there was a commission of the offense charged, there is probable cause justifying the issuance of a warrant." 1992 Supreme Court Annotation

In homicide cases where there is a victim, blood, signs of a struggle, bullet casings, tracks in and out of the scene, and other obvious signs of violation, obtaining a search warrant for the premises is a routine and uncomplicated formality. In the Simpson case, two houses were involved in the crime: the victim's, and the perpetrator's, based on a trail of blood, which ended at the locked gate behind Ms. Brown's condominium, and picked up again at the entrance of Simpson's house. In the Peterson case, from testimony at the preliminary, there was nothing other than the presence of Laci's car, phone, purse, wallet and keys to suggest she did not leave the house of her own volition. There were no apparent signs of struggle, damage, blood, potential weapons, broken furniture or lamps, missing rugs or bedding. Or were there? Something prompted the Modesto police to effectively define probable cause for a judge to grant them a search warrant for the house, Peterson's truck, and the boat within 48 hours.

What was the probable cause for the searches, and the more compelling information to get a second warrant? In California, a search warrant affidavit contains a "Statement of Probable Cause" regarding the property searched and/or seized, how it might be involved in the commission of a felony, or tends to show a felony has been committed, or that a particular person has committed a felony. The warrant has to list a description of the property (single-family residence, address, warehouse, makes and models of both automobiles and the boat) and specifically what items the police are searching for. It cannot be, "We're just going to snoop around and see if anything looks suspicious." The polid3 have to define what they are looking for, such as traces of human blood, clothing, surfaces or material that contain blood, objects that may have been used to inflict injuries (not limited to knives and guns, but also blunt force trauma), computers, receipts for purchases that involve weights, gear, material used to hide or bury a body (i.e., shovels, tools), signs of clean up (bleach residue or results of Luminol). The warrant may also specify items that are conspicuously missing, such as phones, furniture, rugs, bedding, clothing, outerwear, jewelry, documents, personal effects, sentimental items, etc. In the second search of Peterson's home, I believe cataloging missing items was as important as what may have been found.

What do we know was taken, and what was missing? We know they took the boat, Ford truck, Land Rover, mop and bucket, clothing from the washing machine, and computers from the home and office. According to some sources, they also took the contents of the vacuum cleaner bag, scrapings from the fireplace, sink and tub traps, samples of the pool water, pool filter, Peterson's clothing from the truck and some from his closet. Did they take the bag he had packed in the spare bedroom? Noting five impressions of concrete anchors were made from a gallon jug mold in the warehouse, and only one anchor in the suspect's possession gives us reason to believe four of them were used in Peterson's maiden voyage with the boat on Christmas Eve. Laci's clothing on the evening of the 23rd was probably missing, since we believe she was found wearing it. Receipts taken in the first search for purchases of rope, weights, tarp, or other items, which have not been confirmed in court, may have provided further cause to search a second time. Peterson's storage of the tarps, umbrellas and other items originally photographed on the boat were divided between his shed and the warehouse, the most peculiar being the umbrellas back at the house and the boat cover under gasoline-leaking lawn equipment. Those items were mentioned in court, and we can assume they were seized, as well.

Nevertheless, the evidence we know about does not add up to probable cause in my book. It does not define when, where or how a murder occurred. The affidavits had to spell this out and, for reasons about which we can only speculate, have remained sealed for the duration of the case, even beyond the preliminary hearing. By definition (and Constitutional law), the affidavits are required to present the judge with a logical scenario wherein the commission of the suspected acts (in this case, a homicide or kidnapping) took place. Did the MPD suspect immediately that a homicide had occurred? I don't think so, otherwise why involve the FBI, DEA and sanction a search effort? I believe the answers to the mystery of the probable cause and various warrants will be answered once the affidavits for the aforementioned are made public. Until then, we must expect that they had substantial, legally binding cause, or you can be sure the defense would have been victorious in its motions to suppress the warrants and all subsequent "fruit" obtained from the searches, including evidence that was already presented in court: the pliers, hair (and thus mtDNA linking it to Laci), taped phone calls with Amber Frey, GPS data showing Peterson at the Bay, the phone records in general, cash, camping gear, the gun, and items from the boat.

So, the questions remain: What did they find in the house or warehouse that first night (of the 24th) that gave them the green light to go back with a warrant on the 26th? What did they find in Scott's truck that precluded them from returning it, thus establishing it as part of the murder? We await future court filings and publication of the affidavits for enlightenment.

CHAPTER 7: THE ROAD TO TRIAL

DECEMBER 3, 2003
SECOND ARRAIGNMENT

During Peterson's second arraignment, Mark Geragos once again railed against the citizens of Modesto, claiming that they would "lynch his client in town square" if they had a chance. The defense also petitioned to have Peterson's Ford F150 truck returned that has been in police custody since December 26, 2002. The prosecution argued that the truck was vital to its case, because it believes it was the vehicle Peterson used to transport Laci's body to the San Francisco Bay. The driver's side visor and door pocket tested positive for Peterson's blood, indicating evidence of an injury he may have sustained during the murder.

Geragos argued that the Petersons were incurring a financial hardship having to maintain payments on the truck, and that pictures would suffice for the trial. Judge Girolami ordered the State to return the truck to the defense.

DECEMBER 6, 2003
RAISED ON ROBBERY

A person does not simply wake up one day after a life-altering event and become a chronic liar. Deceptive, manipulative, and misleading behavior and thought processes are learned and practiced from early childhood. There are those rare sociopathic individuals theorized as soulless from birth, without conscience or capacity for love, but it's more common that liars are raised in a pretentious environment by conniving, self-centered, and often image-conscious role models whose skills in righteous denial and concealment are exceeded only by their facility with fraud and falsehood.

Like charity, dishonesty begins at home. A child acquires through a sort of social osmosis the values and methods of his parents. By the time he can communicate with words, he has already acquired the nuances and expressions that have assisted in achieving his desires. His first lies are relatively innocuous, such as denying breaking a toy, coloring on the wall, or eating the last cookie. If his parents don't hold him accountable, and instead dismiss his lies out of distraction, laziness, or their own disregard for the truth, the child learns that lying accomplishes freedom from responsibility, increased personal power, and enormous pleasure. The more his lying is rewarded and reinforced by acceptance, sympathy, relief from duty, and escape from blame, the more pleasure he derives. Successful lying is exhilarating and can become compulsive, careless and inconsequential to the liar.

In Scott Peterson's case, it is apparent from his own impetuous, cavalier, and easily disproved falsehoods that he is a person distinctly detached from reality, due to lifelong habit and a severe personality disorder. His parents display similar traits of deep denial, acute insensitivity, and unjustified indignation. We may ask ourselves: how did he get away with his duplicitous behavior for so long? How did he fool Laci, Amber, his siblings, his in-laws, and almost everyone else with whom he came into contact? I suggest that Peterson did not, in fact, fool everyone, and those he deceived were trusting individuals who fell for his handsome, boy-next-door façade, who had more important things to do than investigate his excuses, alibis, biographical inaccuracies or history. He relied on people to take him at face value, meanwhile secretly participating in a parallel fantasy existence, the success of which depended on the players remaining oblivious of each other, like the reenactment of a Shakespearean farce.

How persistently intoxicating this must have been for Peterson, as his cunning little drama played out with seamless precision. Unfortunately for him, because of his obsessive self-absorption and pathological detachment from other people's reality, he severely miscalculated the effect Laci's disappearance would have on the citizens of Modesto, the police, and subsequently the rest of the country. He expected to be believed, regardless of his inconsistencies, irrational behavior, dubious explanations, and alarming determination to resume his preferred activities as though Laci never existed.

One of the many potential difficulties faced by the jury in the eventual trial will be to overcome its suspension of disbelief that a privileged, educated, boyishly innocent-looking man with no history of criminal behavior or previous violence, and with no apparent comprehensible motive, was capable of murdering his pregnant wife, and unflinchingly, relentlessly lying to her family, his family, the media and the world. I propose that Peterson is inherently corrupt, has been lying since before he learned to walk, and was "raised on robbery."

DECEMBER 13, 2003
PETERSON OF THE LIE

A popular and insightful book on evil people by Scott Peck entitled, *People of the Lie* explores, from a spiritual and psychological standpoint, the behavior and motivations of evil people who, more often than not, appear socially acceptable pillars of the community. From the following excerpts from Peck's writing, we are instructed in the devious, amoral camouflaging strategies and vigorous defense mechanisms employed by people like Scott Peterson, who are living proof of the wreckage and malevolence "people of the lie" are capable.

> *The fact of the matter is that we cannot lead decent lives without making judgments in general and moral judgments in particular.*[46]

I believe we have a moral obligation to observe and evaluate what are clearly evil and unconscionable actions, and not succumb to our natural indolence and indifference when it comes to confronting unacceptable behavior, especially by people in positions of power and authority, i.e., the justice system. Those who object to our calling a spade a spade when we characterize people like Peterson, Rodriguez, or Gehring as monsters, in their so-called "expert" but misdirected insistence on defendants' rights, the presumption of innocence, and (bad) law, I suspect that were they or their loved ones a victim of a sociopath, they'd be

---

[46] Peck, M. Scott, *People of the Lie*, Simon and Schuster, 1983.

singing a different tune. The fastest way to convert an intellectually or financially motivated champion of the accused is to have him experience first hand the nature of the beast.

Evil originates not in the absence of guilt but in the effort to escape it.[47]

Perhaps to some this statement seems obvious, but in reality, many who are truly evil are protected by the mental health community, often excused because of some innate inability to distinguish right from wrong, or are justified as defective due to some traumatic childhood experience. I, like Scott Peck, argue that evil people know exactly what they are doing and are fully aware of the potential consequences of their actions. Some may be cloaked in well-developed denial, but are nevertheless absolutely conscious of their destructive nature and choose to perpetrate atrocities anyway. Many of them commit only subtle but consistent acts of willful negligence, sabotage, undermining, deception and scapegoating, and concentrate on their sphere of influence: the family. Others venture out to greener pastures and terrorize entire communities, secure in their distorted notion that they cannot be caught or, if caught, will not be punished.

Evil people hate the light [read: truth] because it reveals themselves to themselves. They hate goodness because it reveals their badness; they hate love because it reveals their laziness. They will destroy the light, the goodness, the love in order to avoid the pain of such self-awareness.[48]

Herein lies a potential motive for Scott Peterson, a young man in his prime who seemed by all accounts to have an enviable life: a beautiful wife, a first son on the way, gainful employment, freedom to travel, a long leash, excellent health, material wealth, an impressive golf score, and good looks. What possible reason, except for a dark, burning hatred for goodness, would prompt a person like him to murder his pregnant wife and risk forfeiting his privileged existence? It is because people of the lie are possessed by a perverse illusion that their reality is not what others see. Their reality is populated by inner demons, jealousy, covetousness, insecurity, pathological selfishness, and greed. Ultimately, people of the lie are thieves, stealing from others their trust, resources, time, love, generosity, forgiveness, and sometimes even their lives.

Truly evil people will take any action in their power to protect their own laziness, to preserve the integrity of their sick self. Rather than nurturing others, they will actually destroy others in this cause. If necessary, they will even kill to escape the pain of their own spiritual growth.[49]

If I am correct in my assessment of Peterson's personality, he is crippled by laziness and dedicated to compulsive self-indulgence at the expense of his relationships (and eventually his freedom). Despite his appearance of busyness,

---

[47] Ibid.

[48] Ibid.

[49] Peck, M. Scott, *People of the Lie*, Simon and Schuster, 1983.

with a cell phone attached to his ear and his frenetic movements during the investigation, he demonstrated pitifully unproductive results of his activities. His family, in all their vehement rallying to his defense, also showed a blatant lack of real involvement in the search for Laci, and instead obstructed the efforts with their toll-free hotline designed to hijack relevant tips that might implicate Peterson.

> *Evil people would be distinguished by these traits: 1.) Consistent destructive, scapegoating behavior, which may often be quite subtle. 2.) Excessive, albeit usually covert, intolerance to criticism and other forms of narcissistic injury. 3.) Pronounced concern with a public image and self-image of respectability, contributing to a stability of lifestyle but also to pretentiousness and denial of hateful feelings or vengeful motives. 4.) Intellectual deviousness, with an increased likelihood of a mild schizophrenic-like disturbance of thinking at times of stress.[50]*

From these criteria, we can conclude that certain Peterson family members manifest the textbook modus operandi of people of the lie. They and their attorneys have attempted to blame inept and corrupt police, serial killers, satanic cults, or even the victim herself for the crime, without a single piece of substantive evidence to support their accusations. Criticism of their son or their own behavior is met with righteous indignation, vicious attacks on the victim's family, condemnation of law enforcement, and pandering to the press. How many times have we heard what a "perfect son" Scott was, statements that his family are law abiding citizens above reproach, or that it was genetically impossible for Peterson to be a murderer? How many times have we seen Mrs. Peterson behave with bitter vindictiveness and then hide behind denial, feigned grief, illness or victimization? Perhaps the apple didn't fall too far from the tree.

DECEMBER 17, 2003
PETITION TO CHANGE VENUE

While I believe it is very likely a venue change for Peterson's trial will be granted, the following is my rebuttal to the petition for a change of venue filed by counsel for the defense, where Geragos attempts to support his motion with the Five Factor Venue Test:

1. The Nature and Gravity of the Offense
2. The Size of the Community
3. The Status of the Victim and the Accused
4. Media Coverage
5. Political Overtones

Of these factors, let us examine the following:

---

[50] Ibid.

#2, The Size of the Community

"Stanislaus County is a relatively small county by California Standards."

Stanislaus County has a larger population than any 10 Cleveland suburbs combined. The diversity of people in the area comprises every cross section of socioeconomic statistic available. Is it really possible that "a majority of potential jurors have formed strong opinions about Peterson's guilt"? How likely is that kind of uniformity in opinion? That majority of people don't even turn out to vote at the general elections. Just for the sake of argument, let's take the population of Stanislaus County at around 400,000; add to it nearby Santa Rosa, San Francisco, Oakland, and San Jose. The total *population of Stanislaus County and* surrounding areas is over 4 million. Of that 4 million people, approximately half the population of the entire state of Ohio, and more than the population of a dozen states in the continental U.S., are we to believe that 12 (or even 20) unbiased people cannot be located? Are these delusions of grandeur, or more preposterous assumptions presented by the defense to move the trial by tantrum? In the last survey taken after the preliminary, only 39 percent of those polled in Modesto admitted to a prejudicial bias against Peterson. Imagine how much smaller that percentage will be when eligible jurors from three of the largest cities in California (San Jose, San Francisco and Oakland) are polled. Why should Girolami move the trial farther than Oakland or San Jose? Or why shouldn't the defense agree to bus jurors in from those areas, thereby sparing the major inconvenience and expense of moving the trial to Los Angeles or Santa Barbara?

#4: Media Coverage

"The media coverage has been undeniably biased against Peterson."

Isn't it interesting that the "extensive and inflammatory" stories that make Peterson look the worst are the simple facts of the case? Most of the unsubstantiated rumors and innuendo dispersed by the media were defense spin: satanic cults, tattoos, partial and out of context autopsy findings, nebulous links to serial killers or other murders in the region, tan vans, mysterious women who were the victims of a cult, blood and duct tape found in the repossessed van, fetal age of the baby, etc. The media, by reporting on undisputed facts about the defendant - his extramarital affairs, the alarming number of phone calls he made to Ms. Frey during the early days of the search, his trading in Laci's car, inquiring on listing the property on Covena Avenue, his change in appearance, cash and suspicious equipment found on him at the time of his arrest - are doing their job in reporting the information. This can hardly be considered "undeniably biased." It's not biased at all. It is one-sided because there are no other sides to present. There is no one, other than the defendant's immediate family, willing to come forward with any information that conflicts with the facts, or submits a viable alternative theory, or presents the defendant in any kind of favorable light. Is it the media's fault that nobody will go to bat for Peterson, or that all the publicity in this case is disparaging to his character?

#5: The Presence of Political Overtones

This is the weakest, if not completely unsupported, factor of the five. To define the Attorney General's statement about the "slam dunk" of the DNA matching as "a political overtone" is absurd. Once again, Geragos wants the public to believe that a successful conviction of the accused is so important that careers will be made and broken on its outcome. This is just another overt attempt to reinforce the foolish and unrealistic notion that some massive conspiracy is underfoot to frame, plant evidence against, and ultimately send poor, "presumed innocent" Mr. Peterson to death row. Similarly, Geragos wants the judge to believe that the Rochas' support of a federal law prohibiting fetal murder has some bearing on the guilt or innocence of his client, or adds political gravity to the case. As if dozens of law enforcement officers, FBI agents, Department of Justice employees, Congressmen and women, and virtually everyone on the County payroll is in cahoots in their mission to nail a nobody adulterous fertilizer salesman like Peterson.

The most amusing citation in the petition is when the defense quotes an indicted (potential) felon, former Modesto mayor, Carmen Sabatino, as additional proof of the political ramifications and impossibility of a fair trial. This is, in fact, further proof that the defense is unable to find anyone of sound reputation, irreproachable morals, or objective detachment to speak on behalf of its client. The overtones in this case are not political, but they certainly are ominous.

DECEMBER 23, 2003
995 MOTION TO DISMISS

Despite the absence of his authentic signature on the document, the *995 Motion to Set Aside Information* has Mark Geragos's hand all over it. Not only was it filed a week past deadline, but it adds insult to injury in typical histrionic fashion: teeming with inaccuracies and redundancies, riddled with non sequiturs, and is as poorly written but with less style and substance than a mediocre high school term paper.

Geragos is fortunate that he didn't have my high school English teacher reviewing his work, or she would have advised him to put a match to his motion. Obviously, the California school system he attended lacked the standards of an average Cleveland suburban public school during the same era. Perhaps that accounts for his abysmally low expectations of the intelligence of the People in general, and the judges in Stanislaus County in particular. Like his narcissistic client, Geragos suffers from delusions of smug intellectual superiority, and insists on portraying his opposition and audience as incompetent imbeciles. Regardless of his continued failure with this attitude and strategy (the recent Winona Ryder case comes to mind), Geragos forges on with his consistently erroneous underestimation of our discernment and acumen.

Let us accept the fact that Geragos thinks we are all idiots, have been asleep for the last year like collective Rip Van Winkles, and that we are too ill informed to refute his conveniently selective memory. Let us not be offended. Let us, instead, rejoice in his misconceptions, and take great comfort in his foolish consistency as verification of the hobgoblins of his small mind. Meanwhile, let us disclose the pathetic impotence and inadequacies revealed in his latest pleadings, which (using his opening phrase) "would be comical if they were not so dreadful."

> *..the People have not only failed to present any evidence sufficient to substantiate even a prima facie case against Scott Peterson, but it is apparent that all real and substantial leads focusing on Laci Peterson's disappearance were dismissed or ignored.[51]*

Consider this statement the main melody that will recur throughout the document like a children's musical round of "Row, Row, Row Your Boat," with equal banality and predictability. For the defense's premise to be true, it would require virtually everyone involved in the investigation and prosecution of the case to be liars and lawbreakers willing to sacrifice their reputations and careers "from the very beginning...to put Scott Peterson on death row." First of all, how did the police (early on) know there was a capital crime committed that would justify the severest of penalties? Was their so-called "single-mindedness" [sic] a result of observing evidence of which we have not yet been apprised? How could the Modesto police be "totally inept", yet capable of "engineering this railroad straight to death row"? How did those bumbling nitwits find their way home at night, much less collaborate on a multilevel conspiracy to frame poor Mr. Innocent? Are they very shrewd and monomaniacal, or reckless and imprudent? Make up your mind, Mr. Geragos; you can't have it both ways.

> *It is a basic rule of law that the prosecution must produce evidence independent of a defendant's own statements, to establish that a crime actually occurred...the prosecution...introduced no evidence that would show that Laci's and Connor's deaths were brought about by criminal means...It appears to be the prosecution's speculative theory that Connor's death occurred inside rather than outside the womb...this wild speculation is unsupported by any evidence...there was no testimony that any evidence was found at the location where the bodies were discovered showing how the deaths were caused.[52]*

This series of excerpts contains some interesting information scattered among blatant inaccuracies, illogical assumptions, denial of scientific laws, and language deliberately inserted to make the People's case appear absurd. Reading between the lines, we can expect that many of the defendant's statements we have yet to hear, either from tapped telephone calls or conversation with witnesses, will be seriously incriminating. If Laci and Connor's deaths were not the result of a crime, how does the defense explain their bodies found three miles from where the defendant claims he was fishing on the day they disappeared? Is a "reasonable person of ordinary caution and prudence" expected to believe that Laci hitchhiked to the frigid and turbulent San Francisco Bay and went for a swim in her street

---

[51] December 22, 2003 Defense Motion to Set Aside Information, p. 2.

[52] Ibid, p. 3.

clothes? If she was fond of swimming in the winter, why not step outside to the backyard and jump in the pool? There is more than enough biological and physical law to support the disparity in decomposition levels between the two victims. In fact, were Connor to have been killed separately from his mother and later put in the water in some sinister and amazingly prescient timing, his condition would have been far more deteriorated, or more likely, his remains would never have surfaced at all.

Regarding the last irrelevant sentence: hasn't the defense continually pointed out, in leaks to the media and in questioning during the preliminary hearing, the tape around the baby's neck as evidence of cause of death? Hasn't the defense insisted that there were footprints and debris located near the baby's remains that would indicate another perpetrator? Has this area of reasonable doubt been abandoned in order for the defense to now claim that A) no crime was committed because there is no cause of death; and/or B) that the mother and baby were separated before death? Talk about wild speculation! Talk about being unsupported by any evidence! I realize the defense does not have to prove innocence, but it would certainly go a long way towards its credibility if it would start making a little sense, here.

> *The reason Scott Peterson is in custody today, and has been held to answer charges that carry with them a possible penalty of death, is that the Modesto Police, at the very inception of the investigation of this case, in the absence of any physical evidence, or any other evidence of any kind, decided that Scott was responsible for Laci's disappearance. They deliberately ignored any exculpatory evidence, and from day one worked only toward putting Scott in the gas chamber.*[53]

Let us take this opportunity to remind Geragos of the real reasons his client is in custody today. Peterson is probably responsible for Laci's disappearance and ultimately her and her unborn son's death. This will be proved in a court of law while he remains in jail without bail. The defense waived its right to a bail hearing knowing full well that Peterson is a flight risk from his well-documented behavior. He is being held to answer because Judge Girolami of the Stanislaus Superior Court determined that the preliminary hearing disclosed enough evidence to support probable cause. This same judge, whom Geragos will have to face again after his 995 Motion is denied, along with the DA and police, were overtly ridiculed as "unreasonable," "failing in their obligations," "biased," "fundamentally flawed," and lacking in "ordinary caution and prudence" by the arguments presented in the points and authorities. Perhaps Judge Girolami won't take this personally, considering the source.

If there was "exculpatory evidence" to suggest another perpetrator, such as the "hostile and suspicious men" with the alleged pregnant woman walking a similar dog on December 24 (who cannot be deemed hostile just because they use foul language - the witness herself stated to police that the trio appeared to know each other and there was no confrontation or forced abduction evident), don't you

---

[53] Ibid, pp. 6-7.

think we would have seen it by now? Don't you think the Petersons and their publicity-hogging attorney would have been shouting it from the rooftops? The Modesto police did not deliberately ignore exculpatory evidence; there simply wasn't any. If this is the best argument the defense can offer to dismiss the charges, you can expect there to be much more evidence presented at trial to connect Peterson to the murder, and the defense is painfully aware of every bit of it.

And by the way, Mr. Geragos, there is no gas chamber in California any more.

JANUARY 7, 2004
CHANGE OF VENUE - TAKE TWO

Since the 1880s, the term "lynching" has become almost exclusively associated with archaic abuse of African Americans and is not limited to hanging, but encompasses any unlawful slaying of a person by a mob. In the Reply to the DA's *Opposition to Motion of Change of Venue* in the case of California v Peterson, upper-middle class Caucasian counsel to upper-middle class Caucasian defendant has employed the racially charged verbs, "lynch" or "lynching" and "hang" to describe the vigilante mentality of the nearly half million (predominantly white, middle-class) citizens of Stanislaus County in his arguments to move the trial. Apparently, invoking the image of the (nonexistent) gas chamber in the recent *995 Motion to Dismiss* failed to elicit enough sympathy and outrage for the unduly maligned and relentlessly reviled Mr. Innocent, thus the tactlessly inappropriate, revolting reference to an ugly and shameful era of civilian injustice. Comparing Peterson's arrest, incarceration and pending trial to racist hate crimes is no less absurd than Mrs. Peterson's previous allusions to Nazi Germany.

Unfortunately, Geragos's provocative accusations demonstrate nothing more than the promulgation of a desperate strategy to portray his affluent, white, scratch golfing, pampered and privileged client as some sort of victim of society. Has Geragos's association with the Nation of Islam corrupted his metaphors? Whatever the reason for his now 44 pages (plus several thousand exhibits) of inadmissible and invalid indictments of the DA and the people of Stanislaus County, it is clear that Mark Geragos is trying his case through his motions rather than subjecting his fallacious arguments to the legal scrutiny of a public courtroom. Ironically, this deliberate incompetence and inflammatory innuendo intended to poison the jury pool are the very sins of which the defense is accusing the prosecution.

For $500 an hour, Geragos couldn't get the motion right the first time around? Even his second attempt, albeit including the occasional relevant citation, could have been distilled to a three-page document that would have neatly laid out a strong, succinct summary of the major points for moving the venue or opening up the potential jury pool to include adjacent counties. Perhaps like Charles Dickens, Mark Geragos is paid by the word. If I were his client, I'd demand a refund.

Let us examine a few excerpts from the *January 6 Reply* and determine which side is, in fact, turning "a blind eye to reality:"

> *The bottom line here is that there is simply no way to conduct a fair trial of Scott Peterson in Stanislaus County...also that the improper bias*

against Mr. Peterson is significantly higher in Stanislaus County than in several other counties...the publicity [has been] hostile and continuous and has infected most if not all of Stanislaus County...it has been highly prejudicial either because of its outright hostility to him and sympathy for the victims, or because it disclosed "factual" information which most of the time was inaccurate but nonetheless likely to create a public belief in his guilt.[54]

Geragos would have served his client adequately with stating the fact that information and sensationalism about the case has saturated the county, and in particular the city of Modesto. That the news is "hostile" to Peterson is really irrelevant and in large part due to Peterson's own behavior and affect during the investigation. Let's face it; he's not a very likable guy, and the crime of which he is accused would incite the wrath of even the most casual observer. However, Geragos is too busy playing the "blame game" to admit that his client is responsible for his own bad rap, not the Modesto police. The "sanitizing" of which Geragos accuses the prosecution (by whitewashing the publicity) is obviously the defense's intent with regard to Peterson's actions before and after Laci's murder. Painting Peterson with the brush of compulsive but innocuous adulterer is preferable to the harsh reality that he is a wife and baby killer. Nobody would want to lynch the poor guy from the nearest tree just for cheating on his wife, right?

anti-defendant misstatements of the supposed evidence which was in turn carried in the local press...relentless campaign by the prosecution and investigators to poison the jury pool...while one arm [was trying] to put out the flames of community passion another arm was fanning the flames...promptly had a meeting with [the Rochas] in order to turn them against him [Peterson]...the press fed the public a steady diet of coverage of the outpouring of grief and sympathy over Laci and Connor's death...orchestrated a campaign to publicly convict Scott Peterson...[55]

Misstatements of supposed evidence? Fanning the flames? Orchestrating a campaign? Is Scott Peterson sitting in county jail without bail because of "supposed evidence"? Are we expected to believe that the arguably minor but incriminating evidence admitted in the preliminary hearing that held Peterson over for trial was a trumped-up phantasmagoric invention of a deranged law enforcement agency hell bent on hanging an innocent man out of laziness, ineptitude or guile? This notion begs the question, "Why?" On the contrary, I conclude that the suggestion of the potential (and alarming) 400 witnesses for the prosecution indicates that there is much more evidence we have yet to hear, and that the case against Peterson is substantially stronger than we have been led to believe by defense apologists and ignorant columnists.

---

[54] January 6, 2004 Defense Reply to the District Attorney's Opposition to Motion for Change of Venue, p. 3.
[55] Ibid, pp. 6-7.

Tomorrow, the hearing for the change of venue will take place in Stanislaus County Supreme Court, and it would behoove Geragos to leave his melodrama at the door, along with his pager and cell phone, so that he can focus on presenting logical and factual positions for a change of venue, which has the potential of being granted if reasonably argued. It would be refreshing to see Geragos earn his keep for a change, instead of squandering his client's resources and the Court's time with supercilious and extraneous public displays of stupidity.

JANUARY 9, 2004
THE SURVEY SCANDAL

From viewing part of the hearing yesterday in the case of The People of California v Scott Peterson, I watched Judge Girolami explain that his ruling for the change of venue was influenced primarily by the pervasive media coverage the case has attracted, especially in Modesto.

Even if they [the reports] were all factual in nature and not inflammatory, this weighs in favor of a change of venue, especially when the coverage is not typical for this type of crime...The jury will base its decision on some facts it learned outside the courtroom."

Girolami conceded, however, that publicity is extensive throughout the state.[56]

It is interesting to note that Judge Girolami said, "Of the surveys, the most thorough was the one conducted by Dr. Stephen Schoenthaler (hereinafter referred to as Dr. Show-and-Tell) and his students at California State University Stanislaus. From the results of his survey, it is apparent that there are residents of other counties that have not formed as strong an opinion as in Stanislaus County."

Dr. Show-and-Tell's survey was termed "professional" and cited repeatedly in Geragos's Motion to Change Venue (Take One).

"[A] Local jury may be willing but unable to distinguish what they heard from the media versus what they heard in the courtroom, and it would be impossible to avoid headlines or news flashes, even if sequestered."

Girolami announced that he based part of his ruling on Dr. Show-and-Tell's declaration, to which the prosecution objected as hearsay. Little did they know it was worse than hearsay; it was fiction! The prosecution was not provided Dr. Show-and-Tell's declaration (survey results) before the hearing; that burden, among many others, was deliberately omitted by the defense.

Let us review some of the (bogus) **Survey Results**:

---

[56] Ryan, Harriet, "Judge Rules to Move Scott Peterson's Trial from Modesto," January 9, 2004, www.courttv.com.

- 68 percent polled in Stanislaus County think Peterson is guilty. (Seven of twelve students on the third floor of the dorm at the time.) Only 44 percent can set aside their bias. These would be the few still hung over from Thanksgiving weekend.
- 59 percent polled in Alameda County think Peterson is guilty. (Three out of the seven parents and relatives that live there, rounded off for authenticity.)
- 50 percent polled in Santa Clara County think Peterson is guilty. (They flipped a coin ten times and got the statistical probability rather than make the phone calls.)
- 55 percent polled in the Bay Area think he's guilty. (Several students called friends at UC Berkeley and asked them to poll their table in the cafeteria at lunch and count the responses.)

The results from Orange or Los Angeles County were not published on the *ModBee* Web site, but I suspect they were no more scientific than the previous statistics reported in the potential venue locations.

Dr. Show-and-Tell's survey, admitted into evidence in a California Superior Court influencing a double homicide case with widespread media attention and venue issues, was conducted by students in his college class who were assigned to call (from the phone book) some 1,175 prospective jurors in late November and early December. He claimed (on the witness stand, under oath, without verifying a single phone number or blind checking a line item result), "From 114 to 122 people responded in each of California's eight largest counties, plus Stanislaus and San Joaquin counties." Is that so?

When several of his students confessed today that they had fudged the results, Dr. Show-and-Tell decried, "I'm stunned, and I find it hard to believe. It seems impossible that I could have missed something like that." I can tell you how he missed something like that: by being so eager to inject his junk science into the frenzy of the Peterson case, he failed to perform the most rudimentary of teaching tasks: grading the papers. I've had sales managers audit my call reports with more scrutiny than Dr. Show-and-Tell invested in his survey results. Why he failed to randomly verify a few phone numbers or call a dozen survey respondents is beyond incompetence; it is tantamount to fraud.

Incidentally, Dr. Show-and-Tell is an international advocate of nutrition and has written academic papers linking behavior (particularly of criminal nature) with vitamin deficiencies. He has received a number of grants from the State of California to conduct experiments in correctional facilities involving adding vitamin supplements to the standard prison diet. His theories, tested over 20 years ago, are far from original, yet he managed to make a name for himself with many intersecting interest groups, including the ADD lobby, criminal psychologists, and health nuts. The results of his studies continue to be used as endorsements for a number of nutritional supplement vendors on the Internet, hawking everything from ginkgo to guanine and other amino acids with guarantees to raise your IQ and improve your memory.

Perhaps Dr. Show-and-Tell should lay off the double lattes and Snickers bars (judging by his girth), focus on his job as instructor, and trade a few points of his IQ for a dose of common sense.

JANUARY 20, 2004
CHANGE OF VENUE: TAKE THREE

We've certainly been getting a crash course on California geography, politics, and demographics lately. Here are a few snapshots of the two major cities in San Mateo County, the new home of the Peterson trial:

San Mateo County: median income for a household is $70,819, and the median income for a family is $80,737.

The City of San Mateo: 63 percent of San Mateo residents have attended college, with a well-trained workforce occupied in the highest proportion of Finance, Insurance, and Real Estate (FIRE) businesses in the county.

Redwood City's largest employer: as of the year 2000, 7,400 people are employed by Oracle Corporation, the world's leading supplier of software for enterprise information management.

Redwood City's weather: it averages 20 inches of rainfall per year, and has an average high temperature of 77 degrees from April through September, and 63 degrees from October through March, with over 160 sunny days per year.

What do these statistics bode for the People and the defense? For the prosecution, the change of venue will initially create a logistical hassle, as it now has to relocate virtually its entire office, staff and case files to a strange facility, with a round-trip commute from Modesto of no less than three hours. Other than the initial inconvenience, however, it must bask in this venue victory, even if it wasn't its first choice. The demographics heavily favor a well-educated, curious jury pool with good analytical skills, a low rate of negative experiences with law enforcement, enough skepticism to dismiss voodoo theories of satanic cults, and indifference to Peterson's country club lifestyle. The average citizen of San Mateo County will regard Peterson as a shallow social climber with inferior breeding, a second-tier education (compared to Stanford or UC Berkeley) and compulsively poor judgment.

For the defense, the move from Stanislaus County and surrounding areas may prove a pyrrhic victory. Granted, it distanced itself from the "lynch mob," but it also forfeited the higher population of middle-class, minority, and working-class people who may have been more impressed with Peterson's clean-cut image and high-profile defense. A less educated (and mostly non-mariner) jury would be more likely confused by scientific testimony, mtDNA and hydrology. The move from Modesto will also leave Judge Girolami behind, thus losing a familiar and somewhat permissive jurist to an unknown and potentially more authoritarian chief.

Obviously, Geragos's arguments to move the trial to Orange County were strictly self-serving, since it is inconsequential to the defendant, who will remain in custody regardless. His pleas that the southern location would benefit

Peterson's family were not only irrelevant, but also insulting and insensitive to the victim's family and the People. Since when does the defendant's family have any standing in this case? Offering to waive Peterson's future petitions for public funding was similar to attempting to negotiate to relinquish child support in a divorce decree in order to retain property or limited visitation. These issues are statutory, and Geragos has no business to play bluff poker with Peterson's rights; it's not only ill advised, it's grounds for insufficient counsel.

Should we interpret Geragos's intimations as evidence that the well is running dry and he anticipates bailing? Redwood City is no Sunday jaunt from Los Angeles, and Geragos has his celebrity clientele close to home. Perhaps the ringmaster is going to pull up stakes and fold his tents and tell the Petersons, "Look, I got the venue changed, I tried my best to get it in L.A. or Orange County, I threw out enough spaghetti that some of it is bound to stick, I filed hundreds of pages of motions that should raise enough reasonable doubt. You have the media to fan the flames of fantasy before the trial. You'll be in good hands with a public defender!" After all, it's just business as usual for Geragos.

FEBRUARY 1, 2004
FEBRUARY 2 AGENDA

Tomorrow morning in San Mateo County Superior Court, the first hearing in the new venue in the case of The People of California v Scott Lee Peterson will transpire. According to documents filed in court this past week, the following issues are on the docket:

Defendant's Brief Re Untimeliness of People's Peremptory Challenge of Judge Richard Arnason - will be dismissed.

Prosecution's reply to above - will be accepted.

Defense Notice of Motion and Motion to Continue - Without access to the document itself, what might be some of the reasons that Geragos would request a continuance, after his belligerent declaration that his client would not waive his right to a speedy trial? Several possibilities come to mind: in order that the People timely comply with as yet undisclosed reciprocal discovery material or copies of witness statements or a finalized witness list; or simply a scheduling conflict with Geragos's other trials.

Joint Discussion Proposal: Both parties have conferred regarding any number of possible issues, but one for certain is their mutual objection to cameras in the courtroom. In addition, according to some news reports, the defense is requesting a jury questionnaire (which is a routine and practical request in the new venue) and to sequester the jury, should they be satisfied with the questionnaire results. It is highly unlikely that its request for sequestration will be granted, but Geragos has nothing to lose by asking for it. Both sides agreed on a four-day week (Monday-Thursday) and their preference that the witness and ultimate jury list be sealed from the public.

Never fear, the media are not going down without a fight, as representatives from California and out-of-state media interests have filed petitions to request cameras in the courtroom, and access to the witness list and jury selection procedures. Court TV (and its affiliate CNN) has filed a brief in *Support of Rule*

980 requesting television coverage of the trial. The bigger media organizations have already invested tens of thousands of dollars leasing tiny plots of real estate from San Mateo County, and have a substantial financial stake in the potential revenue generated from broadcasting as much of this trial as possible. This is capitalism and free enterprise at its most basic level: supply and demand. The Court, however, regards televising trials an exceptional privilege, not a right, and the judge will consider the following relevant factors in his ruling:

- Importance of maintaining public trust and confidence in the judicial system - I doubt this will be an issue, since virtually every aspect of this trial will be publicly dissected, regardless of whether or not it is televised.
- Parties' support of or opposition to the request - Both sides oppose media access to the trial, which will weigh heavily (if not be a *slam dunk*) in the judge's decision.
- Nature of the case - This case has generated unprecedented attention for a non-celebrity, and it may be argued that televising the trial will only exacerbate an already saturated audience with around-the-clock analysis and regurgitation of the trial.
- Effect on the parties' ability to select a fair and unbiased jury - Maybe a California lawyer can explain this to me, but this seems like closing the barn door after the horses have escaped. Nonetheless, I expect both sides to use this argument to ban cameras.
- Effect on any subsequent proceedings in the case - The prosecution may prefer restricted exposure of the trial to prevent grandstanding by the defense, vulnerability to jury contamination, risks of mistrial, and any unforeseen issues for appeal. In the Peterson case, televising the trial would be an advantage to the defense of an innocent client, but avoided at all costs if the evidence is overwhelmingly against him. I conclude that Geragos's natural tendency to seek the spotlight and center stage has been trumped by his professional obligation as an advocate for his client.
- Effect of coverage on the willingness of witnesses to cooperate, including the risk that coverage will engender threats to the health or safety of any witness - This may be a valid concern to the prosecution, especially considering their cryptic points for keeping the search warrant and wiretap affidavits sealed all this time.
- Undue administrative or financial burden to the court or participants - While the court may cringe at the media avalanche, most of the merchants and officials of Redwood City are hoping for a televised trial, based on their lobbying for the venue and their eagerness to cash in on the popularity of this case.

Tomorrow is Groundhog Day, and, according to legend, if the groundhog sees his shadow or not predicts the weather conditions for the remainder of winter. Will Punxsutawney Phil predict the start of the Peterson trial as well? If he sees his shadow, will there be six more weeks of delay? Just in case, let's hope for a cloudy day in Pennsylvania tomorrow.

FEBRUARY 9, 2003
THE WAITING ENDS?

Summary of Hearing

The long awaited and much-delayed trial in the case of the People of California v Scott Peterson is set to begin Wednesday, February 11, one day after the one-year anniversary of the baby, Connor's due date, and nearly 14 months after Laci Peterson disappeared from the lives of her loved ones forever on December 24, 2002.

It seems as though we have waited for this trial with a combination of anxiety, anticipation, and impatience, but in the annals of California murder cases, it is relatively speedy. Neither side seems interested in prolonging the agony, and now that cameras and most of the public have been essentially banished from the courtroom, updates on the trial's progress will be dependent on second-hand information, transcripts (if available), and relying on the interpretations of the few media personalities with seats in the courtroom.

The first order of business will be arguing admissibility of the prosecutor's evidence: GPS surveillance, tracking dogs, hypnotized witnesses, intercepted phone calls, and videos of Peterson's interviews. The mtDNA evidence was already accepted as being scientifically reliable by both sides based on the lengthy examination during the preliminary hearing. The defense has also filed motions to sequester the jury, and for separate guilt and penalty phase juries. After the evidentiary matters are concluded, a tedious *voire dire* will ensue, to which the reporters will have access, according to today's ruling by Judge Delucchi. Both the final jury list and witness list will remain sealed, along with the affidavits, search warrants, autopsy reports, and other documents that have been sealed since early in the case.

Let's hope the light of truth shines brightly on this trial, illuminating the shadows of dark souls who would obscure reason, skew science, and rationalize reprehensible behavior in their ego-driven ambitions to thwart justice for fleeting fame. Let the Rochas feel the collective support of friends and strangers alike, and let justice prevail for Laci and her baby. No more dress rehearsals - it's show time.

CHAPTER 8: PRETRIAL

February 27 – May 27, 2004

The following is a summary and commentary of the February 26 proceedings based on a reading of the official transcripts. I will cite the page number and line when quoting important passages.

The first order of business was to announce that the District Division 2 Appellate Court upheld the exclusion of cameras in the courtroom (from a petition by Court TV, et al.) The second order of business was to hear arguments for and against sequestering the jury and selecting two separate juries for guilt and penalty phases of the trial. In a nutshell (and this is not easy), Geragos's arguments for separate juries included his contention that some "40 to 50 percent" of the jurors would be disqualified immediately because they are opposed to the death penalty. (I don't know where he gets his statistics.) The pretrial publicity has already tainted another 40 percent, and that leaves 10 – 20 percent of which at least half will find excuses not to serve because of the length of the trial. Of those, many have an "agenda" against the defense, and he groused that the jury selection process will be "endless, comparable to the myth of Sisyphus rolling the rock up the hill," an interesting metaphor. If you recall, Sisyphus was a murderer and traitor to the gods. His punishment in Hades was to roll a block of stone up a steep hill, only to have it tumble back down again when he reached the top. Perhaps Geragos should have chosen a more sympathetic character. He reiterated that the penalty phase was really not going to happen, since his client is innocent and will be acquitted, and compared the case to *Sheppard* and the recent decision in Illinois to furlough all death row inmates to life without parole.

Judge Delucchi reminded Geragos that the California Supreme Court, "is not impressed with that argument," and went on to say that he has to "consider the worst case scenario for you, and I have to consider that when we voir dire a jury that we will get to the penalty phase; otherwise the jury voir dire is meaningless." Delucchi conceded that the case has garnered a lot of publicity. In DA Dave Harris's rebuttal to the motion, he stated that, "Counsel's impassioned plea is nice, but, unfortunately, it's illogical and doesn't follow the law." He noted that with two juries the State would not save time, but rather have to try the case twice.

The judge responded by calling the "prejudgment rate of 40 or 50 percent [as] speculative," and that the questionnaire will weed out most of them. From a population of 701,000 citizens in San Mateo County, he is pretty confident he can seat an impartial jury, "so the request for two juries is denied. We will try this case with one jury," (1665:14-15)

Losing the battle for separate juries just inspired Geragos to new heights of hysteria, and in arguing for a sequestered jury, he predicted doom more horrifying than the Biblical plagues. The poor jurors will be subjected to assault by the media, billboards, bullhorns, harassment, paparazzi, and to having their personal information (including their taxes, of course) broadcast all over the Internet! The jurors will be bribed by the tabloids and hounded by "fringe media" who seek an interview and to influence the trial. To this, the judge responded, "I can't control everybody in the world." To which Geragos sniped back, "You can barely control what's in this courtroom!" (1669:20-24) Geragos didn't let the judge get a word in here, and ranted that it won't make the jurors prisoners, but assures that they "remain as untampered [sic] with as possible," which sounds like he was discussing a bottle of Tylenol.

DA Harris retorted with the fact that a sequestered jury would create undue hardships for many jurors with children, and that there is "no constitutional due process or even fairness right to have a sequestered jury...Take the appropriate steps to try and protect the jury as much as possible...admonish them not to read, watch or be involved with anything that occurs outside of this courtroom." (1671-1672) Geragos snapped back that if losing a percentage of jurors was not compelling enough to get his two juries, it shouldn't be good enough to prevent sequestration. He implied the judge is naive and will have no control over what the jurors do after they leave the courtroom, and that, like the Sheppard case, his client requires "unusual preventive measures." To that, the judge stated that locking the jury up and keeping them from TV, radio, their loved ones and other communication would be worse and make them more vulnerable to the press, who would find them and park outside the hotel, anyway. "The only place we could guarantee this wouldn't happen is if we park the jury on Mars." (1675:7-8) The judge made his own dire predictions should there be sequestration: "People are going to be bailing out right and left...jurors get resentful...and they could blame your client for being locked up for five months. He's the one that put them there." (1675) Thus the judge denied the motion for sequestration. There will be 18 jurors: 12 seated and six alternates, who will be sent home every night with an admonishment.

The next item on the agenda was continued direct (by DA Dave Harris) and cross examination (by Pat Harris) of Christopher Boyer, Captain of the Search and Rescue Team for the Contra Costa Sheriff's Office, beginning with some of the testimony of February 25. Defense counsel Pat Harris objected early on that they were not aware that Boyer was going to be a witness, which is why they delayed their cross for the next day. Captain Boyer briefly explained his experience with training dogs and describes what he termed, "scent theory: the chemical, biological, and other processes and behaviors of the dog that allows it to be a scent dog or a scent hound, and how it develops those things, and how to interpret the environment and the scent articles they are using, *or* what they are looking for." (1635) The defense later calls this theory "voodoo."

Boyer went on to describe his role in the Laci Peterson search, which was as a supervisor and a "runner," which is someone who protects the dog and the handler from traffic or other obstructions. Boyer did not personally handle any of the search dogs himself. Dave Harris allowed the witness to emphasize the fact that the dogs consistently led away from the house to the road leading down to the main highway rather than towards the park.

In Thursday's session, Boyer, in continued direct with D. Harris, explained how a dead person can still emit a "live" scent because of what are called "skin rafts": small dandruff-like and microscopic particles shed by humans, that still remain even after "autolysis" takes place, which is when the cells of the internal body begin decomposing. The skin rafts were likened to "Post-It" notes that fall off the body rather easily and are disseminated in the wind. Boyer also attempted to defuse the "cross contamination" accusation by stating that in his experience, scent dogs can differentiate between "predominant" and other potentially mingling scents from imperfect articles that may have been handled by another person.

112

Harris walked Boyer through a brief replay of the Berkeley Marina alerts by Trimble described in earlier testimony from Eloise Anderson.

On cross, the first point Pat Harris made was a gaffe: he asked Boyer if the particulates are called "life rafts," and Boyer corrected him with, "Skin rafts, you idiot! You'd better hope you have a life raft when this Titanic of a case sinks!" (Ok, he didn't say that, but he should have.) Undeterred, Harris continued to show his ignorance of biology by asking, "You know that skin rafts could very well in two weeks end up in San Francisco." Was Harris trying to say that Laci's skin rafts would travel from Modesto to San Francisco without degrading or being consumed by natural forces such as bacteria, or to the exact same area that her husband launched his boat? What kind of molecular phenomenon is that? Is there such a thing as astral projection of skin rafts? Boyer assured him that skin rafts (of which we shed 150,000 per hour) would decompose before traveling that far, to which Harris declared, "So this entire thing we've been talking about for two days is basically voodoo, because these scents aren't capable of sitting there, staying in the location where you claim they are?" (1690) Dave Harris objected; judge sustained.

Pat Harris then tried to discredit Boyer, his team, and the way in which the training logs are verified, as well as asserting that vehicle tracking is an unorthodox method (his words were "it is not a legitimate process") of tracking people, and thus scientifically unsound (therefore should be disqualified for the trial). Boyer defended his confidence in the dogs being able to track a person from a vehicle, but agreed that not all trainers have adopted those methods. For several more pages in the transcripts, Harris attempted to portray the volunteer dog trainers and search team as a bunch of yahoos with no more credibility than people who bring their dogs to obedience school to teach them to heel, stay, roll over and beg.

The gathering of the scent articles from Laci's home, in particular the order in which they were collected and how Peterson responded to their removal, was explored on pages 1713-1720. Boyer recalled that the pink slipper was collected first (and he changed his latex gloves between articles), the glasses in their case collected second, the hairbrush third, and Scott's brown slipper fourth. Pat Harris wanted to insert his belief that the brown slipper was taken between Laci's objects, but Boyer insisted that the brown slipper was last. Boyer also admitted that the collection of Scott's slipper was deliberate and not hidden from Peterson or with any sinister intent, at least not from the dog handler's point of view. To Boyer, it was a standard procedure: "It's common for us to take other family members' clothing articles." Peterson, upon advice from his father and an attorney named Mr. Lee, asked for and received a receipt for the scent articles removed from the home. (Mr. Lee might be Lee Peterson's attorney, but it is interesting that we now have proof of the presence of an attorney early in the investigation.) Pat Harris used this opportunity to point out how cooperative his client was and that Scott was upset that things had been removed from his home without his consent the night of the disappearance, which is why he was asking for receipts. My question is why was he sitting there at the dining table with his dad and a lawyer and not out looking for his wife? This recount also verifies that Scott was sitting in the house when Merlin (the bloodhound) was given the glasses to scent, and if Scott's scent were predominant on the glasses instead of Laci's, Merlin would have loped back into the house and jumped on Scott. So much for the cross contamination hocus-pocus; either the dogs Merlin and Trimble were totally inept, or they were following Laci's scent. Only when given the brown slipper did Trimble follow Scott's "freshest scent" from the warehouse to the highway.

The following exchange is worth reading in its original format to get the full effect. The issue being debated is whether or not the dog tracking Peterson (in this case, Trimble) was actually following his "freshest scent," or some older tracks left from previous trips from the warehouse to the highway, and if Merlin should have been returned to the house to start over again after tracking Laci to the Gallo winery. The questioner is Pat Harris, still on cross (Page 1734 beginning with line 7):

Q: Therefore, the dog does not pick up the freshest scent the first time, does it?
A: That would be predicated that the dog picked up an older scent versus no scent at all on the first time.
Q: That's what I'm asking.
A: So on the first time, we actually have two different scenarios there. The dog could have picked up no scent at all, or the dog could have picked up an older scent, yes, sir.
Q: It doesn't matter which scenario you go. Either scenario the dog did not pick up the freshest scent the first time, did it, in either scenario?
(Page 1735 beginning with line 13)
A: You are assuming there is only one other possibility for the first trail. And there is not, sir. There are two other possibilities for that earlier trail. One could be that, yes, there is an older trail that the dog took, or there is no trail at all.
(Later in the cross:)
A: The dog is trained to pick up the freshest scent.
Q: But it doesn't always do it, does it?
A: It picks up the freshest scent for where it's at the time.
Q: That's not what I asked. The dog doesn't pick up the freshest scent every time, does it?
A: You would have to rephrase that question for me to answer.
Q: I can..
COURT: You are stepping on his answer...Is it fair to say that a dog does not necessarily pick up the freshest scent each time?
A: No sir. Not my experience.
COURT: So your experience is that the dog always picks up the freshest scent?
A: Yes sir, for the point that it's scented at.

This type of questioning goes on for awhile, with Pat Harris trying to make Boyer admit that the dogs don't always follow the freshest scent (and therefore were following an old track Laci put down walking in the neighborhood, or Peterson used when driving for work purposes) with Boyer adamantly sticking to his training methods and experience. Pat Harris then goes over Merlin's tracking from a block away from Scott's warehouse to an unrelated facility, and then starting again at the warehouse itself and tracking Laci to the highway. The questions are designed to be confusing and tedious (or that's just Pat Harris, it's hard to distinguish between strategy and incompetence) and not worth much

114

analysis. More interesting testimony at the end of the day was given by Rick Applegate, an officer with the Modesto Police Department, when he describes Scott's driving up to the barricade to observe the dogs (or throw them off the scent.)

Peterson ignored the motions Applegate made to warn him that the road was closed, so Applegate got out of the marked police vehicle and approached Peterson, who was in Laci's Land Rover, just stopped in the middle of the road. Peterson rolled down his window, and Applegate informed him that the highway was closed. Then *Peterson asked, "What* is the quickest way back to Modesto?" Peterson then made a u-turn, and 15 minutes later one of the dogs (Trimble, who was tracking Scott) started dragging his handler, Eloise, to where the Land Rover had been recently idling.

During the cross, Geragos elicits testimony from Applegate that the barricade was about 10 miles outside Modesto (so it wasn't exactly in the neighborhood) and that Applegate recognized Peterson, but did not acknowledge him or say, "We are blocking traffic to look for your wife." He tries to imply that Peterson was actually driving around posting fliers, and then asked Applegate, "Did you notice any skin rafts flying out the window? Ever seen a skin raft? Those little guys get in with oars?" Geragos once again attempts to inject his theory that the dogs were following Scott's scent and not Laci's, but you can't have it both ways: either the dogs are following Scott the entire time and Merlin completely missed his travels on foot to the park the on the 24th, and didn't smell him 15 yards away in his house, or one of them was tracking Laci. Merlin would not be tracking Laci one minute and Scott the next, although the defense would have you believe that. Needless to say, the defense would have you believe a lot of nonsense, including that their client is "factually innocent," and that they have exonerating evidence to prove this. So far, all we have seen in pretrial hearings is more support for his guilt.

FEBRUARY 29, 2004
CRIMINAL DEFENSE STRATEGIES

Recently I have been reading material on commercial Web sites published by criminal defense attorneys and law firms to gain some insight on how a defense strategy is developed and what are some of the predominant issues, especially when defending someone charged with first-degree murder. I concentrated most of my research on sites that originated from firms in California, and sought out definitions and clarification from generic law sites such as *Nolo* and *Findlaw*.

First, a few definitions: Murder in the First Degree is a killing (or killings) that was preceded and accompanied by "a clear, deliberate intent," that was formed upon preexisting reflection and "not under a sudden heat of passion or other conditions." The premeditation aspect can be over a period of time indicated by planning, or a last minute decision: it is the critical, defining moment when the killer says to himself, if I continue, this person will die; if I stop now, this person may still survive, then makes a conscious, willful choice to proceed.

According to the most frequently used citation, a defense strategy "is a product of a defendant and defense attorney fitting together the *version of the truth* that is most likely to produce a satisfactory defense outcome: a verdict of not guilty, a verdict of guilt of a lesser charge, or an acceptable plea bargain." I emphasize the "version of the truth," because it refers to various circumstances that may be truth in unrelated context, but it does not refer to the truth about the actual circumstances of the murder. For example, we have seen "versions of the truth" in Scott's accounting of Laci's activities the morning of the 24th, when we know she was already dead. He used information that in and of itself was truthful: Laci watched Martha Stewart regularly, she had black pants and a white top on the day before, she probably had ingredients for gingerbread (and the recipe on the refrigerator for reference), and she had, in the past, walked the dog. This is what they mean by a "version" of the truth. It's not the truth about the events of the 24th, but pieces of truth that the defense can use with some substantiation.

In developing a defense strategy, the attorney and client have to determine what is "objectively verifiable evidence" and create an innocuous and credible explanation for most, if not all of it, especially the most incriminating forensics such as blood, fingerprints, DNA, and other physical links to the crime. In the Peterson case, the fact that the defendant and the victim were husband and wife is a big advantage to the defense, since much of the physical evidence (hair on boat, Laci's scent articles, blood in vehicle) can be excused as the residual or transfer of cohabitating people. The defense will attempt to explain Scott's behavior as that of a victim who was duped by police, vilified by the community, and incapable of committing the crime. Expect it to say he was running from the media when he abandoned Modesto, that he changed his appearance in San Diego for the same reason, that he was never told about the identification of the remains and did not imagine they were his wife and baby's, and that his visits to the Bay were prompted by concern for the success of the search, which will be a particularly tough one to sell, especially now that the GPS tracking information is admissible at trial.

When the evidence is not easily explained away, such as Scott's persistent communication with Amber Frey after his wife "disappeared," his conspicuous absence at any organized searches for Laci, the inconsistent statements he made to the media during his publicity blitz, and the lies he told to Amber, the defense will likely argue that Scott was a philanderer and kept in touch with Amber out of ego and loneliness; that his interviews were selectively edited and out of context; that the conclusion that he was lying about admitting the affair is based on a lack of reaction from Laci, and not on provable data; and that his conversations with Amber were hormonally driven and should be disregarded. This strategy is based on the prayerful hope that the jury can relate to this kind of cold-blooded, callous and incredibly detached behavior from a spouse of a missing pregnant woman. It's a pretty big stretch and will ultimately fail to be convincing.

One of the common defense strategies we have already seen implemented is the attempt "to gain the sympathy of a judge or jury," by Geragos's repeated histrionics about how the press "demonized" his client, the accusations of a "lynch mob" mentality of people in Modesto, and characterizing the cops' treatment of Scott as underhanded, unprofessional, conspiratorial and single-minded. This pity party works only if the defendant is remotely sympathetic, for instance, if Scott had behaved similarly to the way in which he was portrayed in the movie, "The Perfect Husband," when he was shown huddling in the dark, hiding from the ferocious media, alienated, abandoned and prejudged. The reality is, however, that

116

other than to the most twisted and mentally tormented individuals, and to his family (perhaps a redundancy), very few normal people will find Peterson particularly worthy of empathy, or his behavior after Laci "disappeared" defensible. It may not prove he killed her, but it proves he is a human mutation.

From a San Diego defense attorney's Web site: "When formulating a defense strategy, an attorney also considers such factors as the reliability of the witnesses, community attitudes toward crime and the police, and a defendant's moral culpability." The change of venue may prove to have harmed the defense in this area. The citizens of San Mateo County are likely to be higher educated, supportive and generally trusting of the police, and acquainted with technology and science. I expect the defense to concentrate most of its questioning and arguments on impeaching witnesses, discrediting the results of any scientific and technological results, and reemphasizing that the Modesto cops were lazy, incompetent and trying to save face by convenience. Again, I believe this is going to be a losing proposition that may even backfire on the defense, especially if investigators appear consistent, sincere, and professional on the witness stand.

Any case involving searches, wiretapping, or surveillance is vulnerable to numerous potential errors in the affidavit process, wording of the warrants, police misconduct, and judicial review. We have seen how aggressive the defense has been to suppress any fruit of the search warrants, GPS, and any dog evidence that supported the wiretaps. You can be sure that every detail of the affidavits, warrants, phone calls, seized property, and tracking results have been scrutinized with a fine-tooth comb to find any deviation from law, because any finding of inappropriate or illegal execution of searches and surveillance would be grounds for dismissal. Since the case was held over for trial, I must assume the warrants were in order, defined the probable cause, and the results of their execution will be admissible. If not, they would have been thrown out a long time ago.

"In deciding whether or not to testify, the defendant may choose to rely on the state of the evidence and upon the failure, if any, of the prosecution to prove beyond a reasonable doubt every essential element of the crime charged against him." The defense is not required to prove its client innocent, or present an alternative culprit; the jury is instructed not to hold the fact that the defendant does not testify against him. It stands to reason, however, that an innocent man would take the stand to explain his behavior, defend his marriage, elicit compassion if not reasonable doubt from the jury, and dispel the notion that he is a "monster." If Peterson does not take the stand in his own defense, it will, whether the jurors openly admit it or not, serve to authenticate his reputation as a heartless, indifferent, self-absorbed punk who thought he could get away with murder.

Let us keep these defense strategies in mind while observing the ongoing trial of the People v Peterson.

MARCH 1, 2004
REVIEW OF DOG EVIDENCE

From what we have learned in the latest pretrial hearings in the case of People v Peterson, the following outline describes the dates, dog, handlers, locations and conclusions of the various canine search and rescue heroes involved in the search for Laci Peterson.

Merlin, male bloodhound, tracks Laci's scent (Cindee Valentin, handler):

Date: December26: Scented on Laci's sunglasses at southern edge of Peterson property. North from 523 Covena Avenue, left on Highland down driveway into backyard of 1326 Highland Drive, continued west on Highland, south on Santa Barbara, southeast on La Loma, west on Yosemite, south on Santa Rosa to Gallo Property (stopped by Valentin).

Conclusion: Laci left the home in a vehicle and not on foot. The freshest scent from her driveway led in the opposite direction from the park where she was said to have frequented when walking her dog. Laci either did not walk McKenzie on December 24, or left in a vehicle after walking the dog, which must, based on the time the dog was returned to the driveway, have occurred between 9:45 and 10:20 am, and would serve to rule out the witnesses who claim to have seen her elsewhere after 10:20 am. One explanation for the odd detour onto Highland Drive may have been that Laci's scent carried from her home to the adjacent backyard, or from the market umbrellas, which were not put "in storage" as Scott claimed, but were propped up against the back fence. It is also possible that Laci handled the umbrellas at some time in the recent past.

Merlin: December 26:Dropped at intersection of Kansas Avenue and North Emerald Avenue. Scented on Laci's sunglasses, south on North Emerald - did not find warehouse.

Conclusion: Dogs don't track buildings, and Brocchini's experiment to see if Merlin would "find the warehouse" was an improper training exercise.

Merlin: December 26: Taken to warehouse at 1027 North Emerald, was scented on sunglasses outside door B-1, headed east exiting warehouse area to North Emerald,
south on N. Emerald across Kansas to Maze Boulevard, west on Maze Boulevard/Highway 132 for approximately one-quarter mile.

Conclusion: Laci was most recently taken from the warehouse in a vehicle headed west on 132.

Merlin: January 4, scented on Laci's sunglasses at intersection of North Emerald and Maze/132, drop trail west on 132 approximately 20 miles to 580, took on-ramp to 580, and Valentin stopped Merlin (pulling hard) at the end of merge lane.

Conclusion: Laci was in a vehicle using a common route to the Berkeley Marina.

Trimble, female Labrador retriever, tracks both Laci and Scott's scents (handled by Eloise Anderson.)

December 28: Scented on Laci's sunglasses, trailed Laci's scent from the boat ramp entrance to a pylon on a pier on the west side of the launch. Twice gave indication of end of trail at pylon.

Conclusion: Laci (or more likely her scent) was at the Berkeley Marina.

Trimble: January 4, scented on Scott's brown slipper approximately 50 yards south of 132 on South Carpenter, west on 132 drop trail, brief detour south onto trail that went down to riverbank, back to highway, continued west. North on ramp to Highway 33 where Scott had just visited in Land Rover, continued west on 132 to 580.

Conclusion: Scott's freshest scent indicated he traveled a common route to the Berkeley Marina, and when he showed up that day near the dogs, Trimble picked up his newest scent at the ramp and had to be taken back to 132 and re-scented.

Twist, female Labrador retriever, cadaver dog (handled by Eloise Anderson): December 27, showed mild interest in interior of boat, dropped her head and tried to get out, which was very unusual behavior, according to her handler. Ran her nose along rim of bow on starboard side, worked three boxes beneath workbench, came back around to boat and alerted, showed frustration by barking. Alerted three times in a small shed at 523 Covena Avenue in an area of the lawnmower, blue tarp and "backpack" fertilizer sprayer, which may have contained fish emulsion. Last alert was after removal of the fertilizer container and the tarp. Searched La Loma Park and found no cadaver scent. Possibly searched in house at 523 Covena; no testimony as to results. According to a tabloid, she also alerted to an area of carpet, to a duffle bag in the nursery, and to an area near the French doors, which has yet to be confirmed.

Twist: January 4, taken two miles from the intersection of Highway 132 and Paradise Rd., worked the riverbank south of 132, worked under the bridge on 132; no alerts at either location.

Water dogs: Used to locate submerged bodies in the water. From information I have received, there were at least four dogs used on boats in the area between the Berkeley Marina and the Richmond entrance channel in early January. One of the dogs alerted to a blue tarp found in the water near Caesar Chavez Park just north of the Marina, which was retrieved for potential evidence. Based on unconfirmed rumors of information derived from his computers, Peterson was researching water depth, tides, and current charts for the area near Brooks Island. According to sources, there were up to 25 alerts in the area of the Richmond entrance channel that directed much of the subsequent sonar searches in that area. According to news reports that were later denied, a body may have been spotted in the entrance channel in mid-March but had moved by the time the weather cooperated and the properly equipped divers could be brought back to the location. Based on expert opinion of the location where Laci eventually washed ashore, if her remains originated at the Richmond channel (near channel marker #4 from which the alleged red paint scraping on the boat may have derived), the Pt. Isabel landing was a scientific probability.

Conclusion: Laci was put in the bay on December 23 or 24, weighted down, in the Richmond entrance channel where the water depth drops from 14 feet to 35 feet. This would account for the decompression that helped to keep her submerged for so long, until she was freed by natural causes or interference with ships, and swept up by the storm that preceded her emergence and discovery on April 13, 2003.

MARCH 7, 2004
MR. PERFECT

It's going to take more than the works of a saint to sterilize the sullied and self-absorbed perception the public has of double murder defendant, Scott Peterson, but in her article, "Portrait of the Accused," in today's San Francisco Chronicle, Kelly St. John tries to do just that. Like her journalist predecessors from earlier in the case, it is apparent that St. John found few people outside the Peterson family who would make anything but generic, noncommittal remarks about Scott, in stark relief to his captivating wife for whom thousands of people mourned and hundreds willingly sang her praises.

> *He was a standout achiever. By age 14, he was besting his father on the golf course. By the end of high school, he was one of the top junior golfers in San Diego.*

How does talent in a game of hitting a little ball around the grass translate into a standout achiever? Golf is a solitary game, not a team sport in the true sense of the genre, ideal for the socially handicapped where good communication and interpersonal skills are not required. If Scott was an All-American ballplayer, an excellent golfer, an altar boy, an entrepreneur, still married to his only wife for over ten years, a philanthropist and active member of the community, regularly attended religious services, adopted an abandoned infant from an eastern bloc country, had impeccable financial and personal credentials and who still socialized with his friends from high school, that's a *standout achiever*, in my book.

"He was like Mr. Perfect," claims his father, Lee, for the umpteenth time. Mr. Perfect? Besides the utter superiority and elitism expressed in that farce, it is insulting to those of us who believe that the only perfect son in human history was the Christ, and to compare Scott to Jesus is beyond hyperbole and borders on blasphemy.

> *But comparatively little is known about Scott Peterson's life before he became the central figure in one of the most sensationalized murders in recent memory -- a case his mother likens to that of Sam Sheppard's.*

I would wager that Mrs. Peterson wasn't even familiar with the Sheppard case before her son went to jail, and probably only knows the selective issues involving the publicity that corrupted the poor doctor's fair trial. The irony of that parallel is that in many people's opinion, especially here in Cleveland, Sam Sheppard was incontrovertibly guilty, regardless of the reversal of his conviction and later acquittal. A more accurate comparison would be to Jeff McDonald, another doctor who staged his pregnant wife's murder and blamed it on a cult.

> *They [Lee, Jackie and Susan] told stories around their dining room table, a stone's throw from a refrigerator plastered with photographs of their children and grandchildren.*

Aren't most people's refrigerators a "stone's throw" or closer to their dining room tables? Is the author trying to symbolize a proximity to sustenance and sentiment? We have already been insulted by the *People* magazine article that depicted pictures of the proud grandparents holding their infant grandbaby only weeks after another grandson, Connor's remains, washed ashore on the banks of the San Francisco Bay.

> *Jackie Peterson's son from a previous relationship was 6 when Scott was born and shared a bedroom with his younger sibling in the family's two-bedroom apartment in La Jolla. Lee Peterson also had three children from his first marriage -- Susan, 12, Mark, 10, and Joe, 9 -- who lived with their mother in San Diego during the week but spent most weekends with their father.*

As I suspected, the older Peterson children were not raised in this faux "Brady Bunch" household. Jackie's naming her dress shop "The Put On" is an accidental metaphor of her favorite fantasy role as a victim and legitimate member of the upper class. "Today, Scott Peterson's mother is reticent about discussing her own life, fearing how it might be twisted by the press." I can't imagine why. Perhaps because the reality of her past indiscretions would taint her reinvented role as den mother and self-appointed arbiter of appropriate behavior?

> *Joan Pernicano, whose youngest son, Andrew, was in the Cub Scout troop led by Scott Peterson's mother, remembers the youngster as a homebody who was "close to both parents equally.*

Is this the best St. John could do to find someone who would comment on Peterson? Someone whose only exposure to Scott was in Cub Scouts? Where are Scott's adult friends? Where are his peers? Where are his coworkers or classmates? A couple of his teammates from high school quoted in this article describe his wardrobe and his mild manner, but offer no vivid impressions to give us any insight into what may as well have been the invisible man. Apparently finding anyone who will admit to being close to Peterson aside from his wife's social circle (who have for all intents and purposes abandoned him as well) is less likely than finding a snow leopard in Siberia.

Let's take a look at some of Scott's ambitious and altruistic endeavors:

By the time he was a teenager, Scott Peterson was working part time at a country club in Rancho Santa Fe, picking up golf balls and filling carts with gas in exchange for lessons and time on the course.

You would think he would be a caddy instead of mucking about in water hazards to retrieve balls in order to play golf. Working as a caddy, however, would require too much responsibility, humility, and social graces in order to be successful.

He was a good student and tutored the homeless all through high school.

Is this the same Scott Peterson who told Detective Brocchini that he rousted homeless people from loitering in nearby Dry Creek Park? Needless to say, claiming Scott helped homeless people ensures that none of them can be tracked down for corroboration! Like the phantom grandmother he adopted as a child, this too is probably more Peterson invention.

Regarding the now debunked golf scholarship, Lee Peterson said, "Nothing was locked in: Scott had spoken with the coach, who had invited him to try out for the team as a walk-on and said if he was good enough, scholarship money might be available." That is a far cry from the original Peterson camp legend that Scott had a partial scholarship to Arizona State where his former teammate, Phil Mickelson, attended. I deduce that neither Scott's golf game nor his scholastic abilities were up to par for ASU, but what has become typical of the Peterson parents' justification, Lee opines, "It was probably a mistake sending him there because it was such a big golf school." What happened to the standout achieving, perfect son?

A quote attributed to Scott by his dad: "Instead of driving a beamer and drinking martinis, I'll be driving a pickup and drinking beers." According to what we have learned since his arrest, Scott zealously coveted the BMW lifestyle, joined a private country club, and kept a bottle of champagne in his overnight bag with which to seduce women along his travels. Scott evidently still fantasized about his original goals to be an international businessman, and pretended to be one to Amber Frey and probably many others, his mother having passed "The Put On" torch to her precocious apprentice. Predictably, his parents minimized his what may be chronic infidelities as "common," and "a far cry from committing murder."

According to his parents, Scott and Laci Peterson considered buying a house in San Luis Obispo, their scenic and relaxed town. They had close friends there, and even dropped by frequently to do their laundry at Scott's parents' Morro Bay home.

Suddenly, here is a guy who, a couple of paragraphs earlier, moves out of the house at age 20 and works three jobs to put himself through college, opens up a restaurant, and after he gets married, "frequently" brings his laundry to his parent's house? This admission belies Scott's virtuous independence and portrays him as an incurably pampered prima donna.

Undeterred by the gag order, Lee and Jackie Peterson vehemently decry Scott's incarceration and, by giving this interview, want as much of the potential jury pool as possible to know that their son is "the victim of an incompetent police department so fixated on a theory...that they ignored other leads and evidence in the case." In marked contrast, I don't see the Rochas giving interviews praising the DA's office or touting Scott's involvement in Laci's murder, although their views would have more impact than the puerile protestations of the defendant's parents.

Jackie recalls the fateful Christmas Eve prior to learning about Laci: "We said a little prayer of thanks, and we're not even heavy prayer people."

It's not too late to start praying.

MARCH 14, 2004
DR. "N" BUSTER: ON PETERSON

A self-proclaimed armchair expert on narcissism based on her extensive research, participation in psychological discussion forums, and unfortunate personal experience in dealing with a classic narcissistic personality, our very own Dr. "N" Buster, returns to answer readers' questions about Scott Peterson.

Is Scott Peterson a Narcissist?

Pathological narcissism is difficult to diagnose, especially if we only have a limited range of behavior to observe as we do with Peterson. It's difficult to diagnose even if we know the subject, work with him or live with him. Most people with this kind of personality disorder rarely, if ever, seek professional counseling unless it is the consequence of an ultimatum from their major "supply." If forced into this excruciating discomfort, they find ways to evade, obscure, charm or con the analyst to avoid sincere self-examination. Additionally, many people misdiagnose malignant narcissism as immaturity, a dysfunctional childhood, or a cultural phenomenon among Gen-Xers that eventually will be outgrown. Meanwhile, these disordered individuals are leaving a trail of destruction in their wake.

There is a dearth of substantive literature on the narcissistic personality disorder, much of it, ironically, from an admitted narcissist, the rest from behaviorists with inadequate experience in treating these individuals. Therefore, we have to rely upon the diagnostic criteria set forth in the DSM-IV (Diagnostic and Statistical Manual of Mental Disorders – Fourth Edition) and our own understanding of human nature to determine if Scott Peterson suffers from a debilitating form of narcissism, or if he was just an arrogant, spoiled, inarticulate buffoon detached from his emotions. In any event, there is something seriously aberrant in Peterson's behavior that lends some support to his narcissism, but to what depth we will never know.

Did Peterson exaggerate his achievements and talents, and expect to be recognized as superior? We believe he misrepresented himself to Amber Frey as an international executive with a glamorous lifestyle. We know from his father that he thought he could play on the Arizona State golf team as a walk-on. Are

123

these isolated incidents, or a pattern of acting upon his delusions of grandeur? Did Peterson entertain fantasies of ideal love, unlimited success and power? We will never be privy to his thoughts, but we can deduce from his performance with Amber that he portrayed himself as a widower and fantasized the freedom and sympathy of that role.

Did Peterson believe he was special and unique and could only be understood by, or should associate with, other special or high-status people? We are all unique, but most of us accept the reality that we are subject to the same laws and moral standards as others. Narcissists believe they are exempt from mundane details like policies, procedures, laws, balanced checkbooks, and vows. Such trivial matters are beneath their dignity to consider, which is why many of them commit numerous preventable lapses in judgment. Evidently, Peterson joined a prestigious golf club, the local Rotary, drove a late-model truck, added a swimming pool, carried an inordinate number of cell phones, and purchased a boat a few weeks before Christmas and only two months before his first child was due. We can surmise he thought he was pretty hot stuff, albeit fiscally short sighted and incapable of deferring gratification. Most young men we know in that age bracket in the same circumstances would be saving money for unforeseen complications, investing in a college fund for the baby, and postponing expensive toys and country club memberships. Possibly the golf membership was obtained by Tradecorp or his parents; nevertheless, his acquisition of these status symbols despite his relatively modest income (by California standards) reveals his sense of entitlement, which is another narcissistic trait from the DSM-IV. If, however, he had an illicit source of revenue from the drug trade or other underworld commerce, then all this speculation goes out the window. Needless to say, Peterson disregarded his wedding vows, and we expect to discover, based on his glib and cavalier *modus operandi*, that his infidelity was chronic throughout the marriage.

Was Peterson interpersonally exploitative, envious of others, arrogant, and devoid of empathy? Of the nine criteria defined for a narcissistic personality disorder, our strongest case can be made for these four. Obviously, he exploited Amber (and others) for ego gratification, narcissistic supply, the exhilaration of her admiration and infatuation, and the fulfillment of his romantic illusions that were unmet by his boring domestic life. Typical of the narcissist's fragile commitment is his "trophy" relationship with an attractive partner along with other tokens of status, but with whom he is dissatisfied, overwhelmed or frustrated. Even if we concede him the presumption of innocence with regard to the murder, we cannot overlook his notable relief when his wife "disappeared." He ducked out of the searches, he relentlessly and recklessly pursued his new "source," and he displayed an alarming lack of grief in his frenzied mission to rid himself of Laci's existence by trading in her car, attempts to list their house, and his abandoning Modesto in pursuit of recreation. We cannot isolate these events and dismiss them as anomalies influenced by circumstances. This was textbook narcissistic behavior.

Wouldn't divorce have been easier than murder?

To a normal person, cutting one's losses and terminating a marriage is an unfortunate but acceptable resolution to an irreconcilable relationship. To a malignant narcissist (or other personality-disordered individuals), the concept of contributing substantial amounts of hard earned cash and forfeiting half of his wealth to obtain freedom is an anathema tantamount to emasculation. A pathologically selfish person with the mentality of entitlement is loath to forfeit his financial power. Permanently eradicating that possibility may have seemed preferable, despite the risks, than a 20-year sentence of scarcity.

Why doesn't he seem to have any close friends rallying around him now?

Narcissists construct extremely superficial relationships, especially with their peers of the same sex. They avoid intimacy and the exchange of confidences that define friendships, in part because they are out of touch with their real selves, and because they fear the potential exposure of their masquerade.

What about the theory that his behavior is a result of a sex addiction?

Narcissists use sex as a means to exploit others and create pseudo-intimacy. Sex is a tool rather than an expression of affection, love, or commitment. Typically, predatory narcissists enjoy the chase and novelty of a new "source," professing their unique and healing love, and tailoring their techniques to the particular emotional vulnerability of their prey. Unlike sex addicts, narcissists don't need sex as a mood-altering thrill. Instead, they are addicted to the supply of attention, short-term unconditional love, and blind adoration of a new source that sex facilitates.

Why was there no history of violence? Did he just blow his top one night, or was he planning his emancipation?

Viewing Peterson from the prism of narcissism, he likely internalized his rage, envy, resentment, and frustration, and probably expressed those emotions in passive-aggressive ways, such as cheating on his spouse, squandering resources, breaking promises, and neglecting responsibilities. At what point his circumstances became unmanageable and thus ripe for the drastic and otherwise unimaginable ("unapproachable") solution of murder will forever remain a mystery. We cannot impose reason on a senseless act.

If he is so grandiose, why did he buy such a crummy little boat?

Objects, and to some extent, people, jobs, and relationships are disposable commodities to a narcissist, who focuses a great deal of energy incessantly seeking replacements. Narcissists are shortsighted, impulsive, impatient, chronically dissatisfied, and operate from an impoverished spiritual core. The more sinister explanation is that he obtained the boat for the exclusive purpose of using it to transport Laci's body to a remote and dangerous body of water after he determined the most effective method of eliminating her from his life.

Why would he initiate an extramarital affair with a single mother only a month before he allegedly murdered Laci, if he didn't want to be encumbered by a wife and child?

Amber was merely the source *du jour*. He had no intentions of making a permanent commitment to her, and we cannot ascribe any compelling motive to her role as lover and unwitting victim of his duplicity. Her emotional and physical demands on Peterson, whether or not Laci was murdered, would have terrified and repelled him within a few months. Had she been an older, childless woman of means, he may have played gigolo for a year or so to enjoy her largesse. When Peterson found himself abandoned by his acquaintances, vilified by the press and subsequently the public, and dogged by the police, his only remaining tenuous source of narcissistic supply was Amber, which is why he maintained constant contact with her until she finally cut him off.

Why does everyone who knew him characterize him an innocuous, nice guy? How did he fool his in-laws and Laci's friends for so long?

This, of course, is the $64,000 question. Adjectives like charming, polite, chivalrous, attentive, and conscientious describe many a narcissist, and most have chameleon qualities and evolved social graces. This façade is a slick veneer concealing an insecure, frightened, angry and bewildered interpersonal parasite. Most victims of narcissists are not naïve, obtuse, or steeped in denial and delusion. Many are simply guileless, generous, gullible people with good intentions and unsuspicious minds. Unfortunately, they may cross paths with this somewhat rare individual maybe once in a lifetime, and are permanently scarred by his (or her) devastating impact. Once a narcissist has victimized you, your former perceptions of human nature are forever altered. Until that experience, most benevolent people are willing to accept others at face value, possibly to their peril.

MARCH 20, 2004
REVISITING THE MEDICAL EXAMINER'S TESTIMONY

(From the Preliminary Hearing transcripts) DR. PETERSON: Let me tell you the process that I went through. When I approached Connor, of course, I had no idea
at that time that he had any connection to Laci at all. This was simply a body washed up on the shore; and the typical forensic pathology question in that type of case was: Is this a stillborn baby or a live-born baby? If it's a stillborn baby the issue simply is one of body disposal, I guess; if it's a live-born baby - that makes it a whole different type of issue.

So the question I typically attempt to address in that type of case is: Was this baby born alive or was he not? And that took place that morning, and that was really the sum of that case. Only later when I had the opportunity to perform Laci's autopsy, and then even later when it become clear that those two bodies were intimately connected, did the other thinking come into place. At that point we're trying to consider where that body was, how it was protected, why the states of decomposition are different. At the time of Connor's autopsy, no, it was simply a matter of stillborn versus live born.

It is important to remember that when Dr. Peterson was assigned the autopsy of the remains of the baby Peterson, he had no information of his provenance. To him, as to those that discovered the body washed ashore, the baby originally appeared fully formed, albeit very small, and was possibly the victim of a stillbirth, abortion, or abandonment by his mother. Nobody would have ever guessed at first that this baby had been recently released from his mother's womb from her underwater tomb. Therefore, Dr. Peterson's first priority was to determine if the baby had ever lived, and if he had lived, how he had died. Without knowing that Laci was connected to this child, he could only examine the remains in isolation of other events of which he was not yet aware. For the defense to use his initial observations to determine the baby's viability and possible birth in exclusion of other facts is misleading and irrelevant once the baby and Laci were connected at her subsequent autopsy.

DR. PETERSON: And I'm referring back to the report now. And I was talking about the loops of tape. Again, one and a half loops of plastic tape there around the neck, there was a knot near the left shoulder, the skin beneath the tape was not injured, and there was approximately a two-centimeter [.75"] gap between the tape and the neck.

DAVE HARRIS: Now, you noted in your report, and you just stated in your testimony, that there was no damage beneath the tape on the skin and that there was a gap. What does that mean from the forensic pathological point of view?

DR.P: My opinion was that this tape, this loop likely existed elsewhere, and the association between the tape and the body was coincidental.

Dr. Peterson's opinion, throughout the questioning, is that the tape was debris and unrelated to the cause or manner of death, since there were no injuries internally or externally from constriction; the tape was not used as a "noose," or any other implement to harm the baby. He determined that the knot preceded the loop of tape going around the baby's head and was not used to fasten anything. He cut the tape off rather than risk damaging the baby's skin (or the tape) by removing it over the head, not because that wasn't possible, but rather because that is standard operating procedure for removing clothing, ligatures and other binding material from a victim at an autopsy.

DR. P: It was possible to see mineral deposit on the outside surface of the body. As it turned out, that was associated with clothing. There was a -- there was a peculiar shredding kind of effect to those trousers. The legs were basically reduced to thread, and within those threads, the calcification, the stone-like material I mentioned earlier, was deposited. Additionally, there was some duct tape, and where I found that was sticking to the front waistband of the trousers. I actually first saw it on the back of her body, because, again, she came in prone. But where it was actually stuck was on the front of the waistband.

After researching various sea minerals and animals that calcify or appear as discrete deposits on inanimate inorganic objects, I have discovered a number of possibilities for the smooth, stone-like material found on the pants that could have formed underwater. Not being a mineralogist or seeing samples with which to compare, it will be up to an expert to determine the exact chemistry at trial. The possibilities include:

Algae, magnesium deposits, limnic material (one of the common components of organic soils and includes both organic and inorganic materials that were either (i) deposited in water by precipitation or through the action of aquatic organisms, or (ii) derived from underwater and floating aquatic plants and aquatic animals), salt deposits, coral, snails, or quartz deposits.

HARRIS: What is your estimate of time in the water for these bodies?
DR. P: I would simply say months.
Q. And Dr. Galloway's?
A. Dr. Galloway, with respect to Laci, said three to six months and --
MR. GERAGOS: There will be an objection. No foundation. Hearsay. I understand he's an expert, but he's already testified that he's not an expert in this particular area, and for --
THE COURT: And expert can also consult with others and get input. So the Court will allow that. Overruled.

Based on the condition of Laci's remains and the professional conclusions of Dr. Peterson (and others we expect to see in the future), the fact that Laci was weighed down, underwater for four months seems irrefutable.

DR. P: The uterus at that point was essentially abraded away and torn. Again, no evidence of cut marks, no evidence of other specific tool marks that I could identify, but the wall there was thin, and it had been more or less rubbed away, and it was empty. Down at the base of the uterus, in the pelvis, the birth canal was closed and appeared normal.

DR. P: My opinion is that that uterus was intact at thetime that this body was deposited in the water or ended up in the water, however it did, and, essentially, I believe that Connor was in that uterus, and that with time --
MR. GERAGOS: Objection. Motion to strike. It's speculation and there's no foundation.
THE COURT: Overruled. I believe he has the expertise

to say that. You'll obviously be able to cross-examine him and try to convince me otherwise.

THE WITNESS: And with the time and tidal action and animal feeding, as the abdominal wall wore away, eventually the upper part of the fundus of the uterus wore away, and at that time, the fetus was released.

Hydrology, physics and physiology will bear out this theory. As Laci's body decomposed and was destroyed by marine life (in particular, large crabs from what I understand), she began to break loose from the weights that were holding her down. Because she was in relatively cool (50 degree) water below 33 feet, the atmospheric pressure and temperature enabled her to stay down longer than she would have if in shallower, warmer water. Most bodies float to the surface much sooner in different conditions.

The underwater investigation, including divers, side scan sonar, and an ROV (remotely operated vehicle, an apparatus that is lowered into the water to locate objects after the sonar has picked up a possible target, and has a built-in high resolution video camera that sends images to a monitor on the boat) detected what they believe was Laci's body on March 12. She was face down on the bottom of an area just inside the Richmond entrance channel, about a mile west of Brooks Island. She was intact except for possibly one lower appendage missing. There was no sign of a tarp or other bundling, and the anchors that held her down were buried beneath her or were sunk in the muddy silt. She was severely damaged from marine feeding.

The divers on board that day lost their way in the murky, limited visibility at the bottom of the bay, and then were thwarted by the ebb tide and currents that regularly churn up the bay waters, which rendered the ROV and the sonar temporarily useless. When they returned the next day, they still encountered various problems, so the captain enlisted another team of divers. By the time the new diving team and the weather coincided to embark on another search 10 days later, the target had moved.

> *DR. PETERSON: In terms of the condition of the bodies, comparing the two together, what I had to reconcile was the fact that Laci's body showed evidence of animal feeding, showed evidence of these external changes associated with exposure to the environment, Connor's didn't so much. Connor was decomposed, and, again, another reasonable term would be macerated, but there was no evidence of animal feeding. There was the one tear in the shoulder, but there wasn't the extensive damage that we saw on Laci. And as I tried to reconcile these two things, the condition of Connor's body and the condition of Laci's uterus, it made intellectual sense to me that his body was relatively protected by the uterus up until the end when the abrasion took away that portion of the uterus and allowed his body to be released.*

Clearly, the baby was protected *in utero* until Laci was released completely from the burden of the remaining weight (possibly only one, based on other evidence we have gathered) and she ascended and the hydrostatic pressure, along with the abraded opening of her fundus, released the baby into the water, from where he was washed to shore within a period of a day or so based on the lack of animal feeding and the condition of his skin. As horrible as this scenario appears, it is much more scientifically feasible and far less macabre than the "plastic bag duct taped to the mother's waistband" theory touted by the defense. That bizarre fiction belongs in a bad horror movie, with a satanic cult cast, not in a court of law.

> *DR. PETERSON: What I saw in the trousers that have been more or less reduced to thread down around the upper legs, there were round, smooth, round to oval deposits of stone. I'm not a mineralogist, I'm not an anthropologist, but it was quite heavy --*
> *MR. GERAGOS: Objection. No foundation.*
> *THE COURT: Overruled.*
> *THE WITNESS: These were discrete deposits. Again, as I tried to consider what possible mechanism might have been involved there, I thought about, again, how a body acts in the water, how it tends to submerge and then resurface. And I think if this happened over a period of time, with alternate layers of wetting and drying, it could have account -- it could account for minerals building up as I saw here.*

From experts I have consulted about this hypothesis, Dr. Peterson is incorrect in his conclusions that the body would rise and sink, or in any possible way dry while in the water. Generally the body sinks, gases form, and if it is not weighted down it rises, never to sink again, but to float on the surface until discovered, eaten, or decomposed by natural processes. Laci's pants could never dry off to *form any mineral* deposits. Those deposits were formed in an anaerobic process by mineral or other biological life underwater.

> *COURT: Can you describe the tape? The width? Is it electrician's tape? Plastic tape? Is it sticky tape, not sticky?*
> *THE WITNESS: Your Honor, it's clear plastic. As I recall from taking this off the baby, there was nothing particularly sticky anymore.*
> *THE COURT: But did it look like tape, the type that you use to tape something or is it --*
> *THE WITNESS: A lot like wrapping tape, Your Honor, boxing tape.*
> *THE COURT: How could that be an item that floated onto the baby if -- I assume two centimeters doesn't get it over the head?*
> *THE WITNESS: Simply because the head's deforming and*
> *the skull plates were overriding, and that's dynamic process. Depending upon what the baby is brushing up against or washing onto, I see no problem with that happening... All I know is this tape was there, and there was no injury to the neck, and I believe it would be quite easy to deform the head enough to fit that tape circle. In other words, decomposition can mask a number of things.*

The clear plastic "boxing tape" described by Dr. Peterson that was found around the baby's neck was also noted to lack any stickiness, and did not match the duct tape found on Laci, or on the mysterious plastic bag near the baby's remains. Based on these principles, I conclude that the tape found on the baby was unrelated debris, and the stray hairs found on the strip of duct tape were picked up in the water.

Whether Geragos will proffer an affirmative defense that includes abduction by beanie-wearing thugs from the park, a crude C-section of the baby, and later disposal in the area where Peterson went fishing in order to frame him for his wife's murder depends on the evidence. If there is no evidence or any witnesses to support this theory, he cannot present it at trial. Without the baby's DNA in the plastic bag, it's a red herring. I suspect there is no physical or circumstantial evidence to bolster the defense's months' long grandstanding about exonerating discovery, and that it will instead hope that the People's case against Peterson is vulnerable to reasonable doubt alone.

MARCH 27, 2004
APPLYING THE LAW

Few of us have or will ever know someone charged with a capital crime; an offense for which a conviction can result in the death penalty or a life sentence without the possibility of parole. Therefore, most of us glean our information about these cases from the media and books, such as with the current trial of The People of California v. Peterson. We tend to apply our rudimentary knowledge of law in a generic way to our speculation and predictions when, in fact, a death penalty case presents a unique set of rules, strategies, and specialization. Because so much of the evidence, affidavits, fruit of the various warrants, and documentation remain under seal by a protective order, we can only gauge the strength of either side's case from court filings, excerpts of arguments, and reasoning until further revelations are made at trial.

Up to this point, we have relied on so-called legal analysts from cable TV news programs, many of whom do not practice in California, or media stories with dubious accuracy and scarcity of useful information. After all, when the theatrics and props are set aside, when the gossip and theorizing diminishes to a tedious whisper, when the hyperbole and ominous theme music are muted, what are we left with? The Law. Let us allow our reading of the California Criminal Law to determine the stark realities of this case, and to provide some illuminating insights into the issues that will be presented at this overly dramatized trial set to begin in May.

At its basic components, this case is not very complicated. Neither the victim nor the defendant is a celebrity, connected to wealthy, elite families with political power, with a flamboyant or glamorous history, or proven to be affiliated with the seamy underworld of contraband. Factually, we have an attractive pregnant woman allegedly murdered by her husband who was carrying on an illicit relationship with at least one woman during the time of the murder. That this particular, rather ordinary case attracted such widespread and enduring attention is something of an anomaly, considering similar tragic homicides unfortunately occur with predictable regularity without the attendant massive press coverage or endless rhetorical discussions about questionable law enforcement tactics, trust, fidelity, fetal gestation, or the degradation of a narcissistic society. An overview of the case, from the standpoint of the law, reveals its essential truths:

Probable Cause, Affidavits, Search and Seizure

Most of the testimony involving the various warrant affidavits and the searches of Peterson's property took place in camera and in redacted motions, so we are not privy to this information until trial. However, since all of the evidence obtained by the warrants, including the GPS tracking, the phone taps, and the forensic findings have been admitted, it is reasonable to assume the warrants were properly executed. The defense has an obligation to challenge all of the evidence, regardless of its gravity, in order to whittle down the State's case against its client. Thus, we cannot automatically leap to the conclusion that the evidence must be terribly incriminating if the defense is vigorously challenging it; that's its job.

Bail

Even if charged with a capital offense in California, there is the possibility for the defendant to be released on bail, contrary to popular belief. Bail is denied only when the standard that "the proof is evident and the presumption great" is met; which implies "any substantial evidence to sustain a capital verdict." Since Peterson's original court-appointed attorney waived his bail hearing in May, and his million-dollar replacement team of Geragos and McAllister never motioned for a bail hearing since then, this sheds a new light on the strength of the State's evidence. If it were as flimsy or nonexistent as the grandstanding Geragos or screaming Peterson apologists have touted, defense counsel would have been remiss not to attempt to obtain his release on bail (even if for a substantial amount of cash) in order to await his trial in the comfort of his own home rather than in a six-by-nine jail cell for the past year.

Defense Counsel

In a death penalty case, two defense counsels are usually the rule, whether appointed or hired. Because there are two phases, the guilt phase and the penalty phase, which require separate trials, if the guilt phase attorney loses his credibility with the jury, the second attorney is necessary to argue the penalty phase. Nevertheless, I expect all three attorneys on the Peterson defense team to argue the first phase. An example of where this general rule would apply was in the Westerfield trial (the convicted pedophile who murdered Danielle Van Dam in San Diego). Steve Feldman, lead defense counsel, would have been smart to bow out of the penalty phase after his appalling and reproachable strategy of vilifying Danielle's parents during the guilt phase. If Geragos loses in the first act, his only remaining scrap of professional redemption is to save his client's life.

132

Exculpatory Evidence

The defense has the right, and - after his many public statements regarding his client's "factual innocence," "evidence of the real killers," and subsequent motion to dismiss the charges in the 995 hearing - a sworn duty to present substantial exculpatory evidence at the preliminary hearing, either by calling his own witnesses or producing the evidence itself.

> *Section 866 requires the defense, at the request of the prosecution, to make an offer of proof that the testimony of the proffered witness, if believed, would be reasonably likely to establish an affirmative defense, negate an element of the crime charged, impeach the testimony of a prosecution witness, or impeach the statement of a declarant testified to by a prosecution witness. The defendant has the right to call a police officer to testify to hearsay that is favorable to the defense, such as the defendant's exculpatory statement.*[57]

If Geragos were actually in possession of highly exculpatory evidence, he was statutorily required to turn that over to the DA and the Modesto police and have it investigated, after which he could have filed for a dismissal. The fact that he did not present any witnesses at the preliminary hearing (like Diane Campos or other "Laci sighters"), or any forensic or other scientific evidence that would have exonerated his client, such as the baby's DNA found in the plastic bag debris found near the remains, leads us to conclude that there is no exculpatory evidence. Based on the law, we would have heard about it by now.

Jury Selection and Procedural Motions

According to the criminal defense "playbook," all of the motions filed by Geragos in the San Mateo venue have been textbook standard: motion to exclude the media interviews (denied, since the statements were voluntary, albeit against the advice of any attorney worth his salt), motion for separate juries and a sequestered jury (denied), and expected motions for additional peremptive strikes or a second change of venue. What is interesting about another change-of-venue motion is that it often generates very adverse publicity; not to mention it is expensive, and unlikely to be granted after the judge has invested time in selecting a jury. The motion must be in writing (it cannot be argued otherwise) and should be presented at least two weeks before trial. If the second change of venue is denied, it is very weak grounds for appeal, and reversal is unlikely. Technically, Geragos can file for a venue change up to the time the jury is sworn *in, but he would do grave if not irreparable damage to* his relationship with the judge if he waits that long. If he does not file this week, I predict he will not file another one in this trial.

We can follow the trial referencing the criminal law, procedure, and practice that will be used by both sides of the aisle. With our new tools, we can analyze the

---

[57] California Criminal Law Practice and Procedure, Edition VI, Section 22.13.

events with factual information rather than continuous speculation or misinterpretation by the talking heads and other uninformed sources. Likely, the defense will attempt (and fail) to create reasonable doubt by refuting every piece of evidence and every incriminating act by Peterson with an alternative "innocent" explanation.

APRIL 10, 2004
A SECOND CHANGE OF VENUE?

It appears from the colorless stories trickling out of the Redwood City courthouse regarding the Peterson trial, and the occasional commentary by legal analysts, that the main topic of conversation is the phantom and legally ungrounded issue of another defense request for a change of venue. Either the media are ignorant of the law, or they are purposely inventing controversy for something to discuss until the trial starts. Let us review the reality of as second change of venue based on the law rather than on specious speculation and scuttlebutt.

Geragos has no case for a second change of venue. The "Five Factors" he argued for the first change of venue in Stanislaus County (which took him two motions, 44 pages, and volumes of documentation of pretrial publicity) were peripherally met and granted. However, those same "Five Factors" do not apply in San Mateo County. The "gravity of the offense" has not changed, nor would it change no matter where in California the case is tried. There has been a significant decrease in publicity since the trial moved to Redwood City, and none of it inflammatory toward the defendant, other than a mobile billboard showing Scott Peterson in shackles and a red jumpsuit with the question, "Man or Monster?" emblazoned in bold letters, advertising a radio station survey, which I still suspect the defense orchestrated. The coverage has been typical of a crime of this nature, but nowhere near the massive publicity demonstrated in Stanislaus County. Geragos will have a difficult time arguing that the size and character of the community in San Mateo County is not diverse and populous enough from which to derive an unbiased jury. Both Scott and Laci Peterson are unknowns in the new venue, and have no constituency, which rules out the fourth and fifth factors. Moving the trial out of Modesto has eliminated the alleged "political factors" as well.

What is clear from the law is that Geragos was derelict in his duty to protect his client from adverse publicity when he accepted the position as his lead counsel back in May of last year. He should have taken steps to reduce publicity, not feed it. He should have requested a protective order immediately, motioned to seal police reports and affidavits, asked for closed hearings and barring of electronic media in the courtroom, and avoided making statements to the press. Instead, he made indignant public declarations to his client's "factual innocence," promised to reveal the "real killers" within hours or days, claimed to have exonerating evidence that would result in a dismissal of the charges, waffled on the protective order and cameras in the courtroom, arguing both for and against them at different hearings, and flamed the fires of adversity with his requests for sanctions, accusations of misconduct, contempt of court charges, and exclusions of judges, the DA, and members of the prosecution team. He was aware, from his previous experience, that controversy creates attention. How well did that serve his client? Was the change of venue actually in Peterson's best interests? I conclude that it was not, and that he is stuck with San Mateo County for the duration of the trial.

It is extremely difficult to have a venue decision reversed on appeal, much less a second request. I believe Judge Delucchi has bent over backwards to accommodate the rights of the accused, and Geragos's frequent belligerence and courtroom antics are self-serving and ultimately damaging to his client. So far, his strategy in jury selection is to assume prejudice, which not only offends the judge, but also serves to delay the trial and continue to give advantage to the prosecution. Delays only hurt Peterson, since he is the one sitting in jail awaiting his acquittal. The longer the process drags on, the more time the State has to continue its investigation and uncover more incriminating evidence. If I were defending an innocent client, I would be chomping at the bit to try my case in that courtroom as soon as possible.

If the defense fails to exhaust all its peremptory challenges, a reviewing court will interpret that to mean the jury, as empaneled, was fair. Geragos's efforts must be directed to selecting the best jury under the circumstances, since he knows he has weak, if not baseless, grounds for appeal. If during the "Big Spin," he concludes that a worse jury might result if he uses all his peremptory challenges, he then faces a dilemma - does he preserve the issue for appeal (weak) or select the best jury from this pool? He will continue to reiterate for the record that while he insists that a fair trial cannot be held in the existing venue, that the jury is tainted, and that he is not satisfied with it, he'll resign himself that this is the best jury that can be selected under the circumstances. At the eleventh hour, he'll ask for additional peremptory challenges and possibly renew the motion to change venue, risking the alienation of the judge, and a virtually guaranteed denial.

If we entertain the possibility for a moment that all of Geragos's actions are designed to further his own career, enhance his high profile status and celebrity, and elicit sympathy from the public for himself rather than his client, instead of performing his professional responsibility as an officer of the court, we realize that he is either woefully incompetent or is implementing an insidious personal agenda to see that Peterson is convicted. Radical? I suggested this was his position when he performed his miraculous turnaround after he was retained as counsel for the defense. Is he, in fact, engaging in a vigorous defense, or is this case more self-aggrandizement and theatrics? Only time will tell.

APRIL 18, 2004
WHAT GAG ORDER?

What has become somewhat a Sunday tradition in the past couple of months, the irrepressible patriarch of the perfect Peterson family has succumbed yet again to the irresistible opportunity to disparage the police and dissemble doubt about the case against his son. In an article printed in the April 18 edition of *The Bee*, by John Cote, entitled, "Peterson's Father is Staunch Defender," Lee Peterson comments:

"We've got the best attorney in the country, and we'll keep him as long as it takes," Lee Peterson said, referring to Los Angeles lawyer Mark Geragos. "They'll (prosecutors and police) end up tucking their tails between their legs and slinking away."

Besides mixing his metaphors, notice the tone shift of this remark, from righteous indignation of a year ago, where he and Mrs. Peterson likened the Modesto police to fascist storm troopers, to an acrid hiss of derogatory references to animals and reptiles. Describing Geragos as "the best attorney in the country" is laughable. So far, Geragos has been called incompetent, a grandstander, out of his league, desperate, ingenuous, preposterous, unprofessional, unimaginative, and unprepared for this trial by his former peers in legal commentary.

Lee Peterson spoke at length with The Bee last week, about the past year of his son's life in jail, the upcoming trial, and the deaths of Laci and Connor Peterson.

The fact that Lee Peterson "spoke at length" with journalists is a clear violation of the protection order, of which he evidently considers himself exempt, judging by the recurring Sunday news articles that feature his and his wife's opinion on the case, and highlight their reverence of their "perfect son." Why the Petersons deem it necessary to speak out about this case to the mainstream media while voir dire is taking place is an indication of their *desperation to plant seeds of doubt* and corrosive innuendo in the minds of the jury pool. If they can influence even one person who makes the final cut on the jury to accept that the police fabricated this case against their son, they have a mistrial. While a mistrial would be considered a victory to the defense, it would not prevent the DA from retrying the case. Of course, three mistrials are as good as an acquittal, and that may be what Geragos is promising the Petersons, which is why Lee says he claims he will continue to pay Geragos for "as long as it takes."

Lee Peterson called his son "an easy target" for police under public pressure after the story of the pregnant woman missing on Christmas Eve blitzed newspapers, supermarket tabloids and cable TV news shows.

"An easy target"? Statistically, the partner is the prime suspect, however, Scott had numerous opportunities to present a different game face to the public and police. Instead, he dodged the press, avoided the searches, denied any involvement with Amber Frey, disavowed any insurance policies, drove to the Bay in rented cars, traded in Laci's vehicle, disappeared from Modesto, and displayed other deviant behavior that served to focus suspicion on him rather than lead investigators in another direction. I am so weary of Peterson's apologists refusing to make Scott responsible for at least some of the negative publicity, his relationship with police, and his deliberate disregard of his lawyer's advice. Face it, Mr. Peterson, your son did not act like an innocent man, and you and your family did nothing to help find Laci except set up your own "tip line," which was a veiled attempt to obstruct justice and collect selective potential exculpatory tips to throw in the investigators' faces.

Typical of articles generated from the Peterson camp, no mention is made of Laci or Connor, or the brutal reality of their murders. No, it's all about poor, misunderstood, maligned and innocent Scott.

He accused police of lying to Scott Peterson's friends in attempts to alienate them from his son, including telling them that Peterson was taking methamphetamine and other drugs. He also alleged that police deliberately leaked false information to the press, such as an inaccurate account of a $250,000 life insurance policy.

Did Scott have any real friends? The people Brocchini spoke to were actually Laci's friends, who may have already harbored their suspicions of Scott's involvement in her disappearance. I have never read or heard about police alluding to Scott's use of illicit drugs, so this has either been a well-kept secret up until now, or it is fiction flung for dramatic effect by the histrionic Petersons. Anyone with any experience with amphetamines could tell that porky Peterson in December of 2002 was obviously not a habitual user!

"Despair and sadness has turned to just anger at these guys," Lee Peterson said. "What upsets me about our legal system is the fact that police are allowed to lie the way they are to suspects, to their friends and their families. They can spread all the garbage they want. They try to isolate you from your family and friends and then break you."

From this subjective remark, apparently Mr. Peterson would prefer that the police invite suspects to tea and crumpets and discuss the weather and the local baseball team, rather than use techniques that include deception, fear, baiting, bargaining and psychological warfare. If Scott is innocent, nothing the cops said to his "friends" or neighbors would have made any difference. They'd have no evidence, no probable cause, and no trial. Keep in mind that all of the affidavits and warrant information remain sealed from the public. We have no idea what the prosecution uncovered about Peterson. Lee's "despair," which has evolved to "anger," simply shows his impotent struggle to accept what he cannot change: that his son is on trial for double murder, and that there is nothing he can do about that except lobby for one juror to be predisposed to cynical mistrust of the police.

"I have adequate resource [to finance Scott's defense.] It's hard to believe," Lee Peterson said, declining to elaborate. "I live very simply, but that's a choice that we made."

I recognize that Peterson's parents are voluntarily suffering significant financial sacrifices to ensure that their son receives the best defense their money can buy; nonetheless, it was unnecessary, since a public defender would have proven competent, experienced in capital cases, and a better choice under the extreme media scrutiny that accompanied this case. From my observations, I contend that Geragos has, in fact, hurt his client, and continues to damage his credibility and presumption of innocence with each diatribe and unprofessional display. Lee Peterson is either blind or brainwashed. Either way, his son's fate is in very volatile hands.

APRIL 24, 2004
THE SKINNY ON "EXCULPATORY EVIDENCE"

There have been media and defense apologist stirrings recently of rumored "exculpatory evidence" contained in a mysterious letter that was sealed and admitted into evidence on April 22, in the middle of jury voir dire in the trial of California v Peterson. This new twist is just the latest in a string of what now appear to be routine episodes of distractions and staged interruptions from anonymous tipsters with information about potential "stealth" jurors, the "real killer," or other allegations that disrupt the proceedings and make headlines. Before we concern ourselves too much with the letter's contents, let us examine the legal definition and nature of "exculpatory" or "exonerating" evidence, two relatively interchangeable terms that apply to any information that tends to exclude the defendant or absolve him from responsibility.

Legally, "exculpatory evidence is applied to evidence which may justify or excuse an accused defendant's actions, or which will tend to show the defendant is not guilty or has no criminal intent." What type of evidence would be deemed exculpatory that could be obtained from an anonymous letter? Legally, none. If there were real evidence that gave the defendant an alibi during times in which the crime was theorized to have been committed, or if there are witnesses to the murder that exclude Peterson, this information would have to be turned over to law enforcement for investigation, and not merely handed off to counsel to the defense for processing. Since there is no justification or excuse for Peterson's alleged actions (i.e., self-defense, intoxication, irresistible impulse, temporary insanity, etc.) the only evidence that could possibly prove exculpatory would be that which points to another perpetrator. I hardly think a letter generically addressed to "Any Judge" will prove to contain bombshell information that will cause a dismissal of charges. To think otherwise is disregarding the laws of evidence and court procedure.

The prosecution was required (and requested) to disclose any exculpatory evidence to the defense last year, and already indicated in court documents that there wasn't any. If Geragos actually found anything in the discovery documentation that exonerated his client, he would have brought it out, either by motioning for a special hearing with Judge Girolami, or during the preliminary hearing through hearsay testimony from officers, or through his own witnesses that he had every right to call. He would not, save with ambitions for professional suicide, have sat on this evidence until trial; meanwhile, implementing various delay tactics while his client sat in custody in San Mateo County jail. Additionally, the defense could have requested any exculpatory evidence that could have adversely affected the credibility of any potential witnesses, law enforcement or officers involved in the case. Instead, we were privy to snide remarks, sarcasm, argument thinly disguised as testimony, innuendo, and leaden trial balloons that led to no substantiated conclusions, but lots of grist for the "innocent until proven guilty" mill.

Based on the law, materially exculpatory evidence is that evidence which "possesses an exculpatory value...and of such a nature that the defendant would be unable to obtain comparable evidence by other reasonably available means." In other words, if the investigation uncovered forensic or physical evidence that linked the murder to another suspect, such as DNA found in the plastic bag or tape debris found near the remains, or Laci's blood or other body fluids found in the infamous tan van, Peterson (through his counsel) would have no access to this type of information without cooperation from law enforcement and the results of any lab testing. Once again, if there were any real forensic evidence that pointed to another killer, Geragos would have brought this out long ago and not be wasting the Court's time (or his client's potential freedom) by sitting on it and intimating that he has all kinds of surprises in store for trial. This is not only a ridiculous notion; it is legally implausible.

Usually a prosecutor does not file criminal charges that are not supported by probable cause. If after filing he comes to believe that the charges are not supported by probable cause, he is legally obliged to inform the Court and move to dismiss the case. To proceed with such a highly visible and media drenched trial without a good case is beneath the standards of even the most incompetent district attorney, and beyond credibility in the People v Peterson.

If a defense attorney is approached by a victim, codefendant, or other witness who possesses evidence that may exculpate the defendant or is crucial to his cause, he will utilize the proper channels to validate this information and vigorously oversee any investigation, should the claims have merit. An anonymous letter, which actually may be more prejudicial ramblings about his client, would hardly qualify for any serious level of scrutiny. I predict the letter is merely another hoax like the two other fruit basket offerings that preceded it.

Peterson's future depends on Geragos's ability to present the best possible defense, which means offering any favorable evidence he can. Technically, there is some "exculpatory" information about Peterson: he has no criminal record, no history of domestic violence, no visible connection to the underworld or shady characters with whom he did business, and other than his moral turpitude and propensity for lying, he is just a typical narcissist with pathological self-absorption. There may be some persuasive constitutional basis for the admission of this type of exculpatory history, but it's going to take a lot more than that to disqualify all the incriminating evidence that will point to his guilt at trial.

Recently, Geragos and co-counsel Ben Brafman told the judge in the Michael Jackson child molesting case that the defense had uncovered "a wealth of clearly exculpatory material" pointing to Jackson's innocence. Soon afterwards, the Grand Jury handed down an indictment for Jackson. I conclude that all this hype about exonerating evidence is, as with Peterson, nothing more than posturing from the pomposity playbook.

MAY 4, 2004
CHANGE OF VENUE - TAKE FOUR

After weeks of threatening and posturing, counsel for the defense, Mark Geragos, finally filed his second "Motion for Change of Venue" two thirds of the way through Hovey voir dire in San Mateo County. As usual, the 22-page document could have been summarized in about three pages. Typical of his signature long-winded motions, Geragos fails to address the real problems with the prevalent publicity and in selecting an impartial jury. There is no "geographical cure" for this trial; no matter where in California it is held, the same major stumbling blocks exist: the length of the trial will still eliminate most of the jury pool immediately, and a significant percentage of the population are predisposed to Peterson's guilt in Los Angeles County. The latter reality would be, of course, blamed on the media.

First, let's call a spade a spade, separate from the law, or the "presumption of innocence," or media spin, or alleged law enforcement corruption, or anyone's particular sympathy for the victims in this case. The fact is that Peterson (and to some extent, his attorney) is responsible for how people feel about him. All along, he has been his own worst enemy. If he had acted in the least bit like a grieving spouse, a person with a heart, a normal mixed-up guy, or even a bit of a zombie bouncing off the walls, most of us may have had some doubts about his involvement. We at least would have maintained a more neutral stance about his personality. Instead, Peterson elicited skepticism, disbelief, shock, suspicion, disgust, astonishment, and various shades of rage in his incredible and appalling behavior from the very first day. Meanwhile Geragos, instead of stifling the public condemnation of his client, exacerbated the situation by proclaiming Peterson's factual innocence, manufacturing cult and other killer theories out of thin air, and repeating a daily hue and cry about virtually everything involved in this case from the delay of discovery to his fantasy accusations of "stealth jurors." If Geragos had practiced a modicum of discretion, at least half of the media reporting on this case would not exist.

Based on my premise that a venue change will not alleviate the problems (but rather is merely self serving and convenient to defense counsel), let us examine some of the $500 an hour arguments from the new motion:

> *As we explain below, more than 96 percent of potential jurors stated they have either read, seen, or heard something about the case, and over 56 percent indicated they had formed preliminary opinions about it...approximately 45 percent of potential jurors said they have already determined that Mr. Peterson is guilty.*[58]

I doubt Mr. Geragos would find the numbers much different in LA County, or any other county in California. In fact, he doesn't even bother to attach a new survey conducted in Orange or LA Counties in order to demonstrate any substantial statistical differences between a southern venue and Redwood City. Why not? Because he knows he'll get the same results. If 45 percent are predisposed to his client's guilt (in any given county), that leaves 55 percent who are not, which translates into hundreds of thousands of people. Among those, if the majority of them were not eliminated right off the bat because of hardship, the population in any given venue would be sufficient from which to derive an

---

[58] May 3, 2004 Defense Motion for Change of Venue, p. 4.

impartial jury. The biggest problem is the projected length of the trial, not the tainted pool.

> *From its onset this case has been the subject of intense media focus which has not diminished....San Mateo County Times and the Redwood City News have covered the case on virtually a daily basis, usually on the front page...re: Sheppard v Maxwell extensive [media] coverage deprived defendant of judicial serenity and calm to which he was entitled...several billboards have asked people to call in and vote whether they think Mr. Peterson is guilty...radio station KNEW currently indicates 87% of callers think Mr. Peterson is guilty.[59]*

This argument is fallacious in its data, in its tired, old Sheppard comparison, and in its farcical scientific validity. There was a lot of intense media coverage of this case on and off since the arrest, but that coverage has dwindled to but an occasional mention on the cable TV news shows, and a few online stories from San Mateo County and the Mod Bee. Since the trial was moved, the media interest has decreased exponentially. Geragos references 300 newspaper stories since voir dire commenced, which is about 20 percent of the coverage from the same time frame last year. I hope the prosecution notes the major plunge in media interest and gets a good laugh from the radio station survey reference. What next, use Howard Stern as a gauge of public opinion? I think Geragos realized the speciousness of his argument, so he proceeds to bolster his phantom statistics with bald assumptions:

> *The extent and nature of the publicity in this case has caused such a build up of prejudice that this court cannot accept at face value jurors' assurances of impartiality. During the last 22 days of jury voir dire, several "stealth jurors" have been uncovered. We believe this to be unprecedented. The prejudice against Mr. Peterson is apparently so strong that potential jurors are willing to provide misleading or false information to the Court just to obtain a seat on the jury in order to convict Mr. Peterson and sentence him to death.[60]*

It's hard to imagine greater irony than Geragos's contention that most of the prospective jurors are liars, harbor an ominous grudge against his client, are willing to forfeit six months of their lives to devote to Peterson's conviction, and of course are secretly hoping he ultimately is put to death as a result of their efforts. Never mind the presumption of innocence or due process when it comes to proving these outrageous allegations against the citizens of San Mateo County. I guess only Peterson is entitled to that! Implementing the strategy that repetition of lies somehow lends them credence, this trumped-up propaganda is duplicated verbatim later in the document.

Junk psychology rears its pointy-head further on:

---

[59] Ibid, p. 5, footnote (2).
[60] May 3, 2004 Defense Motion for Change of Venue, p. 5.

Likewise, in People v Williams...the Supreme Court observed that although most of the jurors in that case had "attested that they could render an impartial verdict," the story of the crime had become "so deeply embedded in the public consciousness" that there was "more than a reasonable possibility that the case could not be viewed with the requisite impartiality." ...given human nature, jurors cannot insulate their verdict from inadmissible knowledge or preconceptions...when pretrial publicity has been injected into the jurors' consciousness, the courts therefore do not give dispositive effect to jurors' assurances of impartiality.[61]

If this premise were pertinent to Peterson, it would likewise apply to all highly publicized cases (Manson, Simpson, Menendez, Bundy, Dahmer, Durst, Spector, Williams, Stewart, Yeats, et al), and virtually no celebrity or other notorious defendant could receive a fair and impartial trial. The only remedy in this (wholly unsubstantiated) situation is to try the case before a judge on its legal merits alone. Moving to LA certainly won't eliminate the "human nature" element. If Geragos were sincerely advocating his client's fair trial rights, and not simply his personal hardship with the commute to Redwood City, he'd waive his client's rights to a jury trial.

Concerning the "five factors" required for another change of venue, the only factor significantly affected by a move to LA County would be #2 - the size of the community. Otherwise, nothing else would be altered: the nature of the offense remains grave, the status of the accused is no better (Peterson is an "outsider" everywhere but San Diego), Laci's posthumous celebrity would be just as prominent, and the media coverage would actually increase rather than be superceded by other news. Obviously realizing the weakness of this argument, Geragos proposes Plan B: grant Peterson an additional 10 peremptory challenges to offset the regional bias. If Judge Delucchi seats 80 jurors before May 17, I expect he will grant these additional challenges. Don't expect that to appease Geragos, however. I predict he will continue to disrupt the trial with the very same "gamesmanship and manipulation of the justice system" of which he accuses the People of California.

MAY 11, 2004
CHANGE OF VENUE - TAKE FIVE

This is now the fifth entry in the Peterson file that discusses a plea, reply, response, or ruling on a change of venue motion. It's hard to fathom how much time, resources, research, surveys, statistical analysis, paper, and ink have gone into the now hundreds of pages that document this seemingly endless debate. If I'm getting weary of it, imagine how the prosecutors feel. Since both the People's Response, including declarations from Ebbesen and Varinsky, and the defense's reply comprise over 100 pages, allow me to summarize the fundamental issues addressed and the glaring lack of substantive data offered by the defense to move the trial to Los Angeles.

---

[61] Ibid, p. 13.

The People's opposition outlines some of the same arguments I posed in my "Take Four" entry: none of the five factors have been affected by the first change of venue to San Mateo County to merit another move and, other than the larger population in LA County, there is no guarantee that pretrial publicity hasn't tainted the jury pool in equal proportion. According to Ebbesen's declaration:

> The defense presented no evidence that they would be any better at detecting jurors who are willing to lie about their opinions in order to get on the jury in venues other than San Mateo County...The defense memorandum presented no evidence to support the idea that "stealth" jurors would be any less able than other jurors to fairly and impartially evaluate the evidence that they hear in trial once they actually participate...The evidence from the jury questionnaire...suggests that no increase in fairness would be obtained by moving the trial to a new venue.[62]

Besides being unable to portray anything about "stealth" jurors, who are by definition hidden and therefore outside any survey or statistics, Geragos fails to submit even a rudimentary survey of the registered voters in LA County to demonstrate a lower bias against his client, a higher percentage of "honest" jurors, or any other measurable data that proves LA County is a better venue. I am mystified as to why he didn't submit any empirical evidence to bolster his argument. If I were so vehement to move the trial to another part of the state (coincidentally my stomping grounds and where my nice, posh office is located, and from where I can go home every night and sleep in my own bed), I would certainly present relevant statistics to support my claim that the new venue would be impartial, less informed of the case, disinterested in my client, and comprised a higher population of honest people with no personal agendas.

Instead, Geragos focuses his reply to the People's opposition on rebuking Ebbe Ebbesen, whose methodology he debases as "pseudo-science" four times in the first 10 pages of his response. Rather than shooting the messenger, why didn't Geragos just include his own survey? Is this due to incompetence? Laziness? No cheap college students available? Or, perhaps is it because the data he may have acquired showed no marked difference from San Mateo County? Geragos, for all intents and purposes, has accused Ebbesen of being part of this vast conspiracy against his adulterous fertilizer salesman client when he states, "Ebbesen's purpose is keeping this case in a hostile and inappropriate venue," as if Ebbesen has any stake in the outcome of the trial or holds a personal grudge against Peterson. This is just another indication of Geragos's limitless ego and delusions of grandeur.

Howard Varinsky, whose motives have yet to be impeached by the defense (but I wouldn't put it past them to try), concludes from his research:

> As for "stealth" jurors, in all of the years and the hundreds, perhaps thousands of cases I have worked on, I have never seen an actual stealth juror seated on a jury. Given this, in my opinion, there is no proof of the

[62] May 7, 2004 People's Opposition to Second Change of Venue, Ebbesen's Declaration p. 5.

existence of stealth jurors. If the defense can prove that a juror is a "stealth," they have remedies available to them both during and after trial. As for the two alleged stealth jurors, the court has removed any juror that appears to have an iota of a problem for the sake of safety and the empanelment of a fair and impartial jury. In this particular case, these same problems would occur in any venue of the country.[63]

We now know why *voir dire* in this trial has taken longer than building the Great Wall of China. Any juror that looks cross-eyed at the defendant, or who intimates even a glimmer of doubt about his innocence is sent home. Based on the 57 pages of compost filler the defense has presented in its two most recent change-of-venue documents, I predict the judge will deny the motion. If he is as appalled at the defense's unprofessional and unsubstantiated arguments as I am, he will also deny any additional peremptive strikes as relief. He may grant six extra strikes if the jury pool grows to 80 by May 17, but I wouldn't expect much more than that.

MAY 25, 2004
DEFENSE MOTION TO ADMIT JACKSON

On May 24, counsel for the defense in the case of The People v Peterson filed their "Motion to Admit Testimony of Hypnotized Witness Diane Jackson," asking the Court to allow them to call Ms. Jackson as a witness, and for undefined sanctions against the prosecution for alleged misconduct. This motion is a joke, and was hardly worth the effort it required to "fisk," but here is the gist of it:

Based on that ruling [to exclude hypnotized witness Dempewolf] the Court may be inclined to exclude the testimony of hypnotized witness Jackson as well. We submit that exclusion of Ms. Jackson's testimony would be reversible error since the violation of Evidence Code Section 795 was the inevitable result of the prosecution's bad faith utilization of Dale Pennington. [challenged hypnotist] as the prosecution must be presumed to have been aware...Consequently, the prosecution committed outrageous misconduct...however the Court has the authority to remedy this situation by granting the relief requested.[64]

Simply put, to prevent the defense from calling Ms. Jackson to testify in this death penalty case would reward the prosecution for its egregious violation of Mr. Peterson's Sixth Amendment right to compulsory process of favorable witnesses.[65]

We recall it was a defense 402 motion to suppress Kristin Dempewolf's testimony that created the potential exclusion of Ms. Jackson's, since the same

---

[63] Ibid, Varinsky's Declaration, p. 7.
[64] May 24, 2004 Defense Motion to Admit Testimony of Hypnotized Witness Diane Jackson, p. 4.
[65] Ibid, p. 4.

disqualified individual hypnotized both women. At the time, Geragos told Judge Girolami that he doubted he was going to recall Ms. Jackson, anyway, as he basked in the brief (and rare) victory of winning an argument for a change. In his latest motion, he refers to California Evidence Code 795, which defines the rules for when the testimony of a hypnotized witness may be admissible (note: prior to January 1, 1985, this type of testimony was not), including if it is limited to events recalled prior to the hypnosis. However, admitting the witness does not preclude the People from attacking the witness's credibility or restrict other legal grounds to exclude the testimony. I seriously doubt the Modesto police enlisted Pennington in "bad faith," considering Dempewolf, obviously pregnant at the time, may have been walking a dog on Covena Avenue the morning of December 24 and saw Peterson loading his truck, thus verifying his whereabouts at a certain time, or perhaps gave Peterson the idea to use the dog-walking scenario in his staging of Laci's "disappearance." It hardly qualifies as "an egregious violation" of Mr. Peterson's Sixth Amendment rights, the cited clause defined in the following:

> The compulsory process clause of the Sixth Amendment guarantees the right to compel the attendance of favorable witnesses through (usually) a subpoena. To exercise this right, the defendant must show that the witness's testimony would be relevant, material, and favorable, and may not be cumulative or redundant.[66]

> The prosecution, not Mr. Peterson, must establish that [their] misconduct in connection with the improper hypnosis does not warrant sanction because the defendant was not prejudiced...Since Ms. Jackson was the only percipient witness to exculpatory events, exclusion of her testimony will necessarily be prejudicial. Hence, the prosecution will be unable to carry its burden and sanctions should be imposed.[67]

Geragos is already referring to the prosecution's "misconduct" as though this is established fact, which it is not; what is particularly interesting is his statement that Ms. Jackson was the only witness to exculpatory events. What happened to Ms. Campos and her witness to foul-mouthed, cigarette-bumming, beanie-wearing thugs in the park, whom he accused during the 995 Hearing? What happened to Maldonado and Mitchell and Chiavetta, the three others who claimed to have seen Laci walking her dog that morning? What about the "mysterious seven" to whom he referred on the record that will exonerate his client? I submit that their stories, as ultimately Ms. Jackson's, have resulted in conflicting geography and time frames that have eliminated their usefulness.

It is only by severe desperation and the defense's desire to influence the 76 members of the jury pool (many of whom may be reading news accounts of the case, now that they have been selected), that it would define Ms. Jackson's

---

[66] Commentaries on U.S. Constitution, Sixth Amendment, Findlaw.com
[67] May 24, 2004 Defense Motion to Admit Testimony of Hypnotized Witness Diane Jackson, p. 5.

completely immaterial testimony as "exculpatory." Here are some excerpts of her "explosive" observations - prepare to be unimpressed:

> She told me that on 1140 hours on 12/24/02 she was driving down Covena towards her house. As she drove by the (V) residence at 516 Covena she saw three short of stature, dark skinned but not African American guys in the front yard of the residence. She stated as she drove by the guys turned and looked at her and that they were standing near a van...the van was parked on the street in front of the house and not in the driveway...two of the individuals were standing at the back of the van and one was standing in the front yard near the van. She thought it unusual that they looked because she initially thought that they were landscapers...and they don't stop and look at traffic going by.

> The back of the van had two doors. The left door was open and the right door was closed...she could not see inside the van... she did not observe any tools... she said that as she passed, they all turned and looked at her..she found this unusual...she had the feeling that they were up to no good. When she heard that the [owner's] home at 516 Covena was burglarized on the Friday after Christmas, she telephoned the police to tell them what she saw.[68]

Wake me up when it gets interesting. How does Geragos submit with a straight face that this testimony possesses exculpatory value? What does Ms. Jackson witness? The van is in front of the neighbor's house, not Laci's, as misreported in news stories today. She doesn't see anyone loading or unloading a van with a person or property; she doesn't see Laci or the dog anywhere in the area (and we know the dog was put back in the yard over an hour prior). This is the morning before a major holiday when many people are off work, or traveling to visit relatives, or are taking delivery of food or packages. How does this connect to Laci's murder? What is the doubt we (or the jury) are supposed to glean from this non-event? I fail to see the relevance.

> Just last week the prosecution turned over reports disclosing an interview with a witness who saw Laci Peterson being pulled into a van by at least two men. This eyewitness, who has been a sworn peace officer, has apparently been known to the prosecution since December of 2002 yet he was only interviewed within the last week. This witness confirmed his sighting of a woman he identified as Laci and her two abductors.[69]

This sounds like a lot more like exculpatory information to me, yet Geragos has already stated that Ms. Jackson is the "only percipient witness to exculpatory events." I don't know how the prosecution knew about this witness in December

---

[68] May 24, 2004 Defense Motion to Admit Testimony of Hypnotized Witness Diane Jackson, pp. 6 – 7.
[69] Ibid, p. 9.

of 2002, unless Geragos is suggesting that the DA was apprised of every lead and interview conducted by the Modesto police. If this witness was a sworn peace officer and did not attempt to interfere in what appeared to be a kidnapping, he was derelict in his duty and guilty of criminal negligence. What I find curious is that this witness was not named in the defense document, and no time, place, or other details are offered in support of his statement; which to me clearly indicates it has already been impeached.

Obviously, Geragos's recent fish wrapping is merely a pathetic, last ditch effort to hurl more spaghetti at the wall to see what sticks before trial, when he will then be restricted to presenting facts in evidence to support his fiction in the press.

MAY 27, 2004
THE "BIG SPIN" AND OTHER SPIN

Final jury selection, referred to as "The Big Spin" by Judge Delucchi, took place today in the Peterson trial where 12 jurors and six alternates were chosen from among the 76 candidates painstakingly plucked after what seemed an endless *voir dire* of almost three months. The jurors and alternates are evenly divided between men and women, the majority of whom are in their 30's.

In other business, the defense motion to allow Jackson's testimony was granted, despite an excellent People's opposition brief filed earlier today, which revealed the fact that the defense witness list includes only 18 names, 35 pages of reports of interviews, one audiotape of Campos's interview, and one videotape of interviews from redacted names. Additionally, the People have yet to receive any discovery from defense experts, presumably Drs. Lee and Wecht, and used this opportunity to make a second formal request for these reports in its motion.

Let us briefly review the final roster of jurors based on information available on their profiles, and the glimpse into the reality of the defense case as revealed in the People's recent filing.

Juror #1 - Male, age 30+, is a head football coach for an undisclosed school. This juror also admitted to not paying much attention to the Peterson case and probably has most of the next three months off work because of the summer, but I would imagine he'll be replaced in August when football practice begins for next season.

Juror #2 - Male, age 50+, is a veteran of juries, having served on two previously. According to news stories, this juror consulted with his priest about rendering the death penalty and was given the green light. Apparently, Geragos objected to this during *voir dire*, so why the defense didn't use one of its strikes on him is a mystery.

Juror #3 - Female, age 30+, Hispanic (the only Hispanic female to survive the defense strikes), is another social worker who is attending night school to obtain her master's degree. I am a little surprised the defense kept her, since I predicted they would eliminate most of the women of Laci's generation, but maybe she is childless or unmarried (or both) and they hope that her minority demographic would imply she was more liberal.

147

Juror #4 - Male, age 50+, a quality assurance manager, former Marine and police officer. This was the man who reportedly got into a fight when he was a cop and had charges brought against him, which he alleges were false. I like this guy because he may think Peterson is a wimp and a spoiled country club boy, but the defense probably thinks he harbors a grudge against police and hopes he'll view their focus on Peterson as being examples of misconduct and corruption.

Juror #5 - Male, age 20+, is on disability from a security job with a local airport and served with the Air Force National Guard. He claimed not to be following the case and watched the news primarily for updates on Iraq.

Juror #6 - Male, age 30+, a fire fighter and paramedic, and has taken classes in law. Apparently he knows one of the potential witnesses (also a paramedic), which could have gotten him excused, so I suspect he wants to sit on the jury for the experience. Maybe he has ambitions in the criminal justice field.

Juror #7 - Female, age 50+, of Pacific Island descent, is a Pacific Gas & Electric employee familiar with the case but willing to set aside the media reporting (as are we all, at this point!) She's not one of the matronly types I was worried would get on the jury and be sympathetic to Peterson, from the descriptions of her in news reports.

Juror #8 - Male, age 60+, and works night shift so will be able to continue working during the trial. His interests are mainly sports, and he did not follow the case. He has served on jury before, and has experience with union negotiations as member of the Teamsters. He has also been the defendant in a civil action. I believe both sides kept him because he is familiar with the court system and appears to have no preconceived notions about Peterson.

Juror #9 - Female, age 30+, works for a biotechnology firm and is the controversial juror whose boyfriend, whom she married when he was behind bars for homicide, was later murdered in prison. She has since remarried and her current husband has no opinion on the case. Much of her voir dire was conducted behind closed doors, and I am very surprised she is included in the panel.

Juror #10 - Female, age 40+, has followed the case to some extent and watched "The Perfect Husband," but advocated the benefits of her high school civics class and has apparently been a victim of some tragedies in her history.

Juror #11 - Female, age 40+, An African American woman who is in the accounting field and had a relative in law enforcement. I can see the prosecution wanting her because of her high analytical skills, where the defense would have dreamed of an entire jury of minority women a´ la Simpson.

Juror #12 - Female, age 30+, a former social worker with children's services, familiar with police investigations and court procedures (and probably met her share of liars). She is a member of the Executive Women's Golf Association and works for an adoption agency. The prosecution may have kept her because of her experience with victims, while possibly the defense hopes she is cynical about law enforcement.

Some of the interesting things we learned in the People's Opposition to Motion for Sanctions (which the judge did not impose) and Request for Discovery filed today include the story behind the mysterious "sworn peace officer" who witnessed a woman he identified as Laci Peterson on December 28, 2002, being forced into a van four days after Ms. Jackson's van sighting and Laci's "disappearance" (murder). No connection was established between the two vans, and the ex-cop described the woman's clothing as different from what Laci was found wearing in April when her remains washed ashore. If anyone believes that Laci would not run or shout for help, even at gunpoint, if she were let out of the van by her abductors within the city limits of Modesto in front of obvious witnesses, then he has rocks in his head. Nobody is going to believe this was Laci.

> In a battle by defense attorneys to allow in previously banished evidence, lawyers said the man spotted Laci going to the bathroom next to a fence four or five miles from her Modesto house. A man was holding on to her with both arms then brought her over to the driver's side door of a van where another man pulled her inside, defense attorney Mark Geragos said.[70]

If this woman were a victim of a kidnapping, she would have had to be subdued by drugs if she did not try to escape. No drugs were found in Laci's toxicology tests, of which we are aware, and I suspect this was not abduction at all, but rather lowlife people who were high or drunk and had to pull over briefly for nature's call. The woman was probably roughly carried into the van because she was too drunk to climb back in without assistance.

Regarding Diane Jackson's statements, the People had the same opinion as I about her merit as a star witness for the defense:

> Jackson's testimony is not exculpatory...She saw three dark-skinned males standing near a van parked on the street in front of 516 Covena Ave...She stated that she initially told the officers the van was white, but that upon thinking about it she believed the van was darker, either a tan, or brown color. That's it. That is all she said. Ms. Jackson had no information regarding seeing Laci Peterson that morning or even that these three people were doing anything improper.[71]

So much for Geragos's claims that Jackson is "the coming attraction" and that "everybody's got this same memory of a van that's in that neighborhood." Would five miles away qualify as the same neighborhood? Are we in Kansas, Dorothy?

> The People hereby move in-limine to prevent the defense from introducing any evidence of third party culpability without a sufficient showing...The People object to any mention of: a cult of Satanists, individuals painting pictures at the Albany bulb, any mystery woman, including Amanda H., any brown van, or of any other third party culpability without the defense first putting forth evidence sufficient to meet the People v Hall standard.[72]

---

[70] Anderson, Brian, "Peterson Jurors Selected," *Contra Costa Times*, May 27, 2004.

[71] May 27, 2004 People's Opposition to Motion for Sanctions and Request for Discovery, p. 3.

[72] Ibid, p. 4.

Part of the above statement could be a best-selling bumper sticker in Modesto. The *People v Hall* standard to which the prosecution refers establishes that "evidence of third party culpability must do more than raise a mere suspicion that another person committed the crime; there must be a clear link between the third party and the crime in question." There is no link between the variously described vans, the beanie-wearing bums in the park swearing about a dog, the sewer pipe at the Albany Bulb, the homeless hanging around Dry Creek Park, or the pregnant woman urinating at the side of the road, and Laci Peterson's murder. I doubt any of these theories will make it to trial, much less any of these characters appearing among the skimpy 18 witnesses the defense intends to call. Opening arguments are on schedule for June 1. No motion or request for delay was submitted today, which refutes yet another media rumor.

CHAPTER 9: THE TRIAL

JUNE 2, 2004
"SAME THING, NOTHING NEW"

"Same thing, nothing new. No evidence," was the terse review of the People's opening arguments yesterday by Lee Peterson, Scott Peterson's father. This cavalier attitude is typical from a family that has repeatedly shown itself to be radically out of sync with normal behavior. If my brother were on trial for murdering his wife and child and I believed he was innocent, I would be devastated at yesterday's detailed chronology and images of the victims. If a reporter asked me, "How did things go today?" I would reply, "This is the most horrible nightmare of our lives. I cannot describe the pain we are feeling for Laci's family and everyone involved. I can only hope and pray that justice is served."

In contrast, ask one of the" Brady Bunch," and you get bizarre, condescending remarks such as, "My kid is going to walk," "I feel like I'm in Nazi Germany," and "They have to have something on me," which are not the sentiments of innocent people. Can you imagine being falsely accused of this crime? Would you have gone out of your mind with grief, rage, indignation and fear? The Peterson family strolls into the San Mateo County Courthouse as if arriving for a casual brunch instead of attending one of the most profound, solemn, gruesome, heart flaying events of their lives.

The following summary includes some of the "same things, nothing new" that were presented by the People yesterday to outline its case against Peterson:

- A scientist specializing in tides studied the location of the remains and concluded they separated just off Brooks Island, the same area of the bay where Peterson said he fished.

This corroborates what I know to be facts: Laci's remains were located by side scan sonar and remote operated vehicle camera in mid-March 2003, in the Richmond entrance channel, approximately one mile northwest of Brooks Island. The sonar discovery was photographed, documented, and later compared to the actual findings and concluded to be Laci. I also know for a fact that the DA has these images and that one of the Modesto investigators may yet testify to their existence.

- In the month after his wife vanished but long before her remains washed ashore, Peterson repeatedly visited a bay overlook with a vantage point of Brooks Island.

Some of the locations we will learn Peterson haunted include the area behind Golden Gate Fields racetrack, just south of Albany; the area near Richmond (from where I believe he launched on the night of the murder) and along the coast, following what he surmised was the current. Clearly, he was extremely concerned about the Bay searches and repeatedly attempted to lead the investigation in another direction, including establishing a search center in Los Angeles.

- A phone tap captured Peterson giving a "low whistle" of apparent relief when he learned through a voice mail that an object detected by sonar on the bay floor was an anchor and not his wife's body.

I'll bet he was relieved. The jury will review many more examples of Peterson's amazing arrogance in upcoming broadcasts of the wiretap evidence.

- A boat cover Peterson apparently used during his fishing trip was found drenched in gasoline in his shed. Another tarp was covered with fertilizer. Both substances destroy DNA and other human biological material and prevent tracking dogs from picking up a person's scent.

Besides the consciousness of guilt implied by deliberately contaminating evidence, I find it odd that Peterson, whose pregnant wife has suddenly disappeared, had the presence of mind to move the boat cover and tarp from the warehouse to his shed, unload the umbrellas from the truck and set them up against the backyard fence, and carry out other reorganizing and cleaning activities before the search warrant was issued on December 26. What innocent person with a missing loved one behaves this way?

- The diamond necklace, sapphire ring, and watch Laci Peterson wore whenever she left the house were found in the couple's bedroom.

Why would Scott report Laci wearing a white top and black pants and descriptions of jewelry of which some was sitting on her dresser? Did he really expect them not to search his house? Why describe her clothing or jewelry at all? Why not say, "I have no idea what she was wearing." The only conclusion we have drawn from Peterson's unnecessary details, his stream of easily proven lies, and his indefensible behavior following Laci's "disappearance" is his irresistible, subconscious tendency for self-sabotage, which is the hallmark of the narcissistic personality disorder.

Today counsel for the defense will present its opening arguments to derail the steady, consistent, dogged track the DA has laid, and to present Mr. Innocent as a falsely accused, confused, and hedonistic young man who only wanted to play around a little, not kill his wife.

JUNE 3, 2004
STONE COLD GUILTY

Appearance is everything to those sad souls with shallow lives, skewed values, and hollow beliefs. They subscribe to the perilous perfidy that material wealth and surface images somehow compensate for their restless, ungrateful, barren existences. It is perfectly appropriate, therefore, that a flashy, Armani-clad, publicity-grubbing, professional liar like Mark Geragos is representing the spiritually vacant, barely human Scott Peterson in the trial for his life. From his opening statements yesterday, let us evaluate Geragos's selective information, his brazen revisionist history, and his outrageously inaccurate and implausible explanations for his client's stone cold guilty behavior after his wife's murder. Frankly, I'm tired of putting quotation marks around the word, "missing," since this was a murder case from beginning.

Perhaps taking a page from his Hollywood cronies, Geragos has reinvented Scott Peterson, outfitting him in a Technicolor dream coat of empathy, sentiment, diligence, discretion, integrity, and self-control. While the jury may be comprised of people who have not regularly followed this case, for those of us who have, Geragos's opening act typically defies the facts and insults our intelligence. Let us contrast Cecil B. Geragos's kaleidoscope illusion with the stark black and white of reality.

- Peterson was "giddy" about the impending birth of his first child, demonstrated by decorating the nursery and participating in Laci's prenatal care.

Yes, Peterson was so giddy about fatherhood he avoided Laci during the times she was fertile, accepted a job which frequently took him out of town, aggressively solicited an extramarital relationship, denied the existence of his wife and unborn baby to his girlfriend and others, discussed his desire for future infertility, and turned his son's nursery into a storage room.

- Peterson was not "going to chuck this entire life" for the masseuse mistress he took out on just four dates.

Nobody has contended that Peterson would chuck his entire life for any woman, since we recognize that he merely uses people and assigns them no value aside from what they can do for him. We know Amber was not the catalyst for murder; she was merely the "source" *du jour*. Peterson's real motivation was obviously economic and personal emancipation.

- The forensic evidence in this case is "zero, zip, nada, nothing."
- The baby could have been born alive a month and a half after she vanished.

Don't expect any evidence of this in the trial. What bewilders me about the abduction theories is that the director fails to flesh out the subplots so the audience can even remotely consider their plausibility.

- Five witnesses bear direct evidence of Peterson's innocence.

Based on an electronically corroborated timeline, there is less than a 15-minute window of opportunity for Laci to be seen walking the dog by all these so-called witnesses in widely disparate locations, and from her agenda, we know that she had preparations to make for that evening's gathering and a Christmas brunch. The idea that Laci would postpone these preparations to take the dog out for a walk in 40-degree weather when she was advised to limit her physical activities is simply ridiculous. We're not talking about Susan Powter or a fitness freak that would never skip her exercise routine!

- Peterson was wrongly portrayed as being indifferent to his wife's disappearance. In fact, the defendant worked tirelessly to find her, handing out fliers, setting up a tip line and even working with his mother to hire a psychic.

Is it a fact that Mr. Innocent worked "tirelessly" to find his wife? Was he looking for her on the golf course? Was he looking for her in Berkeley Hills when he was gallivanting around with his sister and her friends? Was he looking for her at the country club or strip bars in San Diego? Was he looking for her in Bakersfield and Fresno where the GPS located him on numerous occasions? True, I would not portray Peterson as "indifferent"; I would characterize him as jubilant!

- Laci Peterson's hair was in her husband's new boat because she visited it on December 20, not because he used it to dispose of her remains. He said that no one else in the family knew about Peterson's purchase of a 14-foot fishing boat because the couple planned to surprise her stepfather, Ron Grantski, with the news on Christmas.

Even if this nonsense merited momentary reflection, it does not explain how the hair was found crimped inside the pliers, or exculpate Peterson from using the boat as a vehicle for the disposal. For whatever political or professional reasons

153

that few of the commentators will criticize Mark Geragos, much less condemn his opening statements as akin to weaving the emperor's invisible clothing, there isn't an honest person alive who would find his client's behavior justifiable, excusable or "stone cold innocent." Peterson's defense would have been more palatable if it had admitted to his arrogance, lecherousness, and stupidity, and argued that he was too much of a self-centered blockhead to pull off a murder.

JUNE 4, 2004
THE DEVIL'S IN THE DETAILS

In an age of sound bytes, Velcro, hit clips, "billions served" fast food, 10-minute oil changes and instant credit, is it any wonder that the length and detail of Rick Distaso's opening statements in the trial of People v Peterson were widely ridiculed by media pundits and reporters as boring, monotonous, and verbose? Conditioned by the fallacy that "less is more," which only applies to paprika and cosmetics, the ratings-hungry talking heads failed to appreciate the relevance and necessity of Distaso's protracted foundation.

Fortunately, there are those of us with longer attention spans and admiration for detail. We know that life is not constantly exciting, but rather the mundane detritus of our daily events are tedious and banal and, to an outside observer, utterly unremarkable. Some of us learn contract bridge, sit raptly through Shostakovich, read *Moby Dick* for pleasure, or are content to take a year to finish a painting or build a model, adding each piece or color with precision and care. Then there are those with the attention spans of chinchillas, who read headlines and horoscopes, consult the Cliff's Notes, and skip to the last chapter of a book to learn the ending.

The following is a summary of the delicious details either alluded to or enumerated in Mr. Distaso's densely dramatic account of the outline of the Peterson case, which, compared to Mr. Geragos's *misinfomercial*, was like New York cheesecake to lime Jell-O.

- Laci's jewelry, inconsistently reported by her husband as missing, was found on her bedside table.
- Karen Servas reviewed her timeline at Peterson's request, not because of a sinister collaboration with the investigators.
- Laci was frequently photographed between November and December, at various social events and family gatherings, which proved immensely valuable in identifying her wardrobe and jewelry.
- Peterson made quite a few trips to the Berkeley area in rented vehicles and one in particular to the racetrack, which corroborated my consistently impeccable sources.
- Based on his cell phone records, Peterson made relatively few calls on December 24 compared to his average of 30 - 40 a day, and mostly to his voice mail.
- Cash (close to $15,000), several knives, camping gear, his brother's ID, a lot of clothing, and a credit card belonging to Anne Bird were found in Scott's unregistered Mercedes on April 18. Please note his lack of diligence in registering the vehicle. (Anne is Scott's half-sister who was

adopted by the Gradys in San Diego as an infant, and whose adopted brother, Steve, once worked with her half-brother, John Peterson, neither aware of his relationship to her.)

- Plastic material was found on the hair in the pliers that may turn out to be facial wax. Since Laci had that treatment done on December 23, it may be yet another indicator besides the khaki pants of when she was murdered.

- The gun found in Peterson's glove box may have been fired more recently than November, contrary to the defendant's statement.

- Scott's claim that his head and facial hair were bleached by swimming in a friend's pool was refuted by the fact that he never swam in this pool; never mind how silly and impossible that was in the first place.

- Scott deliberately ruined his new boat cover by possibly dousing it with gasoline and folding it under a leaky leaf blower ostensibly to destroy any DNA evidence.

- From retracing Scott's steps from the house on Covena Avenue to the warehouse four miles away, Jacobsen timed the cell phone tower switching to support the prosecution's belief that Scott did not leave Covena Avenue until 10:08 am on the 24th. This would narrow the window of opportunity for Laci to have walked the dog and been seen by anyone in the neighborhood to ten minutes.

- Scott bought a 90-pound bag of concrete mix to make a one-gallon sized anchor. The remaining concrete and bag had mysteriously vanished. What handyman worth his salt would throw out that much spare concrete when there are so many uses for it?

- The reason the second tracking dog (unnamed) did not find Laci's scent where Trimble found it was because the dog wasn't taken to the launch ramp and pier, not because Trimble was tracking Scott.

- The scent item used to track Laci was her sunglasses, but more important, the nose cushion area of the sunglasses, which apparently absorb a great deal of personal scent and are unlikely to be contaminated or confused with a secondary trace scent from someone else handling the glasses.

- A perinatologist has determined to within five days that Connor died between December 23 and December 28. Since we know the baby was alive on December 23 that narrows the time of death and soundly debunks any of the third party theories.

Setting aside the prolonged and incredibly inappropriate affair with Amber Frey, and the inane, albeit intense pseudo-intimate conversations between them, realistically this case will be won or lost on the details.

JUNE 5, 2004
LOWLIGHTS OF THE DEFENSE'S OPENING STATEMENT

Quotes and commentary from Mark Geragos' opening statement:

People often say [opening statements are a] preview of what the evidence is going to show. It's not supposed to be an argument. It's not supposed to kind of spin your side of the case, or anything else.

However, he will try to slip argument, spin, misinformation, non-sequiturs, invention, fancy, revisionist history, and my signature bashing of police as much as possible!

So the fact of the matter is, is that what their theory is, their motive for this crime is the affair with Amber.

Here is Geragos's first major misstatement: In fact, the People alluded to Peterson's motive as financial rather than romantic. The love of money is the root of all evil, and to a man like Peterson, money always represents status, sex and power. With economic freedom, he could change women as easily as golf shoes. Geragos would like the jury to think the People's presentation includes the love spin, because he knows how preposterous that is. Nobody kills his wife to be with a newly acquired "source," but many kill to escape the obligations of domesticity. Emancipation is a very common motive, and we should expect nothing more imaginative or profound with a one-dimensional lout like Peterson.

The fact of the matter is, the police did not believe that he had gone fishing. He was trying to prove to them that he had gone fishing. They didn't buy it.

He was the one who is trying to prove that he was at the Berkeley Marina.

I wonder why nobody believed him? Maybe because he told people he was going golfing and couldn't get his alibi straight? Because fishing 90 miles away in cold weather when there were dozens of closer spots was peculiar? Because his wife was "missing" and he just so happens to be 90 miles away at the time? What are we all, idiots? I still didn't believe he went fishing until the bodies surfaced. I thought he just got a launch ticket as an alibi and was somewhere else. Most people's antennas were alerted by that fishing story.

He had plans -- and everybody will tell you this -- to be back by 4:00 o'clock. And he was, in fact, back by 4:00 o'clock.

Who will tell us this? Nobody knew about his plans to fish. He told Amy he was going to Del Rio, he failed to mention his whereabouts to his father or

156

friends, so who, *in fact*, will tell us about his plans? He was not, *in fact*, back by 4:00. We know from his irrefutable electronic documented cell phone records that he wasn't home until closer to 5:00.

> *She got six -- five or six bags of groceries. Margarita will tell you when she comes and testifies today, Margarita didn't help her with the groceries. She hauled the groceries in herself into the house.*

You have to laugh at his use of the word, "haul," as though Laci is hefting cinder blocks into the house. Based on the list of items she bought, there wasn't anything very heavy: salmon, pastry, cereal, and a bottle of liqueur. It doesn't take much to spend $90 at Trader Joe's.

> *And she was walking. She was concerned about her weight. She was concerned about the swelling of her ankles...you are going to have a succession of witness who saw her walking, and saw her walking the dog.*

Here is an example of selective truth inserted into the story as though this were still valid. *In fact*, according to her medical chart, Laci was experiencing dizziness and nausea while walking and was advised to curtail that activity in early November. The "succession of witnesses" will all describe her in black pants and a white top (not even a coat, mind you) and at various places in the neighborhood that will contradict the physical reality and the weather. The "succession of witnesses" will also have to fit Laci's sighting into the 10-minute window allowed by Scott's actual departure time and the dog's return to the yard.

> *The fact of the matter is, the evidence will show you, he went to every single appointment; and, as I indicated before, was excited enough that he was one who built personally built that nursery that you saw the pictures of yesterday.*

I am skeptical that Scott, the traveling salesmen who causally spent two days in a row with his new girlfriend, was able to attend "every single appointment" of Laci's prenatal care. Pay attention when the medical staff testifies to see if this claim is true. Based on Geragos's track record, it would not surprise me to see him continue to throw out blatant lies that he knows cannot be shown by the evidence, and may even be refuted by testimony, without a care in the world. It's rather unnerving, but it must thrill the prosecution.

> *There is no way that - if there is a pregnant dead woman with weights in it, that you would not see it....In fact, those witnesses have been located. And witnesses who were there, who saw him put the boat into the water, were located. In fact, one of them remarked that he laughed at Scott, because he kind of hit one of the pylons.*

Is it true that these witnesses saw Scott launching the boat, or did they see him when he was taking the boat out of the water? If the boat cover were still on the boat when he put it in the water, or pulled down just enough to allow him to step in, nobody would see Laci in the boat, either. Remember, the boat cover later doused with gasoline?

> *Now, the fact of the matter is, that was the basis for the search warrant to put in the trackers, and to tap his phones, because he has lied about the meringue.*

Does Geragos expect us to believe that the probable cause for the search warrants, GPS tracking and phone taps was "there was no meringue segment on Martha Stewart?" I submit there was much more than that to obtain a judge's signature, including a series of inconsistencies and lies the defendant told that first night.

> *Now, the prosecution will then say well, ah-hah, there was a fourth and fifth visit. Why were those? The suggestion was, yesterday, that he went up there, some kind of return to the scene of the crime.*
>
> *So instead of just seeing this story here, he went to the Berkeley Marina. And if that's suspicious, understand it in context. He was going anywhere he thought he could find or promulgate a search for Laci.*

By my count, there were seven visits to the marina between January 5 and early March, not including trips he made in Ann Bird's Mercedes, and several of them were to remote locations where no one in law enforcement or on the search team would be aware of him. Why would he visit the area to stay only five minutes? Why would he rent vehicles instead of using his own? I conclude it was to verify that the searchers were in the wrong place. He saw that they were nowhere near the shipping channel where he submerged Laci's body, and drove away thinking they would never find her. How did he "promulgate a search" for her with these peculiar visits?

> *The interesting thing about that is that he's been portrayed as somebody where -- he's been portrayed as somebody who was not doing anything. And, in fact, what the evidence will show you is that he was somebody who was trying to do everything that he could to find Laci.*

This is going to be as easy to disprove as the fictitious receipts Geragos claimed Winona Ryder possessed from her shoplifting trial.

> *Quoted phone conversation between Peterson and Frey: "I would hope that you know me well enough, as does, you know, our families who know that there is no possible way I could have had anything to do with this."*
>
> *"There is a lot of reports of people who are at least thinking they saw her in the park and walking the street. I do not know where she is. I wish I did. I love Laci. I loved Laci, no question."*

Did Geragos really use this excerpt in defense of his client? How would Frey, after only "four dates," know him "well enough," or the families involved at all to judge Peterson's capabilities? And then Scott goes on to say, "I loved Laci" in the past tense, which indicates those feelings were history.

> *This baby lived beyond December 24th. And the evidence is going to show you that this baby was born alive. And it's going to be based upon the combination of the size of the baby, the growth of the baby from the last time it was seen, which was December 23rd.*

> *We do have Dr. Yip who will come in here and testify that on December 23rd that baby was 32 weeks. That's what Dr. Yip, the OB-GYN, put in their records on December 23rd.*

> *We have now a situation where there's going to be three other experts, or at least two other experts -- three others, that are going to tell you that this baby lived beyond 32 weeks. If that happened, then Laci was alive, or the baby was born alive and kept alive, one or the other.*

There is not an iota of evidence that will show that the baby was born alive, and as far as the miracle growth to "full term," which alludes to the idea that Laci was kept alive for a period of time after being abducted, there are no facts in evidence to support that theory, and we will not hear from any witnesses who support that fantasy, either.

> *The evidence is going to show you that she was alive on December 24th when Scott went to the marina.*

> *The evidence is going to show clearly, beyond any doubt, that not only is Scott Peterson not guilty, but Scott Peterson is stone cold innocent.*

After tossing out allegations implicating homeless transients, Amber Frey, Kimberly McGregor, dark-skinned van occupants and burglars, this is Geragos's affirmative defense that will have absolutely no evidence to support it. The best he can hope for is reasonable doubt based on "expert" testimony regarding the baby's size, and just one ambivalent juror who believes Laci was seen on December 24 despite the pants, timeline, weather, and Laci's condition.

JUNE 6, 2004
FIRST DAY OF TESTIMONY

The first full day of testimony served to diagram the parameters of the prosecutors' case, establishing that Laci bought food specifically for the brunch she was planning for Christmas, and that she wore two different outfits on December 23: black capri pants and a pressed white long-sleeved shirt (over which she wore a black sweater) during the day, and khaki pants with a black print blouse (over which she wore a car-length black coat and a white cashmere scarf) in the evening. Based on Amy Rocha's account, the black print blouse Laci last wore was later found "wadded" in a top bureau drawer during the second search of the Covena Avenue home in February.

Besides confirming that Peterson's description of Laci's clothing actually matched what she was wearing the day *before* she was reported missing, and possibly showing that Laci had completed her shopping (thus refuting that item on the agenda her husband invented for her the morning of the 24th), three of the witnesses described Laci as "not herself," or "tired," and less ebullient than usual when they saw her that day. I believe what the prosecution is attempting to demonstrate are Laci's lack of energy and the fact that she wore either a black sweater or coat over her outfit, and therefore would not likely be seen walking the dog the next morning, much less in a white top (a detail consistent the with all the erroneous Laci sighters) without a sweater or coat. If any of the Laci sighters described her in any color pants and a black coat, even though she was ultimately found in khaki pants, there might be a sliver of credence to their sightings. As it is, I believe their statements are nullified by the fact that Laci would have worn something over that white top on a 40-degree morning, if she were walking the dog regularly, which at that point the prosecution is convinced she was not.

What is simple but effective about the prosecution's blueprint so far is that while its opening statements primarily focused on the defendant and his behavior (lies, inconsistencies, avoidance of involvement in the search, severing his ties with Modesto and his past, and inferences of premeditation and planning), the presentation of evidence has redirected the spotlight onto Laci, applying hue and dimension to our sketchy knowledge of her personality and lifestyle. It is simultaneously impressive and poignant. Here is a young woman with sophisticated taste, enviable talent, impeccable grooming (even in late term pregnancy, which is no small task), and carloads of friends willing to instantly abandon their holiday activities to help find her. Only Scott hated Laci, and the vast scope of her loss is becoming clearer with each span, stud, bracket and buttress added to the architecture of the People's case. The centerpiece of this structure is a woman whose heart was passionately in her home.

JUNE 7 2004
TAKING A PAGE FROM RUDOLF

It is hard to avoid making comparisons between Peterson east (Michael Peterson's murder trial last summer in Durham, NC) and Peterson west. They both involve an outwardly "perfect couple" with no history of domestic violence; both defendants were engaging in surreptitious extramarital liaisons; both couples seemed financially sound with secure income sources; neither murder included witnesses, and both were committed in the couple's home; and it appears that both defense attorneys are employing a similar strategy to create reasonable doubt by portraying the investigators as inept and single-minded, and by suggesting (but not quite defining) the culpability of a variety of phantom perpetrators.

From high-profile defense attorney David Rudolf's signature "Top Ten" list presented as his closing arguments in several recent murder trials, it is already apparent as early as the second full day of testimony that Geragos is setting a similar stage:

- *No murder weapon/cause of death.*

160

The media pundits and forensic experts continue to belabor this issue, even though the State is not required to prove exactly how the victim died, only that she was murdered. Many defendants have been convicted even without a body. Last year in California, Bruce Koklich was convicted of second-degree murder (after two trials) of his wife, Jana, whose body has never been found.

- *There is no credible motive.*

Geragos has already misstated the prosecutor's theory of motive as being centered on Amber Frey, and while he eschews the financial issues surrounding Peterson's extravagant lifestyle (reminiscent of Michael Peterson), he attempts to demonstrate that Laci had recently inherited some valuable jewelry and stood to gain a sizeable settlement from the sale of her grandmother's home. Ironically, this may backfire as it did for Rudolf, when it becomes clear that the spouse was worth much more to the husband dead than alive.

- *The couple was happily married with no history of violence.*

How either of these attorneys can attest to this nuptial bliss with a straight face, knowing full well that their clients were chronically unfaithful, steeped in secrets, polished in pretense and arrogance, and, in the case of Scott Peterson, shamelessly persisting in his pursuit of his girlfriend, merely confirms their reptilian ancestry.

- *The defendant's grief and shock were sincere.*

Neither Michael nor Scott Peterson was capable of sustaining any level of manufactured panic after the early hours of the investigation. Beyond that, both men hit the fast track to forging their newly emancipated lives without so much as a backward glance. Michael Peterson cashed in his wife's life insurance policy (which is currently in litigation), and Scott ditched his wife's car, tried to sell their home, and blew town as quickly as his new wheels would take him.

- *The information and documentation from the crime scene are not reliable.*

Expect to hear many weeks of testimony and cross-examination regarding the police investigation, attempts to impeach their findings, exaggerating their mistakes, and refuting their conclusions. We can also look forward to endless hours of nauseating, conflicting expert witness testimony dueling over the baby's gestational age and condition.

- *The State relied on junk science, emotion, guess, and conjecture.*

The mtDNA results pointing to the statistical probability of it being Laci's hair in the pliers on the boat, plus any other potential forensic evidence in this case will be thrashed by the defense as though the People of California have suddenly sanctioned alchemy.

- *Investigators suffered from tunnel vision.*

When your client is unquestionably guilty and you have no substantive exculpatory evidence, accuse the police of tunnel vision, a rush to judgment, misconduct, or being fixated on your client; any variation on that predictable, frayed, familiar fight song will do.

Be grateful for this ineffectual and unimaginative defense strategy. It flopped for Rudolf, and it will likewise bomb for Geragos.

JUNE 8, 2004
WHAT PRICE, FREEDOM?

To a narcissist, freedom is more than a whimsical ideal; it is a vital necessity. Freedom from accountability, financial constraints, domestic obligations, and any obstacles that hinder his relentless pursuit of supply is as essential as oxygen. When his freedom is impinged upon by employers, demanding family, impending fatherhood, or economic recession, the narcissist begins to devalue and discard those areas of his myopic world that threaten his (false) self-image of superiority to life's prosaic burdens he deems unworthy of his attention.

From this week's testimony in the trial of California v Peterson, we can begin to see the ruinous but predictable progression of the defendant from attentive, involved marriage partner to detached, anxious, restless and disconnected stranger. As his world began to close in on him, he felt stifled and trapped, and years of internalized aggression and rage culminated in one night of tragic brutality.

We learn from Brent Rocha that during the summer of 2002, Peterson complained of his disappointment with his sales job at Tradecorp and hoped that a new employee would achieve greater success; read: "I want out!" He misrepresents himself as an international executive and widower to Amber Frey, tearfully confessing that the upcoming holidays would be the first without his "lost" wife; read: "I will make this happen, and I want out!" He spends more time off with his new girlfriend, or with his family at Disneyland, buying a boat, in Carmel with his parents and Laci, driving to Sacramento, and disappearing for days than he does performing his employment duties; read, "I don't care about this job, and I want out!" He gives notice to the landlord to end his lease on the warehouse in mid-January, and moves his personal property to a rented storage unit; read: "I'm getting out!" He trades in his "missing" wife's car, inquires about selling their house, and abandons Modesto before the end of February; read, "I'm out!"

Of course, Peterson's apologists would argue that the police essentially evicted him from his home by confiscating all his important possessions and that the media drove him underground with their harassing attention, but I submit that he intended to eliminate all traces of his former life regardless of what anyone did. That was all part of his original blueprint for freedom: stage Laci's abduction, lie low for a month, string Amber along until a better source materialized, and blow this backwater cow town once and for all. What about the Del Rio golf membership? Why would he invest in that or in the nursery if he were planning to relocate? Because the country club membership was nothing but a prop and was easily replaced by his former seaside courses in San Diego. Besides, compared to the potential thousands of dollars in child support and losses in a divorce, $25,000 was chump change.

The defense attempted to eliminate the financial motive for the murder by clarifying the terms of Laci's inheritance, but they failed to camouflage the underlying eagerness with which Peterson sought his freedom. He stood to gain nothing from allowing Laci to live; in fact, the closer she came financial independence, the more threatening she became to his position of control. While

162

her death would not immediately reward him monetarily, his subsequent freedom from the abhorrent doom of domestic servitude was priceless.

JUNE 11, 2004
IT'S TOO LATE, BABY

As expected, we are learning from a number of witnesses today that Peterson's demeanor after he reported his wife "missing" on Christmas Eve, 2002, was anything but consistent with a man who had recently experienced personal tragedy. Instead, he appeared unconcerned, remote, evasive and cagey. He erected an emotional fortress around himself, not to conceal his deep sentiments (of which he has scant), but rather to avoid annoying interrogation by Laci's friends and family. Sharon Rocha's cousin's husband, to whom Laci referred as "Uncle Harvey," testified that he followed Peterson from the search center to a mall parking lot and to the Del Rio country club, where perhaps we are to imagine Peterson hung missing posters in the locker room while having his cleats cleaned.

Karen Servas, the next-door neighbor who previously testified at the preliminary hearing, reiterated the steps she took to confirm the time she returned Laci's leashed but unattended dog to the backyard at 10:18 am. She corrected her initial recollection of leaving again later in the afternoon to 4:05 pm, but despite Geragos's attempts to impeach her highly destructive evidence to the defense's imaginary timeline, the electronic corroboration based on her cell phone records and the Austin's receipt will remain an invincible cornerstone of the People's case.

I predict we will hear many more accounts of Peterson's unique style of mourning, especially during the months of March and April, where we know he was basking in the high life with his sister and nouveau friends in Berkeley and San Diego.

JUNE 13, 2004
EXPLORING THE EAST BAY

Under a cloudless sky and deceptively cool sun, I spent my second day in the Bay Area exploring (mostly on foot) the scenes we as Peterson case followers have come to know almost as well as our own neighborhoods; or so we thought. While it is said that a picture is worth a thousand words, seeing something in person is encyclopedic in comparison.

We headed out to the Albany Bulb, an undeveloped, scruffy landfill, part of the East Bay Regional Park system that resembles an abandoned island of some lost primitive subculture. Scattered throughout the rough terrain of brush, wildflowers, crabgrass and weeds are exhibits of junk art created with scrap metal, trash, toys, concrete slabs, plywood, rusty bicycles, debris, car parts, driftwood, hangers, sewer pipes, rebar, Styrofoam, spray paint and stencils. In one area was a circular clearing with an assortment of odd sculptures we couldn't quite decipher, along with the renowned row of murals, which, after careful inspection, I have concluded have nothing to do with Satanism and everything to do with the most common art themes of history: death and sex.

Because we were unfamiliar with the layout, we hiked for quite awhile around the bulb, what seemed several miles more than we needed to in order to see what we came to see. We ended up retracing our steps and walking in circles, finally finding a path down to the opposite end of the archipelago where the most interesting artwork stood, but it was an amusing adventure nonetheless. From where the "SNIFF" artists have their "gallery," it would be impossible to float a test buoy to Richmond, since it's on the wrong side of the park. On the Bay side of the bulb is nothing but concrete landfill and rocks. No mystery sewer pipe could be located, and my sunburn and rubber legs can attest that we covered most of the potential territory. I am happy to report that I slipped only once down an embankment, and even that without serious injury.

There were no evil vibes at the bulb, and although there were a few makeshift campsites, we saw no homeless denizens lurking among the bushes or performing any occult rituals. However, we did see a few other curious explorers, and several times interrupted a young couple in the early stages of performing what may be termed an ancient ritual. From due northwest of the bulb, you can see Brooks Island, and north along the coast, you can see Richmond. Just south above the bulb is the race track where Peterson was noted to visit, based on the GPS evidence, probably because from that vantage point you have a panoramic view of the entire East Bay area and, on a clear day, can observe every boat for miles. With a pair of binoculars, you could easily scan the east shoreline for anything unusual washed ashore.

Just south of Albany is the Berkeley Marina. Being from a waterfront city near a yacht club, I found the marina quite beautiful, with its impressive array of elegant watercraft, motorized cranes for large craft, well-maintained facilities, and unmistakable nautical flavor. In some ways, boaters and fishermen have their own subculture as well, with a set of rituals and lexicon unique to their hobbies. Unlike in December of 2002, the marina was crowded. Several customers were launching fishing boats (all much larger than a Gamefisher); members of the sailing club, dressed in bright yellow rain gear, paraded down the pier like baby ducks behind their instructor, and in the distance, we could see a regatta of sailboats, with dozens of colorful spinnakers aligning the horizon, originating from San Francisco.

We took some pictures of the area where Peterson allegedly launched his boat and the route his boat would take in order to motor to Brooks Island if, in fact, that is where he went. Seeing it for ourselves, we determined it would have taken him every bit of an hour and a half just to make the round trip, so I'm not even certain that's what he did the afternoon of the 24th, as he claims. It is apparent now that he took two trips and originally launched from an area farther north, not so much because of the issues of being seen in the daylight, but because of the distance and the time it would have taken for him to reach the Richmond entrance channel, submerge Laci's body, and return to Berkeley, which was logistically impossible to accomplish in a one-trip time frame.

When we returned from investigating the area, we came across some fishermen who were cleaning the day's catch: an 80-pound sturgeon, a halibut the size of a round kitchen table, and a few smaller bass. Needless to say, the sturgeon caught our attention, and we couldn't resist the opportunity to interview the fishermen about what bait they used and how they landed that monster fish, which was larger and 20 pounds heavier than my eight-year-old daughter. They were more than happy to discuss these details, of course, and informed us that they had used anchovies as bait and a 20-pound test line, and that it had taken two men (a man and his son) to reel in the sturgeon. Their boat, a 30-foot vessel, dubbed "For the Hall-o-bit," easily held five men and gear and probably a number of ice chests and beer coolers. Up close, a sturgeon is a marvel of ecological efficiency, with catfish-like whiskers, reptilian skin, and a collapsible throat that acts as a miniature vacuum cleaner hose to feed from the silty bottom. We asked the fisherman what they were going to do with their catch, and their enthusiastic response was that they were going to cut it into steaks for future grilling.

JUNE 14, 2004
RUBBING ELBOWS WITH "CELEBRITIES"

I woke up to the faint beeping of my Mickey Mouse travel clock at 6 am and resisted the urge to sleep another half an hour, knowing I may need the extra time to get lost. After a quick shower and pouring my coffee from the single-serve cone device into my road mug (not nearly enough), I applied a little lipstick in the bathroom mirror and recited my newest daily affirmation: "I have a good sense of direction...I have a good sense of direction" and headed south on Sunset around Lake Merced to the Brotherhood Way onto 280 South toward Redwood City. Not sure of where exactly I was going, I exited on the second Redwood City turnoff and headed east. Soon I saw what appeared to be a cluster of office buildings, banks, and commercial lots and pulled into a public parking lot where I saw a local man walking toward me wearing a backpack. I rolled down the passenger side window and asked him if he could tell me where would be the best place to park to attend court. He told me the lot I was in had 10 hour meters and that I was only three blocks from the courthouse. I was prepared to pay big bucks to park, but needed only two dollars in quarters. I parked at a meter and walked across Broadway to a little coffee shop, bought a badly needed second cup of coffee and got change for the meter.

When I arrived on the front steps of the courthouse, there were no people in line for a lottery ticket, and the woman handing them out said she thought most, if not all of us, would get a seat. That looked to be the case until a little after 8 am, when another dozen people arrived and the morning odds went up about 3:2. When the first 25 out of 30 tickets were picked and my number still hadn't been called, I started to get a little nervous. A gentleman standing behind me offered to hold my ticket for good luck, claiming that he had the magic to will my number to be called. I happily handed him my ticket, which he blew on and whispered to, and he told me to sit on the "lucky bench" to await the last five numbers. My number was the third last to be picked and would have been the last had not two people been absent when theirs were called.

The public has to enter through the back of the courthouse, on the opposite side of the ticket area, and there I ran into Stan Goldman. He looks younger and better looking and (as with most of the media personalities I met today) much smaller in person. I chatted with him for a few minutes, and he spoke highly of both his former students, although he admitted that Mark Geragos took four years to finish law school. I remarked, "Why doesn't that surprise me?" After I went through a metal detector and my purse was x-rayed, I took an escalator upstairs to wait in line with the rest of the media and public. In line I met a few local people who were interested in the trial and a writer from *The National Enquirer*, Don Gentile, an obvious New Yorker from his accent, and who became my (unwitting) straight man for the rest of the day.

When the jury filed in from the front of the courtroom, I first noticed a woman juror with an interesting shade of red hair and earrings as large as hula-hoops. A couple of young men were in the last two seats in the back row nearest the gallery and sat through the entire proceedings without taking a single note. I tried to guess from the profiles who was sitting where in the jury box, but I didn't have a very good view of them from where I sat.

The first witness of the day was Derrick Letsinger, a well-spoken, neatly groomed, blond with a mustache, who was on patrol the night of the "disappearance." He walked us through the layout diagram of the Peterson home and talked about the duffel bags in the spare bedroom closet that he saw on his first inspection of the home. One of the duffel bags was on the floor, upside down, which may imply that Peterson was either putting things away or taking something out in a hurry. He testified to the conversation he overheard in the hallway (a very small area) when Peterson could not answer questions from Officer Spurlock about what he was fishing for or what type of bait he used. Apparently, this conversation was not in his report, and this sticky point became the main thrust of Geragos's objections and tantrums regarding officer testimony throughout the day. Letsinger also noticed the bucket with water around it and the two damp mops outside the door, and considered them "suspicious." Letsinger participated in the search of the vacant house to the right of the Peterson's house, which was owned by Greg Reid, and for which Geragos insisted that only Peterson could have provided the information that it was vacant. Why he kept bringing this up over and over again is beyond me, but perhaps he just wanted to emphasize that Peterson was cooperating and helpful to the police that evening.

A series of pictures of the interior of the house was shown, and in none of the pictures of the kitchen could be seen the pizza box or the ranch dressing listed in the original report. However, an open telephone book was photographed from two different angles, and according to the scuttlebutt, it was open to a colored page insert of advertisements for criminal defense attorneys, which remains to be verified in future testimony. If I had had my binoculars, I might have been able to read the page from my seat. I could see Mr. Innocent rifling through his notebook and pretending to look industrious, but we never made eye contact.

On cross, Geragos pointed out the picture showing the curling iron in the bathroom, implying that it appeared that Laci was curling her hair that morning into a "fun flip," which was objected to by Distaso and sustained by the judge. Since he is never going to put his client on the stand, Geragos proceeded to testify for Peterson, tossing in comments like, "We both know there was no evidence on those mops," and wasn't it possible that Peterson was upset that his wife was missing and not that he was frustrated over being asked to leave the house as an explanation for throwing the flashlight and swearing. The flashlight/cursing issue came up again later in Spurlock's testimony, which was when Geragos made a formal rule 1054 objection regarding the discovery of the two officers' accounts of this event, which was not in their filed reports. Evidently, this new information was reviewed over the weekend when the DA was preparing Letsinger and Spurlock for testimony.

Already so much has been made of that incident today, but I will offer what I saw from inside the courtroom. When Spurlock testified on direct, he talked about the phone book, the open bottle of ranch dressing, and the balled up wet towels that had sand and dirt on them and were on the top of the washing machine. He reviewed the search of the house, including finding Laci's tennis shoes and sandals outside the French doors, which made me think that all of her shoes were accounted for, once again refuting the dog-walking scenario and explaining the daisy sandal scandal during the Dalton days. Spurlock mentioned the overflowing laundry hamper (and Geragos had to debate whether it was a laundry *basket* or a *hamper*, things that must drive the jury nuts), and then the now infamous flashlight tossing, cussing incident when Scott was asked to leave the house. At this point in the testimony, Geragos shot up from his seat, blasted an objection based on rule 1054 and demanded the judge admonish the jury that it should be struck. The judge sent the jury out of the room for the two sides to argue. Geragos acted furious (and I mean acted, because it was just another side show as far as I'm concerned), and complained that the story was a "cheap shot among a never ending series of cheap shots!" He claimed it was a "huge discovery violation" and that this information was not in the reports.

The judge ruled that he could cross-examine the witness about the incident and that he wasn't going through this "rigmarole," and that it was not a gross violation. Then, to everyone's amusement, Geragos demanded a mistrial, which drew some laughter from the spectators, at which he insisted the judge remove the violators from the "peanut gallery." I didn't laugh, but I did shake my head a few times at Geragos's outbursts and facetious questions throughout the day. The motion for a mistrial was denied, and Judge Delucchi (who seems to have no patience with Geragos) stated, "Testimony of the defendant's demeanor cuts both ways. I don't think it's a big deal." I don't think it's a big deal, either. Why would Geragos constantly object to stories of his client's temper? If anything, it humanizes him. Why would he want the jury to think Peterson was an automaton?

When the jury returned, Geragos cross-examined Spurlock and used the photos to attempt to create a scenario wherein Laci was home the morning of the 24th. The table was set with Christmas napkins ("Did you set the table?" he asked Letsinger and Spurlock); the baby's room was decorated with blue walls, a little life preserver and a sailboat mobile, and there was a shopping bag on the dresser with some unpacked baby gifts, presumably. ("Were there things *stored* in the baby's room?" Geragos asked Spurlock; it's obvious where he is going with this.) We reviewed the curling iron, the dry floors, and the somewhat rumpled, hastily made bed in the couple's bedroom, on which Geragos tried to imply Spurlock sat while searching the purse, to which Spurlock corrected him. If Geragos was trying to make these Modesto police officers out to be bungling idiots, he did a very poor job. Both men were poised, professional, articulate and consistent. I was impressed, since I didn't know what to expect after so many months of law enforcement bashing on the various Internet crime forums and in media reports.

The final witness of the day was Phillip Williams, a representative from Motherworks, Inc., which is the company that owns Motherhood, Mimi's, and Pea in a Pod maternity clothing. In response to a Modesto Police request, Motherworks provided the style information on clothing Laci bought at a Motherhood retail store in Modesto. Catalog photos of the clothing as well as

167

several of Laci wearing some of the outfits were shown on the overhead projector. One particularly difficult shot was of the waistline and tags of the tattered remains of Laci's pants found on the rocks of Pt. Isabel. The question of the pants Laci was found in seemed to be finally resolved. They were cropped, with pin tucks (a crease down the middle of each leg) and what might be termed a "mock cuff," which was actually just decorative stitching about four inches above the hem. The debate on the color code ensued, with Geragos claiming that #25 was tan, while #24 was "stone," and what was the difference? Why didn't the witness bring swatches or the color chart? To which Mr. Williams stated that "stone" was a version of tan and that different styles had different color codes. On redirect, Dave Harris pointed out that no matter what the color code, the pants were not black.

When court recessed for the public and the jury due to an in chambers discovery argument, possibly in reference to tomorrow's testimony from Sergeant Cloward (who was involved in the underwater search efforts) and Detective Beuhler (who was Amber Frey's contact in the MPD), I saw Phillip Williams sitting on a bench in the hallway, looking visibly flushed and somewhat shaken. I stopped and assured him that he did an excellent job and I could attest that his company had beautiful maternity clothes. He looked up at me and said, "It's too bad I have to be here for something like this."

Besides meeting Stan Goldman and Don Gentile, I also had an opportunity to speak to Gloria Gomez, a very pretty reporter from Sacramento who conducted one of the interviews with Peterson right after Amber Frey came forward. I didn't get a chance to meet Gloria Allred yet, since I did not want to interrupt her on the phone or talking to someone I assume was an assistant, but I did meet Ted Rowlands, and I asked him how he liked his new job at CNN. I told Ted I ran a Web site that discussed the case, and that I had composed a little quiz where one of the questions was about his new job after leaving San Francisco's KTVU, with the one of the multiple choice selections that he was offered a square on "Hollywood Squares." He laughed.

JUNE 15, 2004
HINDSIGHT IS 20/20

As a general rule, the cross-examiner should aim for one or more of the following goals during cross-examination:
- *Impeach the witness with prior inconsistent statements*
- *Discredit the witness's direct testimony on substantial issues;*
- *Corroborate matters that are significant to your case*
- *Establish bias, interest, or motive for the witness's testimony*

Attorneys should keep in mind that cross-examination is not required. Sometimes the best cross-examination is counsel's statement, "No questions, thank you." ~ California Criminal Law Procedure and Practice

For defense counsel in a trial where there are potentially hundreds of prosecution witnesses and volumes of discovery, cross-examination is critical to establishing its case; often through attacking testimony and unraveling the weave of circumstantial fabric that binds the State's evidence. Cross-examination is not designed to reiterate previously covered territory in direct, inject testimony from yet unheard witnesses, practice stand-up comedy, or insult the witnesses. Apparently, Mark Geragos skipped the classes in law school that covered the vital tools to effective cross, as was demonstrated today in his questions to Jon Evers.

It never ceases to amaze me that this high-profile, highly paid, and highly touted Hollywood huckster continues to merit accolades and admiration from the legal pundits and some reporters. For the past year, he has filed inadequately researched, legally ignorant, verbose and redundant motions, most of which were denied. He has stood in front of microphones proclaiming his clients' "factual innocence" (both Peterson and Michael Jackson), and threatened those who would defame him with a "ton of bricks." The only bricks I am seeing must be in his head, because he is incredibly ineffective as a cross-examiner. I have not personally witnessed many trials, but based on what I have seen in the last two days, I consider Mark Geragos to be one of the poorest excuses of a trial lawyer in California. It's positively embarrassing. I might be wrong, though. Maybe most of them are this bad.

Yesterday's outburst and motion to dismiss were only symptoms of this man's withering incompetence. Today we were punished with a long, pointless cross-examination during which many in the gallery struggled to stay awake. Let us briefly review the major points covered in Jon Evers's testimony, and the subsequent cross-examination that was probably completely lost on the jury and only served to annoy those of us who have followed the case closely. Similar to his tactic in the preliminary hearing to isolate events out of context in order to diminish their impact, Geragos attempts to impose clairvoyant powers on the police officers at the scene.

Evers was the first officer to arrive at the park, after getting the call from dispatch, which originated from a 911 call from Sharon Rocha's house in Modesto. Evers initially headed toward the Rocha's and then diverted to Dry Creek after further instructions. He arrived at the park a little after 1800 hours (6 pm) and met up with a group of people, including Sharon and Scott, at 1811. This time clarification solves the mystery of the 9-1-1 call Peterson allegedly made shortly after 6 pm, based on his cell phone records. From Evers's testimony we learn that Scott told him at the park that he had been fishing in the Bay and that Laci was planning to walk the dog down at the park. This is very important because it shows that of all the things we have heard about Laci's agenda for the day from Peterson, he tells the *first* officer on the scene about the dog walking plans. Upon further questioning, Peterson says he left the house at 9:30 am, that Laci was planning to walk the dog, shop for groceries, and prepare a holiday meal (note the order he gives), and that he arrived home at 4:30. This is just one long series of lies that have already been exposed. Why would an innocent man lie about the time he left and the time he arrived home when it could be so easily disproved? What would he have to gain from that?

Peterson said he arrived at the marina at "around noon" and fished for two hours. In fact, later when he produces his launch ticket from the ashtray of his truck (upon request of the officers), it indicates he bought the ticket at almost 1:00 (12:54, to be exact). Again, why lie about when he arrived? Why give himself more time at the Bay rather than less? I have already concluded that he could not have accomplished the dumping mission in the time frame between buying the launch ticket and making that 2:15 pm cell phone call from the Berkeley area, so why would he want the police to think he was there for over two hours?

We learn that the patio doors (the French doors leading out to the backyard) were unlocked, the dog was on his leash in the backyard, and that nothing in the house looked out of order, burglarized, vandalized or showed signs of a break-in. Again, why would Peterson attempt to stage his wife's abduction and upon finding the dog back in the yard, not mess up the house a little? We learn that Peterson had trouble answering questions about what he was fishing for, what bait he used, and why the duffle bag in the closet was upside down on the floor. He shrugged it off and said, "I'm just a slob." A slob? Besides the full laundry hamper, the house was pristine. Apparently, at that time, there was also a conversation about weapons in the house, but Evers did not elaborate. Expect to hear more about the weapons from Detective Brocchini.

Evers filled out a missing persons report based on Peterson's information: Laci was last seen wearing a white long sleeved shirt and black pants, diamond earrings, a diamond ring, and a diamond necklace, and that she had a scar on her abdomen and a sunflower tattoo on her left ankle. There was no mention of Laci's planning to mop the floor, which indicates he came up with that one for Brocchini *after* the police took the mops and bucket. Evers was present at the warehouse during the fictitious power outage and eventually was sent to Moose Park early in the morning hours of December 25 to search.

Now for the classic Geragos cross:

First, we were subjected to another presentation of the slides of the interior of the Peterson home, which we have seen four times in the last two days. When the picture of the muddy, sandy rags on top of the washing machine was shown (and several were quite blackened with dirt, which may be one of the reasons they questioned Ms. Nava about cleaning the outside windows), Geragos asked Evers, "How many times were you in the home? Did you ever talk to Marguerita Nava?" How was Evers, the night of the 24th, supposed to know about Ms. Nava? So what if he did not notice the rags on top of the washing machine or consider them suspicious at the time? Then Geragos asks, "Did you think they were used for cleaning up a homicide?" To which Evers replied, "I drew no conclusions about them."

Geragos asks, "Was there any evidence on the rug? Any blood? When Peterson straightened it out, did he say, 'hey look over there!' while he did it?" Evers responded that he felt the explanation about the dog and cat playing was reasonable at the time. Geragos forwards to his favorite picture, the main bathroom with the curling iron on the counter, and asks, "Did you notice the curling iron? Did you know she was at the salon the night before learning how to do a fun flip?" to which Evers (keeping a straight face, which was a miracle) said, "No." Then Geragos goes on to quiz him about the house: "What is this a picture of?" To the master bedroom picture, he asks, "Did you notice this large black item was a dog bed?" "Did you know that Ron Grantski went fishing that day?" "Did you have keys to the warehouse?" "Did you see this hamper in the corner?" "Did Scott tell you the house next door was vacant?" And other idiotic questions until we were all bored stiff. I am sure the jury was totally confused and saw no rhyme or reason to this line of questioning.

170

Where was this questioning leading? What was his purpose? Does he expect these policemen to know Laci's grooming routine, or the original layout of the house, or anything beyond what Scott tells them at the scene? Are they all supposed to be Amazing Kreskins, put the rug to their foreheads and summon the reason for its scrunching? This cross-examination did not impeach the witness, since Evers's statements are consistent; they did not discredit him, since he appeared sincere, objective, and nonjudgmental; it did not corroborate anything substantive, since the curling iron could be left out all the time (as is mine), and the fact that Grantski went fishing was unknown and irrelevant to Evers. What bias or motive did Evers exhibit? None! He was merely accounting everything that happened at the time.

In hindsight, Evers drew different conclusions about the events of December 24, as did officers at the scene. Meanwhile, Geragos continued to confuse the jury, confound the gallery, and waste everyone's time with ill-prepared, disorganized, and incohesive questioning. If this is a million-dollar defense, it is one of the greatest cons perpetrated in recent judicial history.

Other courtroom observations from Redwood City

- There are two artists in court, a woman with watercolors, and a French gentleman who sits on the far right seats along the wall.
- Pat Harris has done no cross-examination this past two days. He chats a little with Peterson, but otherwise sits like a potted plant.
- Peterson looks taller and thinner in person compared to his ubiquitous photographs.
- The lead court reporter is slim, elegant men in his early 60s, dressed in a jacket and tie, and seems very savvy. He sits just in front of the witness stand, below the judge's bench.
- The chairs in court are similar to those in a movie theater: metal backs with cushioned seats, but the second to last row are wooden arm chairs, where I have been sitting, because they are slightly higher and you can see above the rows in front.
- There was an *in camera* hearing first thing this morning regarding a discovery issue, possibly the same one that caused court to be recessed early yesterday.
- The deputies in court watch the crowd like power-drunk hall monitors. You can't chew gum, read, or nap, and if your cell phone goes off during the proceedings, you are escorted to the door. That happened yesterday to one of the media people.
- The bailiff constantly has to yell at the gallery to be quiet when they return from breaks or just before court resumes. Considering it is a room full of attention-deficit extraverts, it gets pretty rowdy in there.
- People come in and out of the courtroom at will during testimony, which I found a little unnerving at first. We don't have to rise when Judge Delucchi enters or leaves, and the court in general is relatively relaxed and casual. There is a metal detector when you first enter the building. I don't have any problem with the watchdogs, and I have found all of the court staff and security to be pleasant, courteous and helpful.

171

Although Redwood City (dubbed "Deadwood City" by some in the Bay Area) is a bit run down and the courthouse is kind of rinky-dink, the people in town have shown me nothing but good manners, good service, good food, good coffee, and good directions. The streets are clean, the weather has been spectacular, and while there is not a lot to do there, it does have its charms.

JUNE 16, 2004
THE EMERGING SHAPE OF GUILT

After reviewing some of my notes and observations this morning of the last three days of court in the trial of California v Peterson, a number of things began to solidify in the seeming pointillist landscape of the circumstantial evidence. As in the early stages of a sculpture, imagine the case against Peterson as a solid block of marble, being chiseled and chipped away until a recognizable form begins to emerge.

The house was too neat. This would, of course, never be said of my house and would ordinarily reveal the occupants as admirably conscientious. However, in this instance, it made the crumpled rug, upside-down duffle bag, mops and bucket, and sloppily made bed more conspicuous. It also indicated that Laci was not home that morning, or there would have been signs of baking, cooking, eating or other indications of use. It certainly ruled out any invasion by strangers (burglars, vagrants, etc.) or forced abduction from the home.

When Scott was arrested, he was definitely in disguise. Unless you were very familiar with Scott Peterson (as Amy Rocha or his family would be), his dyed hair and goatee rendered him radically different in appearance. After seeing him for myself, I can attest that most casual observers or strangers would have found him completely unrecognizable on April 18, 2003. Thus, the controversy over whether or not he was intending to flee, based on the camping gear, cash, and weapons found in his unregistered, recently purchased car, seeing the difference between his altered appearance and his normal appearance removes any ambivalence in my mind, whatsoever.

Peterson had a short fuse. Despite fables to the contrary, it is becoming rather apparent that Scott had a temper. There isn't a true narcissist around who doesn't have an impulsive personality, prone to mood swings, unpredictable bursts of temper over trivial matters, mysterious disappearances, and constant duplicity. Why should we expect Peterson to be any different? The barbeque story and the much ballyhooed episode with the flashlight are what I believe only previews to numerous occasions of volatile behavior.

Scott had other weapons in the house. We heard from Lee Peterson last year that the police confiscated Scott's guns (besides the handgun in the glove box), but after Evers's testimony yesterday, there is more to come on other weapons Peterson owned.

Peterson washing his own clothes was suspicious. With an overflowing hamper in the master bedroom (and it was finally determined to be a hamper, not a laundry basket), the fact that Peterson washed only the three items he wore to the Bay, and left the dirty rags and other laundry unwashed, pointed to a clean up. We have yet to hear about what bleach evidence exists from the house that was examined in questions during the preliminary hearing.

Laci bought only one pair of tan maternity pants from Motherhood. The pants she was found in were the pants she wore at the salon the night of the 23rd, regardless of Amy's uncertain memory. Who remembers details like creases or cuffs? Amy is a hair stylist, not a fashion consultant. Unless Laci borrowed another pair of tan cropped pants with a Motherhood label from a friend, those were the only ones she owned.

The dog-walking story originated from Peterson, not Sharon Rocha. He embellished the story with each telling, adding new errands Laci intended to run, until she had an entire day's worth of activities, which would preempt an explanation for why she didn't answer the land line during the day and why he would not be concerned.

Scott did not call the hospitals or the OB/GYN office, and made only a cursory search of the neighborhood before calling Sharon. He was in a big hurry to get this inconvenience over with and get on with his new life.

So far, we have heard no testimony of Scott's attending Laci's doctor's appointments.

Expect to hear more from Sergeant Cloward. He will probably be recalled later in the trial. Today, he laid the foundation for the story of finding Laci's body in March, and the divers' inability to retrieve it, by discussing the difficult searching conditions of the Bay. He was on the boat when the sonar spotted her, and participated in the video documentation of those searches. There were also other items found in the searches that have not come into evidence as yet.

The Gossip

- Kim McGregor lied to the police about stealing the video camera. She originally denied it, and then she admitted to taking it and throwing it in the grease barrel behind Fast Eddie's. She was interrogated by Detective Brocchini and asked to take a polygraph. She did pass a polygraph in regard to Laci's disappearance, but word on the street was that she was only a neighbor who may have had a little crush on Peterson. Her first visit to the house was precipitated by the canvassing of the neighborhood that night. Someone from Laci's family knocked on her grandmother's door (in whose house she lives) and asked if she had seen a woman walking a dog and showed her Laci's picture. Prior to that, she had never been to their home on Covena Avenue. She may have used Scott's publicized visit to LA as an opportunity to break in the house and insinuate herself into this drama.

- Anne Grady Bird visits Scott in jail occasionally, but she has not been to court. She is testifying for the defense instead of the prosecution, according to Ted Rowlands, but the People originally subpoenaed her. She has some good probative information about Scott's demeanor during the months of March and April. According to another source, Anne attempted to sell Scott's letters and private correspondence to the tabloids.

- Mark Geragos's young son fell asleep in court today, and Geragos swatted him awake with a file.

Who says you have to be inside the courtroom to get all the news?

JUNE 22, 2004
SELF-INCRIMINATION AND SELF-SABOTAGE

As students of the routinely undiagnosed and rarely treated narcissistic personality disorder, we have learned that malignant narcissists are virtuoso self-saboteurs. The glitches and short circuits in their wiring often result in a complete disconnection from reality. Besides the absence of any veracity in their repertoire, they tend to leave a noticeable trail to their misdeeds, as if imposing their peculiar myopic oblivion onto others. In the case of the defendant, Scott Peterson, his actions and demeanor following Laci's "disappearance" were so exceptionally shortsighted and arrogant, we can only conclude that he operated from a compulsive, subconscious desire to get caught or, in the very least, be the focus of suspicion.

Since the media pundits and defense counsel have continually attacked investigators, Laci's family, and various witnesses for their lack of prescience, let us apply that same 20/20 hindsight to some of Mr. Blow-it-All's major blunders.

Scott gave the investigating officer too much detail. By elaborating on Laci's clothing, jewelry, plans to walk the dog, the meringue segment on Martha Stewart, and specific times of departure and arrival, Peterson left himself wide open for conflicting facts. Instead of being so adamant about the details, especially within a short time of discovering his wife was "missing," he should have said, "I don't remember what she was wearing. I don't know what her plans were for the day, and it didn't seem strange that she didn't answer the phones, so I wasn't worried." But no, Peterson traps himself in a timeline and details that are handily disproved by cell phone records, tan pants, and the dog being returned to the yard so quickly.

His purported whereabouts are inconsistent with the facts. Obviously, Peterson, in his wildest dreams, never imagined that his cell phone records would betray his geography. If he had stayed off the phone the entire day, his alibi may have been more difficult to disprove, and he could have told Brocchini with impunity that he left the house at 8 am, arrived in Berkeley in the morning, and decided to launch the boat at around 1 pm when other fishing spots were unfruitful. But, Peterson couldn't stay off his phone, checking his messages like a teenager who has snuck out of the house.

By far the most detrimental habit Peterson refused to stifle was his constant, neurotic contact with his girlfriend while the entire county was looking for his wife. Had he terminated that relationship in the first phone call after Laci's "disappearance" and refused further communication, he may have taken some of the heat off. Amber Frey's life would have been a lot easier, too. But, no, he needed his fix and, like a junkie, couldn't stop himself from perpetuating the romantic ruse, telling her he was in Europe and who knows what else, straight from *Adultery for Dummies.*

After Laci's murder, several of the principals of Tradecorp paid Scott a visit and effectively terminated his employment. Instead of using that opportunity to invest his freedom into the search for his wife, he continued to lie about having to

174

work, using that as an excuse to trade in Laci's Land Rover and to avoid confrontation with Laci's family and other accountability in Modesto.

When the remains of his wife and baby washed ashore, did Peterson rush back to Modesto to oversee the identification or be available for the tragic news? No, he was in San Diego, with a newly purchased Mercedes packed with camping gear, cash, knives, clothes, credit cards, his brother's ID, sporting his newly dyed hair and goatee. Is this not a classic example of self-sabotage? The only things he was missing were a bandolier and a large sombrero.

Those of you familiar with *MAD* magazine may recall the monthly comic, *Spy vs. Spy*, that pits a white-cloaked spy against his black-cloaked nemesis, with each trying to outsmart (and ultimately destroy) the other, using booby traps, secret weapons, and other subterfuge. The spies' behavior mirrors Peterson's alleged antics with the surveillance, which encompassed renting cars, erratic driving, dropping bogus clues, and hiding behind his lawyer, Kirk McAllister. If Peterson were really concerned about Laci's fate, why would he behave like Butch Cassidy? I believe it was because he never expected the bodies to surface and figured the police would never collect any hard evidence against him. His arrogance was only exceeded by his stupidity.

We can choose to be appalled or grateful for the deeply ingrained character defects of recklessness and irresistible impulse Peterson and his ilk possess. It makes it so much easier to remove them from society where they can no longer wreak destruction, heartbreak, callous cruelty, and chaos.

JUNE 23, 2004
STEALTH JUROR NO. 5

After seeing and hearing dismissed former Juror #5, Justin Falconer on MSNBC's "Abrams Report" this evening, I have several suggestions and observations about the ex-juror's remarks and where I believe the prosecution should focus its presentation of evidence from now on.

Falconer thought Peterson's excuse that he "just wanted to put the boat in the water" was reasonable. Either he slept (or played with his Gameboy) during the part in the People's opening statement about how many waterways were closer to Modesto than the Bay, or the People need to re-emphasize this fact. I wonder if Falconer would drive 180-mile round trip with $2.35-per-gallon gas prices merely to put his new toy in the water?

Falconer protests that Peterson is simply "unemotional in a crisis." The People need to demonstrate Mr. Innocent's lovey-dovey overtures to Amber Frey to show his ability to turn on and off his emotions like a faucet when they suit him. As a narcissist, he can't fake that of which he has no comprehension; namely: grief. The taped conversations with Frey will dispel that illusion pretty quickly. They need to bring those into testimony as soon as possible.

When Falconer expressed skepticism about how Peterson's boat was used to dump the body in the Bay, it tells me that the People need to show those sonar images of Laci in the bay from March 2003. If there was any hesitation prior to this interview to admitting those images, there should be none now. They need them as proof Peterson weighted her down there, that she was not alive and planted after the search was ongoing, and an expert in hydrology must clearly

175

demonstrate how she wound up on the east coast shoreline. This has now become vital evidence.

The one-trip theory, however deliberately vague, needs to be scrapped. The prosecution must go out on a limb to present a two-trip theory. While many in the jury may concede that the boat is ample for transporting the body to the channel, they may not be able to reconcile the timeline or the daylight factor.

Regarding Peterson's story about his "lost" wife and the impending holidays without her, Falconer quipped, "Guys say stupid stuff to women all the time." Well, maybe guys like Falconer say stupid stuff to women all the time, but in the context of these conversations, this statement shows Falconer to be an obvious oaf and Peterson apologist of the first order. He also goes on to make the same specious and irrelevant arguments that Geragos has emphasized: the meringue segment, Peterson's behavior not convincing that he is guilty of murder, that Laci could have changed her clothing prior to the dog walk, and that "pregnant women are crazy. One day they'll be bedridden, and the next day they think they're fat and will want to run a marathon." Apparently, Falconer resents his ex-wife and has projected his misogyny onto Laci Peterson, while completely ignoring all the issues that relate to Laci's difficulties with mobility and fatigue.

Even when asked if he heard Frey's testimony that Peterson lied to her about his wife, Falconer makes excuses for his buddy, indicating he hadn't heard it as evidence and could not judge that. Yet, he is willing to judge the police for testifying about the flashlight-throwing incident and condemn them for not putting that in their report. Typical of many of the Peterson apologists, Falconer has a double standard: one for the defendant and another for law enforcement.

As Dan Abrams pointed out, Falconer was "parroting" the defense; he would never have been convinced, perhaps without a video of the murder, that Peterson was guilty. The prosecution, meanwhile, needs to begin providing more substantial evidence earlier than it originally planned, and present its case with a more cohesive structure. It needs to remember that the jury has not been living this case for the last 18 months, and that it is not always aware of how to connect the dots.

While the Defense may be sorry that Mr. Falconer was dismissed today, we and the People should all breathe a sigh of relief and learn from this cocky dimwit that even though he didn't take notes or pay attention, he heard and remembered all the wrong things. This is a pivotal event for the prosecution, and it would behoove it to reconnoiter its strategy and heed the warning.

JUNE 72, 2004
LACI'S LAST DAY

December 23, 2002 was a clear, cool day in Modesto, California, high temperatures barely 50 degrees. It was a short day, with sunset at 6:30 pm. It was the last day that anyone would see Laci alive.

According to her mother, Laci generally arose around 7 am, perhaps alone, perhaps later than her husband, who either had not been home or had left before 8:30 am when the cleaning woman, Margarita Nava, arrived. Laci was dressed in her preferred maternity "uniform" of black capri pants and a white long-sleeved shirt. She hadn't accumulated a great deal of maternity clothes, and appeared in numerous photographs between November and late December wearing the same handful of outfits. She rested on the sofa with her swollen feet elevated, and watched TV or read until 9:45, when she left to go to Trader Joe's to buy specialty food items for the brunch she was hosting on Christmas day, including smoked salmon, a bottle of Grand Marnier, and a box of gourmet, all-natural cereal. The receipt from Trader Joe's indicated she checked out her purchases at 10:06.

An unverified report suggests Scott Peterson was at the warehouse by around 8:30 that morning. Also, based on another rumor, Peterson made a phone call to Amber Frey from the Sacramento airport sometime that day, telling her he was catching a plane to Maine or Alaska, or as far away in the Continental US he could fraudulently place himself to discourage Ms. Frey from calling him the next day.

Laci brought the groceries back home, carrying them in one or two bags at a time, put them away, and fixed herself something to eat at 11:30 am. She missed seeing Scott stop by briefly at 10:00 am to pick up a FedEx envelope that had been delivered that morning. After lunch, Laci went to Sweet Serenity Spa, arriving about 15 minutes early for her 1:00 facial waxing appointment, which took approximately 20 minutes. She was still wearing the black-and-white outfit, with the only noticeable jewelry a gold and silver watch on her wrist. She wore black, Mary Jane flats, and a black sweater over her shirt.

According to Ms. Nava, her cleaning was completed by 2:30, but Laci must have already been on her way to her monthly obstetric appointment, which was a routine examination that probably took only a half hour. According to the nurse practitioner who examined her, Laci was weighed and the usual vitals were taken, and she heard the baby's heart beat, reassuring and uplifting, knowing that she only had a little more than a month left before he was born. The last two months in any pregnancy, let alone during the holidays, always seem to take forever. There was no testimony in the trial to corroborate that Scott accompanied her to the appointment. She returned home before 4:00 to hear from her sister, Amy, who called from Vella Farms for suggestions about what to put in a gift basket for their paternal grandfather. At 4:45, Laci called her close friend, Stacy Bowers, to wish her a Merry Christmas, and that was to be the last time Stacy ever spoke to her. Meanwhile, Scott rented a mailbox at the (now) UPS store in Modesto just before 5 pm.

Sometime between 5:30 and 5:45, Laci and Scott arrive at Salon Salon to meet Amy in order for her to cut Scott's hair. Laci had changed her clothes sometime before or after her doctor's appointment, for she now wore tan capri pants and a dressy black blouse with a beige pattern. She was still wearing the black flats, along with a black car-length coat and a soft, cream-colored scarf. She consulted her sister about curling her hair, and practiced with the curling iron in the mirror for a few minutes. She was seen relaxing on a black leather sofa near the hair dryers, and turned down an offer of some tulips from the owner, who was going out of town for the holidays. She ordered pizza from a phone at the salon, and we can presume they picked up the pizza and went home after the haircut. The last person beside her husband to speak to Laci on December 23 was her mother, at 8:30 pm, when Laci called to confirm the couple's presence at the Rocha's Christmas Eve dinner the following evening.

177

We can theorize that Laci commenced undressing for bed, and Scott strangled or suffocated her while she was still wearing her undergarments and the tan pants. She may never have worn the diamond pendant that day, since it was found on the nightstand along with her everyday ring (a sapphire/diamond combination) and her watch. However, the 2-carat diamond earrings have never been found, and we can only surmise that she rarely, if ever, removed them.

Based on this itinerary, testimony from people who saw her that day, and phone records that revealed the geographical proximity of both Laci and Scott, there was no evidence of her being at the warehouse or office on the 23rd, or that they were together before 5:30 pm for the salon appointment. It appears that Scott was busy making preparations for his future life of freedom, and avoided being with Laci until early evening. At that point, he offered to pick up the basket for Amy because he intended to play golf the next morning to give himself a convenient alibi when he staged Laci's abduction, after he had completed his trip to the Bay late on the 23rd or early on the 24th, weighting down her body in the deep waters of the entrance channel off Richmond. Something compelled him to return to the Bay the next morning rather than go to Del Rio County Club as he originally planned.

Just as we can never truly appreciate Laci's anticipation, melancholy, or fear on the last day of her life, we will never know for certain what motivated Peterson to formulate his horrific scheme to annihilate his beautiful wife and unborn baby and destroy her dreams. It is now, during the trial, that we begin to comprehend the terrifying reality that the image of the perfect son and doting husband was a calculated charade concealing a cold-blooded killer.

JULY 2, 2004
"DUCTGATE"

With all the media attention, melodrama, hand wringing, and fanfare over the recent allegations that Detective Brocchini embellished (with the addition of "duct tape") on the information he received in a tip on Scott Peterson's purported statements to a friend about disposing a body in the ocean, what are the legal aspects of this issue?

At the beginning of the trial, Judge Delucchi instructed the jurors that: "An opening statement is not evidence; neither is it an argument. An opening statement is simply an outline...of what he or she believes or expects the evidence will show in this trial." In Distaso's opening statement, he mentions duct tape in one instance when showing Laci's remains: "She was also found with a line of duct tape running up her body, and we're going to talk about that later but not now." Other mentions of duct tape so far in the trial occurred when Distaso asks Brent Rocha:

Q: When he [Peterson] comes back with the duct tape, about how much time has elapsed from when he said he was leaving to go to the warehouse until he comes back with the duct tape?

And then:

Q: When you were done putting up these posters with the duct tape...

178

Later, during the cross-examination of Brocchini, Geragos introduces a number of potential "witnesses" through information and tips Brocchini received during the investigation, and counsel for the defense essentially testifies to those tips, although they are not intended to be offered as the truth. I don't know if the jury understood that disclaimer, but the judge reiterates these instructions during the redirect on June 29:

> "Yesterday or the last two or three days, Mr. Geragos was asking questions of this witness as to information he received. As I told you yesterday...that information is not being offered for the truth because it's not hearsay. This is information that he received and the issue here is to the reasonableness of his conduct and also to his state of mind...So that stuff that's not being offered for the truth that that's in fact what they saw or that's in fact what he heard or that's in fact what he said, it's what he was told..."

Subsequently, under Distaso's questioning, Brocchini proceeds to narrate a tip the police received from Miguel Espidia (who may, judging by his name, be a dark-skinned, not African American, male, and should be on Geragos's ever-expanding suspect list), an alleged acquaintance of Peterson's who describes a frighteningly familiar body disposal method:

> "He [Peterson] said that he would tie a bag around the neck, the neck with duct tape [sic]. Put weights on the hands, throw it in the sea..."

The mention of "duct tape" in this context would entail simple logic, since how else would you seal or fasten a plastic bag over a head in order to submerge the body in water? It's not as if this duct tape was being described as "running up the body," or wrapped around the legs, or layered, mummy-style. The specific use of duct tape (if Mr. Espidia said the word "duct," to specify the type of tape) in this instance bears no resemblance to its reference in Distaso's opening remarks. Therefore, how is the mention of duct tape any more prejudicial than the description of the body's being weighted down and thrown in the sea?

Based on the law, the opening statements are not evidence. The reiteration of tips through second- or third-hand accounts is not evidence. Therefore, there has been no perjury, no misconduct, and no misstatement of the "facts," since the Modesto police, and now the judge in the trial, have already discounted Espidia's story as evidence. Thus, I see no legal grounds for a mistrial. If Geragos plays an audiotape of Espidia's tip in order to impeach Brocchini with facts not in evidence, it will only serve to further prejudice his client to the jury, and return to haunt them once the forensic experts testify to the condition of Laci's remains. That would be beyond stupidity, incompetence, and perhaps even the netherworld of Geragos's standards of decency. I see "Ductgate" going by the way of "Pawngate," (the bogus pawn shop ticket receipt intimated to be Laci's Croton watch) and "Warehousegate," (the promised witness who saw Laci in warehouse December 20). In other words, up in smoke.

SUMMARY OF THE PEOPLE'S CASE - HALFTIME

The following is a summary of relevant testimony from witnesses in the trial of The People of California v Scott Lee Peterson, with some redundant testimony and Detective Allen Brocchini's marathon session omitted.

The purpose of this table is to outline the People's case so far. From a synopsis of the transcripts, I have distilled what I believe to be the most important information elicited by the prosecution, and its evidentiary value in proving their case against Peterson.

Witness	Salient Testimony	Probative or Evidentiary Value
Fred Eachus Manager, Trader Joe's	Showed receipt for Laci's purchases at Modesto store on Dec. 23.	Laci already shopped for her brunch; shows Peterson lied about Laci's needing to shop again on Dec. 24.
Tina Reiswig Sweet Serenity Spa employee	Said Laci appeared tired early afternoon of the 23rd; wore white top, black pants, black sweater to the spa.	Laci was too tired to walk the dog; Laci did not leave the house without an over garment.
Sharon Rocha Laci's mother	Detailed events of the 24th; Peterson's behavior; Laci's health; the couple's relationship history, growing suspicions of defendant.	Scott did not act like a grieving spouse; avoided confrontation from the family; did not participate in the searches; used language indicating consciousness of guilt.
	Laci complained of nausea and dizziness when walking the dog; was advised to curtail that activity, at least until later in the day.	Although Laci was probably not walking the dog since her problems in November, that was where Sharon thought she might have fainted or become disabled, which

		is why she went to the park after Peterson's phone call.
Ron Grantski Sharon Rocha's partner	Spoke to events of the 24th; his fishing habits, history with Laci, growing suspicions of defendant. Later supported by Harvey Kemple, Ron didn't believe Laci to be capable of walking steep path in park. Scott left expensive rod and reel in Grantski's garage after fishing trip previous winter. Recounted how Scott said he wanted Ron and Sharon to spend more time together as a family with Laci and him.	Scott kept the boat a secret from his in-laws and related unlikely fishing story to an avid fisherman.
Brent Rocha Laci's brother	Reiterated activities involving the search for Laci; couple's lifestyle, growing suspicions of the defendant, eventual confrontation about affair. Scott took two hours to retrieve duct tape from office/warehouse. Peterson told Brent the previous summer he hoped that the new salesman he hired (Olsen) would be more successful than he. Inconsistent information about where Scott and Laci got down payment. Brent understood it to	Indicates Scott ducked out of searches; took pains to avoid the press and the police; distanced the Rochas, and initially lied about affair. Peterson couldn't tell the truth about ordinary events, thus many of his statements lack credibility. Peterson was hinting that he was having financial difficulties or that the job was not as lucrative as he had hoped, thus implying financial

	have come from Lee & Jackie — $40,000 (20% down payment). Scott said that he had to cash in retirement portion of life insurance policy for down payment.	hardship and motive to eliminate the economic burden of a wife and baby.
	McKenzie was protective of Laci — barked aggressively at Brent.	
	Scott was not privy to details of trust; may not have been aware that he would not receive Laci's share of inheritance.	If unaware of the conditions of the trust, suggests an economic motive for the murder.
	Scott was not home at 2:00 am, 12/25 after his interview with Brocchini.	
	Scott told Brent that media and police were following him. Brent asked how he could tell the difference. Scott said that police drove Dodge or Chrysler and had dark tinted windows.	
	Scott told Brent that he made only one anchor and used the rest of the concrete on his driveway.	
Rose Rocha Brent's wife	Recalled remarks Peterson made about "hoping for infertility".	Peterson did not want a baby. Points to motive.
	Recounted that Scott was not shy in front of large groups or a camera — he gave a spontaneous 10-minute speech on video at Brent and Rose's wedding.	His sudden desire to be out of camera range seemed out of character, and he had other reasons to avoid being photographed.

Witness	Salient Testimony	Probative or Evidentiary Value
Sandy Rickard Sharon Rocha's friend	Remembered calm demeanor of defendant the night of the 24th; Peterson told her "he wouldn't be surprised if they found blood on the truck". Laci had complained of being "tired and heavy".	Peterson injured himself in the process of the crime and disposal. Laci was not walking in the recent past. Peterson lying about dog-walking scenario.
Gwen Kemple Sharon's cousin	Asked Peterson what Laci was wearing that morning (Dec. 24), and he said black pants and a white top, tennis shoes. Also asked Scott if he were ready for his son, and would he be teaching him sports, etc. Defendant said he had friends who would do that.	Inconsistent with clothing in which Laci was found; Scott did not look forward to fatherhood — points to motive.
Harvey Kemple Gwen's husband	Asked Peterson where he was all day, Peterson told him he was golfing (not fishing). McKenzie was protective of Laci. Kemple followed Peterson from the search center to the mall and to the country club; never saw Peterson hang fliers or participate in searches; testified that Peterson had a short fuse.	Peterson lied about his alibi; Laci was unlikely kidnapping victim; Peterson played golf and laid low rather than search for his wife; inference is that he knew she was dead, was not mourning her, and therefore may be responsible.
Karen Servas Laci & Scott's next-door	Discussed critical timeline of finding dog in the street at 10:18 am	Narrows the window of opportunity for Laci's abduction to 10 minutes

neighbor	Dec. 24; retraced her steps and receipts to confirm her itinerary. Found the side gate open when she went to put the dog back. Her concern about the time she put the dog back in the yard was prompted by a phone call from the defendant asking her if she was sure about the time.	from Peterson's cell phone call in the vicinity at 10:08 to the time the dog was returned, which demonstrates improbability of Peterson's story. Grass on leash shows dog was in recently cut lawn and not park. Side gate open may show Peterson left it open so the dog would wander out.
Bill Austin Owner of Austin's store	Testified to Christmas store receipt timestamp.	Corroborates Karen Servas's timeline.
Amie Kringbaum Neighbor	Routinely parked a white Ford Astrovan, with a Siemens logo on the side, on Covena Ave, across from the Peterson house. Noticed that the outdoor Christmas lights came on in the early evening in the Peterson's yard. Peterson told her he had been golfing all day.	Lays the foundation that the Siemens van may have been one of the vans in the neighborhood sighted by various defense witnesses yet to testify. The Christmas lights may have been left on from the night before and were not noticeable until dusk, inferring that Peterson never unplugged them. Or the lights were on a timer and Peterson lied about them. Peterson can't keep his stories straight whether he was golfing or fishing, implying that he was a careless liar or deliberately confused people.
Terra Venable	Noticed a package in the	Their house is close to

Witness	Salient Testimony	Probative or Evidentiary Value
Neighbor	Peterson mailbox when she and Amie returned from the store at 4:15–4:30, the afternoon of the 24th. The blinds at the Peterson home were closed all day, and neither she nor Amie had seen Laci all day.	the park entrance where Laci would have passed to walk the dog either in the park or around the neighborhood; thus they would have seen Laci if she had walked by before 1:00, during the time when any abduction could have occurred.
Susan Aquino Sharon Rocha's sister	Recounted that two police officers came by the Peterson home Christmas day in the early afternoon and notified the defendant that two witnesses claimed to have seen Laci walking in the park over the bridge. Scott told Susan that "Laci didn't walk that way," and didn't get excited about the possibility of Laci's being seen in the park.	Defendant knew Laci was not seen, which may indicate cognizance of her demise.
Witness	**Salient Testimony**	**Probative or Evidentiary Value**
Russell Graybill Postal carrier for that area	Calculated based on scanner records that he delivered the mail to the Peterson home between 10:35 and 10:50 am, the morning of Dec. 24. Described McKenzie as a territorial dog who would bark at him but not go beyond the front yard or follow him outside his boundaries.	If any abduction or suspicious activity was taking place in the neighborhood that morning (such as an abduction), the mailman would have been witness to it. Note the dog does not leave its territory, thus would not be wandering around the neighborhood with a leash attached. This refutes the defense claim that McKenzie was the dog seen running in

		the park without its owner.
Susan Medina Neighbor across the street	The Medinas left their home on Covena to visit their children in LA at 10:33 am on Dec. 24. They returned late afternoon of Dec. 26 to find a lot of police cars on Covena and that their house had been burglarized. Some of their property was quickly recovered.	Did not see Laci walking the dog and witnessed no abduction or other suspicious activity on the street. The burglars were already apprehended because of all the publicity about Laci, and were ruled out as having anything to do with her disappearance.
Byron Duerfeldt MPD Officer	Said that it was "unusual for a detective to be assigned to a missing person's case" but that based on what the officers at the house told him, it was his decision to have a detective respond early in the investigation. While he was the only officer in front of the house, after sending the three cops to the park and standing guard until the detective arrived, Duerfeldt was fielding emotional questions from Laci's family and friends, but Peterson never spoke to him.	Duerfeldt was the first of several officers who became immediately suspicious of the defendant, based on experience, instinct and observation. This was not a rush to judgment by Brocchini, but a collective impression by a conscientious group of experienced LE officers. Peterson's behavior was very odd for a man whose pregnant wife is missing. Reasonable people may infer this was because he was aware of the truth.
Craig Wend MPD Officer	Flew in the helicopter that searched the park with spotlights and heat sensing devices from around 8:30 pm until 10 pm.	Shows that the MPD used all available resources to search for Laci, and its response was thorough, rapid, and well organized — not the actions of an inept and

		sloppy department.
John Hodson MPD Officer	Was dispatched to work overtime the early hours of Dec. 24 to assist in the search at the park. He came across some homeless encampments at the park and the people there were cooperative when he asked to search the area, although some were upset because it had been the third time they were disrupted that evening.	Laci was never taken to the park or from the park. The homeless who camped near the river had nothing to do with her disappearance.
David Corder MPD Officer, formerly (at the time of the murder) assigned to the K-9 unit	Searched the neighborhoods, the creek bank, and the areas near the park entrance with his dog. Found nothing of evidentiary value. Described other resources used to find Laci: fire department, rafts, and all-terrain vehicles in mineshafts in La Grange.	No evidence of Laci in the park — refutes Peterson's story and infers that he staged Laci's disappearance. Further evidence of the major undertaking the MPD invested into finding Laci.
Derrick Letsinger MPD Officer One of the first officers who walked through the house to search for any sign of Laci or foul play	Observed and noted the guest bedroom closet in disarray (upside down duffel bag), the damp mops and recently dumped bucket of water, the dirty rags on the washing machine, and the "scrunched rug" against a side door. He overheard Peterson unable to answer questions about what he was fishing for or what bait he used.	The first impressions of a seasoned police officer were important in establishing that something was wrong with Peterson's accounting of events. It is clear from the officers who testified that no one had a personal agenda against Peterson, none of them had ever met or heard of him before, and they conducted themselves with utmost

		professionalism.
Matthew Spurlock MPD Officer	Arrived at the park at 6:11 pm (after Peterson had made a 911 call from his cell phone), and then went back to the house on Covena by 6:25. When doing a security check of the house with Evers, noticed the mops and bucket and moisture around the bucket as if it had been recently used. Noticed the phone book open to a color page, which we now know was an advertisement for a criminal defense attorney. Noticed the rug scrunched up against the door jam. Saw the rags on top of the washer that were still wet and dirty with sand and dirt. Saw two pairs of Laci's shoes: tennis shoes and sandals, outside the door in the patio area. He and Evers found Laci's purse with all her personal property (including her keys) hanging in the closet. Recounted that Peterson was unresponsive to questions about where he was, what bait he used, and what he was fishing for. The house appeared	The wet mops and recently emptied bucket indicated recent cleaning activities. Peterson may have been looking up criminal lawyers before the police arrived. Rug looked out of place in neat house — appeared to have been underneath something possibly dragged out of the house. Out of place disarray in a neat home made him and other officers suspicious. (It is their job, after all, to be suspicious.) Scott said that Laci wore her white tennis shoes when she went walking: those shoes were on the patio, inferring that Laci did not take a walk. Laci would not run errands without her purse, or likely leave the house without her keys. No sign of break-in, vandalism, or struggle in the house, therefore no burglars, vandals, or violent abduction scenario. Peterson has a temper, gets frustrated when things seem to be slipping out of his control,

| | neat, which made the guest room closet and the rug more conspicuous.

When he asked Peterson to leave the house, Peterson threw his flashlight and swore through gritted teeth, in apparent frustration. (At this part of the testimony, Geragos had the judge make the jury leave the room, objected to the fact that this anecdote was not in Spurlock's written report submitted in discovery, and motioned for a mistrial — which was denied). | as does his lawyer. |
| --- | --- | --- |
| **Witness** | **Salient Testimony** | **Probative or Evidentiary Value** |
| **Phillip Williams** Representative of Motherworks, Inc., a maternity clothier. | Explained how the style number sent to him by the MPD was tracked and a duplicate pair of maternity pants was sent to compare with those found on Laci's remains.

Other purchases Laci made were displayed, many of which looked familiar because of previously published photographs of Laci wearing them to various events. | Laci only owned one pair of tan, cropped maternity pants made by Motherhood. Therefore, the pants she was found in were the only ones she owned of that style and color, and most likely the ones she was wearing the evening before to the salon, unless the defense can produce another pair. |
| **Jon Evers** MPD Officer First to be dispatched to the park from | Evers filled out the missing person report, with details supplied by Peterson, including the clothing and jewelry she | Peterson lied about when he left the house, when he arrived at the marina, how long he was fishing, and changed his story |

the 9-1-1 call; first to speak to Peterson about fishing that day and that Laci was planning to "walk the dog," and the rest of Peterson's timeline, which will later be shown to be false based on cell phone records and other documentation.	was last wearing — which was also proven to be false. Evers accompanied Brocchini and Peterson to the warehouse and witnessed the cursory search of the office and warehouse, the boat and Peterson's behavior.	several times about what Laci was doing before he left. Peterson's inconsistency in his activities, yet the excess of details (under stressful circumstances) regarding Laci, and then the easily disproved details (jewelry, timeline) shows him to be curiously (if not pathologically) dishonest. A reasonable person can infer he was reciting a rehearsed scenario. Peterson did not behave like a person in distress.
Lisa Martin Nurse with the OB staff where Laci received her prenatal care	Testified to the dates of the sonograms and various details about Laci's pregnancy. Determined the EDC (estimated date of confinement) or due date of the baby was 2/10/03, and remained that date after the second ultrasound.	Gestational age of baby will be a factor to the defense; thus this witness establishes the documentation that Connor's due date was 2/10/03, putting the baby at approximately 33 weeks' gestation on 12/24/02.
Stacey Josephson Receptionist at the OB office who retrieves messages left on the answering machine	There were no messages left regarding Laci Peterson from the afternoon of the 24th, until the morning of the 27th when the office reopened.	Scott never called the OB's office to inquire if Laci had called or was in labor. Inference: he knew she had not.
Victoria Guadamuz Employee of Motherhood	Testified to what Laci bought at that store in August.	Laci purchased only one pair of stone (tan) cropped maternity pants from Motherhood — the

Maternity in Modesto		ones in which her remains were found.
Amy Rocha Laci's sister	Had a close relationship with Laci, cut Scott's hair on the 23rd, never noted any overt problems with the couple that night or any time.	
	Recalled Laci wore "cream" or stone cropped pants and a black top with a small cream pattern that night, but was unable to unequivocally identify the pants that matched the ones found on Laci's remains. She said Laci also wore a black coat and cream scarf.	Fact: Laci wore cream/stone cropped pants the night of the 23rd. Fact: Laci's remains were found in cream/stone cropped pants. Fact: Laci had only one pair of tan maternity pants from Motherhood. Inference: Laci was murdered the night of the 23rd while still wearing those pants.
	Laci complained about being tired and had not mentioned walking the dog since the nausea incident in November.	Laci did not leave the house without a coat or sweater.
	Peterson offered to pick up a fruit basket at Vella Farms, a store near Del Rio, because said he was golfing on the 24th. Vella Farms called the afternoon of the 24th to say nobody had picked up the basket. Amy called Scott's cell phone and he did not answer. She picked up the basket herself.	
	Amy had never color-treated Peterson's hair.	Peterson's dyed hair in April of 2003 was an anomaly.

| | Amy never spoke to or saw Laci anytime on Dec. 24.

At a search of the house in February, Amy found what she thought could be the top Laci wore that night of the 23rd, wadded up in a dresser drawer. She found what she believed to be the cream scarf, and the shoes, but not the black coat, and the issue of the pants was muddled by cross-examination, so it is unclear what she saw in the house. | Laci's lack of communication to anyone on Dec. 24 indicates she was dead.

There may be other issues regarding the jewelry Laci and Amy inherited that will be elaborated in future testimony. |
| **Margarita Nava** Housekeeper | Said Laci wore black/white in the AM on Dec. 23rd, appeared tired, did not walk the dog, had already done the shopping for her brunch, and that the floors had all been cleaned, left the dirty rags in a bucket on top of the washing machine. | Refutes Peterson's story about the floors needing mopping. Shows Peterson emptied out the rags from the bucket in order to use it on Dec. 24. Dog walking not part of routine anymore. |
| **Witness** | **Salient Testimony** | **Probative or Evidentiary Value** |
| **Mary Anna Felix** Jeweler employed at Edwards Jewelers, Modesto, in 2002 | Saw Laci as a customer 10 to 12 times, and was working with her to redesign a wedding ring using the diamonds from her ring combined with a large diamond from her grandmother's ring she had inherited. The value of the finished ring was estimated at $55K.

Testified that Laci wore a | The bezel pendant, repaired watch, and the sapphire/diamond ring |

	reconfigured bezel diamond pendant at every visit, and claimed never to take it off, not even to have it cleaned. Laci told her that of the jewelry she had inherited, she was going to keep one of the watches (which she had repaired), the diamond earrings, the bezel pendant, and the sapphire/diamond ring she wore in lieu of her wedding ring while the new ring was being made.	were found in Laci's bedroom, inferring that she had never left the home on Dec. 24. But the earrings and one other watch were unaccounted for after her disappearance, implying she was wearing them when she was murdered, or they were taken off afterwards and hidden, thrown out, or pawned.
David Fernandez Agricultural trade associate	Attended conference where Peterson and Sibley met in Oct.; was present at dinner during the sexually explicit exchange between Peterson and Sibley and excused himself as quickly as he could after he ate dinner.	Even a male peer found the conversation uncomfortable, which shows how extreme Peterson's vulgarity and deplorable manners.
Eric Olsen Peterson's employee at Tradecorp	Worked out of his home, rarely visited the office/warehouse, never saw the boat. Was aware that Peterson was married and his wife expecting a child, and was present for the trade show dinner and described the conversation between Peterson and Sibley as "inappropriate." When Sibley contacted him weeks later to verify Peterson's marital status, Olsen refused to comment, considering he	The person most likely to see Peterson's boat was never told about it or saw it, either. Provides another account of Peterson's overt flirtation with Sibley. Peterson was letting his responsibilities slide in early December (or prior), which indicates he had other priorities, including possible murder preparations. Begs the question: did

	was still employed by Peterson at the time and wisely sensed a conflict of interest. He resigned his position with Tradecorp effective Dec. 26, due to the fact that he got another job offer from a larger company, that Peterson was slacking in his duties as manager, that "things were not getting taken care of," and that his health benefits never materialized. The sales job he and Peterson shared never entailed working with farm equipment or anything more elaborate or dangerous than an electric pump. Noticed a "partial bag of concrete" in the warehouse in November. After his resignation, Olsen met with Peterson and the new employee to review sales notes, and Peterson bragged that Geraldo had interviewed him.	Peterson have health insurance and maternity benefits? If not, lends to motive since an uninsured childbirth would be a major debt. Peterson lied about cutting his hands all the time to Diane Sawyer, saying he worked on farm machinery. Where is the rest of the concrete? Peterson was more interested in his new celebrity than he was in finding his "missing" wife. Indicates his knowledge, if not participation in her death.
Mike Almasri Agricultural trade associate	Interviewed with Peterson for a sales position with Tradecorp in the summer of 2002; was not made an offer. During the course of lunch at Applebee's in Fresno, defendant mentions he is married	Shows how Mike would know about Peterson's marital status.

	and just bought a home in Modesto. Later in December in another conversation with other associates, including Shawn Sibley, Mike mentions that Peterson is married, and there is not more than one Scott Peterson with Tradecorp.	Peterson evidently never expected Mike and Shawn to be comparing notes, which points to his self-centered and careless nature.
Shawn Sibley Agricultural trade associate	Met Peterson at a trade show in October 2002 (dates have been confused in testimony from Oct. 14 or 24, but more likely was the 14, 15.) During dinner exchanged inappropriately intimate conversation of a sexual nature with Peterson; spent the evening with him until 3:30am drinking, talking. Peterson misrepresented himself to Sibley as single, wealthy, living in Sacramento (one of two homes he claimed he owned), formerly a principal at another company for which he had a business card (bogus), and that he was looking for a long-term meaningful relationship with an intelligent women, and that he liked thin women. Peterson and Frey meet, spend their first date	Peterson is a predatory adulterer, not simply a "cad" or someone who has a weak moment when opportunity arises. He sought out an extramarital relationship and aggressively pursued it once it materialized. He has no qualms about denying the existence of his wife (and impending baby), or fabricating real estate and employment holdings, which indicates he routinely manifests his fantasy with strangers without any regard for the truth. One can infer he has a lot of practice in this game, which points to a motive of desire for emancipation.

	overnight, and are later seen at a social event held by Sibley. In early Dec., when Sibley learned from Mike A. that Peterson was married, she confronted him via telephone and threatened bodily harm, as well as telling Amber. She also subscribed to a search service to locate marriage licenses in California counties. She started her search in Sacramento, but never searched Stanislaus county because Peterson called her and begged through racking sobs to let him tell Amber that he had lost his wife, that it was too painful to discuss, which he promised to before Dec. 9. Sibley claims she remained suspicious of him, and on Dec. 29 at a birthday party where Amber was present, Amber received a phone call alerting her that Peterson was the same man in Modesto whose wife was missing. Sibley and Frey contacted the police immediately.	His claim that he "lost" his wife was either clairvoyant or the panicked words of a pathological liar who has been cornered. He slips up by revealing his plans to really "lose" his wife. Clearly points to premeditation.
Witness	**Salient Testimony**	**Probative or Evidentiary Value**
Jeff Shumacher Jeweler with Edwards Jewelers	Was involved in designing Laci's new ring (combining the stones), repairing some items, and appraising the value of the jewelry Laci	Laci's response to the value of the jewelry was that her husband would be "very happy," implying a potential motive. We have already learned all

196

	brought to him and Ms. Felix, which was valued at over $100K.	of the most valuable jewelry was accounted for except the diamond earrings and possibly a watch (later possibly accounted for). This suggests Peterson removed Laci's jewelry, or she was removing it prior to bed. It also casts doubt on the abduction theory, since Laci normally wore at least the sapphire/diamond ring, and the diamond pendant, along with the repaired watch, and her diamond earrings.
Robin Rocha Dennis Rocha's sister, Laci's aunt, daughter of Helen Rocha and co-trustee of her estate	She distributed her mother's jewelry to Laci in Nov. 2002, and was asked to identify any missing pieces when Laci was found murdered. She noticed the diamond earrings (with threaded backs, thus hard to remove), and a watch was missing. Ms. Rocha identified a photo from an E-bay listing (presumably Laci's listing) as the missing watch.	The picture from an E-bay listing suggests the watch was not missing, but rather was sold on E-bay prior to Dec. 2002; thus the defense's pawn shop ticket concerning a "Croton" watch is a red herring. The threaded backs on the diamond earrings make them difficult to remove. Did Peterson leave them because of that, or did he remove them, only later to dispose of them or pawn them in another city?
Mike Imelio Pool service technician	Serviced the Peterson's pool every Tuesday (except Christmas eve), and testified that the dog always barked and was very protective of Laci.	No way would that dog allow anyone to abduct Laci, without vociferous barking and possibly a major attack on the perpetrator. Unless, of course, the perp was his master.

197

David Brooks	Recounted that Laci	Pawning jewelry implies
Owner, local	came into the shop twice	there was a cash flow
pawn shop	in Dec. 2002, once on	problem and that quick
(Brooks Pawn	the 10th and again with	cash might be needed,
& Jewelry),	Peterson on the 14th (the	especially for Peterson's
Modesto	same date as the	date on Dec. 14. The
	Christmas party with	conclusion that Peterson
	Amber).	used the proceeds of his
		pregnant wife's pawned
	She sold some gold	jewelry to entertain his
	chains on the 10th for	new girlfriend is really
	$140.00, and some rings,	beyond the pale.
	a charm, and some	
	chains on the 14th for	
	$110.00.	
Victoria	Confirmed Laci's visit to	Since Laci didn't bring
Brooks	the pawnshop and did	her ID, can infer that the
Co-owner with	not bring her ID, so	money was going to
husband,	Peterson signed for the	Peterson, and that she
David, of	loan/sale.	was annoyed by having
Brooks Pawn &		to sell the jewelry that
Jewelry		day.
	On redirect (after	
	Geragos asked about	We can only imagine
	problems between Laci	how annoyed she would
	and Scott) that Laci	have been had she
	appeared "agitated" and	known for what purpose
	"hesitant towards him"	he needed it.
	when the defendant	
	rubbed her belly.	
Stacey	Recounted Laci was	If a person tells her best
Boyers	getting dizzy and sick	friend she is having
Laci's best	from walking and was	difficulty walking and was
friend, since	told not to walk any more	told not to walk, chances
childhood	in November. She never	are she is not walking
	personally walked with	any more.
	her during the	
	pregnancy.	
	When Laci came to her	
	Christmas party on Dec.	
	14 (the night Peterson	
	was with Amber at	
	another party in Fresno),	
	Laci told Stacey she was	
	exhausted from having to	

	walk from where she parked a few houses down.	
	Testified that Laci told her she was depressed about the holidays and that she was too tired all the time to entertain, as was her custom.	Why would Peterson be concerned about a "clean house" when his wife was missing? This behavior may indicate a pathological need to clean as an obsessive/compulsive consciousness of guilt. Peterson's aversion to using his pictures implies he was hiding from someone, most likely his girlfriend, and didn't want her to put two and two together.
	On Dec. 25, after the chaotic night before, witness went to Peterson's home and observed him vacuuming the area around the washer and dryer and saying, "I can't keep the house clean enough". Peterson made the rule that the media could not enter the volunteer center until 9:30, and by then he was usually gone.	
	Another "rule" Peterson made was that no pictures of him could be used in media shots or hung on the wall of the center, and he wouldn't allow any wedding pictures to be shown/published.	
	Stacey was not aware of Peterson's affair with Amber from Laci.	
Lori Ellsworth Laci's friend	Reiterated Stacey's recollection of the events at the party and Scott's "rules" at the volunteer center.	
	The only interesting thing	The fact that Laci's friends embraced rather

	to come from Lori's testimony was the fact that after her press conference for the MPD, Amber was an overnight guest at Lori's house, and was befriended by some of Laci's other friends	than shunned Amber indicates their acceptance that she was a victim, and bore no culpability for Laci's disappearance.
Debra Wolski Laci's yoga instructor	Laci enrolled for 10 yoga sessions, and was the last student on Dec. 20 still pregnant, and she complained of being very uncomfortable. Debra eliminated all the exercises except deep breathing and relaxation. Narrated that Laci remarked that her dog "must think she is mad at him because she no longer walks him", and that she never leaves the house without her cell phone. Later when asked to identify jewelry Laci wore, she did not identify the "E-bay watch" as one Laci wore to yoga class. Debra also testified that Laci needed help to her car because of her weak condition, but this testimony was struck from the record after stipulation by both sides because the witness had never told the investigators this information prior to the trial.	Laci was not walking the dog. The E-bay watch was not one Laci wore, thus would not be an item pawned by her phantom abductors.

Timothy Helton MPD Officer, supervisor of the equestrian unit at the time of the incident in 2002; second in command to Cloward in charge of search efforts	Investigated the Tracy tip in which a person said Laci was being held in a building there — no findings. Located some of the stolen Medina property and was involved in the arrests of Steven Todd and Glenn Pearce, the now convicted burglars. Also recovered the Medina's safe, which was damaged from being forced open and hidden under a wooden crate where the burglars were apprehended.	Shows more of the comprehensive search undergone for Laci, including the equestrian unit, follow- ups of numerous realistic tips, and the enormous manpower and resources devoted to the case; not the actions of a rush-to-judgment.
Ron Welsh Criminalist – firearms expert	Testified that Peterson's pistol — seized from his glove box Dec. 24 (a Llama .22 caliber semi-automatic handgun) — was not jammed and fired normally under testing. The gun uses a .22 long rifle cartridge, the same used in rifles, and was loaded with 8 rounds (a full magazine) when confiscated. The gun was dusty and debris, fiber and hairs were adhering to the exterior (handles were removed) and were found inside the barrel, but not enough to cause it to jam.	Peterson lied to Brocchini about the gun's misfiring/jamming and when he last used it. Why were the handles removed from the gun? Were they broken when the gun was used as a blunt force object? Were the hair(s) and debris collected from the interior and exterior of the gun tested? Peterson had long guns (rifles) in his home, which do not require registration, and also admitted to owning another handgun that he claims was stolen from his vehicle some time past. The gun information suggests there may be more evidence to come

		regarding forensics.
Ronald Cloward Sergeant with the MPD, Search Incident Commander in charge of the search for Laci Peterson	Organized search using volunteers, LE agencies (allied agencies from other counties), search dogs, K-9 units, ground officers, fire department personnel, divers, helicopters, boat teams, side scan sonar, equestrian unit, explorer scouts, and in his words, "the biggest [effort] I have ever been involved in." Recounts a sampling of how they followed up on numerous tips. Searched vacant houses and eliminated as many known local offenders as they could track down. Testified that Todd's sister was wearing one of the stolen necklaces from the Medina burglary, and detailed some of the circumstances surrounding Pearce and Todd's arrest on Jan. 2, 2003. (They were cooperative.) Directed search of abandoned mines and other areas outside Stanislaus County. Regarding the search of the SF Bay, noted the extreme currents at flood tide, the poor visibility, the difficult conditions, the vastness of the Bay, and continuous frustration with boats,	Demonstrates the huge effort in manpower and logistics the search for Laci Peterson entailed. Clearly, all possible resources were used, including time and talent from agencies throughout the state, and professionals recruited from all over the country to assist in providing technology and equipment for the massive undertaking. Peterson's numerous trips to the bay belie his statements to Cloward that he was only going to focus his efforts on looking for a live Laci. He certainly spent a lot of time, expense, and trouble in renting vehicles and driving to the East Bay a half dozen or more times. Once again, his actions speak louder than words. The Bay was far too large a body of water to search thoroughly with any degree of success. By the time the bodies washed ashore, the divers, sonar and boats had covered only a fraction of the potential areas where she could have been submerged, although there is reason to believe she was

	equipment and sonar maintaining position on target areas. For whatever reason (and I may know why) the direct and cross-examination skips over the March 13 sighting of Laci's body by sonar in the Richmond entrance channel. This may yet come out in Detective Owen's testimony. On redirect, recounted that Peterson called him and indicated he was searching for Laci in places where he would "find her alive," which precluded the water searches the family organized.	sighted in March. Hopefully, more details of that sighting will come out later in the trial from Detective Evers or others involved in the investigation.
Dr. Tina Edraki Laci's OB/GYN	Confirmed that Laci's first ultrasound was July 16, 2002, and the second was September 21 (at around 20 weeks.) Laci called on November 6 complaining of dizziness, shortness of breath, and nausea symptoms when she walked. The doctor advised her not to walk or exercise anymore.	Laci had a routine pregnancy without complications and expressed concern about carrying the baby full term because of her childhood surgery. She was obviously very much looking forward to the birth of her child. Based on her conscientiousness and obvious regimen of pre-natal care, was likely following her doctor's instructions.

203

JULY 6, 2004
GERAGOS V BROCCHINI

Traditionally, there is an expected professional, albeit somewhat artificial, enmity between a criminal defense lawyer and a lead detective in a murder investigation, especially if the defense is purporting that his client is "factually innocent." Peterson's counsel's objectives are not simply to defend him, but to avenge him with vehement indignation and accusations of misconduct. Geragos isn't satisfied with fabricating reasonable doubt based on weak evidence; he has to attack the people in the case against Peterson in an effort to reinvent his client as a wronged and falsely accused victim.

The three days in which Detective Allen Brocchini suffered aggressive and inflammatory cross-examination from Geragos served as a trial within a trial that temporarily transformed the courtroom into a boxing ring, with Geragos hoping to portray himself as the underdog contender fighting for his life against the heavily favored bully, the "rogue cop." Of course, this was absurd fiction, since Peterson is as guilty as sin, and it is laughable to consider him much more than a sneaky, lying, arrogant sociopath without morals, conscience or an iota of social graces. However, giving Cecil B. Geragos his due, let us cut through the illusion and examine the real reasons that Peterson (through his million-dollar thespian/director) hates Brocchini with the white-hot intensity of a uranium reactor.

What does Peterson (judging by the questions from his fitting proxy, Geragos) hate most? Having a person with power and authority calling him stupid, injuring his false ego, demeaning his social status, questioning his integrity, emasculating his virility, and curtailing his compulsive whims. Who inflicted the most damage to his image with his friends, family, and ultimately the world? Brocchini! I imagine that from the moment Brocchini laid eyes on Peterson the night of December 24, 2002, he said to himself, "This guy is a lying, sniveling, murdering little weasel, and I'm going to take him down if it's the last thing I do." Geragos would have us believe the detective's mission was some kind of crime. It was more the impetus of well-honed intuition and street smarts, developed from years of experience in dealing with creeps.

At the time, Laci's family, friends, and neighbors were paralyzed by shock, and their natural naiveté, based on their personal ignorance of sociopaths, required a painful but unfortunately necessary wake-up call. Brocchini essentially told them, "Forget all your previous notions about Peterson being a good husband, and a nice, harmless guy who wouldn't hurt a fly. He has been a walking time bomb, living a double life and harboring violent fantasies, and is more than capable of murdering his pregnant wife and sinking her body in the sea without skipping a beat." The smiling, soft-spoken, country-club boy's mask was peeled off, and behind it was a hideous monster.

So, what did Brocchini do to deserve Peterson's wrath, recently manifested in Geragos's vicious defamation campaign? From the beginning, Brocchini didn't take Peterson's word for anything, and made him prove every aspect of his alibi. He took Peterson's gun, took his mops and bucket, took pictures of his boat, took

204

his statement, eventually took his truck, boat, computers, clothes, cell phones, and finally took his freedom. You don't take things from narcissists; they take things from you! Obviously, there were many others involved in the decisions to search his home and confiscate his property, but Peterson blames Brocchini. The other nameless, faceless law enforcement that participated in the investigation were merely following Brocchini's vindictive directive. Far be it for Peterson (or his lawyer) to take any responsibility for the actions or prejudicial opinions of the DA, media, or public. It's all Brocchini's fault.

Brocchini is an easy target for Geragos's tirades, too. He has less than perfect work habits, his documentation leaves a lot to be desired, he was unapologetic about his desire to plant seeds of doubt in people's minds early on, and he's defiant and uncooperative. However, he will not lie down on the altar to be slaughtered as the scapegoat for the defense, despite the media experts' predictions. Nor will he be responsible for a mistrial or grounds for an appeal. In contrast to a lifetime of escaping responsibility and a career of dodging blame by impugning other people or circumstances, and fierce, habitual denial, Peterson will finally face his Waterloo, with Brocchini as his Wellington.

JULY 15, 2004
THE PARENTS' MEDIA PRESENCE

In light of the current arguments in the trial of the People v Peterson regarding Scott's media interviews, and the recent appearance of Peterson's parents on ABC's "20/20" with Barbara Walters, I recalled several interesting reported statements from Lee and Jackie Peterson. While the parents' statements to the media will not be used against them in a court of law, we certainly have the right to evaluate their veracity and intentions based on their inconsistencies and obvious departure from what we now know to be the truth.

Jackie Peterson: [Regarding the police deliberately alienating Scott from the Rochas] "They know it too. They [Laci's family] supported him fully until the police misled them, and that was to divide and separate him from them. He was their support. They were his support."
How could Scott's affair with Amber Frey (and his denial) be received in any other way but as a bitter betrayal by the Rochas? How could the news of a life insurance policy, easily substantiated by documentation, cause antagonism? A reasonable person would instead ask her son why he lied about the affair and the policy when it served to only make him seem uncooperative and duplicitous.

Lee Peterson: "They worked strictly on a theory that was dreamt up by this lead detective within the first eight hours, and they've pursued it backward from there and they have neglected so many good leads."

Perhaps detectives "dream up" theories all the time, but the statistics regarding domestic murders, or the lack of cooperation from Scott, or the fact that he mopped the floor and got all cleaned up before he called anyone could not be overlooked by attentive officers at the scene. Never mind that he was hiding under a baseball cap (I wish it had been his cowboy hat) and not allowing his face to be visible on camera or pictures of him published. Forget the fact that he didn't walk a single block to look for Laci after the first night. His blatant lies to the media, to the Rochas, and to investigators were misunderstood. Besides, if Brocchini were not the kind of man to rely on his immediate instincts, he's in the wrong profession.

> Lee Peterson: "And one of these gentlemen - and they are prominent people - he's a three-term council member up there and an attorney, and they saw her and they know her and the police have disregarded this. If it doesn't fit their theory, by God, they don't want to investigate it. I just can't be any more emphatic than that. And we're gonna pursue this thing."

This statement refers to Bill Mitchell, who was channel-surfing for a football game on December 24, and who, in fact, did not know Laci Peterson or see her face that morning. If his late wife's testimony was so pivotal, Geragos was remiss in failing to formally depose her.

> Jackie Peterson: "Now conveniently, the body has been found where he told them he went fishing. Why would he go 80 miles fishing, come home with a receipt and buy gas and food along the way, have a receipt of the dock and tell the police exactly where he went fishing - and the body would be there! That does not make sense. It's too damn inconvenient for that."

Au contraire, the bodies surfacing where they did were *very inconvenient* for Scott. Did she mean to say "convenient," as in the police planted them? Does she actually expect anyone to believe that someone intentionally placed those bodies in the Bay to frame her son, or that law enforcement somehow hid the decomposing human remains for months only to later place them in the marsh and on the rocks at Pt. Isabel? This might work as the plot of an "X-Files" episode, but is beyond the most macabre imaginations, except maybe Geragos's.

> Jackie Peterson: "No drugs. No financial problems. He worked three jobs to put himself through college and put his wife through college. They both worked hard to get everything they had, and they were enjoying it to the hilt. And they adored each other."

No drugs? We now know Scott carried Viagra and sleeping pills, and there are rumblings from the defense camp that he was on tranquilizers, although he claims he never took so much as an aspirin. No financial problems? I suspect that when Peterson's bank statements and financial records come into evidence, they will reveal (similarly to Michael Peterson) a man swamped in debt and in jeopardy of losing his job. His promise to Amber that he would be altering his traveling requirements by late January was in part due to his impending separation from Tradecorp.

Lee Peterson: "They'll see the police have just bungled this investigation from day one. They can come after me. That's fine. But they've bungled this case."

Jackie Peterson: "I think every man out there should be in fear if this is the way the police worked. If a crime happens to your wife, you'd better know you're with six people and they weren't drunk and they are good friends who are going to be able to put up with this. If they have any kind of shady character, the police will dismiss them and you'll be ruined."

Certainly, Lee Peterson hopes that Geragos can convince the jury that the Modesto police "bungled" the investigation, but I believe that evidence of the enormous efforts expended by numerous agencies, and the major investment of resources and dedicated personnel will refute this argument and satisfactorily compensate for several mistakes made by individuals involved in the case. Jackie Peterson's statement is still puzzling, since we now know Scott has no friends, drunk or otherwise, and that he has no exonerating alibi for the date of Laci's disappearance. In fact, he has the world's worst alibi.

Jackie Peterson: [In reference to Scott inquiring about selling the house] "That's not what he said. He said he didn't want to live there anymore. He said he didn't want to bring Laci home to that and what would they get out of it. He did not sign a listing. He did not go to a realtor."

It's probably true that Peterson said he didn't want to live in Modesto any more, but it wasn't because of his worrying about Laci. He may not have signed a listing (and that's because it was not legally possible, or he would have), but from the trial we have learned he consulted with two realtors. It seems rather obvious from where Peterson derived his careless lying habit.

Lee Peterson: "Did you folks know that there's another pregnant lady that was floating in that bay in January? Another torso and two other pregnant women missing in that area. And that place is polluted with parolees."

So far in trial, Geragos hasn't brought up the Evelyn Hernandez case (if this is Lee's reference), but we are barraged with countless possible suspects for the murder, most recently the half dozen or so sex offenders from the controversial discovery list.

Jackie Peterson: "I will tell you exactly what happened. He sold his car because his job has changed. He doesn't have to haul stuff any more. And he couldn't afford it. He was making a payment, and we loaned him a car to drive instead. Apparently from what we now hear, the police had a device attached to it...His attorney knew where he was at all times. We talked to him every day...They lost him."

If Scott didn't have to "haul stuff any more," why trade in the Land Rover? It was paid off and would have served his transportation purposes nicely. Instead, he continues to be obliged to make the monthly $650 Ford truck payment, and then incurs yet another car payment for the new Dodge truck. Does that make sense? Who's paying the freight on these vehicles?

> *Lee Peterson: "It's just not in him," [to murder his wife] "I've never seen him mad. The only time I've seen him mad is - if he misses a golf shot, he might get a little mad."*

> *"It was a relief when we heard he was arrested. That sounds strange, but at least we knew where he was every night and that he was safe, relatively safe."*

Perhaps Lee is projecting his own image onto this scenario, saying, "It's just not in *me*;" thus it could not be in his son. No parents want to believe their child capable of such a horrible act, but the outlandish notion that Scott never showed anger or had a temper is characterizing their son as some kind of robot. The lack of demonstrative rage and despair from this alleged "innocent" family is extremely disturbing. This may be a well-defended denial system in place, but I read between the lines that their "relief" at Scott's incarceration is tantamount to saying, "At least from there he can't do anything too stupid or dangerous or harm another person." When trying to glean the truth from people, it's often what they don't say that is more significant than what they freely admit.

JULY 18, 2004
REGARDING HENDEE

Henry Dodge Hendee, a detective with the Modesto Police Department since 1993, spent the better part of July 13, 14 and 15 on the witness stand in the trial of the People v Peterson, and most of that on cross-examination. I was hoping to find some significant scraps in the nearly 500 "pages" of the transcripts, but there were slim pickings, to say the least. I did notice some consistent strategy from the defense to concentrate on where evidence was *not* found, versus where evidence may have been found and was not elaborated upon. I also noticed that, as usual, media reports and misinformation about Hendee's testimony abounds, including more alleged defense "bombshells" based on out-of-context or incomplete reporting about the gallon pitcher and the anchor found on Peterson's boat. Based on what remains compelling evidence of cement residue on the trailer work surface, and clothing found in both Peterson's home and warehouse, this may deem relevant to sketching the details of a two trips to the Bay theory. Here is a quick overview and my analysis:

Search of the House December 26 and December 27, 2002

- Two pairs of black maternity pants were found in a white shopping bag in the nursery. The pants looked "unused," but did not have price tags on them as has been misreported elsewhere. Black pants were one of the items listed on the search warrant, along with specific jewelry. The search warrant affidavit was not testified to or published on the court update site.

- A Louis Vuitton purse (not a wallet, and not a wrapped gift) was in the living area. No further details about its contents, if any.
- The police found no blood evidence, but the FBI did conduct a Luminol test. The results of that have not yet been revealed.
- Hendee found the boat cover (which he describes as a tarp) in the shed under the leaf blower, smelling of gasoline.
- A duffel bag (how many of these does Peterson own?) was found in the nursery closet containing men's clothing and unspecified "camping gear." It appeared to be a quick "getaway" bag.
- An ultrasound photograph on the dresser in the nursery was taken into evidence. Earlier in the trial, Geragos asked Brocchini about Kim McGregor's saying that Peterson was supposedly upset about this. Since it was triple hearsay at that point, we will have to wait for McGregor to hear the rest of the story.

Search of the Warehouse December 27, 2002

- There was what appeared to be blood stains on the man door inside the office that later tested negative.
- There was concrete spilled in a large area of the warehouse.
- Samples from the shop-vac proved not to be concrete mix but possibly lime; however, that came from Geragos, so it remains to be verified. Lime powder may be used to reinforce the concrete mix used to make anchors, or it could have been an old spill. We know Peterson is a slob, so everything on the floor isn't evidence.
- A camouflage jacket was found in a duffel bag (this one canvas) on the back of the boat. Disassembled fishing rods, the yellow-handled pliers with the hair twisted and crimped in the teeth, a small jack, a spare tire for the trailer, an oar, and other junk were found on the boat. I think Peterson threw everything in there after he returned, and much of it wasn't with him on his "fishing trip."
- A concrete anchor in the shape of a pail, with a small rebar loop encased, was found on the boat. A water pitcher with concrete residue and dirty water was on the wooden trailer next to a dustpan and spilled concrete mix, where several (at least four) circular voids were apparent indicating other molds for other anchors.
- In a bucket nested inside another bucket, they found a plastic bag with black boots, a black knit watch cap, and one blue glove. (Maybe Michael Jackson has the other one.)
- A roll of chicken wire and a claw hammer with what appeared to be more concrete residue was in the Ford truck bed, near the Greenlee toolbox.
- Hendee found several blood spots inside the Ford truck, probably all Peterson's.
- The FBI conducted a "Hemoglow" test on the inside of the truck.

- Marble-sized concrete chunks were found in the bed liner, and a receipt from Home Depot for "concrete products" was found in the glove box.
- More men's clothing, unspecified but appearing "new" was found in a bag in the back of the truck cab. Peterson has more luggage and clothes than any 10 people!
- Yet another cell phone was found plugged into the lighter outlet of the Ford truck.
- A collage of pictures and paper (collected and then admitted as evidence for the defense) covered the window between the office and warehouse, so it was undetermined if the boat could be seen by someone standing in the office looking out.
- The auxiliary wheels were on a pallet in the warehouse, described by Hendee as "training wheel type things." It is not clear if they were taken into evidence, but it answers the question as to why Bruce Peterson wasn't asked about them.
- Only one life preserver was found, and a pair of orange (rubber?) gloves from the bottom of the boat.
- The Gamefisher boat, manufactured by Sea Nymph and marketed by Sears, had a 500-pound capacity.
- Peterson had a drill press or jigsaw in the warehouse, and of course the mortising machine. He was just another Bob Vila!

Looking for Laci in all the wrong places

The San Francisco Bay, an estuary within a larger system that includes San Pablo Bay, Suisun Bay, the Carquinez Strait, and other river tributaries, is over 480 square miles in area, with 12 islands and two trillion gallons of salt water. Most of the bay is relatively shallow, compared to the ocean or deep lakes, with some natural and intentionally dredged deep channels that range from 40 to over 100 feet deep. Because of its shallowness, the bay has a volatile personality, and can swiftly change from calm to turbulent, becoming a treacherous place for small craft and divers. The daily tides affect the depth around the shoreline anywhere from three to 10 feet. For example, at low tide, the water around Brooks Island is four to six feet, and 10-12 feet at high tide. Wading from Brooks Island to Pt. Isabel is not recommended unless you have a wet suit, fins, a mask, and a good immune system.

It was apparent from Hendee's testimony that the hydrologist from the USGS, Dr. Ralph Cheng, based his "high probability area" on investigators' suggestion that Brooks Island was a focal point in Peterson's fishing trip. Therefore, much of what encompassed the intensive search of a two- to three-square-mile area of the Bay was probably a couple of miles south of the actual disposal site, which was in the deeper water of the Richmond entrance channel. In direct and cross-examination, most of the testimony involved the underwater searches after Laci and Connor's remains were found, and there seemed a deliberate attempt to avoid describing the sonar searches in March.

Geragos spent a great deal of time pointing out the fruitless efforts of the searches by numerous agencies using high-tech equipment, but he carefully avoided any queries about the events of mid-March, and only once revealed his knowledge of the findings in a June 15 question regarding the sonar manufacturer, Marine Technologies' offer to assist in the search.

It is almost certain that Geragos is aware of the sonar and ROV images of Laci in the Bay, but until witnesses who were on the boats involved directly testify, he can pretend they don't exist. Concrete anchors as small as the ones Peterson made and the other remains for which the divers and equipment scoured the targeted areas would have been difficult to locate in a calmer, clearer body of water. In that churning, silty Bay, with its strong currents, low visibility, difficult diving conditions, and unpredictable weather, it was virtually impossible. It didn't help that they were looking in the wrong places.

<h1 style="text-align:center">JULY 21, 2004
DR. "N" BUSTER - ON PETERSON</h1>

Dr. "N" Buster, our exclusive specialist on narcissism, returns to explain recent revelations about Scott Peterson's activities before and after his wife's "disappearance."

Why did Peterson leave such a big mess of concrete in the warehouse and those tell-tale circular voids that show he was using molds to make anchors?

Peterson is a selective neat freak. His primary concern is appearance, which pretty much begins and ends with himself: his grooming, his truck, his clothes, his material possessions, his imaginary employment, and his air of mystery. With all the energy and time he spent balancing his predatory sexual pursuits with his domestic duties and occasional work days, he didn't have time to organize his warehouse, clean the spills, empty out his duffel bags, drive all over town throwing away potential evidence or doing a full load of wash. Instead of cleaning up after himself or washing clothes, he just bought more stuff.

How could Peterson afford to accumulate so much junk and have four cell phones, a new truck, a new boat, dozens of pairs of shoes, camping gear, and stacks of cash?

He couldn't. Chances are he was carrying a great deal of debt, had several credit cards that were charged to the limit, or nearly, and he was "borrowing" money from Tradecorp by cutting himself expense checks. Obviously, Tradecorp wrote off the embezzling rather than entangle the company in Peterson's debacle. This explains Laci's need to pawn some of the jewelry and his growing panic over their financial situation once the baby arrived.

Why did Peterson rent a post office box the day he planned to murder Laci?

In typical narcissistic disorganized fashion, he simply ran out of time. He had probably promised Amber Frey an address and had hedged beyond the point of her patience. A post office box in Modesto was anonymous, could be connected to his business, and would not reveal where he lived. It would also prevent any embarrassing mail from arriving at the home on Covena Avenue, especially after his wife disappeared and he knew his mail might be searched or confiscated. He actually believed Frey would not recognize him as Laci's husband and would be in the dark for a month. His self-delusion was one of his major handicaps.

Why did Peterson continue to contact Amber Frey after Laci disappeared?

Peterson is an addict; his drugs are approval, admiration, attention, blind devotion, and the pursuit and conquest of new supply. When everyone seemed to turn against him, his only remaining source of affection was Frey. He couldn't stop himself. He was completely powerless over his compulsion. This addiction had long been unmet at home, and the idea of a new baby's commanding Laci's attention and unconditional love loomed as a terrifying threat to his self-image. He derived all of his sense of being from others and could only reflect what was given to him. He exists vicariously through others' esteem. Being in his skin without some external source of narcissistic supply is tantamount to starvation. He literally withers away, depressed, despondent and bitter.

What's with packing the Vitamin-V for his getaway?

Not surprisingly, Peterson probably suffered from chronic impotence. This is a very common malady among narcissists, based on a biological short circuit with their subconscious. On the surface, they appear bon vivant, experienced in romance, and have a number of well-rehearsed lines that boast of their prowess between the sheets. In reality, they are insensitive lovers, premature to finish, have difficulty faking or sustaining arousal, and often avoid intimate encounters when the fairy dust settles after the first few weeks of a new romance. Vitamin-V helped stave off what was certain to be a disappointing display of lackluster performances. Also, he had no intention of becoming a monk on the lam.

Did Peterson pull off the "perfect murder"?

I believe the demise of the People's case has been greatly exaggerated. Peterson will prove to be the classic narcissist: devoid of sincere emotional concern, notable antipathy for others, a false superiority complex, disregard for others' opinions and observations, and colossal short-sightedness and self-sabotage that are the hallmarks of these types of individuals. Chances are, he also left a big, fat trail in his recklessness and arrogance.

JULY 31, 2004
REVISITING THE "LOVE SPIN"

In light of Amber Frey's inevitable and impending testimony in the Peterson trial, and the renewed media intensity on the pseudo "Love Spin" as Peterson's motive for murdering his pregnant wife "only a month" after meeting Amber, let us adhere to the realities of Scott's personality and expose this romantic hype as myth. Peterson's intentions were predatory, opportunistic, devoid of sincere emotional attachment, and amoral to the core. His relationship with Frey was about anything but "love." Her early infatuation with him served several purposes: to stroke his ego, supply him with a fresh, uninformed source of attention, and possibly as reinforcement to his fantasy of being a single, unencumbered male on the prowl. I believe he was planning to abandon his wife and unborn child long before he met Amber, and that his intent to eliminate any future financial and messy social obligations was an undercurrent to his methodical, murderous mission as early as the summer of 2002.

Peterson instantly recognized Amber's weaknesses as a lonely, inauspicious single mother with ambitions of building a better life for herself and her child. He pretended to cultivate her dreams of financial security, reciprocal devotion, emotional and physical compatibility, and most important, stability. The irony of his total inability to provide any of that for her was inconsequential to Peterson. He expected her to believe his fantastic fiction and never to question his veracity. When she began to doubt him, he retaliated with the tearful, tragic invention of his "lost" wife in order to disarm her and elicit her sympathy. It's patently transparent to those of us who have been on the receiving end of this kind of charade.

Many of Peterson's supporters and the commentators on this case continue to raise the question of why would he be so imprudent as to reveal his plans to rid himself of his wife to his nouveau lover? Why would he continue to call Amber after Laci "disappeared," having some semblance of common sense that this relationship would be the bane of his credibility? What will the upcoming tapes of phone calls between them disclose? I need not glance into a crystal ball to guess the answers for those uninitiated in his mindset and motivation.

Why would he reveal his plans? I believe it was partly from a subconscious desire to be punished for either conceiving or entertaining the idea, or for actually implementing it, as he stands accused. I suspect Peterson is at heart a self-saboteur, capable of squandering countless opportunities and discarding worthwhile employment, relationships, and possessions because of his irrational self-destruction. The "lost wife" scenario also temporarily derailed Amber's suspicions until (he thought) he could make it a reality and be seen as pitiful and sincere. So what if the dates would be inconsistent? That's merely a petty detail easily obfuscated with the next victim. Amber was going to be history after a few months, anyway.

Why do the Amber Frey conversations exist? Because the narcissist clings to any possible supply he has, regardless of its inherent risks to his reputation, culpability, or social acceptance. I expect the conversations between Scott and Amber to be circular, illogical, strewn with impassioned pleas for reconciliation and increased pressure for Amber to meet with him in person or let him come over to her house. He was desperate to see her face to face where he knew she would be most vulnerable to his charms. I doubt he ever realized that the phone calls were intercepted, and we can relish the fact that their broadcast in court will be extremely mortifying to him. Those who anticipate the gravity of hearing Peterson in action will not be disappointed. Those of us who have heard it all before will not be surprised.

The prosecution won't impose a "love spin" on the Frey affair, nor do I expect it to base it evidence around Peterson's philandering; at least I hope not. It would be wise to introduce Frey's testimony (and the tapes) as a window into Peterson's state of mind: his lack of grief, his frosty emotional disconnection to Laci's disappearance, and his relentless and brazen promiscuity. Anyone who can behave that way after his pregnant wife of five years disappears on the holiday is obviously void of conscience, which will finally abolish the humane but misplaced "cad" label and replace it with the more accurate depiction of a murderer.

AUGUST 2, 2004
PETERNOMICS

Based on witness testimony today in the Peterson trial, the defendant was hardly "sitting pretty" as Geragos claimed, with $22,000 in credit card debt alone. According to recent reports, "the couple's total debt of $210,000 included $168,000 owed on their Covena Avenue home, $22,000 in vehicle loans and $21,000 on credit cards." Mark Geragos, in cross-examination of Mansfield, stated, "So, in actuality, his expenses are about $3,000 a month?"

In *actuality*, what we can gather so far the accounting resembles more realistically the following, including reported income and expenses, and those Peterson conveniently omitted from the ledger:

- House payment – actual $1,250 (does that amount including property taxes or homeowners' insurance?)
- Ford 150 truck payment – actual $650
- Auto insurance (both vehicles) – *estimated unreported* $400
- Gasoline expenses for 4,000 miles/month (according to his expense reimbursement of $1,400 at .35 per mile) - $450/month using 18 mpg @ $2.00/gallon
- Credit cards - $750 according to Peterson – but in reality more like $150 minimum payment per month on six credit cards totaling a $20,000 balance = $900
- Heath insurance - Unpaid until December 24, *estimated* $400/month
- Utilities - $150? Does this include water, electric, gas and landline? Corrected to *$300*
- Satellite dish and ISP - *unreported estimate* - $65
- County club dues - actual $390
- Cell phone - $50 per Peterson, which covers one phone; with four cell phones = $200
- Business expenses: hotels, meals, entertainment - $500 *estimate*
- Federal withholding income tax, FICA, Medicare: *very conservative estimated* 22 percent - $1,200
- Premiums on two whole life insurance policies and Roth IRA contributions - $450 *per testimony*
- Miscellaneous expenses Peterson called "home improvements" (pool maintenance, upkeep, power tools) - $500
- Food: actual figure from Peterson - $600
- Wine clubs, subscriptions, entertainment, yoga classes, vanity treatments, prescriptions, and miscellaneous expenses - $200 (very conservative *estimate*)

Total revised monthly expenses – over **$8,000**

Mark Geragos: So he's got roughly disposable income, after all of his expenses, of how much? $2,300 a month?

Mr. Geragos, I think you need a new calculator.

Gross Income: $5,000 (essentially unearned) draw + $1,400 expense reimbursement = $6,400
Net loss per month ~ over $1,600
Net loss per annum ~ over $20,000

Even adding Laci's modest income (less than $1,000 per month) covers only the groceries and utilities. The inheritance she was expecting at age 30, per California law, would not go to Peterson if they were no longer married, so the mounting debt coupled with the unpredictable (and hefty) expenses of a new baby were hanging over Peterson's head like a black cloud. How *convenient* if he could wipe it all out by "losing" his wife. The prosecution so far has woefully downplayed "Peternomics" as an interrelated motive for murder, while the defense continues to radically misrepresent Peterson's solvency. Thank goodness, there's an accountant on the jury!

AUGUST 5, 2004
PETERSON'S ART OF SEDUCTION

What are the secrets to Peterson's seduction techniques? From what we have gleaned from testimony, phone transcripts and anecdotes, Peterson compressed the courtship process on his very first date with Amber Frey, with her cooperation, naturally, and managed to enchant her with trite but effective manipulations for about three weeks. What were some of his mesmerizing methods?

First, he had to break the ice and develop a cozy sense of trust. He arranged for a private room in a Japanese restaurant unfettered by distractions and unwelcome spectators. Building upon his awareness of her criteria, he portrayed an image of accessible sophistication with an air of alluring mystery.

With his lack of imagination, Peterson resorted to some rather vapid, vanilla props like champagne and strawberries, although he may have had ulterior motives with the fruit. Popular men's magazines advise that observing the way a woman eats a strawberry is an indicator of her potential sensuality. I imagine people with lust on their minds can find inflating a bicycle tire sexy.

Flattery and formality were his favorite weapons, as well as playing dress-up, renting limousines and flashing cash. No doubt he simpered about searching for a woman of substance in contrast to the "bimbos" of his revisionist romantic history. He expressed his disappointment with all the girls he had met, awaiting the "one" who would rise like cream to the top. This is such a tired old line that I am always amazed by its success. Of course, his date believed she was smarter, deeper, prettier and better than her potential rivals. His intimations of discriminating selectivity aroused her natural competitive instincts, and she wanted to be the one to lasso the lonely stud. He went to great lengths to make Amber feel "special."

Peterson dispensed with any lofty ideals of courtly love or other romantic illusions; his was purely a game of sexual conquest. Borrowing from popular cultural motifs, he offered clichés like "You complete me," "You're the woman I've been waiting for all my life," and "You're my soul mate." This sophomoric

215

swill would be innocuously sappy coming from anyone but a malignant narcissist. To the predator, it is beguiling bait.

Another common tactic used by the player is sudden unavailability, which will test the victim's desire and reaffirm who's running the show. Depending on whether "absence makes the heart grow fonder" or "out of sight, out of mind" is the resulting effect, the narcissist can gauge his control. Peterson announced early in December that he would be away for the holidays and beyond, but assured Amber that in late January they could be together. This technique served two purposes: to buy him a month to allow the dust to settle on Laci's disappearance (woefully underestimating the impact of that event), and to employ his favorite head game with Amber. In the meantime, he proffered a post office box in Modesto where she could send him packages or letters, and ordered her a star theater for Christmas, presumably so the interactive comet and meteor maker reminded her of his electrifying virility.

AUGUST 8, 2004
"FAIR AND BALANCED" FALLACIES

With the epidemic of misinformation, partial information, titillating teasers, and ridiculous banter from the media lately, allow me to remind the readers that despite news stories and ignorant opinion to the contrary, recent testimony in the Peterson trial has important probative value in demonstrating the defendant's premeditation, financial recklessness, deception in all areas of his life (not only in his marriage), and yet more of his inconsistent statements. Meanwhile, the media and defense apologists suggest "innocent" but implausible explanations, and their constant intimations of law enforcement impropriety are based on peripheral but common errors at best. Essentially, the defense is not merely suggesting alternative scenarios for Peterson's unconscionable behavior, creative bookkeeping, or curious purchases, but is actually perpetrating totally false information. Bolstered by his puppets on cable TV news programs and Web sites or crime forums that shamelessly enumerate fictitious, slanderous allegations against Laci's family and Amber Frey, Geragos and his wraiths actually attempt to indict the Modesto police and, by association, the prosecutors for his client's transgressions.

The average viewer will come away every night believing that Peterson is going to be acquitted, that there is no evidence against him, that the prosecution is inept and corrupt, and that every witness the People introduce is useless or actually benefits the defense. Why on earth would the networks want people to believe this? Is it to maintain suspense? To create controversy and conflict entirely manufactured out of a Hollywood imagination? Has reporting the truth become an archaic and trite convention? Court TV is the only network covering the trial that produces any consistent pro-prosecution editorial. After witnessing for over a year the appalling tabloid reporting and insidious misogynist bias on Fox News, I can only charitably regard that network as a macabre and disgraceful display of malicious propaganda. Perhaps a little accountability is in order.

The media is more concerned with strictly stylistic differences of the prosecution's presentation. They make ratings by second-guessing the investigation that entailed months of painstaking efforts by hundreds of individuals and every available technology. They want the viewers to wring their hands in despair over the pundits' dire predictions. In reality, we should be outraged by a system of justice that allows a criminal defense attorney to make a mockery of the People. We should be incensed and very concerned that the media has manufactured "news" and has inadequately reported on the facts of the trial.

AUGUST 10, 2004
TGI FREY-DAY

When we think of landmark events in our lives, we think of graduations, weddings, buying a new home, births, deaths, divorces, and career changes. I would venture to guess none of us aspires to be a key witness in a widely publicized murder trial, much less labeled the "other woman" to the defendant. Yet, today is a pivotal day for Amber Frey, if she in fact sits in the witness box in Redwood City for the first day of her long anticipated and excessively speculated testimony. So much synthetic fluff has been made of the relationship between Peterson and Frey that the essential truth of their romance has been buried in hyperbole and scintillating but groundless aspersions to her character. At its essential core, this is a boy meets girl story with a twist. If this case weren't headline news every day, the world would have long forgotten Amber and her ill-fated rendezvous with the Ice Man.

This morning, Amber will wake up in a San Mateo hotel room, after a likely fitful night, perhaps to the sounds of her baby boy's hunger. She'll go through the motions of her tasks in a surreal, automaton warp. Part of her must dread the imminent event, and she cringes at the thought of countless cameras, flashes, microphones, shouting reporters, and Gloria Allred's steel grip on her arm as she escorts her to the courthouse. Another part of her is relieved that the day has finally come and she can put this nightmare behind her once and for all. Most of us walk away from a doomed relationship sadder but wiser, able to close the door and allow the memories to dissolve into the nebulous, pastel past. Not so Amber's brief, bitter taste of the noxious sycophancy of Peterson's compressed courting style, and his relentless, desperate attempts to prolong the illusion despite its catastrophic consequences. Amber will have to relive the relationship practically moment by moment, as accurately as distance and dizzying interim events will allow.

So many lives have been suspended by this trial, as though the families have stepped off the mellow carousel of the course of daily events into a warped and horrific fun house with distorted mirrors, cackling clowns, moving floors, rotating walls and disorienting darkness. Peterson, a selfish, unimaginative, underachieving, lecherous and lying fertilizer salesman is still taking hostages with his ersatz innocence and Hollywood trappings. Even when his sickening words are played in court, he will sneer and stare ahead and sit smugly as if saying, "So what?" We can expect his family to dismiss his inopportune and injudicious hound dogging as merely attention-seeking lust, but what will the jury think? No matter how the defense tries to impeach Amber, no matter whom Amber dated, no matter when she found out that Peterson was married, no matter what color her hair or the shape of her figure, no matter how idiotic her father has

217

behaved, no matter what the despicable apologists have implied about her criminal past, Amber will crystallize for the entire world how loathsome, unmoved, single minded, unconcerned, irresponsible and manipulative Peterson was.

Though a picture is worth a thousand words, in this trial, Peterson's words spoken in his own voice are worth a thousand mentions of duct tape, concrete residue, broken hairs, or tidal chart downloads. We hope Amber will stay strong and hold her head up, that she ignites the room with the light of truth, and that the sight of her sears Peterson's heart like molten lead, and he spits gritty, charred ash for weeks to come.

AUGUST 13, 2004
MORE EPIPHANIES

From the recordings of calls between Peterson and Amber Frey heard in court today, interesting fruit can be plucked from the orchard of obfuscation that sheds some light on the real Scott. As outlined in a previous analysis of one of the phone transcripts of January 6, known as the "Day of Epiphany" or the 12th day of Christmas, these phone calls reveal Amber's transformation from gullible, infatuated "source" to a woman in control of her destiny.

Excerpts from the first call: January 6, time: 2216

Amber mentions to Peterson that her friend, Saki, has left her a disturbing message on her voicemail, from the airport during a layover in Chicago. No doubt Saki saw something about Laci Peterson's disappearance on the news. Amber pretends not to know what the message is really about, and tries to see if Peterson will indicate that he has an idea. Instead, he remarks:

Scott: You don't need anything else tough in your life. I mean, people can make it better. And I don't mean your life is bad. I'm just saying, you know, quality people."

After a discussion of Amber's daughter's future potty training and the expense of diapers:

Scott: God, I love talking to you. You make me happy.

Elaborating on the Pasternak poem, "Hops:"

Scott: And my hands around your waist like anchors for people. I like the first stanza because it sounded so much like two people providing shelter for each other. Holding onto each other in crisis...You would hope you wouldn't need the other person to protect you from the storm or take shelter with in the storm. You'd hope the relationship wouldn't have storms, outside, inside, any time."

Scott: You know how I tell you how special you are, how unique and everything? And how much I need you? And I'm not just saying it? And you need to know how true that is, how wonderful you are. You are amazing! Call me if you need me."

Amber: But you never answer.

Scott: Yeah, I'll answer.

A few minutes later, he calls her back:

Excerpt from the second call, January 6, time: 2302

Scott: It's the worst thing. I'm so sorry that this has happened and I'm so sorry that I am going to hurt you this way. I don't want to do this over the phone. I want to be there in person to tell you this, but I'm sure that's why Saki called you.

For the past two weeks I've been in Modesto with her family and mine searching for her.

(As if he doesn't live in Modesto and implying Laci went missing absent his involvement. He is still denying his relationship with Laci, even in his sudden admissions.) Amber's reaction is odd, since you would think she'd at least pretend to be shocked and outraged but she just says, "Ok," and mumbles "Uh huh" after he tells her these incredible things after just a few minutes ago he was quoting her Pasternak and telling her how much he "needs" her.

Scott: You know, I'm destroyed, and I hope so much that this doesn't hurt you.

Finally, Amber starts to interrogate him:

Amber: You told me you lost your wife...and now all of a sudden your wife is missing?

Scott: I never cheated on you.

What he is saying here is that he wasn't sleeping with his wife since November 20. In his warped mind, this constitutes sexual fidelity.

Scott: There's different kinds of loss, Amber.

This is a perfect explanation for the narcissist's common practice of "devalue and discard." The loss he describes is the loss of Laci as a "supply" for him some time in the past.

Scott: You will thank me for not explaining it now... not thank me, but understand.

Excerpts from the third call, January 6, time: 2329

AF: "What purpose did I serve in your life this last month?

SP: Amber, you are, you changed me this last month. You have, you are so special; you are amazing.

AF: And so what? Are you telling me your wife was not?

SP: I cannot explain it all to you now.

AF: There's a lot of things you're not wanting to explain to me now.

SP: No, I want to but I can't.

Then she asks him to elaborate on his use of the word "loss," after hammering him about the "coincidence" of the timing and how everything appeared to be on his "time frame."

AF: Again, what loss and sense are you speaking of?

SP: There are many types of loss.

AF: And what kind of loss was that?

SP: Sweetie, I can't tell you.

(Regarding ever trusting him again:)

AF: The only way I would ever change my mind is if she is found or she comes forward or whatever.

SP: God, I hope she is found alive.

This is the only reference to any concern about Laci that Scott makes in all three conversations, which comprise about an hour and a half of calls. He never says he loves his wife, he never explains the "loss," he never admits the baby is his, and he denies any involvement yet refuses to elaborate on the so-called "whole story" about his marriage.

AF: So why is it you have such a hard time with the truth?

SP: I don't think so. But I lied to you and I hate myself for that.

AF: You didn't think you knew you lied to me?

SP: No, no, no. I have always told you the truth.

AF: Oh, really?

SP: Let me...well, no. With exceptions, maybe.

220

AF: Oh, truth with exceptions, huh? That's a new one for my book...!

AF: I'm listening. Just tell the truth.

SP: I can't. I want to.

AF: What's stopping you?

SP: The situation's stopping me.

AF: That makes no sense.

SP: Ok, yeah, I thought I lost you...I can't say any more.

AF: Well, it can't get any worse.

SP: True. It's better than it is, than it sounds.

AF: What's better than it is?

SP: Well, the situation is terrible, Laci is missing.

"It's better than it is?" This statement is mind-boggling. My first impression is that he is not that upset about it (obviously) and that he thinks that the ultimate resolution will be to his benefit, that Laci won't be found, eventually granting him his emancipation and his "simplified life," elaborated in the following:

AF: So let's see here. Let's read into this a little bit more, Scott. You can't tell me now, but of course you couldn't tell me then about your missing wife, or not about missing but that you lost your wife until you came back from Europe. Now everything has a delay. Is this for you to come up with something really good, like your New Year's resolution? It has to be really good?

SP: And I deserve that all...I can't give you any answers.

AF: You can't give me any answers because it's not what's in your best interest.

SP: It's in no one's best interests.

AF: The whole point of the European trip was so you could have a life and not travel and not have to work so hard...

SP: The whole point of the business negotiating...are [sic] to simplify my life. This situation changed all that.

AF :Really?

SP: And I'm obviously not working.

221

Thank you very much. I have been saying this for 18 months. Now his and his family's excuse for him trading in Laci's car and his trip to Mexico will be revealed for the putrid fertilizer it was.

AF: So if you trust me then why can't you share this information with me?

SP: Because you would share it with everyone.

AF: I would share it with everyone?

SP: You would. And you would have to.

That's a pretty darn incriminating statement if I ever heard one. And the *piece de resistance*:

SP: I just hope you know how special you are. I hope you know that assholes like me and the previous guys who lied to you don't change you.

AF: Well, that's gonna be a hard one for me to work on.

SP: Don't let them change you. God, don't. (crying)...don't let people lie to you like I've lied to you, don't change.

Don't let people lie to you? As if Amber is somehow responsible for the lies her former boyfriends and Peterson told her? This is textbook narcissist *modus operandi*. The lengths to which Peterson goes to detach from his wife, his unborn baby, the circumstances, his personal responsibility in any of the events, and even his victimization of Amber can only be described as purely sociopathic.

AUGUST 16, 2004
THOROUGHLY MODERN MATA HARI

At a second gathering of friends and trial watchers in San Francisco, all of whom I had met in June during my previous visit, at the scenic and spacious second floor Romeo walk-up flat in the Mission district, with its only slightly obscured view of The City due to the tree cutters from the Tenderloin having lopped off the wrong branch, which dangled perilously over the highway for weeks by the nylon threads of a borrowed rope and an extension cord (that was promptly stolen), we discussed Amber Frey's testimony and recent news stories appearing in the San Francisco *Chronicle* and the *Modesto Bee*.

The *Chronicle* article was relatively flattering to Frey for a change, depicting her as a complex woman with honorable intentions; a radical departure from months and months of disparaging, spurious character sketches based on rumor, sensationalism and what has become predictable defense bias. Nevertheless, the *ModBee* quoted Amber's former boyfriend, Anthony's, mother claiming Amber was lying about the visitation arrangements between her daughter and her "I'm not

222

just a gigolo" son. In addition, *Newsweek* reports of allegedly 16 calls Amber made to Scott on December 24 and characterizes her as a "stalker."

Vigorous and enthusiastic debunking ensued. Frankly, Frey's domestic issues are none of anyone's business, nor do they have probative value in this trial. Besides, they are a "he said, she said" argument unless the defense sees fit to subpoena any corroborative documentation to undermine her integrity in some way. Regarding the phone calls and any obsessive hounding on Amber's behalf, we have already read (and heard) for ourselves the tenor of Peterson's reckless and desperate conversations with her, however circuitous and unintelligible his responses. We believe the fictitious story of phone calls on Christmas Eve (is this "Phonegate?") is likely to be nothing more than media spin orchestrated by Geragos, similar to *Ductgate*, *Pawngate*, and *Warehousegate*. *Newsweek's* teaser merely provided the belated weekly red herring typically reserved for Thursdays.

We unanimously agreed that Peterson was oblivious of the phone taps. If he were aware that this inane dialogue, akin to a badminton match between toddlers, were being recorded for posterity, he would have done one of two things: either stopped calling her altogether, or engineered his excuses to bolster his protestations of innocence. He does neither. Peterson might know what "genre" means, but his common sense is severely undeveloped.

The consensus of Amber's probable impressions on the jury is that she is very credible, courageous, selfless, sympathetic, and clever by turning the tables on Peterson, usurping his former persuasive powers, and seizing the reins of the relationship, as the horses changed back into mice and the gilded carriage into a pumpkin.

More taped phone calls between Frey and Peterson will be entered this week in court, as well as the long-anticipated and heavily hyped cross-examination by the defense. How will Geragos counter Frey's role in the motive? How will he minimize the impact of Peterson's mention of a "lost wife" and his availability in late January? How will he downplay his client's persistent and puerile communication with Amber after Laci's disappearance, much less after Frey's press conference? The million-dollar strategy remains to be seen.

AUGUST 18, 2004
FORMER STOMPING GROUNDS

During the eight years that Peterson sporadically attended college, he lived in Arizona for about six months, and then returned to Morro Bay, California, where his parents resided in the early 90s. After allegedly working seven jobs to support himself (although I am only aware of two), he eventually landed in San Luis Obispo to complete his marathon academic career at California Polytechnic State University (Cal Poly). In my recent trip to California, I was able to visit two of Peterson's former hangouts: Morro Bay Golf Course and The Shack.

Morro Bay reminded me a little of an island in Lake Erie called Put-in-Bay, which is mainly a summer resort area for boaters and college kids; although, there are some fulltime residents who take the ferry to the mainland to work in Port Clinton (home of the Davis-Besse nuclear power plant), or other industrial areas near Sandusky. As in Put-in-Bay, unless you have a boat, a bicycle, or golf clubs, there is really nothing to do in Morro Bay. Even the Morro Bay visitors' bureau sends you to Hearst Castle or recommends water sports (kayaking, sailing, or fishing) for entertainment.

As you stroll along the weathered docks by the marina, you notice the air is rife with the rancid smell of deep fried fish, rotting kelp, and stale beer. The décor in the restaurants is late "punch palace," and the bordering houses, while no doubt very expensive, resemble low income housing in one of our ragged midwestern neighborhoods. When the Petersons made Morro Bay their home, it was a number of social notches below Rancho Santa Fe. The golf course is well maintained and nestled among some beautiful topography with a view of the ocean and that ugly and useless Morro hump in the middle of the harbor. We ran out of interesting things to photograph and explore after about 10 minutes.

On a separate excursion, we visited San Luis Obispo, which, compared to the splintered boardwalks and faded facades of Morro Bay, is the drop-dead, knockout prom queen. If Peterson was hoping to return there some day, either because it reminded him of happier, carefree times, or because it was so much sexier and scenic than Modesto, I can appreciate his sentiment. San Luis Obispo must be the best-kept secret on the central coast: ideal climate, an eclectic mix of architecture and culture, and the sophisticated informality of a college town. I could elaborate on how gorgeous San Luis Obispo is, but I'm afraid I might incite a stampede of visitors and refugees from Morro Bay. I understand it's not a cheap place to live (is anywhere in California?), but if you are going to spend the big bucks to live out there, that's one location that may almost be worth it.

We shopped at Trader Joe's in San Luis Obispo, where there was "Turkey Jerkey" available (contrary to Geragos's observations), and stopped at The Shack, the restaurant originally owned and operated by Scott and Laci Peterson. It was a cookie-cutter sports bar in a small strip mall that was practically empty during the lunch hour. I presume during the academic year it is packed; but the locals didn't seem to care much about it, judging by its vacancy in mid-August. There were no lingering signs of Laci's creative touch in The Shack, but I took some pictures of its interior and of the campus of Cal Poly for a photo essay on the area that will highlight some of the lovely scenery that was probably familiar and endearing to her. Frankly, I don't know how she ever wanted to leave San Luis Obispo. I suspect there was serious trouble in Paradise to make her uproot from the palm tree-lined boulevards, rolling green hills, flowering trees, charming neighborhoods, and urbane population, to return to bucolic, banal Modesto.

AUGUST 26, 2004
DEPRAVED INDIFFERENCE

"When you look into an abyss, the abyss looks into you." –Nietzsche

There's a kind of hush among the Peterson apologists today, a kind of strained mumbling, as if struck by reluctant laryngitis. The more aggressive defenders, protected by anonymity on crime forums and chat rooms, are reaching for the withering vines of excuses that they hope will swing them across to reasonable doubt before shredding in their sweaty grasp, sending them into the dark, oily depths of Peterson's mind.

Imagine the squirming in the courtroom today, people shifting in their seats, straightening the seams on their linen slacks, rubbing their chins and staring at their hands. Imagine the collective reaction of extreme discomfort while listening to Scott Peterson blithely lie to his family and friends, casually delete unheard messages, and chuckle over the incompetence of dedicated searchers diving in the Bay or combing the countryside for his "missing" wife. The agitation was unanimous and deep, as the profundity of Peterson's inhumanity resonated throughout the room.

Laci's mother exited in disgust. Peterson's mother wept. Geragos scrambled for phantom phone calls for deliverance, but there was no redemption for Peterson today. His callous indifference to all who helped him, loved him, sacrificed and sympathized, offered friendship and assistance and prayer, was as dramatic as if he had hurled a gallon of black India ink from a second-story window onto his supporters below. It was painfully obvious to even the most strident defender that Peterson despised his wife and held nothing but contempt for those who searched for her.

From recordings of phone calls between Scott and his family, it seemed that the Petersons were not very fond of Laci, either. What did Laci do to deserve the disdain of her in-laws? Was she too bold, too outgoing, too bossy or demanding? Did her vivacious personality and focused ambition constantly remind them of their character defects, of their insipid dullness and their shameful mediocrity? Did her sudden absence elicit a sense of relief to them? As early as mid-January, they seem more concerned with trivial matters than with her well-being. Curiously, they never mention the baby and exhibit a peculiar dislocation from the fact that she was pregnant. Perhaps they are the kind of people who don't acknowledge or attach to a child until he is born, since, after all, he cannot reflect them until he is visible and bears a resemblance to the clan.

Blatant evil is always a terrible thing to witness, especially in people we trusted, or in our own flesh and blood. Our initial reaction to the exposure of the ugly underbelly of the human condition is to cover our eyes or look away, deny its existence, or invent rational excuses for its evolution. The defense faces an

225

impassible chasm in justifying Peterson's behavior in the early months following the murder.

And it's only going to get worse.

The howling defenders who fail to vilify Amber Frey, who cannot expunge the images of Laci and Connor's remains washing ashore from their murky grave near where Peterson took his boat on Christmas eve, whose condemnation of the investigators and the prosecution obscures the simple facts of this case, are suddenly stifled by Peterson's pathological apathy that curdles the milk of human kindness and suffocates their sympathy.

AUGUST 27, 2004
THE IMPORTANCE OF BEING EARNEST

Almost three months ago, which must seem like a year to the jury and participants in the Peterson trial in Redwood City, Mark Geragos presented his opening statement outlining the defense position on Peterson's "stone cold" innocence. To merely declare that the People of California would fail to prove a substantive case against his client was not powerful or dramatic enough for the blustering, pompous purveyor of pretense; he had to overstate his case.

Previously I critiqued Geragos's remarks with the facts as I knew them at the time. Now, after 45 days of trial, we can review the defense's barefaced mendacity, which seems only too appropriate, considering the defendant's chronic and treacherous duplicity. It is no surprise that Geragos has asked for (and received) many delays during the trial so far, no doubt to distance the jury's memory from the numerous inaccuracies, deliberate misstatements, and fabricated revision in his opening remarks. Allow me to enumerate the lies so far:

> ...at the time that Scott supposedly makes the decision to kill Laci, he had had exactly two dates with Amber. And total, he had four dates. And the evidence is going to clearly show you that Amber was upset with Scott for not calling. She was upset with him for not giving her a Christmas gift. And she ends up calling sixteen times on December 26th.

Perhaps this is arguing over semantics, but none of us would qualify the overnight visits and days spent with Frey as "four dates." Geragos makes it sound as if they took in a movie and went out for ice cream; never mind Peterson's stories about his "lost wife" and their future plans he painted. Amber was upset with Scott for not calling? You mean she wanted him to call her 350 times instead of 300 times? By the way, based on the newly published phone logs, she called only 14 times on December 26 (which we already knew), and Peterson called her twice. He also sent her that goofy star theater and, while not a very expensive or elaborate gift, was nevertheless a gift!

> And he was, in fact, back by 4:00 o'clock. They had plans that evening to go over to Sharon's house for Christmas Eve.

No he wasn't. He wasn't back, by his own admission and the neighbors' testimony, until almost 5:00.

But the idea that he was not an avid fisherman is just belied by what the evidence is going to show you.

He was such an "avid fisherman" he didn't pack the right gear, rods or bait, and he went to the wrong area to troll, illegally, for fish that were not there.

But you are going to have a succession of witness who saw her walking, and saw her walking the dog. And she would tell people that she was walking the dog. And that's what she did for exercise.

So far, we have heard from all the neighbors who lived near Laci, and none saw her walking the dog that day, or any other day with any regularity. The only person who claims she was walking the dog for exercise is Geragos.

The fact of the matter is, is that he arranged his work schedule to improve the chances of the pregnancy.

Unless Peterson takes the stand, this bit of devoted behavior will never be proven. Pardon me if I don't believe it, and neither will the jury.

The fact of the matter is, the evidence will show you, he went to every single appointment; and, as I indicated before, was excited enough that he was one who built personally built that nursery that you saw the pictures of yesterday.

He built the nursery? His mother complained when Sharon Rocha took the crib she bought. As far as going to the doctor's appointments, none of the staff of Laci's OB/GYN have testified to seeing Peterson there "every single" time, and the question was never asked of Laci's doctor. I wonder why?

Now, this idea that he's apathetic about his wife's disappearance. Understand what Scott's life had become. You have to put this into context, because it's very difficult to understand.

We have recently seen it in context. He never searched for her. He lied to his friends and family about his location and his activities. He went to the golf course and drove around California, clearly avoiding the searches. It's not difficult to understand in the context of a guilty murderer's behavior.

They had just purchased this country club membership. They spent quite a bit of money...It was in excess of $20,000 to buy the country club membership. Was excited about that.

Peterson's parents bought the country club membership. Geragos knows this. Why does he insist this is some kind of valuable investment that would preclude Scott from leaving Modesto or murdering his wife? He tried to sell the house (a bigger investment); why not sell the membership, too?

> *She [Laci] was there at the warehouse on December 20th, had seen the boat, was in the boat...She was worried about getting anywhere near that liquid fertilizer*

This makes no sense, and again, unless Scott testifies, we will never hear anyone say they saw Laci in the boat, and the fact that the boat was surrounded by pallets of fertilizer product kind of refutes the idea that she would go anywhere near it if she saw it.

> *He drove all the over Northern California...And you will see all the different places he went posting flyers, every time he got a tip, or anything else...Then there was also the -- he organized search teams. He tried to pursue the search...what the evidence will show you is that he was somebody who was trying to do everything that he could to find Laci.*

This is just laughable after hearing the recent phone taps.

> *...the evidence is going to show that the pants that she was wearing on the 23rd were the pants that she was found in are just -- is just plain not true.*

It is true. Laci only owned one pair of khaki (stone, whatever) Motherhood maternity slacks. The other pair of tan pants found hanging in the closet was not Capri style. In any case, she was not wearing the black pants Peterson insisted, emphasized, underlined and highlighted on every report.

> *The people who were burglarized believe it was on the 24th, in the morning, the Medinas, and they will tell you that.*

No, she didn't. Ms. Medina testified only to when she left that morning and when she returned, not to when she thought the burglary took place. She could not be certain. She was also not clear on what cars were in the Peterson driveway at 5 am, only that there were two.

> *...there's no way you can tip it over because the boat would capsize, because it's only a little twelve foot aluminum Gamefisher.*

Even the most casual observer of this trial knows that the boat is 14 feet long, and that you could easily push a body off the bow without capsizing. The boat and fishing expert testified to this as well.

Interestingly enough, Geragos never mentions the anchor or the missing concrete items (evident by the mess of residue left in the shop), the location where the bodies were recovered, Peterson's ersatz Maine and European furlough during the holidays, what was discovered on his computers, that Laci's jewelry (the lure to a mugger) was still in the house, and a number of other inconsistencies with his "innocent" client's story.

I appreciate that the task of a defense attorney is to create reasonable doubt and vigorously protect his client from slipshod or corrupt investigative practices and prejudicial bias. However, it's another matter altogether (and unlikely the Founding Fathers' ideal) to dispense deliberate dishonesty. I believe it is important to be earnest in defense of a person, especially in such a highly publicized case. It can only backfire, otherwise. All the praise heaped upon Geragos for his strategy should instead be withering scorn for his complete lack of integrity.

Expect his forensic promises showing the baby as older or was born alive, that Laci wasn't in the bay for almost four months, or all the witnesses he will parade who claim to have seen Laci walking the dog the morning of December 24 to be similarly deceptive and dismissed as fiction - the same fiction as the "glorious" marriage and describing Peterson as "giddy" about the prospect of his son. He was so "giddy" he denied him, deleted him, and disposed of him like an empty ink cartridge.

AUGUST 28, 2004
A SPIRITUAL BATTLE

It has become clear that there may be a divine purpose for the massive interest and publicity of the Laci Peterson murder case. While reporters and pundits argue over the superficialities of reasonable doubt and the psychology of the defendant, and networks capitalize on the ratings and revenue generated by their coverage; as crime followers in forums, living rooms and around office water coolers debate the detritus, the battle lines are being drawn. What began as a garden-variety spousal murder with mystical, symbolic timing in the dates of the disappearance and reappearance of the victims has become a paradigm for spiritual warfare. Where you align yourself may have eternal consequences.

Consider the mythical symbolism in this case: a beloved Madonna with child is murdered on Christmas Eve and figuratively resurrects during Holy Week, in what many regarded as a miraculous ascension from the soft, stubborn silt of the bottom of the cold waters of the San Francisco Bay after being weighted down with concrete anchors and ravaged by scavengers. The "high-profile" attorney from Los Angeles, the city of fallen angels, leads the defense of the demonized husband, an unrepentant, conscienceless cur who represents the most grievous sins of modern society: overindulgence, materialism, moral bankruptcy, impulsivity, pathological perfidy and self-centeredness.

A criminal trial is, by definition, an adversarial contest designed to render justice, but the rigid demarcation between the white hats and the black hats is generally blurred. The system itself is a quagmire of gray area, fraught with speculation, nebulous motives, unproven theories and ulterior agendas. However, in the Peterson trial, the gulf between good and evil, light and darkness, and intellectual integrity and manipulative distortion has widened so distinctly as to dramatize the tormenting human onus of free will. With every new development characterizing the prosecution as incompetent, it appears that the powers of darkness will envelope us all.

The underlying malignant tone of the trial, like a modulating bass line beneath the dissonant melody of the media sound bites, reinforces our despondency and etherizes hope. But armed with the spiritual weapons of truth and commitment to our defense of innocence and all we deem holy, we will endure this test of our faith. Good will triumph over evil, as millions of witnesses observe the outcome of this trial and are reaffirmed in their convictions. Trust that there is a higher order to the universe. Trust that our prayers and diligence have not been in vain. Imagine the glory of a purifying, spiritual victory in the wake of our current state of disillusionment, distrust, fear and war. So much good has already come of the horrible evil prevalent in this tragedy, I am fully confident that sovereign righteousness will prevail. Keep the faith.

CHAPTER 10: JUSTICE

September 8 – November 3, 2004

SEPTEMBER 8, 2004
BACK TO THE BASICS

The following are excerpts from an article by Gregg O. McCrary, Supervisory Special Agent with the FBI on "Staged Domestic Homicides,"[73] and their relevant application to the Peterson case:

> *There was nothing in Marilyn Reese Sheppard's lifestyle, such as criminal activity, drug use, etc. that would have elevated her risk for becoming the victim of violence, nor were there any situational dynamics that unduly escalated her potential for becoming the victim of a homicide.*

Similarly, there was nothing in Laci Peterson's lifestyle or neighborhood (despite defense hypotheses to the contrary) that would predispose her to a violent crime, abduction or assault Christmas Eve morning in Modesto.

> *[The Sheppard] crime and crime scene have many elements of staging. Staging can be defined as the purposeful alteration of the crime and crime scene by the offender. Staging is a conscious effort by the offender to mask the true motive for the crime by altering the crime scene to suggest false motives. The offender's goal in staging a crime scene is to misdirect the investigation and conceal his involvement in the crime.*

We believe that Peterson staged his wife's abduction with the leashed dog, artificial morning itinerary, and insistence that Laci was preparing to "walk the dog" after mopping the floor. The bucket of recently emptied water was possibly another prop to cover what cleaning he may have done prior to calling the police.

> *The more time an offender spends at a crime scene the higher the probability that the offender is comfortable and familiar with that scene. Offenders who spend a great deal of time at a crime scene often have a legitimate reason for being at the scene and therefore are not worried about being interrupted or found at the scene.*

From recent testimony, it has been verified that Peterson returned to the Bay (where he submerged his wife's body) on numerous occasions and took pains to visit inconspicuously in rented vehicles, staying only long enough to reassure himself that the underwater searchers were in the wrong location. I submit that Peterson's research of the Bay area and exploration of launch sites and locations of deep water in the channel provided him with a level of comfort when he ultimately took Laci's body to the Bay sometime on December 24. It was not a dry run.

---

[73] McCrary, Gregg O., "The Assignment," Court TV Crime Library, December 1, 1999.

232

This offender will further attempt to steer the investigation away from him by his conduct when in contact with law enforcement. Thus, investigators should never eliminate a suspect solely on the grounds of that person's overly cooperative or distraught behavior.

How often did Peterson complain that the police were wasting time and manpower searching the Bay and that their efforts would be better spent elsewhere? Did he not try to bring the search to Los Angeles, rather than to the more logical city of San Francisco? His cat-and-mouse games with the surveillance were another indicator of his smug defiance and arrogant disregard for their efforts.

An offender who stages a crime scene usually makes mistakes because he stages it to look the way he thinks a crime scene should look. While doing this, the offender experiences a great deal of stress and does not have time to fit all the pieces together logically. Inconsistencies will begin appearing at the crime scene, with forensics, and with the overall picture of the offense. These contradictions will often serve as the "red flags" of staging and prevent misguidance of the investigation. The crime scene often will contain these red flags in the form of crime scene inconsistencies.

The "red flags" initially noted by the officers at the scene: the house was almost too clean and looked as though no one had been home all day; no signs of baking or food preparation; the dog was put in the yard by a neighbor; no sign of a struggle except a scrunched area rug; the hastily made bed and the duffel bag upside down on the floor in the guest bedroom; and no one had seen or heard from the victim since the evening prior. Peterson's inconsistent statements to people regarding his whereabouts, and the long distance fishing trip in weather too cold for golf added up to a suspicious scenario that alerted police to the prospect of foul play almost immediately.

Eventually, when the bodies were recovered, there were major inconsistencies with what Peterson said Laci was wearing when he left her in the morning with what she was found wearing. The most incriminating evidence of all was the proximity of where the remains washed up to Peterson's inconvenient fishing location.

When an offender stages a domestic homicide, he frequently plans and maneuvers a third-party discovery of the victim. The offender often will manipulate the victim's discovery by a neighbor or family member or will be conveniently elsewhere when the victim is discovered.

In Peterson's case, he did not expect the dog to be returned to the yard so quickly, failed to anticipate the media attention his "missing" wife would attract, and hoped beyond hope that her body would never be discovered.

Other Crime Scene Indicators:

233

- *The murder weapon, fingerprints and other evidentiary items often removed.*
- *The crime scene often involves the victim's or offender's residence, as the offender typically has control of the scene and therefore can spend time staging the scene without worry of being interrupted.*
- *An offender who has a close relationship with his victim will often only partially remove the victim's clothing (e.g. pants pulled down, shirt or dress pulled up, etc.) He rarely leaves the victim nude.*

Perhaps instead of spending so much time romancing his new girlfriend or on the golf course, Peterson should have been studying the FBI criminology and profiling literature, widely available online and in libraries. Rather than criticize the Modesto police for its "tunnel vision" and its focus on the husband, the defense should do its homework. The police were acting on statistically reliable information derived from decades of criminal investigation techniques, professional training, and good instincts.

SEPTEMBER 12, 2004
THAR'S GOLD IN THEM COMPUTER FILES!

Based on media reports and trial pundits, you probably thought the computer testimony from Detective Lydell Wall was disappointing, lacking in incriminating details and void of scandalous secrets uncovered in Peterson's Internet habits. When I finally got around to reading all of the transcripts for the direct and cross-examination (which was delayed by three weeks), it became clear once again that the media (and defense camp) woefully underestimated the significant probative value of this testimony.

Here are some critical discoveries:

- December 7 - (the day after Shawn Sibley discovered his marital status), Peterson is searching for boat sales in Modesto and Fresno.
- December 8 – his searches include: "boat, ramp, Pacific, Watsonville" – using Yahoo as a search engine (which explains why he was in Yahoo weather on December 24 – Peterson routinely used Yahoo, as some of us habitually use Google. Are we to assume that Laci used Yahoo as a search engine, also? The defense would certainly like us to.)

Why Watsonville? It's over 130 miles from Modesto on the central coast, so we can surmise that Peterson was looking for places to "fish" that were about two hours from Stanislaus County. He researches Bear Valley near Yosemite, and Antioch Dunes, near Alameda, both state parks with lakes and remote wilderness preserves. He also looked at Coyote Reservoir, a 22,000-acre foot deep, fresh waterway known for its lively bass population.

- Admitted into evidence: numerous e-mails for slpete1@email.msn.com from Shaw Sibley and Eric Olsen – dated December 5 and other dates in early December. This was an active e-mail account used exclusively by

Peterson during this time period. Laci had already set up a separate MSN account in her own name.

- E-bay listing – "Amazing Diamond Bezel Ladies Croton Watch." With that overused adjective that begins with an "a" in the headline, I don't think there can be any argument about who listed that watch!
- December 8 - more searches for "map, San Francisco Bay, chart, fish and game codes, and Central Bay current velocity maps." Current and tidal information also includes depths of the Bay. One of his search results downloaded (printed) included: "navigation chart shows soundings SF Bay area," and, of course, soundings indicate depth. This bolsters my theory that he was looking for the closest, deep water in the east Bay.
- December 8 at 9:53, on the "Dell Laptop Home," Peterson enlarged (zoomed) a map of Point Portrero Reach, Richmond entrance channel, just north of Brooks Island.

This is exactly where Laci Peterson's body was sighted by side-scan sonar March 13, 2003. We now have corroborative evidence that Peterson researched the area, the tides, currents and depths, and by his own admission, revisited this area on December 24 when he claims to have been "trolling" near Brooks Island.

- December 15 – Peterson exchanged more e-mail to E-bay prospects about the Croton watch, using the MSN mailbox.
- Friday, December 20, "Slpete1" received confirmation that a Star Theater II was shipped to Amber Frey. Additionally, there were E-bay exchanges regarding buying a magazine (ammunition for a gun) and several regarding Laci's grandmother's watch. If Laci were selling the watch, why wasn't she answering the inquiries if she had access? Clearly, he was handling the E-bay correspondence, and even if he had her blessing to sell the Croton watch, she was not involved.
- December 24 activity on "Dell Laptop Home" which, by the way, indicates the laptop was originally seized from the home, not that it necessarily was being accessed from the home. Laptops are, after all, portable, and it is obvious from some of the above e-mail downloads that Peterson was probably not home when he was accessing Shawn's e-mail addressed to "HB." From direct questioning, Wall notes that another e-mail to slpete1 was opened on December 24 regarding another E-bay transaction. The laptop was active from 8:40 – 8:45 am. Five minutes. Later that morning, the "Dell Work PC" was accessed from 10:30 – 10:56 am.

From what we have learned from the information above, let us now address the cross-examination, and the so-called "bombshell" that has been ridiculously touted as irrefutable evidence that Laci was on the computer the morning of the 24th, and therefore alive and not lying at the bottom of the Bay or in Peterson's toolbox awaiting transportation to the Berkeley Marina. No reasonable juror will draw that conclusion.

Geragos is extremely uncomfortable with the introduction of the map of the shipping channel and Point Portrero, so he immediately tries to dissemble it

235

in cross-examination. He devotes a stupor-inducing amount of time to the map, as well as to the fishing sites Scott skipped over like a stone during his research on December 8. I'm surprised a single person was still conscious by the 3:00 break.

> MG: Does it appear to you that Brooks Island had been...all of Brooks Island has been zoomed in? Or does it appear that the Southampton Shoal has been zoomed in?

> LW: It's a general area. I don't know what the intent of the zoom was ...

> MG: Well, you indicated before that you recognize from the map that you had, this one that you recognized it on one of the maps you saw here?

> LW: That's correct.

> MG: Doesn't appear to me -- you tell me, does it appear to you that all of Brooks Island is there?

> LW: No.

> MG: Okay. Does it appear that all of the Southampton Shoal is there?

> LW: Not being familiar with all of the Southampton Shoal.

Geragos goes on to try to further discredit the incriminating map by suggesting the .gif image was uploading as Peterson continued surfing to another site, due to the slow speed of his dial-up modem. When Wall reiterated that Peterson had also clicked on the map to zoom a portion of it, Geragos struggles to understate it by noting that the Web site had not been saved in Peterson's "favorites," and that the image was not printed. Geragos spends from Line 139 to roughly Line 500 from the transcripts trying to diffuse this map, which only serves to draw a great deal of attention to it, and you can be sure the jurors took note to review that part of the binder of computer evidence during deliberations. It would behoove the prosecution to clarify the nexus between that map and the sonar sighting in March with an upcoming witness before its significance is lost on even the most astute juror.

Geragos tortures the jury, the judge, and the gallery the rest of the first day of his cross-examination going over all the "fishing" sites Peterson checked, including search results for "Sturgeon Fishing Tackel [sic]," fishing reports, USA Fishing, Moss Landing and Monterey Bay, and various places Peterson peripherally peruses that have something to do with sturgeon fishing. The irony that must escape Geragos (with his incredibly tedious presentation, painfully boring to read in transcript form, so I can't imagine how brain-numbing it was in person) is that his client went to the Bay on December 24 totally unprepared for sturgeon fishing. He brought the wrong rod, the wrong bait, and illegally trolled in the shallows near Brooks Island where none of the fishing sites he browsed would *have recommended! What purpose did the sturgeon or other fishing research* serve? I submit it was to find a match for where sturgeon can be found to where he wanted to dispose his wife's body. When he found no perfect match, he improvised, assuming nobody would be the wiser.

On the second day of cross, Monday, August 30, Geragos finally gets around to the December 24 computer activity, from the "Dell Laptop Home" computer and later the office computer labeled, "Dell Work PC." On the laptop, at 8:40, on Yahoo (Peterson's preferred search engine, possibly even his home page), the user entered a zip code for a weather forecast, and also San Jose (nearby areas to the first zip code entered, possibly.) A Yahoo shopping site was accessed where a digital weather station and a garden weather vane were listed. In my experiment, I went to Yahoo and typed in a Cleveland zip code, and the result took me to a new page with a sidebar giving other options for weather for "nearby locations" and other weather-related items, including "Back to School" merchandise and "Late Summer Fun." One of the items allegedly accessed that morning was a "sunflower-motif umbrella stand," for a few seconds. Immediately following this brisk shopping spree, the user logged into an MSN e-mail account (surprisingly enough, slpete1) and read an exchange between Scott Peterson and a Mr. J Shockley.

If any were still awake, a reasonable juror would conclude that Peterson was the user that morning. Why would Laci check the weather in San Jose in order to take a walk in Modesto, as if by daily habit (as Geragos tries to imply later in the cross)? Why would she "shop" for fewer than three minutes? Why would she log into an e-mail account she had not used in over a month, but which her husband was using to exchange suggestive e-mails with Shawn Sibley, conduct work correspondence, and verify the shipment of a present to his girlfriend? What is the likelihood he had been sharing that e-mail account with her recently? Zero, zip, nada! While this may not prove Laci was already dead that morning, it makes no case to show she was alive.

SEPTEMBER 17, 2004
BLASTED WITH BOULDERS

In the Peterson trial this week, there was quite a lot of talk of sand, pebbles, fly ash and other aggregates found in concrete mixtures, along with some figurative stone throwing by the defense to try to show that Peterson's driveway repair matched the material of his homemade anchor, and to diminish the relevance of the powdery residue found in the boat cover. Since Geragos's favorite metaphor is to threaten his adversaries with "a ton of bricks," and we all agree that the apologists who constantly justify Peterson's behavior must have rocks in their heads, it is time for us to drop a few boulders of our own. As a connoisseur of nuance and innuendo, *double entendres, subtlety and* subtext, it will require a certain stylistic departure for me to employ such a crude image as a boulder to make my points. Nonetheless, after this week's powerful testimony, I have imagined Geragos as Wyle E. Coyote, self-proclaimed genius, standing beneath a rumbling pile of boulders that are about to crush him under their thunderous mass.

For all intents and purposes, most, if not all, of the defense balloons floated that Laci was seen walking McKenzie in the park or in the neighborhood the

237

morning of December 24 have been punctured by the narrow window of opportunity created by Peterson's admitted (via Martha's mention of meringue) whereabouts, his voice mail retrieval from within a few blocks of his home based on cell tower records, and Karen Servas's confidence that she returned the dog to the backyard at 10:18. The People's parade of women who walked dogs or walked for exercise while pregnant at the time didn't help, either. To quote several of the trial pundits, "The timeline *kills* him."

From Amber Frey's prodigious credibility and candor on the witness stand, bolstered by irrefutable evidence from Peterson's own words that he consistently lied to her about virtually everything, it won't take a leap of logic for the jury to infer that he planned to be a widower, and seems transparently ingenuous in his denials of involvement in Laci's "disappearance."

Peternomics, pooh-poohed as underwhelming to the amateurs, predicted a fiscal disaster and proposed the oldest motive in the book: financial gain.

The phone call excerpts depicting Peterson's depraved indifference toward his wife, family and domestic responsibilities obliterated whatever semblance of sympathy remained for his self-inflicted circumstances.

Al Brocchini, like the elusive Roadrunner, manages to escape any substantive damage or capture, despite Wyle E. Coyote's obsessive fixation and fervid attempts to vilify him. On the contrary, Brocchini emerges unscathed, pecking casually at the proverbial birdseed as the Coyote maneuvers his speeding truck, aimed for the hypothetical holes in the prosecutor's case, off a steep canyon wall.

O'Neill, the petrologist who testified this week, concluded that Peterson's anchor was probably made in a bucket, that the ingredients matched the debris found in his truck bed, dining room, bottom of the boat, and in the boat cover, and was intrinsically different from the mix used on any repair work or fence posts in the Covena Avenue driveway. O'Neill recreated from dried pieces a possible second anchor cast in the plastic pitcher found in the warehouse, which was originally thought to be the mold for the remaining anchor on the boat. The result of this testimony, coupled with the photograph of five voided circles found on the flatbed, suggests that there was more than one anchor made, and that Peterson lied to the police and Brent Rocha about what he did with the leftover premix. Geragos, who is not much of a lawyer and even less of a mason, tried to insist that Peterson poured the mix on top of gravel to create the disparity between the sample taken from the driveway and the anchor material. O'Neill discredited that process as unfeasible, much to Wyle E's ire.

Testimony from medical experts confirmed that, based on the condition of Laci's remains, she had been in the cold saltwater of the Bay for three to six months, and that the disarticulation could have very well been caused by being weighted down. It was obvious that she had recently released her baby into the water prior to washing ashore on Pt. Isabel, and that the baby was protected in her womb for the duration of her dark submersion. Without elaborating on the morbid details, there remains little credence to the preposterous and ghoulish theory that she was murdered, the baby was "born," and later both were planted on the shore a mile apart to frame her husband. Similarly, Connor's condition belies any notion that he was removed from his mother by human hands.

Seismic eruptions are often followed by aftershocks. Before the dust settles on Wyle E. Coyote's muzzle, upcoming testimony is expected from a hydrologist who will verify through current and tidal patterns in the East Bay the location where Laci's body was unceremoniously discarded; a perinatologist will certify Connor's age through calcium tests done on his bones; and lead detective Craig Grogan will tie up all the loose ends. The People's case will conclude with an avalanche of boulders that will make Geragos's "ton of bricks" seem like a shower of ping-pong balls.

SEPTEMBER 21, 2004
A TREMENDOUS MESS

In yesterday's testimony, lead Detective Craig Grogan describes the spilled concrete mix, dirty pitcher, scattered powdery residue, and the general state of the warehouse as a "tremendous mess." The tremendous mess left in the warehouse is an apt microcosm of Peterson's clumsy efforts to accomplish what the apologists frequently mislabel as "the perfect crime." In fact, a tremendous mess would accurately summarize Peterson's entire life and legacy.

We learned recently that Peterson told police that Laci had ersatz diplomas printed and framed on the wall in honor of Peterson's marathon college attendance, a duration in which serious students could have obtained several degrees. We can only imagine the disconnected disarray he made of his academic career; yet, it seems to be in character. From photos of his backyard sheds, warehouse area and closet, we conclude that organization and neatness are not Peterson's strong suits; thus, we would expect him to leave a lot of *loose ends in his baneful blueprint. We are discovering that he, indeed, left a tremendous mess.*

My suspicions that Peterson was in no hurry to properly register the boat, out of typical procrastination or because he intended to "lose" it, were confirmed when Grogan attests that Peterson failed to complete that particular paperwork. It's not significant in isolation, since he had a month to conform to the law, but it presents one more indicator that the boat was a secret and that Peterson is a careless, self-absorbed narcissist who considers petty details beneath him.

Calling "Peternomics" a tremendous mess would be an understatement. The couple's debt, spending habits and lifestyle compared to their radically decreasing income was an impending disaster. In three years when Laci's inheritance became available, the Petersons could easily have been $300,000 in debt with no equity left in their home from which to borrow. If Scott and Laci divorced, Peterson would lose access to the inheritance, and still be responsible for potentially a quarter-million dollars in child support over the course of 18 years. Similarly, Peterson's career had spiraled into ruin when he failed to meet even 25 percent of his sales quota for 2002. Meanwhile, he lined his pockets with fraudulent expense reimbursements and neglected to pay the health insurance.

Behind the pastel picket fence of the "glorious marriage" was a tremendous mess of infidelity, deceit, economic adversity, and poisonous power struggles. With geographical and career changes failing to cure the cancerous relationship, the prospect of a baby created the catalyst for catastrophe. Another tremendous mess was the cruel and tragic timing of Christmas that guaranteed a holiday tradition of mourning and interminable grief.

A tremendous mess is inadequate to describe the condition of the remains of a beautiful, healthy, spirited young woman on the brink of the most fulfilling moments of her life - after nearly four months in the ruthless, unprotected environment of the Bay. Seeking justice for her and her unborn baby, the State of California is being condemned for making a tremendous mess of this trial, but I disagree. The cumulative effects of the series of shameful shambles that Peterson has made of his life and the botched bunco to "lose" his wife will be enough to convince a thoroughly repulsed jury to render a unanimous guilty verdict.

SEPTEMBER 23, 2004
THE GROGAN FACTOR

For continued theatrical effect, the legal analysts of the Peterson trial have been imposing dramatic stylistic differences between Modesto Detectives Grogan and Brocchini, attempting to portray them as "good cop/bad cop," aggressive maverick mollified by congenial homeboy, or Harry Callahan versus Andy Taylor. Since I have read every word of both detectives' testimony in the court *transcripts, I contend that this* comparison is as bogus as the perennial myth of Mark Geragos's cross-examination prowess. Instead, I see Brocchini and Grogan as being very similar in their disarming styles, in their dogged pursuit of evidence and information, and neither was very confrontational or surly with the suspect. I estimate Brocchini and Grogan logged more hours in the first three months of investigating Laci's murder than most people work in an entire year. Thus the "rogue cop" melodrama and the insinuations that there was pervasive corruption or a perfidious conspiracy to entrap Peterson are simply absurd. The search for Laci Peterson and the investigation of her murder constituted the biggest case that either officer had ever seen or ever will see again in his career. With over 300 officers and 90 law enforcement agencies involved, the notion that there was a collective decision to focus on Scott Peterson and ignore leads that implicated other individuals is patently ridiculous.

We need to keep this reality in mind when the defense presents its case in chief and persists in its fabricated accusations of law enforcement tunnel vision and incompetence.

From Grogan's September 21 testimony, we have learned a few interesting things:

- Peterson made several trips to the Berkeley marina that did not coincide with a news story appearing in the *Modesto Bee* or phone calls from Grogan. In fact, in one case to which Geragos previously referred, based on tracking data, Peterson was in Berkeley at 8:00 am, three hours before Grogan called him to apprise him of the search.
- During the second search of the Covena Avenue home in February, cops found a couple of duffel bags that Peterson had packed, containing a little over $2,000 in cash (in Ziploc bags), his watch and wedding ring, a bottle of wine, and a lot of clothing. They let him leave with those bags, contrary to their unmerited reputation as thugs.
- The search warrant for Peterson's home specified drugs, poisons, receipts, bedding, and, interestingly enough, fishing periodicals or

240

literature, of which they found none for the "avid fisherman." For even my most casual hobby, I have a few books or magazines around.

- From a search of the backyard, there was no chicken wire found around any of the trees, although one of the cats was seen to scratch on the trunk of a tree while the cops were there. Apparently, Peterson was one of those guys who starts a lot of projects and never finishes them. For example, he bought a mortising machine, and Laci gave him a 10-inch table saw for Christmas, as if he had impulsively decided to become a carpenter.

- The "LACI-INFO" tip line administered by the Peterson family (specifically Mrs. Peterson and Scott) was not forwarding tips to the Modesto police, as Brocchini noted in previous testimony. If this isn't obstruction of justice, I don't know what is.

- Juxtaposing the phone calls between Peterson and Grogan against Peterson and Amber Frey, it is clear that the defendant can tailor his emotions for his audience, obviously a practiced skill from years of affectation.

He's not fooling anybody any more.

SEPTEMBER 24, 2004
"ULTRA" SOUND REASONING

According to Dr. Greggory Devore, renowned maternal-fetal expert who testified September 22 in the Peterson trial, the first trimester ultrasound that shows the crown-rump measurement is "the most useful and accurate" in determining gestational age of a fetus. Laci's July 16 ultrasound showed the baby's crown-rump length as 32 mm, which, based on Devore's calculations, put the baby's age at ten weeks and one day, based on the standard 40-week calendar that dates the pregnancy from the first day of the last menstrual period. The second ultrasound, performed in September, included measurements of the femur bone, the head and abdomen circumference, the head diameter, and the level of the liver. From his reading of the second ultrasound, Dr. Yip, one of Laci's obstetricians, moved the baby's due date from February 10 to February 16. Dr. Devore disagreed with Yip's interpretation and explained why he believes the first ultrasound to be the "gold standard" in determining fetal age.

The following excerpt from trial transcripts outlines Dr. Devore's calculations to determine the baby's age upon death:

D. HARRIS: In terms of relating this to looking at Connor Peterson's age, having that first trimester ultrasound, having that second trimester ultrasound, does that mean something? DEVORE: Absolutely. It's key. I think to try to understand to -- for example, the femur bone that we have at the time, that we have from the pathology specimen, to its true perspective.

HARRIS: So you looked at the medical records and, at some point in time, you were himself given the femur bone from Connor Peterson?

241

DEVORE: Yes, I was.

HARRIS: And did you perform some type of examination on the femur of Connor Peterson?

DEVORE: I did.

HARRIS: What type of examination did you conduct?

DEVORE: On February the 8th I went to the Coroner's Office in Contra Costa County, and I was given the femur bone. And what I did was, I placed the femur bone into a water bath. It was a tank. And I then had a portable ultrasound machine that I use in the hospitals, for example, when I do consults in the hospitals.

And I put the femur in the water bath. And I then placed the ultrasound called transducer in the water. And the depth was about this deep. And I then measured the femur bone with ultrasound to see how close the ultrasound was to the actual measurement. I repeated that exam three times, obtained three different measurements.

DEVORE (Continued): So I will just go through this for each of these. Excuse me. 64.7 equals 33.15, equals 33 weeks and one day, which equals, I think, December 23rd...65 equals 33.28, which equals 33 weeks two days, which equals December 24th. And the average is 64.5, which equals 33.06, which equals 33 weeks one day, which equals December 23rd.

THE COURT: Those are the estimated dates of death, right?

DEVORE: Yes. Dates of death, yes.

In cross-examination, Geragos reminds me a little of Maxwell Smart:

DEVORE: I think the key thing that the ultrasound is telling us, for example, is that we are looking at a time frame when this baby most likely died. And we have focused in on a period of time of a couple days. And it's consistent with the concept of when some people think this baby died.

GERAGOS: It's consistent with. It's also consistent with the -- that the baby could have died plus or minus five days after that?

DEVORE: I don't believe so.

GERAGOS: [Would you believe] Plus or minus three days?

242

DEVORE: Well, if what you have is, you have -- from the measurements, you have three-day window. And if it died three days later, or died on the 24th at 12:00 o'clock, it's not going to be that precise to the hour to tell you

exactly. Gives you a time frame of several days when the death could have occurred based upon the measurements.

To muddy the waters further, Geragos attempts to discredit Devore's alarming conclusions by asking him about other studies not used in the calculations and the unusual circumstances of the underwater environment:

GERAGOS: Is there something -- did you take into account what happens to the bone if it's been in water? Did you build in any factor for that?

DEVORE: No, I didn't build in a factor for the water.

GERAGOS: Did you talk to Doctor Galloway and ask her what her experience is with bones that have been immersed in water?

Does Dr. Galloway have any data on this? What happened to the defense claim that Connor was born and was protected by a plastic bag, and other apologist theories that have the real perpetrators placing the baby on the marsh just before discovery? It appears that Geragos is stepping on his own hypotheses in order to extend the baby's date of death beyond December 24.

Dr. Devore explains Dr. Galloway's and Yip's methods and how they differ from his:

When Dr. Galloway was given a bone to measure, her job was to try to ascertain what was the age of the fetus at the time of death. And so she gave you a mean and then she gave you ranges. And the reason for the ranges was because they don't know how old that fetus was exactly and they didn't know what the growth potential for that fetus was, therefore, what they basically said was fetuses with bones of this length can fall within this range. The average age of the fetus for this measurement is, say, for example, 35 weeks or whatever she may have used as her average...[However] We have a very accurate way of determining that. [Based on knowing the exact age of the baby from the first ultrasound.]

So, therefore, what we do, and we still use the same equation, therefore, the fetus is of a certain percentile, which we determined in the second trimester femur length, I can use my equation of approximate data age for that measurement, I can then say, hey, now, what would you be expected to be if you grew along that profile, to the 50th percentile out someplace in the distant.

GERAGOS: So you and Dr. Yip are on different pages in terms of that interpretation of the ultrasound; is that correct?

DEVORE: Well, I would say that I've had certainly much more experience with doing this than Dr. Yip has.

GERAGOS: Have you ever met Dr. Yip?

DEVORE: No.

GERAGOS: Do you know how many ultrasounds Dr. Yip has done?

DEVORE I doubt she's done 75,000 of them.

DEVORE: Secondly, the use of the crown-rump length dating the pregnancy has less variability than does the second trimester study. And if you have a first trimester crown-rump, you're going to use that as the reference point versus second trimester study.

GERAGOS: But she didn't –

DEVORE: She chose not to do that, that's correct.

GERAGOS: Well, so you have a different interpretation than the actual OB/GYN in taking care of the baby?

DEVORE: Yes, I do.

Finally, Geragos delivers another one of his famous "hypotheticals" regarding the date of conception, which only serves to make the baby 34 to 35 weeks old, confirming Dr. Galloway's estimate, which then refutes his earlier "reasonable doubt" that the baby was "too young" on December 24 to have died that day.

DEVVORE: [Based on the first ultrasound] We know how old it is. We don't have to answer that anymore. We have to simply say how much did it grow and does that growth represent an age at the time of the death.

GERAGOS: So if I understand this, what you're talking about is once that first part on this bell-shaped is kind of established and you're saying that's that gold standard, the fixed point that you're satisfied with the ten week, Is that correct? Does that mean that the nineteen weeks, four days on femur length, which produced at least for Dr. Yip, the 2/16 change, does that mean that that's a reasonable interpretation of what the age was at that point?

DEVORE: No.

GERAGOS: And can I ask you one other question?

DEVORE: Yes.

GERAGOS: As long as you're saying that's not a reasonable interpretation, does your ten week, one day that you locked in; does that mean that she, that Laci had to conceive on May the 6th?

DEVORE: I don't know.

GERAGOS: Okay. So if the actual conception was prior to that or after May the 20th, how does that affect your calculation?

DEVORE: You'd have to adjust accordingly.

GERAGOS: I mean, does that mean that it could go out into January?

DEVORE: Well, if that were the case you'd have a very abnormal fetus from these measurements from the examination to be that delayed.

GERAGOS: Well, if date of conception was not May 20th, but May 16th, would that make Dr. Yip and the second ultrasound on 12-28 the right date?

DEVORE: It would shift it four days, yes.

GERAGOS: It would shift it four days and the date of death would be the 28th of December?

The latest date Geragos can get Devore to concede to the baby's death is December 28, and by his own blustering incompetence, that's the outside margin of error of five days. Yet, he can't insist the baby was too "young" to die on the 24th (his original line of questioning to Drs. Peterson and Galloway), and then turn around and move back the conception date to May 13 or May 16 in order to make Dr. Devore's calculations show a later date of death. Whatever the strategy, it failed.

SEPTEMBER 26, 2004
THE FINAL DAYS OF FREEDOM

Throughout the trial of California v Peterson, certain people's testimony intrigues me more than others, because I believe they have important evidence to disclose, or their area of expertise is so scientifically significant that they enhance or refute my personal theories, or in the case of California Department of Justice Special Agent Quick, they confirm my "inside information." I was very interested in Peterson's behavior after the bodies of the unidentified baby and woman surfaced in mid-April, because I knew from a person close to his family that he was in Berkeley with his sister, Anne, with whom he had been staying intermittently since February. Apparently, Peterson had enlisted quite a bit of assistance from family members. By April 4, he was driving his father's Ford

245

truck, and by April 16, he was driving the Grady's Lexus while his brother, John, was driving the white Dodge Dakota he bought when he traded in Laci's Land Rover. For a "stone cold innocent" man, it seems odd that he would continue to play "musical cars."

The most important fact brought forth in Quick's testimony was that when a woman's remains were discovered on April 14, law enforcement was not aware of Peterson's whereabouts. Aside from members of his family, a few friends and us, nobody knew where he was, least of all the media! We knew by April 14 that Peterson was back in San Diego, and as I speculated, his behavior that week was indeed very telling. Agent Quick recounts tracking him to Ocean Beach because of a landline call he made to his cell phone voicemail (his brother, John lives there), then to Escondido (his brother, Joe lives there), and to La Jolla (where the Grady's live.)

At 6:00 (unconventionally early for him) on the morning of April 18, Peterson is seen leaving what I assume is the Grady home, with bleached hair, eyebrows and goatee, and led the surveillance, in his newly acquired maroon Mercedes, on a five-hour pleasure drive north to Orange County and then south again (conveniently omitted by the defense advocates), until he is pulled over near the Torrey Pines golf course where his family allegedly has a membership. Curiously, he has no golf clubs or golf shoes in his impressive cache of camping gear, clothing and shoes; thus, the defense's rationale for his trip to the club to meet his family for a round of golf via Los Angeles County seems rather dubious.

Unfortunately, Peterson's life of leisure had come to a screeching halt, and he became a busy little beaver buying equipment, collecting cash, and rising at the crack of dawn to evade arrest. Notice there were zero, zip, nada press personnel gathered near any of his hideouts, nor were there any vans with satellite dishes or media personalities following him on the highway that day, although he took down license plate numbers and car models for his then attorney, Kirk McAllister. Doubtless, Peterson knew they were cops, especially when he saw a few agents with "buzz cuts" when he stopped for gas, and they didn't run up to him with microphones, screaming questions, dragging hapless cameramen behind with trails of wires and lights.

The balance of Grogan's direct, and the first part of the cross-examination from September 23 revealed some important defense "red herring" debunking, a few interesting facts, and tied up a few loose ends:

·   Peterson stayed in or near Lake Arrowhead (where he wanted to meet Amber Frey) in February.

·   The Croton watch, filmed at two different times in the video, appeared not to run. A Croton watch pawned in Modesto was ruled out as Laci's watch because there was no mention of jewels on the face, and it was scratched. The pawned watch fetched only $20 in a loan, which implies it wasn't as valuable as the Peterson's watch, for which they were asking $700 on E-bay.

·   Dodge Hendee, Phil Owen and Al Carter were dispatched to Richmond when Laci's remains surfaced. Possibly Owen or Carter is on deck to testify in the trial.

·   Detective Grogan requested that Dr. Peterson perform Laci's autopsy; he preferred the continuity of the same pathologist conducting both hers and the baby's.

246

· Live by the cell phone, die by the cell phone: Peterson's cell phone betrayed his location in San Diego, just as it had betrayed his location on the morning of December 24, among other geographical inconsistencies exposed in the wire taps. Perhaps if Peterson had ditched his phones on December 23, he might be a free man today.

· In his cross, Geragos repeatedly refers to the "12-foot aluminum boat." It's the incredible shrinking boat defense. By the time he gives his closing arguments, the boat will be the size of a tin cup.

· Peterson returned for credit some quick-setting concrete mix he bought for fence posts in November 2002. No matter how Geragos tries to confuse the issue, with hearsay testimony about a tipster who saw Peterson's flat bed trailer with fence posts and cement mix bags earlier in the fall of 2002, he cannot get past the fact that the anchor was not made of that material, or the fact that his client told people he used the leftover mix to patch his driveway, samples of which do not match the anchor, either.

· Modesto police officers Buehler, Carter and Brocchini accompanied Grogan to San Diego to make the arrest. We have yet to hear from Buehler or Carter but can expect one of them to elaborate on the contents of Peterson's getaway car in upcoming testimony.

OCTOBER 6, 2004
A "MAZE" ING

I was never a big fan of mazes; they were either too simplistic or a strain on the eyes, and two-dimensional nonverbal puzzles were boring. After the advent of computer adventure games, however, mazes evolved into more interesting challenges and were integrated with riddles and logic and multi-dimensional graphics. In the more complex mazes, there are several entrances but only one exit, which is analogous to the Peterson case: despite vague defense rumblings alluding to various potential perpetrators for Laci's murder, only one suspect completes the maze from start to finish without hitting blind alleys, traveling in circles, or getting lost in the thorny brambles of irrational deductions, and that is the defendant. Only Peterson can navigate the labyrinthine path of motive, means, and opportunity defined in this crime.

Let us examine some of the "suspects" foreshadowed by the defense, and follow the factual evidence (as opposed to fantasy theories) from Point A, Laci's last undisputed contact with someone other than her husband on December 23 at 8:30 pm, to Point B, the discovery of Laci and Connor's remains on the east shore of San Francisco Bay the following April.

The Renfro(e) connection: One of the vans seized and later cleared during the investigation belonged to the Renfroes, reportedly a homeless family with no criminal history or motive to abduct a pregnant woman. Should "Deanna Renfro," who borrowed $20 against a Croton watch, turn out to be related (although her last name is spelled differently), she subsequently retrieved the watch, and no nexus between her and Laci has ever been established. No one can place the Renfroe's van at the scene, there was no evidence that Laci was in the van, and the Croton watches do not match, based on the descriptions available from the video and E-bay listing compared to the pawn ticket. This mouse hits a dead end.

247

Kimberly Ann McGregor: Granted, McGregor is a disturbed woman, lived in the neighborhood, and had access to the Peterson home, yet her bizarre activities all occurred after the fact. Prior to Laci's "disappearance," she did not know the couple, had no reason to harm Laci, and once her Hawaiian friends' alibis were verified, that eliminated any possible wherewithal she would have to abduct, murder and take Laci out to the bay to frame Peterson. This mouse reaches a blind alley.

The dark-skinned men with the van across the street: These mice go round and round the same section of the maze and never make any progress. If they were in front of the Medina house at 11:40, assuming they were somehow involved in the burglary, despite the fact that two Caucasian men confessed, were convicted, and sentenced for the crime, McKenzie had already been returned to the backyard over an hour before, even if we grant another 15 minutes to Karen Servas's timeline. Is it reasonable to suggest that Laci was concealed in the van and the perps were standing around across the street an hour later, with the van doors open, allowing the postman, the neighbors, the UPS driver, and all those scruffy, homeless vagrants wandering up and down the street (according to Mrs. Medina) easy visual access?

The park tramps: Touted as the most likely suspects during the 995 hearing, Geragos has since abandoned his original theory that the beanie-wearing, cigarette-bumming, shrub-dwelling thugs in Dry Creek park, observed by Diane Campos at 10:45 that morning as they flanked a pregnant woman along the path and swore at the dog, were responsible for Laci's murder. There were several major problems with this sighting in the first place: the description of the woman's clothing didn't match, the fact that the dog was returned to the yard 15-30 minutes prior, and the fact that Ms. Campos is a smoker, and you know you can't trust smokers. Seriously, the only way that story flies is if Laci took her walk after 10:18, allowing for her to change into the tan pants in which she was found, invalidating that 10-minute window altogether. Unfortunately, the mice hit a dead end when Peterson finds McKenzie in the backyard at 5:00, with the leash still on and the gate closed. What is the likelihood that another neighbor put the dog back in the yard later in the day and never reported this to the police?

Pierce and Todd: One of the theories bandied about by the apologists is that convicted burglars Pierce and Todd, who were found with stolen property from the Medina house (including the safe that Jackson supposedly claimed the dark-skinned men were carrying to the van at 11:40), cut a deal with the Modesto police to cop to the burglary in exchange for immunity for any involvement in Laci's murder so that the police could nail Peterson, even if that required hundreds more man-hours, dozens of law enforcement agencies, wiretaps, GPS, surveillance, and millions of dollars to try an innocent man.

Random Serial Killer: An incredibly lucky and clairvoyant serial killer just happened to be in the neighborhood to grab Laci during her walk (in the maybe half-hour window from the time Peterson left to the time the dog was put back in the yard), knowing her husband would be gone all day, passing up all the easier victims who weren't walking dogs that might bark like crazy or even attack, and went to the unprecedented and extensive inconvenience of transporting her body to the bay after learning a few days later her husband's alibi location, just for the fun of it. Never mind the unnecessary risk and ludicrous logistics involved in such a caper. How many dead ends can one mouse find?

Transient Jewelry Thief: This is Scott's theory that a bum, apparently familiar with Laci's routine and the value of the jewelry she wore regularly, seized upon the opportunity to nab her during her walk and, although desperate enough to kidnap a person for jewelry, somehow had the means (and the stomach) to take her remains to the bay at some point. Perhaps he was disappointed that Laci wasn't wearing her diamonds and engineered this gruesome vendetta to spite the husband. I don't think this mouse finds his way out of the maze, either.

We know Laci was not taken from her vehicle. She didn't have her purse, phone or keys. She wasn't wearing black pants and a white top, a jacket or scarf, and she was found without a blouse. The dog was put back in the yard before 10:30, and the sightings of her beyond that time confound the fact that the dog was not put in the yard again later. No ransom note or contact with the family was ever made, nor did an informant call in a conclusive tip to collect the sizeable reward. The only viable suspect is Peterson. He had the motive (financial and sexual freedom), the means (a boat), and the opportunity (unlimited access to Laci from 8:30 pm on December 23 until 5 pm December 24). Even if we disregard his abhorrent behavior, Amber Frey, his evasive maneuvers, and his desire to rid himself of Laci's property, by the process of elimination, he remains the only mouse that can enter and exit the maze.

Bring on the mice, Geragos.

OCTOBER 8, 2004
EXPROPRIATING ANY DOUBT

Reinvigorated and heated debates involving "reasonable doubt," one of the most misinterpreted and misrepresented concepts in jurisprudence, are predictably active with the Peterson trial followers this weekend. In anticipation of the upcoming defense case, much of which has already been presented through cross-examination, let us review the areas of vulnerability in the State's case and anatomize the logic that would refute the points we expect to see in the next two weeks.

There was no motive, no cause of death, no weapon, and no history of domestic violence. Geragos will attempt to convince the jury that Peterson had no financial or romantic motive to murder Laci, although most of us would dispute that with Peternomics and the defendant's behavior. However, the State is not required to define a motive in order to prove its case. The condition of the bodies obscuring any cause of death works as a double-edged sword for the defense: there is also no evidence of injuries that would have left blood, signature of a serial killer, tool marks, dismemberment, deep puncture wounds, amateur surgery, or any indication that the baby lived, breathed, or ate. Consequently, there is no evidence that another perpetrator, much less a disorganized, random lunatic, was responsible either.

The baby was older than 32 weeks gestation. An inexact science at best, the expert testimony that Connor's measurements show him to be above average size at the time of his death, or that the medical examiner, anthropologist and perinatal specialist do not concur on the precise age does not necessarily prove exculpatory

249

for the defendant. The theory that Laci lived beyond December 24 and was killed later, the baby removed, and both bodies were taken to the bay requires an unreasonable suspension of disbelief. If the baby were the valuable target, why was he later found dead? If Laci was mistaken for a neighboring Deputy District Attorney who resembled her, why would her killer go to the trouble (and enormous risk) of transporting the bodies to frame Peterson? Logically, if the baby were the prize, either for organs or black market adoption, he would not have been found practically unscathed on the marsh in Richmond. Similarly, it is highly unlikely that Laci would have suffered extensive damage from being underwater for so many months.

There is no physical evidence connecting Peterson to the murder. This is actually the most troublesome issue in the entire case, but once again it cuts both ways: there is no physical evidence connecting anyone else to the murder, either. None of the tarps, plastic bags, twine, kelp, fabric, hair or other debris disclosed another perpetrator's fingerprints, criminal profile, or modus, and as Distaso said, "This is not an episode of CSI." That Peterson left no compelling forensic evidence in the house, boat, warehouse or truck is explained by the fact that finding any of Laci's DNA in her own property or that of her husband would not be remarkable. The hairs clutched in the teeth of the pliers are the only incriminating clue, and even that is weak. The jury may conclude that the crime was bloodless and quick, and that she was wrapped in a tarp or the (later gasoline-soaked) boat cover during the journey to the bay.

No anchors were found despite comprehensive searching. Geragos will vigorously challenge the concrete evidence, intimating corrupted samples (alluding that Brocchini deliberately sent material from the warehouse and not the driveway), and producing bags of post mix and proof of concrete work around the house that will rationalize the missing concrete mix and the mess in the warehouse. Nonetheless, this will not refute the scientific reality that Laci was weighted down in the water; otherwise she would have surfaced much, much sooner. Those five voided circles are going to be difficult to ignore as well.

"Tunnel vision," police incompetence, conspiracies, neglected leads, ignored sightings, and various allegations of impropriety demonstrated a bush league investigation that failed to explore other avenues. I believe the testimonies of Cloward, Grogan, and Brocchini rebut this feeble (and rather desperate) claim. It is unreasonable to expect the police to follow obviously counterfactual leads or expend resources to research every missing woman, every murder, every burglary, every van or every suspicious vagrant, mail thief, drug gang, and registered offender in Modesto to substantiate a thorough enough investigation to satisfy the defense in this case.

Reasonable doubt does not mean any doubt or beyond the shadow of a doubt. It means the alternate scenario has to make sense and align with the facts in evidence. Because, if Peterson didn't murder Laci, who did? It's not enough to show that certain pieces don't fit perfectly or that there are other innocent explanations for Peterson's behavior. The jury will be instructed as to the specific definition of the law, and barring obstinate ignorance or stealth agendas, the jury will enter deliberations with unequivocal proof for a conviction.

OCTOBER 9, 2004
RELIANCE ON SCIENCE

Today's juries have been spoiled by science and technology. Less than 20 years ago, identifying a victim's blood type at a crime scene was considered state of the art and served as very damaging evidence at trial. Given the fact that a specific blood type in the ABO group can comprise over 20 percent of the population, fans of "CSI" and "Forensic Files" may be surprised to learn that such imprecise blood evidence was decisive to securing guilty verdicts from juries for decades. On a scientific timeline, identifying human blood itself, separate from animal blood, paint, chemicals, or organic material, was a relatively recent major leap, enabling investigators to locate blood on a variety of materials and in places never before possible.

Hair strands found trapped in a pliers under the bench of Scott Peterson's boat have been identified as being probably Laci's by its mitochondrial DNA: an advance in science so selective, it can narrow down the donor to the one in thousands, as opposed to blood typing, which includes candidates in the tens of millions. Is this not sophisticated enough? Is the defense going to argue that some other person's hair was in Peterson's tool? Judging by the lengths to which Geragos attempted to suppress both the science and the hairs, suggesting they were tainted or planted, and attempting to place Laci inside the boat in December (somehow shedding her hair so that it was captured inside a tool), we can appreciate his discomfort with the inference the jury will make with the mtDNA evidence.

Prior to the computer and cell phone age, tracking phone calls was cumbersome and unreliable, and easily evaded. With as many calls as Peterson made on his five cell phones, even without the wiretapping, it would have been relatively easy to determine whom he was calling, how often, and for how long. The People have shown his phone habits as another illustration of his state of mind after the murder and his propensity to lie to everyone, including his family. The documentation was incriminating enough without the tapes, but the tapes brought to life the chameleon personalities Peterson donned, based on to whom he was speaking. Other than hooking him up to a voice analyzer, which Geragos would call "junk science," it just doesn't get much better than this for revealing the defendant's multiple layers of deceit and fantasy.

Before GPS or other sophisticated surveillance techniques, consistent cooperation from adjoining law enforcement jurisdictions, substantial manpower and resources used for stakeouts, and physical tracking were employed to follow a suspect who was gallivanting around as much as Peterson. Nevertheless, it was done, with laborious record keeping and long, boring hours with stale coffee and binoculars. Today, modern law enforcement will seek to substitute, wherever legally feasible, less labor intensive and more reliable means of tracking a suspect, which not only save tax dollars, but are actually less intrusive than personal reconnaissance, which belies the defense's posture that the surveillance was a violation of Peterson's rights.

Bloodhounds and cadaver dogs have no agendas, are not privy to politics or bias, and are not personally attached to the outcome of a search. Their impressive skills and proven accuracy in locating bodies, scent trails, and human detritus are widely accepted and applauded as a reliable investigative tool. The dogs trained in Contra Costa, while not perfect, are famous in the region, and their dependability would pass muster in any court in California. The defense, however, has already reproached the remaining tracking dog evidence as "voodoo," and we can expect to see one of the dog handlers (Ron Seitz) testify that his dog didn't pick up Laci's scent at the marina. We need to remember that Seitz's dog wasn't taken to the parking lot and boat launch area where Trimble picked up Laci's scent and tracked it to the end of the pier.

With all the technology and scientific advances at our disposal, there remains a research gap with regard to data on submerged pregnant women and the state of their fetuses in a body of salt water for several months. Fortunately, there are not enough subjects to study this phenomenon, but it leaves the argument entirely subject to speculation and assumption. Nevertheless, common sense should prevail, as it did for hundreds of years before forensic science became a make-or-break issue in a criminal trial.

OCTOBER 20, 2004
TIMING IS EVERYTHING

Media pundits with selective opinions, defense apologists, and Peterson groupies have filled the airwaves, newspapers, and *cyberspace* with "innocent interpretations" of Scott Peterson's activities and behavior before and during the investigation of Laci's murder. His advocates continuously remind us that, according to the law, the jury will be instructed to accept explanations that point to the defendant's innocence. They conveniently fail to include the rest of the instruction, which explains, "If one interpretation [of such evidence] appears to be reasonable, and the other interpretation appears to be unreasonable, you must accept the reasonable and reject the unreasonable."

In isolation, some of Peterson's activities and decisions appear perhaps irresponsible, insensitive, shortsighted, or warranted. In the context of the mosaic of events between November 2002 and April 2003, however, there are no "reasonable" explanations for Peterson's most incriminating behavior that point to innocence; on the contrary, as we will see, timing is everything.

Peterson tells Amber Frey on December 6, 2002, that he "lost" his wife and the upcoming holidays would be the first without her. Fellow cads and women who look the other way at adultery claim that this odd statement was merely a pickup line to secure a short-term sexual relationship with Frey. I accept that men lie about their marital status and tell outrageous stories with ulterior motives, but the fact that three weeks later Peterson's wife "disappeared" and he spent Christmas without her was a little too coincidental for most. What would ordinarily qualify for a yellow flag from the dating referee became a full-scale red alert.

A few days after telling Amber about his "lost" wife, Peterson was researching tides, currents, and deep-water areas in the San Francisco Bay. He was also investigating other deep, fresh waterways at least 200 miles from

Modesto, and glancing at a few sites relating to sturgeon fishing. His ardent defenders minimize the significance of the Bay research, claiming he was merely looking for a place to catch sturgeon. However, Peterson travels a considerable distance to the Bay (a very inconvenient place to fish for an hour when you have plans in the early evening), and his wife and baby's remains are found in the exact location he had researched and visited. It appears as though Peterson was really planning to lose his wife, and the decision remained where, exactly, should he lose her? In context, this information is evidence of premeditation.

The next stage of the plan required a vessel: a method to transport a body to one of the researched waterways. Peterson wasn't wasting any time. Despite the fact that barely a week before he had joined a country club with numerous recreational offerings; or that Christmas was three weeks away and his wife would, the very next day, undersell a few pieces of jewelry for quick cash; or that the couple was expecting their first baby in two months and no telling what urgent financial demands that may bring. No, Peterson was purchasing a boat and trailer with $1400 in cash on December 9. Never mind that he kept the purchase a secret from his friends and family.

Ten days later, Peterson buys a few fishing props and a legitimate two-day fishing license with the added ocean stamp, and fills out the dates as December 23-24. Clearly, he was planning a visit to a salt-water area on one or both of those dates. By then he knew his work schedule (which was generally wide open), and when he would have the block of time necessary to make the trip(s). Yet, on the evening of the 23rd, he offered to pick up a fruit basket the next day for his sister-in-law, Amy, because he said he would be in the area playing golf. What is an innocent explanation for Peterson planning a fishing trip (by filling out the dates), not going on the 23rd, and then telling his wife and her sister that he's golfing the next day, the remaining day on the license that he took pains to acquire? There isn't one.

So, Scott drove 200 miles, spent four hours in a truck on his day off when he practically lives in the truck as part of his job, to spend about an hour fishing. Then he forgets to bring the right rod on board. In isolation, this decision seems like poor planning and a huge waste of time and gas. In the context of prior and subsequent events, this decision was obviously unavoidable. Whether Peterson's original plans were to golf on the 24th, after using his new boat to dump his wife's body the night before, or whether he changed his mind and took only one trip to the Bay on the 24th, the fact that he placed himself 90 miles away on the very day his wife "disappeared" and then, a few months later, hers and their baby's body surface in the same area is far too great a coincidence to explain away with fruitcake theories.

Meanwhile, Amber Frey was still in the dark about Peterson's marital status, his missing wife, and his actual whereabouts. On New Year's Eve, when thousands of people gathered to pray and lend support to Laci's family and him during a candlelight vigil, Peterson dialed up his gal pal and gleefully recounted, "I'm in Paris! Listen to that crowd! There are fireworks over the Eiffel Tower!" as he held the cell phone out for Amber to hear the noise. I would not be surprised to find out some day that this specific act alone clinched a guilty verdict from one of the jurors.

253

People buy and sell automobiles and homes every day, but not usually within a month of their spouse's going "missing," and the property just so happened to be hers. When we learn that Peterson was so eager to get out of their house on Covena Avenue that he was willing to sell it furnished, in the context of the big picture here, the timing is simply atrocious.

Like a moth to a flame, Peterson was repeatedly drawn to the Bay. He rented cars and stayed five minutes. When did he go - on a leisurely Sunday afternoon in warm weather? No. He went when he knew there were underwater searches taking place.

In April just before his wife and baby's remains were discovered, Peterson dyed his hair, bought a Mercedes with his mother's name, packed the car with camping gear, clothing, $15,000 in cash, and his brother's ID, and appeared poised for flight. During his last week of freedom, he remained incommunicado and never once inquired about the unidentified woman and fetus found on the east shore of the Bay that everyone with reading comprehension above a first-grade level suspected was probably Laci and Connor. His defenders offer the lame excuse that he was avoiding the media, yet the media hadn't seen him for over a month and didn't know where he was. Detective Grogan didn't even know where Peterson was until he checked his voicemail and was traced to San Diego.

Several other odd things occurred in which the timing was significant. Peterson obtained a post office box on December 23, almost as an afterthought, three weeks after being advised by a Tradecorp officer that the a check was stolen from the warehouse complex mail box. The day after his wife "disappeared," Peterson had an attorney sitting at the dining room table when the dog handlers arrived. He promised Amber that he would be more available to her by late January. Kim McGregor burglarized his home the night he publicly announced he would be down in Los Angeles organizing a one-day search center. He admitted to making a concrete anchor December 18 and left a big mess on the flat bed indicating a major project. He moved the boat cover to the shed under a leaky leaf blower the day after he went to the Bay. The electricity was mysteriously off in the warehouse the night of the 24th when Brocchini asked to see the boat. He arranged media interviews only after Amber's press conference exposed their affair. He paid his overdue health insurance premiums on December 23. He threw his "fishing clothes" in the wash when he arrived home, ignoring an overflowing hamper of dirty laundry in the bedroom. He asked Brocchini about grief counseling, cadaver dogs, and his missing handgun the night of Laci's disappearance.

Are these events rationalized by innocent, reasonable explanations, or are they the sinister, calculated, and occasionally obtuse actions of a ruthless killer? In a case predominantly comprised of a series of interrelated circumstances, timing is everything.

OCTOBER 24, 2004
THE HARD SELL OF THE DEFENSE CASE

A good defense attorney has to be a good salesman. He has to build rapport with the jury, establish trust, overcome its resistance and objections to his "product" (his story), and ask for the sale: the verdict of not guilty. In the upcoming continuation of the defense *case, Mark* Geragos faces what would be considered in the sales lexicon a "hard sell." His approach will be characterized by aggressive criticism of the investigation, manipulation of events and circumstances, and compelling drama that will grab the jury's attention and persuade it of the merits of his case.

Salespeople undergo various styles of training, but every seminar and manual share similar techniques. Let us explore some of the common denominators of a successful sales strategy and evaluate the potential outcome of Mr. Geragos's objectives.

The pivotal role of trust

Trust is rarely established on the initial sales call; it is earned or lost over the course of the relationship, since good salespeople strive to develop relationships with their customers. In fact, a good relationship can overcome many unforeseen mistakes in the process, such as late shipments, incorrect or defective products, and price increases. Customers are far more willing to give you the benefit of the doubt if they like you personally and trust that you have their best interests at heart. You teach customers to trust you through your consistency in actions and by keeping your promises. Has Geragos kept his promises? Judging by his opening statements, he hasn't. Instead, he's resorted to "bait and switch" maneuvers with regard to the pawn ticket, the witnesses who saw Laci walking the dog, the forensic proof of a live birth, and other exculpatory evidence he claims to possess. If the jury's trust in Geragos has eroded over the past few months, the hurdles of its resistance and skepticism will be extremely difficult to overcome.

Building rapport

By employing humor, sarcasm, and indignation, Geragos attempted to endear himself to the jury and to establish common ground with what (he hoped) was its aversion to accepting the police investigation of his client at face value. If he misread most of them, and instead repelled or bored them with his behavior, he has too much ground to reclaim at this point to reestablish their good will. Similarly, if his product (Peterson) is beyond redemption in the eyes of the jury, which is very possible, he's fighting an uphill battle.

Sell the "benefits" not the "features"

255

Geragos struggles to sell the "benefits" of Peterson's acquittal. Are there any benefits to letting Peterson walk? Beyond the parameters of their legal obligation, the jurors will need to leave this time-consuming trial feeling good about their decision. Will they be able to face their families, communities, and selves with that verdict? Or, will they, in good conscience, balk at a unanimous decision and delegate a retrial, with all its attendant taxpayer costs and prolonged agony to the victims' family, to another jury of their fellow Californians?

Will they acquit Peterson based on shadowy transients, tan vans, unreliable hearsay, sympathy for Peterson's devoted family, inexact scientific conclusions, or unsubstantiated allegations of police misconduct or incompetence? I submit that the only win-win conclusion to this trial is a guilty verdict, because the defense will not and cannot demonstrate any reasonable doubt as to who murdered Laci and Connor Peterson.

No murder trial is perfect; no investigation is perfect; people are flawed and prone to mistakes and faulty memories. The prosecution's "sales" presentation was disconnected, overly detailed, cumbersome and confusing. Nevertheless, the jurors, like consumers, will be forced to choose between "buying" the story from a humble, mousy, soft-spoken nebbish with two left feet, or that of a flashy, Hollywood huckster in Armani suits.

The question remains, will the jury buy an innocent client from this man?

NOVEMBER 1, 2004
BY JOVE, I THINK THEY'VE GOT IT!

As a lifelong Cleveland Indians fan, it's practically second nature for me to anxiously watch ballgames between the fingers of my hands covering my face and wonder, "What are they *doing*?" Observing the Peterson trial in person and reading the transcripts have evoked similar dread. Some of the People's decisions regarding the batting order of witnesses, switch-hitting theories, prolonged pitching slumps, and bottom-of-the-ninth strategies reminds me of a World Series ballgame that has gone into extra innings. Just when I think the agony will never end, Rick Distaso rips a two-run double in his closing statement enlivening the sluggish crowd and earning the MVP award for the game.

From key excerpts of Distaso's closing emerge the crux of the People's case against Peterson:

> ...*the biggest part of this case [is] the betrayal aspect of Scott Peterson. Laci Peterson had no idea what was coming from this man. And, in fact, she probably*
> *trusted him more than anybody else...*

The victims' vulnerability and accessibility to the defendant highlight the fact that only Peterson had the opportunity and means to accomplish his lethal intentions within the constricted timeline.

> *The only man -- or only person that we know without any doubt that was in the exact location where Laci and Connor's bodies washed ashore, at the exact time that they went missing, is sitting right there.*

Distaso reminds the jurors early in his remarks of the most incriminating circumstantial evidence against Peterson: the location where the victims were discovered within a relatively short distance to where Peterson admitted to "fishing" on December 24. Finally, after months of nebulous inferences, Distaso outlines the People's theory of the murder:

> *The defendant strangled or smothered Laci Peterson the night of December 23rd, or in the morning while she was getting dressed on the 24th. I can't tell you when he did it. I can't tell you if he did it at night. I can't tell you if he did it in the morning. I'm not going to try to convince you of something that I can't prove. I don't have to prove that to you. I only have to prove that he did it.*

Actually, the People could have convincingly made a case for Peterson's making two trips to the San Francisco Bay based on his cell and land line records showing no phone activity from before 9:00 pm on December 23 to just after 10:00 am December 24, along with using Gene Ralston's side scan sonar images of a body in the Richmond entrance channel taken in mid-March. However, the People chose instead to propose a less specific scenario for reasons I will postulate in a later entry.

> *After he gets the weights attached, he puts the cover on the boat. Here's what it looks like. You can't see into the boat with the cover on. He puts the bungee cords on, straps it down, and he drives off to the Bay. Nobody can see a single thing that this man has done.*

I agree that Peterson most likely transported Laci's body in the covered boat, which is why he doused the cover with gasoline and left it under a leaky leaf blower in his shed for the police to find on December 26.

> *He drives out to Brooks Island. He dumps Laci out. It takes him all of, what? He gets there at 12:54. We know from his cell phone records he's back at the marina at 2:12. So it takes him less than an hour.*

This is where the People take liberty with the facts (as they know them), but since the jury is unaware of the sonar images, Distaso can propose this hypothesis in order to narrow the geography down to the areas of Brooks Island, where Peterson has admitted to trolling on December 24, and Pt. Isabel and Richmond, a mile east of the island where the victims' remains washed ashore.

> *Let's talk about who is going to suspect him. Everybody thinks he's the perfect husband, right? [The] perfect couple. They're living the American Dream. They're madly in love. We heard all of this stuff. Well, you know what? Show me something that's perfect and I'll show you something that's not.*

Distaso illuminates Peterson's heart of darkness that conceived and concocted this cataclysmic course of action:

> *Here's how well the defendant in his mind was perceiving himself. Not his fantasy world, because we're going to talk about that, but this is how he felt about his reality. He thinks he's facing midlife. The guy is turning 30, but he thinks he's facing midlife. But that's what he tells Amber in one of the calls. I'm old, he said.*

> *He tells Brent Rocha, you know, I'm doing bad at my job, I'm turning 30 and becoming a father all in the same year. Boy, life really stinks for Scott Peterson. You know, most people would be overjoyed to have this. Maybe not the lousy salesman part, but the rest of it for sure. But not this guy.*

If this were a musical composition, Peterson's myopic mindset is the prelude, and his dual life is the fugue with the recurrent narcissistic melody of grandiosity, delusions of wealth and status, and affected egotism.

> *The two lives of Scott Peterson. Peterson created a fantasy life for himself. Scott Peterson, in his fantasy world he was rich, he was successful, he had a beautiful girlfriend, he was a jet setter. Remember, vacations in Kennebunkport, fishing in Alaska, jetting off to Europe?*

> *He actually says he owns Tradecorp. He says one of my nametags attracts women. I'm rich. Horny bastard. Remember that that was his nickname, HB, in every one of his e-mails. And this I think is the most important thing, though, of all those things I just told you. First off he tells her he's looking for another relationship. Okay, we got that. Then he tells her this...I was once with a woman who was my soul mate, but I lost her. He's talking about Laci then in October. Laci Peterson was dead to Scott Peterson a long time before he actually killed her.*

> *Two lives catching up on Scott Peterson. He wants, in public, everybody to think he's doing the right things. He's the grieving husband. He's cooperative with the police. He is helping out. He's doing the things. None of it is true.*

> *Two lives: Private life, public life.*

Despite media "love spin," and Geragos's sneering references in his opening statement and cross-examination to the notion that Amber Frey presented a component of the People's proposed motive for Laci's murder, Distaso distinctly disowns that theory:

> *I don't think he killed Laci Peterson to go marry Amber Frey, though. Amber Frey represented to him freedom. Freedom is what he wanted. The end-of-January comments is important because he knows what he's*

going to do and he figures -- you know, he's not a stupid man. We've seen that. He knows there's going to be some uproar, some hoopla, over Laci going missing. He has no idea it's going to snowball into this huge mass that it became. He had no idea that was going to happen. No one did.

He thought: Yeah, everyone's going to, you know, a couple weeks will goby, everyone is going to be worried, looking for her, the police will do their standard thing, fill out a missing persons report, nothing will happen and that will be the end of it.

Distaso reiterates Peterson's statements, behavior, and actions that define premeditation and lines them up like damning dominoes:

He tells Amber throughout the month of December, you know, he doesn't want any children, her child's going to be enough for him. It's a perfect relationship, of course, because her child doesn't mean anything to him. He has no connection to it, he has no responsibility to it, he can do whatever he wants. He can leave and show back up whenever he wants.

This is on December 6th: I told her the truth that I lost my wife. Of course, he hadn't lost his wife until he actually killed her, but in his mind, you know what? Maybe that was the truth. She was dead to him a long time before he killed her.

Recently dead. That's what he said. Those are his words. On December 7th he researches boats, waterways in Northern California, both freshwater and salt water. On December 8th he looks up Bay charts and fishing information. This short period of time in December is the only fishing and boating information on his computer. So the avid fisherman apparently never needs to look up any information at all about fishing. And we're going to talk about his fishing abilities in a minute.

So December 9th he buys a boat. On that same day he goes down to Amber's home crying, tells her that he's sorry, he's lied to her, he actually had been married and he lost his wife. In marked contrast to that, to the defendant's actions in putting this plan into place to kill Laci, the two lives going on here.

Was the revelation of his murky marital status the catalyst for Peterson's frenzied activity in early December, or did it merely solidify the deadly design he had been harboring in his implacable imagination for months? Based on Distaso's opinion that Laci was "dead to him a long time before he killed her", we can conclude that the prosecution believed that murder was brewing in Scott's mind soon after he learned of his impending fatherhood and the restrictions on his reinvented parallel life such a burden would impose.

Distaso delves a bit into Peterson's psyche and sketches a portrait of a person of the lie: someone who is facile at lying, who lies without regard to logic,

259

and who lies sometimes seemingly without purpose. At the same time, people of the lie expect to be believed because of their credible and upright image in their sphere of influence.

> *He's not lying just because he can't tell the truth. He can tell the truth. Some things he said was true. He did go to the Berkeley Marina. The reason he's doing this is, he has to keep his supporters on the hook to keep his support base behind him, to keep the pressure off of him, and the suspicion away from him. That's why he's doing this. That's why these lies were important, not just because he's lying, because of who and what he's lying about.*

> *He told the news media for sure that he told Laci about his affair with Amber in early December. He says she knew all about it. I don't think there's a single person in this courtroom who believes that. Except for maybe him.*

> *I expect people to believe that. I'm Scott Peterson. I expect people to believe anything I say. That's what this guy wants you to believe here. You think -- there's no arguing? No, not at all; I can't even say -- well, I can't say she was okay with it; but it was not any big deal with us.*

> *...but he's a good liar. He comes up with a story quick. Much quicker than me. You can tell if I'm lying. It's all over my face. Not this guy. He can look Diane Sawyer straight in the eye and tell her a bald-faced lie.*

When confronted with the indisputable and awkward revelation of his affair with Amber Frey, Peterson resorts to the common justification that accused rapists employ: he insists his predatory sexual exploits were consensual to both women.

> *He bought this two-day license [yet] he told us and he told Detective Brocchini that it was a morning decision to go fishing. Do you remember that? It was either go to play golf at the club or go fishing. It was that morning he decided to go. If that's true, why is this license filled out for December 23rd and December 24th? Why would you fill out a license on the 24th for the day before?*

Peterson purchased the two-day license (with an ocean stamp) on December 20, four days before, along with several lures and a small fishing rod, which indicates he at least had the props to appear to be going fishing, if nothing else. Devising appearances is his chief priority, for example, imitating an international business tycoon to Amber, telling her he was in Maine for the holidays, and staging Laci's "abduction."

> *So [according to Peterson] she puts on all of her jewelry to then, I guess, go mop the floor. Because he says, when he says he leaves, she's mopping the floor, she's got on a white shirt and black pants, and she's barefoot. So she has to have put her jewelry on, finish mopping the floor,*

put on her shoes and socks, change her clothes -- because remember, when she's found, Laci Peterson is not wearing black pants. Laci Peterson is wearing a pair of pants just like these. No one confuses these pants with black. Except for maybe him. Because that man confused Modesto with Paris, Brussels, Normandy, France, and everywhere else.

Distaso closes the ten-minute window with a resounding slam.

Nobody -- I don't care how upset you are, nobody forgets that they just got home from fishing at the Berkeley Marina. That didn't happen. So why did he tell them golfing? That's a much more important question, because that's where the defendant was originally going to go. He was going to get out there, dump Laci, get back, go hang out at the club, maybe have a drink at the bar, you know, screw around a little bit. It just took him longer than he planned.

He was going to say: Yeah, I was at work checking my computer; yeah, I was there, see? And I went to the club and, you know, you'll have some people that saw him, and that was it. He just screwed up. He screwed up his alibi. That's all that was.

I agree that Peterson was planning to go to Del Rio Country Club on December 24, but not later in the day to have a drink or hang around. I believe he intended to play golf in the morning, because he expected to have accomplished his task by then. That's why he procured a fishing license for December 23 and 24, so he'd have an extra day to tie up loose ends in case he had to go back. If he had planned to dispose of Laci's body on the 24th, he never would have frittered away the morning at the office.

The Bay is huge. He thought he got her into deep water. You heard what the experts say, you get her into the deep-water channel, she's going out under the Golden Gate. You heard how difficult it was to search the Bay. We're going to talk about that. It's no big deal to tell them: I was out fishing in the San Francisco Bay; how are they ever going to find her.

Distaso fails to bring up the charts showing that Peterson researched water depths of the East Bay and the shipping channel near the Point Portrero Turn where he actually dumped Laci's body in relatively deep water, hoping it would be carried out to sea or destroyed beyond recognition.

Is it a risky thing to go out in the San Francisco Bay by yourself in a boat you have never used before? Yes. Is it a risky thing to kill your wife and you have to get rid of her body? Yes. If you are going to take someone out there, get rid of them, you will take the risk. If you are just going out for a pleasure cruise, your maiden voyage, no way. No way one can believe that's true except for maybe this guy, in his fantasyland kind of mind, he might believe it's true.

261

It's also very risky to lead a double life, live beyond your means, and to consistently disappoint your employer; but to Peterson, this was standard operating procedure.

> *Can't [live a free-wheeling bachelor life] when he's paying child support and alimony, and everything else. It's not like this guy was rich. Although his parents gave him a ton of money. I guess they could bail him out. But he wasn't making a ton of money. He didn't want to be tied to that kid for the rest of his life. He didn't want to be tied to Laci for the rest of his life, so he killed her. It's as simple as that.*

> *[Scott tells Amber Frey] "I never had a prolonged period of freedom like that from responsibility, and this is interesting to me, and something you could incorporate into life." Remember he is still in Europe, still working the plan. And in Scott Peterson's kind of fantasy world, things were going to work out for him. Never had that prolonged period of freedom from responsibility. That's what this guy wanted. That's what this guy had just gotten.*

> *The reason he's doing all these things [trading in Laci's car, trying to sell the house, ordering pornographic channels on the satellite dish] is because he knows she's not coming back. And he's just separating his life from Modesto, his life from Laci, his life from Connor, and he's starting anew. It was all part of the plan that he started way back in October.*

Here, Distaso alludes to Peterson's proclivity for metamorphosis and attempts to illustrate for the jury a somewhat arcane concept: suicide by proxy. Peterson commits a kind of suicide by killing his former life so that he can reinvent his new life with a clean slate.

> *He's never told [Amber] he loved her. I don't think Scott Peterson did love her. Scott Peterson doesn't love anybody but himself. Didn't love Laci. How could he have done all the things he did and love Laci? Didn't love Amber. Didn't love his parents. He lied to them constantly. His friends, he lied to them too. Scott Peterson loved himself, no doubt about that.*

Distaso never labels Peterson a "narcissist," but he characterizes him as one in this statement. Perhaps he didn't want to articulate a categorical personality disorder on the record that a psychiatrist could exploit to excuse Peterson's behavior somewhere down the road; yet behind closed doors when scripting its closing remarks, you can bet the prosecution team called him the "n" word, among other things.

> *You know why I played that [New Years Eve] call? Listen to his demeanor, and then put it in the context with what's going on in Modesto at that time. He's laughing. He's happy.*

You know, there is no playbook for grief. That's what people have told me when I talked about this. I agreed with that. Everybody grieves differently. **Nobody grieves like that.**

This is not a guy who is intimidated by, really, anybody, or anything. He's certainly not intimidated by the media.

[In the Brocchini interview] Calm, cool, collected, chuckling at times. Where, where is any concern at all? Oh, she told me what she was going to do for the day. You know, no big deal. Yeah, she's gone. No big deal. He can turn the tears on when he wants to, though, can't he?

It's a pity Peterson didn't fake grief a little better, or stay off the cell phones from early December 24 until the bodies of his wife and baby surfaced. He may never have been arrested, much less be facing a murder trial.

And what their expert said is No, he had all this money, he had tons of money to spend, look at this chart. Remember they put this chart up where it looked like he had two thousand dollars a month, you know, of free money just to spend away. And all of a sudden we asked him Is that gross or net? You know, we all got to pay taxes. Oh, well, yeah, that's -- that's gross, so, you know, immediately cut -- cut that down by a third, cut this down, cut that down.

It was not an accurate portrayal of these people's finances.. What the defense   expert presented to you was just not correct.

The prosecution continues to understate the importance of Peternomics. A more accurate bottom line would show that Peterson was deep in debt, had little equity left on his home, was performing substantially below par in his sales job, and was barely covering the monthly interest on his credit cards. In fact, according to his credit report, Peterson had nearly reached the spending limit of at least one of his VISA cards, and the alleged credit lines to which Geragos referred were mostly inactive or closed accounts.

There is no disputing that he had recently acquired camping equipment, a shovel, a water purifier, a mask and snorkel, a camp saw, knives, a rope, camp axe. You have seen the pictures of all the things he had. He had a hammock. He had his -- he had Anne Bird, his sister's, credit card. He had his brother John's ID.

Remember what the testimony was about why he had the ID? That's ludicrous also. Here's a guy with $15,000 in cash in his car. He is just carrying loose. He's going to get his brother's ID so he can go rip off Torrey Pines for 25, or what was it 25 or 30 bucks? Does anybody believe that? Do you think he believes that?

This is from a family that gave him $30,000 for that Del Rio membership. Was it like 20 or 30 -- I don't remember exact number. Some significant amount of money 20 or 30 thousand, something like that for a down payment on the house. Lee Peterson gave him $5,000 in January.

Remember his mom testified on April 8th she gave him six or eight thousand dollars. And then she gave him another -- on April 17th -- $10,000. But we're supposed to believe that for 25 or 30 bucks or 50 bucks, whatever the testimony was, he's going to be ripping off Torrey Pines? That's. That's ludicrous. He's got his brother's ID.

He said, well, yeah, his brother John, or whoever, was just dying to have Scott's truck, so he had to sell it, had to run off and try to buy a Saab in his mom's name, then a Mercedes. You know, I think it was clear that his family would do what they have to do to protect him from being prosecuted in this case.

Here we have a summary of "Scotty's Roundup," and uncomely details of his family's eager complicity in his escape. The issue of saving money at the golf course reminds us of Peterson's excuse to Grogan that he made anchors from $3 worth of concrete mix rather than spend $20 on a more utilitarian metal version. This is a man who spends $30 on a pipe wrench at a Bakersfield Sears, and $20 on a bicycle lock at K-Mart, and is found with over $2,000 in cash in plastic zipper bags in his duffel bag in February; but he's too cheap to buy an anchor?

And you heard about this neighborhood. You heard about all these -- you know, you are wondering why we are putting on all these pregnant ladies up on the stand to testify about walking the neighborhood. Because a lot of people, a lot of pregnant women walk their dogs in that neighborhood, and nothing ever happens to them. Some of them even look like Laci Peterson.

That some of the neighborhood women resembled Laci Peterson is at least as important as the reality that none of them were abducted or harassed by the vagrants, tramps and thieves that Geragos claimed were an omnipresent menace in Dry Creek Park. Many of us theorized that seeing women (pregnant or wearing bulky clothing) walking dogs in the neighborhood inspired Peterson's abduction scenario .How many of these coincidences does the defense want you to swallow and have you still call yourselves reasonable people? If the explanation for all of these facts taken together is not reasonable as defense is trying to present, you must reject it.

If the evidence as we present, as I have argued it today, is reasonable, you must accept it and find this man guilty of the murder of his wife and son.

Peterson's apologists misinterpret Distaso's final remarks as unfairly placing the burden of proof on the defense. However, according to the definition of "reasonable doubt", the jury was within the law to reject unreasonable explanations of Laci's murder that contradicted logic, opportunity, witness testimony, and the surfeit of evidence demonstrating Peterson's culpability. The fact that Mark Geragos failed to present any witnesses who saw Laci walking the dog, visiting the warehouse, sighted in Tracy, confronting homeless people, or wearing tan pants and a black coat that morning confirms what we have suspected for months: there weren't any.

NOVEMBER 2, 2004
"DO YOU ALL HATE HIM?"

Who better to defend a "14-karat jerk" than another 14-karat jerk? Mark Geragos began his closing arguments today in the Peterson trial with the following question to the jury:

Do you all hate him?

Did the jurors nod their heads, or were they shocked at what Peterson might define as an "unapproachable" defense? Why would Geragos concede not only that his client was a cad, but that the jury should also have reason to hate him? Is this the best defense $1 million can buy?

This guy's the biggest jerk that ever walked the face of the Earth, the biggest liar on the face of the Earth, and you should hate him, hate him, hate him.

Did Geragos warn Peterson that he was going to vilify him in his closing, make him out to be an idiot, a liar, a philanderer and an "asshole?" (Yes, he used that word.) How does a narcissist like Peterson sit through this ego-bashing ridicule in smug silence?

Don't bother with the fact that the evidence shows clearly he didn't do this. Just hate him, because if you hate him, you'll convict him.

On the contrary, the evidence summarized in Distaso's closing yesterday was substantially convincing that Peterson murdered his wife and unborn son and that the entire nation has just cause to despise him. Similarly, we have reasons to censure his defense team and the misled supporters who have spread lies and allegations pointing suspicion toward Laci's family or Amber Frey for the past six months. We have collective contempt for the media pundits who have misstated the evidence or presented preposterous ideas that skew reality and common sense, just to make a buck on this tragedy. We have reason to detest the Peterson family and their wretched behavior and violation of all that is decent and honorable among victims of homicide and their loved ones.

The only thing they're banking on is you'll hate him, and if you hate him you will suspend rationality.

265

While Geragos complains about suspending rationality on one hand, in the other, he is waving his wand with its magic pixie dust, hoping he can transfix the jurors to suspend their disbelief of his fantasy theories about vagrants, tramps and thieves who had a motive to murder Laci and then transport her body 90 miles away to frame his client. So far, his sleight of hand tricks failed as miserably as his impotent case-in-chief, which sputtered like a defective sparkler on the Fourth of July.

He was a gentleman who, unfortunately, when [his wife and unborn child] went missing, was having an affair. Everything afterwards can be explained by virtue of that.

A gentleman? Surely you jest, Mr. Geragos. Either your client is a jerk and a liar, or he's a gentleman. You can't have it both ways, as you and your lackeys are so fond of saying. Are you suggesting it was merely an issue of bad timing that Peterson was soliciting a serious, committed relationship a month before his wife "disappeared"? Is the jury to believe that all of these startling coincidences were merely unfortunate timing? Cause and effect, the laws of physics, and logic defy this explanation.

He said investigators worked from the assumption he killed his wife and that belief colored every interview they conducted and every report they wrote.

We expected the defense to blame the cops for tunnel vision, and we are not disappointed. This record is so worn, the grooves have grooves in them, and the sound is warped.

Clearly she was not a victim of a soft kill.

Then what, pray tell, Mr. Geragos, was the cause of death? Do you have a surprise last-minute witness to pull out of your pointy purple hat and show the world how Laci was murdered, when several forensic experts, including your own celebrity specialists that never testified, were unable to arrive at any conclusion? Did your experts opt for guest spots on "What's My Line?" instead?

First [the motive] is [mistress] Amber [Frey], then it is financial, then it is 'Because I want to be free,' then it's 'because I don't want a kid,' he said.

The reason the prosecution solidified its motive in closing is because it finally figured it out. Most of the people who have followed this case have been relaying the motive all along: emancipation, pure and simple. It's a very common motive. As Rick *Distaso said in his closing* several times, "There is no mystery here." Emancipation is the whole package: financial, emotional, no baggage, no future obligations – the narcissist's dream.

266

He's not the smartest tool in the shed.

Unfortunately, the other rake, Geragos, is prolonging the agony of his closing arguments and will wrap it up tomorrow, followed by the People's last word, which will pull the plug on the holographic dragon of the wizard's defense; the worst defense $1 million ever bought.

NOVEMBER 3, 2004
PEERS, JURORS, CALIFORNIANS

The following are selected excerpts from trial transcripts of Mark Geragos's closing arguments (in italics), with my commentary.

Peers, jurors, Californians, lend me your ears. I come to defend Peterson, not to praise him!

> *Grogan didn't know what Hendee was doing,*
> *Hendee didn't know what Owen was doing,*
> *Owen didn't know what Jacobson was doing,*
> *Jacobson didn't know what Brocchini was doing.*

"And the cheese stands alone," quipped Kimberly Guilfoyle-Newsom, commentator on Court TV. What we have here is a failure to communicate that precludes a conspiracy, doesn't it? It rules out the possibility of collective tunnel vision. It refutes Geragos's original and repetitive accusations that every officer of the Modesto Police Department was out to get his client.

> *Laci carried groceries in five bags at a time.*

First, it was one or two bags at a time; now it's all five at once. After Jackie Peterson's testimony that she and Laci walked miles in Carmel, I wouldn't be surprised if the defense argues that Laci was a triathlete.

> *She suggested to Scott, "Take the umbrellas out of here." But did anybody ask this question?*

Who could they ask?

> *When he's printing out this master plan for the Bay, she's printing out a recipe for crème brulee.*

Contrary to media reports, the recipe download occurred on December 9, not December 24, and there is no way to know if Peterson or Laci printed out the recipe. For all we know, Peterson was planning to impress Amber Frey again with his culinary talents. Since Laci went to cooking school in France, I would think she already knew how to make crème brulee and would not require a recipe.

267

They keep their shoes outside, so she steps outside the unlocked door, she puts on her shoes, and at that point goes to, I assume, walk the dog. They didn't find any shoes. Where did the shoes go? Nothing is there.

Note Geragos conveniently forgets the women's tennis shoes Officer Spurlock saw December 24 on the patio.

Clearly she was alive. Clearly she is not a victim of a soft kill.

To whom is this clear? Where is the evidence of the cause of death?

Nothing consistent with strangulation.

Unfortunately, the parts that would reveal this are missing.

No evidence there were weights on the body.

Then how did Laci remain submerged in the water for several months, and how do you explain the disarticulation?

He won't be paying child support when she comes into this money, she'll be paying him!

Did Mark Geragos sleep through Domestic Law classes, too?

Because there is no motive, and if there is no motive, that in and of itself means that he could be not guilty.

When the actual law is not on your side, make up your own.

And the next thing you know, they're suggesting that you are embezzling money, when you are dealing with an employer who is already probably not real thrilled with the amount of scrutiny that you are getting.

Peterson's employer was not real thrilled with his redline productivity, either.

If he was going to leave town, why borrow $25,000 for a country club membership?

Peterson's mother has already testified that the club membership (or the money used to buy it) was a gift, but the defense thinks it looks better if it calls it a loan. Geragos also hopes the jury will impute value on the club membership rather than realize that to Peterson, it was meaningless and easily discarded.

Laci does not like him coming home with his clothes, putting his clothes in her hamper after he's either been work around fertilizer or in the Bay.

268

Yet Laci approved of all his other clothing overflowing from the hamper; clothes that he wore to work, presumably, when he actually went to work, that is?

Why does he go to the marina? Simple thing. There are newspaper articles that say the search of the Bay, and he's looking for the witnesses. Now, they say why didn't he stop in the office? Well, what they then find out in the testimony was, is that his investigator stopped there in the office to see if they could find him.

Whose testimony explained Peterson's five-minute visits to the Bay? Why did he send an investigator if he made the trip five, six, seven times, staying a few minutes and leaving? How does "locating witnesses" correspond to the Bay searches? I don't quite see the connection.

Yet they still perpetuated basically this false idea from this witness stand with these witnesses that he would come in [to the search center] at 9:00 o'clock, or he would come at seven. He's out of there by 8:45, that he is just gone, just wasn't true. The uncontroverted testimony is this guy searched more than any other human, any other human, and rightfully so. It's his family that he is looking for.

True. It is difficult to controvert testimony that does not exist.

Remember his erratic driving down in Bakersfield; he is circling the parking lots. Remember that? We produced two exhibits. You will get them, the receipts he went inside the store and he bought items.

There are no K-marts or Sears in Modesto?

I don't fish, but apparently those who do think nothing of driving the 90 miles to go fish.

Do they drive 90 miles to fish for an hour with the wrong gear, no bait, and in cold weather?

Then Grogan says, what did you base the fact that Laci knew about the boat? And he said based on the statement, because Rosemary Ruiz said she had been over there in the industrial complex and had come in to her unit to use the rest room. That was December 20th. That would have been the Friday before she disappeared.

Speaking of assuming facts not in evidence, where is Rosemary Ruiz? Who offered this testimony? Are we accepting double hearsay as evidence?

Do you remember who Doug Phelps was, was going into Scott's shop? He's a competitor who doesn't like the fact that Scott is taking away some of his competition and some of his clients. So this guy comes out. You noticed there were four-by-four fence posts and bags of what I could assume is concrete on this trailer back in the month of September. Did you ever let the petrographer know that?

The jury never heard from him. Yet more facts not in evidence and more double hearsay inserted for the truth.

They would have you believe, they presume his guilt, that somehow that this cement that got over there came from the next door neighbor, flew over the fence, or seeped under the fence. Just so happened to be in the exact same formation as Scott described to Brent on the phone a year and half before.

Has that "exact same formation" ever been defined? When did Peterson point out to Brent, or to anyone for that matter, where he did this sprinkling concrete magic?

And Vladimir tells you, here it is right here, that Vladimir tells you, by stipulation, that this was their on August 9th of 2004, in the middle of this trial. That no work was ever done, because this particular fence, which is not the one that Scott did the fence post work on, but the existing one, was not in concrete.

What fence post work? I thought you just told us there was an "exact same formation" where he used the leftover concrete mix in December about which he told Brent? Never mind the fact that Peterson returned unopened fence post mix in November.

To me, to my mind, that in and of itself not only gives you reasonable doubt, but tends to show you, unless you believe that it's just an enormous coincidence that within a week somebody's pawning a Croton watch in Modesto, that in and of itself is reasonable doubt.

This is "Crotongate," the watch someone named Deanna Renfro borrowed $20 against at a pawnshop and later retrieved. Where is the evidence that this was Laci's watch? How is reasonable doubt elicited from facts not in evidence or from anecdote? This doesn't even qualify as hearsay!

There was no history of any specificity as to that car. In fact, the testimony was that [Laci] wanted a new car, and that that's what she was looking for.

Who testified to this? Who on the witness stand said that Laci wanted a new car? Are we confusing Peterson lore with evidence again?

It wasn't even his knife. The guy who sold him the car left the double-edged knife that, if we hadn't asked the question, could be just another nail in Scott Peterson's coffin by the Modesto PD investigating this case and -- and attributing it to my client.

270

With all the other knives, cutting tools, camping ax, shovel and rope Peterson had in the Mercedes that *did* belong to him, I don't think the police really needed the double-edged knife as another "nail" in his coffin. I don't know how the prosecutors kept a straight face during this moronic monologue.

And they knew that. Here's his handwriting on the document. This is one of those documents that's sealed -- and you get it but we're not putting it out to the public -- where he's writing down the license plates and, you know, what it turned out, every single one of those DOJ people said those were their cars, that's what he thought he had. He had written on that "private investigators."

How does "private investigators" translate into the press or the media? How does that explain Peterson asking several officers what agency they were with?

He purchased Easter books for his nieces and nephews. You saw that.

We saw from evidence photos that the books were in the Dodge Ram in February, and I believe they were gifts for Connor that he gave to Amber's daughter.

They had the baby on the way. The nursery you saw was something that Scott built. They have not proved that Scott Peterson did anything except lie. And that's -- and they give you really no reason as to why he would lie.

Scott "Bob Vila" Peterson didn't build anything; the nursery furniture was all factory stock. On the contrary, the People gave us a lot of reasons as to why he would lie.

That's why we didn't find the other anchors. That this body obviously was exposed to the air or the elements. That's why you had the evaporation.

Geragos is referring to Dr. Brian Peterson's preliminary testimony, of which the jury is not cognizant. The mineral deposits were not discussed at trial, and the barnacles on the duct tape and Laci's remains indicate a lengthy anaerobic process.

Scott Peterson would not -- do you think he's just out there manufacturing this kind of concerned husband and running around doing the searches, and putting up flyers, and putting up posters, and living out of his car, all because it's part of his master plan to become a jetsetter? Does that make sense to anybody?

Yes, it makes sense to anyone who has ever been a victim of a narcissist or who has known someone like him. It makes perfect sense.

271

There is absolutely no history of domestic violence, or anything else. And that one day he just snaps, and all this -- all this happens and, gee, coincidentally, there is no evidence?

Does the name Mark Hacking ring a bell? Michael Blagg? Michael Peterson?

I think if he didn't expect Laci to come home, he would have made a lot different decisions than the ones he made.

If he didn't expect Laci to come home he would have tried to sell the house, traded in her Rover, ordered pornographic channels on the satellite dish, abandoned Modesto, exchanged hundreds of phone calls with his girlfriend, and dyed his hair a Crayola clown color. Of course, that's exactly what he did!

I think that what the reality is, the stark reality is, is this is a guy who literally got caught with his pants down, and he did what he thought he had to do, because he fully expected her to come home. He fully expected Laci to come home.

He was caught with his pants down? He did what he had to do? Does this explain Peterson's behavior? Is this what passes for exonerating evidence? Geragos's excuse for a defense closing argument in a capital murder trial makes me wonder if he has intentionally thrown this case so that Peterson has the issue of insufficient counsel for his appeal.

CHAPTER 11: THE VERDICT

November 9 – November 30, 2004

Buying a wrench down in Bakersfield
Hoping the tools of your plot aren't revealed,
Well, another crazy ride, you run but you can't hide
And forget about everything.

Their silly searches make you feel so cool,
They've got so many people, but they've got no clue,
And because you're Mr. Clean, you sanitized the scene
And you thought about everything.

Right down the street there's a new Kmart store,
You buy a new lock; you've got some things to secure,
When they ask where you've been
You tell them you're in pain, and you thought about counseling.

You had a dream about riches and fame,
You're gonna shake off your duties and that ball and chain,
And then you'll get to leave the city you deceived
And forget about everything.

Calling your friends when in Bakersfield
Praying they won't sense the bliss you conceal,
Well, another crazy drive, you hurl 'em all your jive
And forget about everything.

This turning 30 made you feel so old
There is no sign of Laci and the trail is cold,
And by acting nonchalant you'll get just what you want
You're entitled to everything.

NOVEMBER 9, 2004
JURY DEADLOCK?

According to the trial transcripts, in case of a jury deadlock, one of the instructions Judge Delucchi will give the jurors includes the *People v Moore* (upheld in California appellate court). Here is the *Moore* instruction and its application to *Peterson*.

Your goal as jurors should be to reach a fair and impartial verdict if you are able to do so based solely on the evidence presented and without regard for the consequences of your verdict regardless of how long it takes to do so.

Evidence in this case does not include (single, double, triple) hearsay testimony from people who saw dog walkers, Laci in a warehouse, fence posts and concrete on the flat bed, Peterson mourning in private, pawn tickets for Croton watches, witnesses at Berkeley who saw Peterson launch his boat, forensic proof of the baby's birth, or any other indirect anecdotal information brought forth in testimony from law enforcement in order to judge their actions, not for the truth of the matter. A great deal of the defense's cross-examination and the entirety of either side's opening and closing statements are inadmissible in jury deliberations. Therefore, we are left to wonder what reasonable doubt exists as "evidence" or facts in this case?

In the course of your further deliberations, you should not hesitate to re-examine your own views or to request your fellow jurors to re-examine theirs. You should not hesitate to change a view you once held if you are convinced it is wrong or to suggest other jurors change their views if you are convinced they are wrong.

This instruction advises the jurors to leave their egos, projections, assumptions and speculation at the door of the deliberation room and abandon personality issues. It's a daunting, if not somewhat unrealistic, order for 12 people, but I compare it to being in an orchestral ensemble. Each musician has his interpretation, tone preference, taste in genre and personal style, but when brought together to play the score, the instruments are subservient to the blend. Imagine if everybody played his part as a soloist, with his own interpretation, dynamics, articulation and intonation. It would not resemble music, but noise.

As I previously instructed you, each of you must decide the case for yourself, and you should do so only after a full and complete consideration of all of the evidence with your fellow jurors. It is your duty as jurors to deliberate with the goal of arriving at a verdict on the charge if you can do so without violence to your individual judgment.

Media reports about evidence requested so far indicate that the jurors are reviewing the issues of premeditation, means, opportunity; the defendant's conversations, and the potential crime scenes: home, warehouse, boat, and the

Bay. This appears to be consistent with a thorough analysis of the pieces of the circumstances from early December through the discovery of the victims' remains in April.

> *As I previously instructed you, you have the absolute discretion to conduct your deliberations in any way you deem appropriate. May I suggest that since you have not been able to arrive at a verdict using the methods that you have chosen, that you consider to change the methods you have been following, at least temporarily and try new methods.*

> *For example, you may wish to consider having different jurors lead the discussions for a period of time, or you may wish to experiment with reverse role playing by having those on one side of an issue present and argue the other side's position and vice versa. This might enable you to better understand the other's positions.*

People do not assimilate information in the same manner. Some people require linear layouts, visual reinforcement, repetition, analogies, or other means of drawing conclusions. In this trial, we have audiotapes, photographs, calendars, maps, phone logs, GPS plots, receipts, diagrams, videos, and tangible items like clothing and concrete. There are no weapons, a cause of death, substantial blood or other signs of obvious violence, or irrefutable forensics that connect the defendant to a murder. However, the fact that a murder occurred is not in dispute. Will there be enough information to conclude Peterson murdered Laci with premeditation?

The decision the jury renders must be based on the fact[s] and the law. You must determine what facts have been proved from the evidence received in the trial and not from any other source. A fact is something proved by the evidence or by stipulation.

> *You must accept and follow the law as I state it to you regardless of whether you agree with the law. If anything concerning the law said by the attorneys in their arguments or at any other time during the trial conflict[s] with my instructions on the law, you must follow my instructions.*

Other "sources" would include hearsay, attorney questions or argument, alternative theories, assumptions, phantom perpetrators, media commentary, rumor, innuendo, unsubstantiated explanations, and material that was not admitted by the laws of evidence, such as video of boat demonstrations, pawn tickets, Laci sightings, French toast recipes, dog sightings in the park, plea bargains by burglars, missing shoes, phone tips, Kim McGregor's eccentricities, Ron Grantski's fishing habits, Peterson's presence at the doctor's visits or his willing participation in the searches, or anything that was not directly testified to as fact.

Given that this instruction and the law disqualifies the majority of the defense case (and some of the People's), the jury is prohibited from deliberating all the preposterous hypotheses and Geragos's attempts to testify for his client (through questioning and hearsay). The only hope Peterson has at this point is that one or more of the jurors will not find the People's case sufficient to convict him beyond a reasonable doubt. I maintain that this will not be the outcome and that the jury will render a unanimous guilty verdict today or tomorrow.

NOVEMBER 10, 2004
THE LATEST PURGE

I was wrong about expecting a verdict yesterday or today; but, as usual, there is never a dull moment in the Peterson trial. Three jurors have been dismissed since June, two in the past two days during deliberations, and a new foreperson was selected today. Reviewing what we know about the removed jurors let's examine the altered dynamic of the existing panel.

The first juror to be dismissed was Justin Falconer, a mirror image of his hero, Scott Peterson: a divorced, X-Generation, former baggage inspector who said, "Pregnant women are crazy." He has poor social skills, he's a careless liar, and he is rumored to be a deadbeat dad and a fraud. He was ideal for the defense and, according to Varinsky, managed to fool the prosecutors during voir dire. Unfortunately, he sabotaged himself with his inability to avoid his own publicity. His removal was a good thing for the prosecution and was no accident. Why any of the mainstream or cable TV talk shows continue to feature him on their "legal panel" resembles theater of the absurd. Ironically, Falconer has managed to parlay his failure into prolonged celebrity because of the media's constant desperation to have something to discuss and because reading the trial transcripts would be too much like work.

The second juror to be shown the exit door was #7, Fran Gorman, the PG&E employee in her late 50s who graduated from UC Berkeley in 1968. My instinct about the People's preference for striking jurors was to remove that particular demographic: women who were old enough to be Scott's mother, because many of the most vociferous of Peterson's defenders on the Internet are in that age group. The fact that she attended Berkeley during the most anti-establishment era in modern history should have eliminated her from the outset as a bad risk. If this were a horse race, a savvy handicapper would have scratched her.

Replacing Falconer was the first alternate, the JD/MD Dr. Gregory Jackson, a man who either could not make a career decision or who could not cut it in the professions for which he invested years of study and capital. He has practiced neither law nor medicine and perhaps has very little practical experience in the real world. My guess is that he bogged down the deliberation process, intimidated some of the other jurors with his education, and may have had difficulty seeing the forest for the trees, which would be problematic in a circumstantial case that requires a macro view of events and evidence.

Juror #6, who has been on the main jury since the beginning, was elected foreman today. His background is in public service as a paramedic and fireman, and I and others observed him to be indifferent during the trial, not taking notes, and seeming bored on many occasions. Apparently, the tealeaf readers overlooked his leadership skills, because most of the pundits expressed surprise when his new position was announced. His quiet, unassuming presence and apparent sympathy for Laci's family will be a positive force and that he will cut to the chase in deliberations. Perhaps discretion is the better part of valor, and he's a man of action.

Alternate #3, an older man with a tangential connection to Scott and Laci's restaurant in San Luis Obispo, "The Shack," statistically would be a good pick for a prosecution juror, with old-fashioned values, respect for the system, and skepticism toward the sleight-of-hand tricks played by the defense. I doubt he is very sympathetic toward the defendant, but we hope that the evidence presented lines up with his interpretation of the law. Jury selection is a crapshoot; it's subjective, and it's totally unpredictable.

Word on the street indicates that new foreman #6, alleged to be pals with Falconer, is actually wearing a white hat and will propel this new panel into a swift verdict of guilty on both counts in the first degree. This may be wishful thinking, but I intend to remain optimistic for justice for Laci Peterson and her baby. The world is watching, and despite all the hoopla to the contrary, I believe these jurors are serious about returning a verdict and will not abandon their duties with a mistrial.

NOVEMBER 11, 2004
STUPID IS AS STUPID DOES

Definitions of stu·pid:
1. Slow to learn or understand; obtuse.
2. Tending to make poor decisions or careless mistakes.
3. Marked by a lack of intelligence or care; foolish
4. Pointless, worthless

In my home, using the word, "stupid" is forbidden, along with the command, "shut up," because these expressions are particularly demoralizing and dismissive. Nevertheless, there comes a time when employing the word "stupid" to describe someone's behavior or state of mind is appropriate and necessary. It should now be conclusive to every reasonably intelligent person who has witnessed the events in the Peterson case over the past 18 months that Mark Geragos has either intentionally assisted in Peterson's conviction (which would be cause for disbarment), or he is a stupid man.

Throughout the case commentary, we have heard nothing but accolades, admiration, approval and professional endorsements for Geragos's alleged skills, except for the random criticism from fellow defense counsel, Geoffrey Fieger. I shake my head and wonder how it is possible that Geragos's media peers actually believe what they are saying. Are they reading the defense motions? Are they reading the transcripts? Are they watching the same man? It is not possible for an honest person to describe Mark Geragos as anything better than a 14-karat jerk with a boilerplate defense strategy in which one size does not fit all, and that's the nicest thing you can say. Some may agree with me, after this most recent boat prop incident, that the man is not only an incompetent lawyer; he is also obscenely insensitive. In my opinion, this man is both wicked and irrational, and that's a very dangerous combination.

Let's review some of the areas where "stupid is as stupid does" in Mark Geragos's defense strategy, based on the various definitions above, from the time he accepted Peterson as a client in May 2003 to the present boat debacle in Redwood City. First, who could forget the "satanic cult," the "carved up" dismembered body, and the baby strangulation theories that Geragos fed to his pal, Geraldo Rivera, and that Fox News ran with as though it was based on authentic information. Fortunately, Rivera got wise and dropped Geragos like a live grenade and has taken up the People's banner in this battle. That was a smart move on his part, because it will become apparent in the near future that any journalist or media person who aligned with Geragos will suffer professional embarrassment and other negative karmic repercussions.

If the introduction of a mythical cult, mythical van, mythical mystery woman, and mythical Oakland Raiders fan was not foolish or pointless enough, Geragos then announced to the public that his client was "factually innocent," that he knew who the "real killers" were, and within days or hours would present this exculpatory evidence to free his falsely accused client. Did anyone take that seriously? Didn't that resemble a Monty Python skit or something from a Mel Brooks movie? After that performance, with Geragos surrounded by the solemn-faced Peterson family and Kirk McAllister, was there another straight face in the house? For a high-profile attorney to publicly make that kind of claim and then fail to produce even a semblance of exonerating evidence ever, in the preliminary hearing or in trial, he has to be a fool. He cannot expect that blatant demonstration of promoting fiction not to harm his credibility.

Perhaps this is just pathological self-sabotage, typical of the narcissistic personality, which seems to characterize Mark Geragos's displays of grandiosity; his seeming exemption from rules, orders, or professional standards; and his despicable lack of empathy and decency toward the victims of this horrible tragedy and, to some extent, his fellow media pundits.

What other poor decisions did he make? His opening statement in the Peterson trial is a good example. The statement, while it was not offered as evidence, nevertheless laid out what he intended to prove to the jury, including the "facts" that Laci sat in the boat, was alive the morning of the 24th, was witnessed by many that morning walking the dog, that the baby was born alive, and that Peterson was framed by an obsessed police department and a mysterious vagrant murderer who planted his wife's body in the Bay after learning of his alibi.

That's what he said. If this weren't such a travesty of jurisprudence, if this weren't such an insult to our intelligence and that of the jury's, if fellow lawyers weren't commending his statements and strategy, this would make a hilarious farce, and some people might even think that we made this up. Nobody could be that stupid in real life and make $500 an hour, right? The concept defies reality. Some of us may even want to live in a cave after this because we cannot wrap our minds around the idea that people think Mark Geragos is a clever, skillful media wizard and brilliant trial practitioner.

After routinely feeding tidbits of misinformation to his media weasels throughout the trial, his sycophants were only too happy to oblige: Jim Hammer, Aphrodite Jones, Richard Cole, Daniel Horowitz, Michael Cardoza, and other lesser minions with a laptop or a microphone disseminated his defense detritus like road apples. We heard about "bombshells" and "secret witnesses." We waited for the celebrity forensic experts we were promised. We waited for Detective Brocchini to be handcuffed and hauled off to jail. We waited for Geragos to eviscerate Amber Frey and prove Kimberly McGregor had motive and opportunity to murder Laci. We tapped our feet awaiting his earth-shattering case-in-chief promoted with more ballyhoo than the presidential candidates' campaign promises. We waited and waited, and then what did he do?

Zilch. Nada. Nothing. Pull the curtain aside, what have you got? A fraud. The flim-flam man. A clown in an Armani suit and Ray-Bans.

When denied presenting to the jury most of his legally inadmissible evidence and his video reenactment of a body dumping scenario he proclaimed could not exist in the first place, Geragos engineered his *coup de gras*: he parked a replica Gamefisher boat, with a dummy victim inside with anchors attached to its limbs, in the parking lot of his newly purchased office building in Redwood City two blocks away from the courthouse. Is it possible to imagine anything more inappropriate, brutish, foul or inhuman? Are these the actions of a talented and capable media manipulator, or those of a deranged man?

He should be run out of town on a rail. Instead of dubbing him the darling of his fellow criminal defense attorneys, he should be the laughing stock of the entire legal community. The Peterson case should be a prototype for law students of the worst, most ineffective defense strategy in a high profile murder trial. Let us hope some of the jurors see Mr. Geragos for what he really is: a disgrace.

NOVEMBER 12, 2004
THE VERDICT AND AFTERGLOW

The early evening was already dark with a winter chill off the lake as I drove home from work, two hours after the jury handed down the verdict in the five-month trial of People v Peterson. Suddenly, it felt as if a thousand days had passed since I walked along the warm, tree lined sidewalks outside the San Mateo County Courthouse in the dry California sun in June and August. It seemed a thousand more since I first read about Laci Peterson's "disappearance" and immediately suspected her husband was responsible. When I pulled into the parking lot, I opened my window to look up at the sky and saw a single star above me, surrounded by charcoal clouds and lavender wisps, and just at that moment, the bells of the church a block away began to peal. The bells chime every day at 6:00 pm, but most of the time their timbre fades into the background of my routine, and I rarely notice. Today, I paused at the sight of the star and the sound of the bells and imagined them symbolizing the clear, pure beauty of the melody of justice, as sonorous as a lone golden trumpet in a candlelit chapel.

Today's verdict was a triumph for truth, love, righteousness, faith, and all that is inherently good in humankind. Although her family and friends can never recover the lives of Laci or her baby, they can reconstruct their future with the peace and comfort of justice. It is the only restorative closure to an otherwise shattering tragedy. As in nature, with all action, there is an equal and opposite reaction. We observed this dynamic throughout the trial and the months preceding it, with the forces of darkness and chaos battling against the hopes and passions of light for the upper hand. The last scrimmages, with the losses of two jurors in two days, and the hideous replica boat transformed into a shrine for the victims, proved to be the final moves guided by a divine will that navigated this case from the beginning.

There was never any doubt in my mind that the jury would convict Scott Peterson. I eschewed the pervasive doubts, parodied the media pundits, disparaged the pompous defense, and condemned the ghoulish apologists and their fantasy allegations aimed to defame the victims and derail the natural design. I knew in my heart that truth and right would prevail over the tabloid reporting and the routine creation of imaginary drama and controversy from fiction and spin. I was only surprised at the large turnout for the verdict outside the courthouse on such short notice, when most of us expected deliberations to last until early next week. Otherwise, nothing surprised me: the defendant's demeanor, the juror's nods to Sharon Rocha, Mrs. Peterson's eleventh-hour breakdown, or the tears of relief, grief, and gratitude that followed.

Where was the devil today? Mark Geragos and Lee Peterson were conspicuously absent for the reading of the verdict, one of the most important days of this prolonged trial where delays and *in camera* hearings, illnesses, holidays, evidentiary matters and excused jurors disrupted the flow. We know the devil is a seductive liar who recoils from love and light, but he is also a coward, and he knew that he was defeated today. He campaigned mightily for this cause, enlisting his horde of black-hearted wraiths underground and his vociferous lieutenants on the airwaves to promote his vile agenda. He and his feeble followers were trounced, smashed, sent scuttling away under the moldy rocks and filthy swamps from whence they crawled to lick their wounds and whisper in hissing malice their vicious little schemes for appeal, revenge, and vindication. They'll be back, however weakened, emasculated, and anemic.

For now, we bask in their defeat. We raise our faces to the stars and the sun in praise for this confirmation of the ultimate power of truth. The church bells toll for Laci.

NOVEMBER 16, 2004
THE (HYPOTHETICAL) NOTICE OF APPEAL

The first thing Mark Geragos will do after the penalty phase in the trial of California v Peterson, scheduled to begin November 22 is move for a new trial, attacking both the guilt and penalty verdicts. When that (and *his predicted motion for a change of venue for the* penalty phase) is denied, the second thing he will do is file a notice of appeal.

According to California Criminal Code, the notice of appeal for felony convictions must be filed within 60 calendar days after rendition of judgment. A common tactic, especially for a chronically late filer like Geragos, is to bring the notice of appeal and possible request for the appointment of pro bono counsel for his indigent client to court when Peterson is sentenced and file it before he leaves the courthouse that afternoon. Most attorneys file a notice of an appeal for any conviction, whether they have legally binding grounds or not.

Whoever is assigned Peterson's appeal (or in the unlikely event his parents ante up for an appellate lawyer) will review the record, which includes trial transcripts, voir dire, in Limine motions, evidence hearings (402s), objections to evidence, sentencing issues, jury instructions, and matters of judicial notice such as if there were a documented investigation of juror misconduct (as opposed to rumor and media speculation), and perform what is termed "issue spotting." The appellate counsel must then determine which issues are arguable and meritorious that may result in a reversal or modification of the judgment. Basically, all of Geragos's objections were made on the record to preserve any possible issues for appeal, for example, his most recent objection to the dismissal of the original Peterson jury foreperson.

Once Peterson becomes the appellant, the burden of proof falls on him to show that Judge Delucchi committed legal errors that, if not for certain decisions, would have resulted in an acquittal or a lesser degree of charges or sentencing. What are some of the possible issues for appeal in Peterson's case? Let us examine the law concerning procedural errors, prejudicial errors, and erroneous rulings that may constitute fodder for appeal, keeping in mind that *although the appellate court can review whether the evidence was substantial, all factual presumptions are in favor of the judgment.* (Criminal Law Procedure and Practice, Seventh Edition, Section 42.34)

Generally, appellate issues fall into two categories: procedural and evidentiary. From the history of this case, dating back to the former venue and judge, there have been some recurrent actions from the defense that give us an outline of the potential areas of arguments for reversal, retrial, or reduction of the penalty.

Procedural Issues

- While Geragos was denied most of his motions during the pretrial, preliminary and trial phases, expect him (or his successor) to cite the fact that Judge Girolami denied the defense motion to close the preliminary hearing to the public to prevent tainting of the potential jury pool from prejudicial pretrial publicity. Considering the fact that the defense was partially responsible for the publicity and that closing preliminary hearings in California is extremely rare, this is a very weak issue.
- Denial of second venue change – Another very weak issue, especially since the only difference between L.A. County and San Mateo County is the size of the population, and Geragos failed to demonstrate any statistical differences in terms of public opinion of his client's presumption of innocence.
- Denial of separate guilt/penalty juries – This was an unreasonable request in the first place, and if the jury sentences Peterson to life without the possibility of parole, it will become a moot point.
- Denial of jury sequestration during trial – The greatest challenge both sides faced in empanelling a jury was the length of the trial. They lost over half of their prospective jurors because of hardship. If the additional suffering of sequestration were added to the burden, nobody but the homeless and transients would have been willing to serve.
- *Voir dire* – Both sides hired high-profile jury consultants, and for the first four months of the trial the defense seemed very pleased with its selection. Jo-Ellan Dimitrius commented on various news programs how

282

confident the defense team was with the impartiality and intelligence of this panel. An appellate lawyer would be hard pressed to argue that *voir dire* was improperly conducted, especially since Geragos did not use all his strikes.

- First and second degree charges given in jury instruction – It is my understanding that this is the law, regardless of Geragos's admonition to Judge Delucchi that he would include these choices in the jury instructions "at his peril."
- Dismissal of jurors and foreperson during deliberations – Until we learn more about the circumstances surrounding the dismissals of Falconer, Gorman and Jackson, I remain confident that in issues of appeal, unlike in trial, the judge rather than the defendant receives the benefit of the doubt.

Evidentiary Issues

- Dog evidence – The only dog evidence that survived two separate 402 hearings was the one tracking golden retriever (Trimble), who followed Laci's scent to the pier at the Berkeley Marina. Trimble's findings were corroborated by Peterson's admission to being at the marina on December 24, so there is no mysterious voodoo or precedent set in what was a cautiously conservative ruling by Delucchi. Did the dog interpretation provide a critical piece of evidence that convinced the jurors of Peterson's guilt? I submit that the location where Laci and Connor's remains surfaced was appreciably more probative.
- Mitochondrial DNA and the GPS – There will be no appellate issues regarding the inclusion of mtDNA evidence or the GPS results, because these technologies are widely accepted science. The occasional skewed results of the GPS signal indicating unapproachable speeds do not disqualify the other reliable data that revealed Peterson's whereabouts.
- Affidavits/Search Warrants- What seems very curious to many of us, the affidavits and warrants issued during the investigation of this case continue to remain sealed; thus we cannot determine their liability as an issue for appeal. Virtually all the "fruit" obtained by the warrants, including the GPS tracking, the wiretaps, and the flimsy forensic findings, were admitted in trial. Since these areas are the weakest links in any criminal process, the fact that they held up during pre-trial and trial is a good indication that they will hold up in an appeal.
- Wire tap evidence – Of all the intangible circumstantial evidence in this case, the wire tap issue is the most vulnerable to scrutiny. Because of the rarity of their use in a domestic murder investigation and the several incidents where police were privy to attorney-client conversations, the wiretaps are the Achilles heel of this case. I don't think the information obtained from the phone calls was that useful, certainly not probative enough to risk reversible error. However, admission of the wiretap evidence passed muster with two Superior Court judges, thus the politics

involved in overturning those rulings prohibits the likelihood of that event.

- Media interviews – Geragos made a big stink about the admissibility of the media interviews, including several obstreperous objections and arguments to their viability as evidence. The fact that Peterson willingly gave these interviews (saved forever for posterity) was tantamount to him testifying on the witness stand. Let this be a lesson to all future murderers: don't say anything on camera that you think can be used against you in a court of law! Live by the media; die by the media.

- *In camera* hearings regarding evidence denied the defense – I believe there were a number of *in camera* hearings regarding evidence and witnesses the defense wanted to use in their case-in-chief that Delucchi denied for legal reasons. Those apologists who protest that Geragos's case was hamstrung by prejudicial rulings are unfairly assuming that Delucchi doesn't know the difference between admissible and inadmissible evidence. I expect most, if not all, of the evidentiary issues denied the defense should withstand any further review.

- Boat reenactment – The alleged video reenactment of a failed body dumping is so preposterous, I cannot see anyone using it in the appeal. How could Geragos credibly recreate a scenario he purports never occurred? He knew going in that his video would be denied, and when he parked his demo boat in the highly visible lot of his newly acquired building, he made himself the target of contempt and ridicule from the legal community. Geragos's boat is a non-issue and will never see the light of day again.

- The unknown – With as many rulings that took place in chambers on the record but sealed from public view, there are undoubtedly a number of unknown issues that will surface in the notice of appeal. Nevertheless, let us keep in mind that appellate judges are political animals appointed by elected officials who are responsible to their constituents. Overturning the Peterson conviction is about as attractive to a California appellate court as paroling Charles Manson.

NOVEMBER 21, 2004
WHAT THE DEFENSE SHOULD DO

As Scott Peterson's defense team prepares for the penalty phase trial it denied would even take place during pretrial hearings last spring, what would be its best approach in convincing the jury to spare its client's life? For over a year, the defense accused the media of "demonizing" Peterson, which they claimed tainted the jury pool and destroyed the presumption of innocence Peterson deserved during his trial. The defense now faces the challenge of humanizing Peterson to the same jurors who unanimously agreed that the he murdered his wife, Laci, and their unborn son with premeditation and malice aforethought. The defense also faces the daunting task of recovering a modicum of credibility after its farcical case-in-chief failed to present exculpatory evidence, reasonable doubt, or numerous witnesses promised in Geragos's opening statement.

I suggest that the only possible redemption for the defense in the penalty phase is to have Mr. Hollywood vacate the concertmaster position and defer the final trial and closing arguments to his co-counsel, Pat Harris. Eugene Patrick (Pat) Harris is a mellow country boy from Arkansas, a graduate of The University of Michigan (so he can't be all bad), who has remained out of the spotlight, refrained from making any obtuse public statements and has seemed close to the defendant throughout the trial. If a nice guy like Pat Harris can attest to his affection for Peterson, he may be successful in breaching the wall of antipathy and allowing a few rays of pity to flicker through.

It may be important to diminish the underlying conflict of interest that a significant financial relationship exists between the Peterson family and Geragos that may preclude his objectivity. Pat Harris can present Peterson's family as loving, supportive, loyal and unwavering, thus worthy of compassion and mercy. The jury may be more receptive to Harris and his affable, vanilla manner, in contrast to its possible antagonism toward Geragos.

The defense has never heeded my advice before, and I doubt Geragos's pride and ego will allow him to sit second chair during the penalty phase. He may insist on carrying the torch of "lingering doubt" and "stone cold innocence" to the bitter end, possibly dooming his client to condemnation. I predict he will remain consistent in his grandstanding, bad judgment, and bad lawyering, and seal his client's fate with spectacular artlessness.

NOVEMBER 27, 2004
WHY SCOTT PETERSON SHOULD NOT GET THE DEATH PENALTY

There are over 600 men on California's "Death Row" housed in three units in San Quentin called "North Segregation" (or the "Old Death Row"), "East Block" with a Bay side and a yard side, and the "Adjustment Center" or AC, for those prisoners who present disciplinary problems. Many of the condemned on Death Row committed homicide under special circumstances, such as multiple murders, murder while committing another felony, or a particularly heinous act that merited the ultimate penalty.

According to January 2004 statistics from the California Department of Corrections, approximately 40 percent of condemned inmates are white, 35 percent are black, and 19 percent are Hispanic. Ironically, over 30 percent were tried in Los Angeles County where Geragos attempted to move the trial venue three times; whereas San Mateo County represents less than 3 percent of the total. The majority of inmates are over age 40, and a substantial number were convicted between 1992 and 2000. Since 2001, the current population of Death Row grew less than 10 percent. Judging by these statistics, it is apparent that in the last four years the trend for California jurors to sentence a man to death has decreased dramatically.

Based on his age, socioeconomic background, geography, clean criminal history, and the prevailing reluctance of California juries to condemn defendants, statistics alone indicate Peterson's improbable arrival to Death Row.

There are condemned inmates whose crimes were no more depraved than Peterson's, but because most of them could not afford expensive defense counsel or had a criminal record (or "sheet") as thick as a Harry Potter book or because

285

any slim potential for them to return to the streets some day was so abhorrent to the jury, they were sentenced to death. In contrast, Peterson had a million-dollar, high-profile attorney who kept his case on the front page of newspapers, magazines, cable TV, and the tabloids. In fact, Peterson has become a celebrity. The public and the jury have grown accustomed to his face. He appears clean cut and innocuous, perhaps a bit cocky and cold, but far from the image of a detestable monster whom we can envision writhing in agony shackled in a chair under a metal cap hooked to thousands of organ sizzling volts. (Or strapped to a gurney connected to an IV in the arguably more humane method of lethal injection.)

It will be difficult for the jury to disregard Peterson's affluent good looks, tasteful suits and ties, elegant demeanor, and his loyal, resolute family who attended trial daily. The depravity of the crimes of which he has now been convicted tends to be obscured by lingering disbelief that a young man with his upbringing and privileges could resort to such a desperate and despicable act.

I expect the prosecution will present a strong case for the ultimate punishment, reminding jurors that Peterson not only murdered a vulnerable woman and his helpless, unborn child, but that he ruthlessly led the authorities and eventually the entire country on a wild goose chase, defying anyone to "get something" on him, and privately snickered at their attempts. They will present Laci's family to narrate the agony of their loss and resurrect Laci Peterson's irreplaceable personality through photographs and anecdotes. Will it be enough to convince the jurors to override their natural aversion to condemning a man like Peterson, who could have been their son, their golf partner, their fraternity brother, or their college roommate?

Scott Peterson may be an easy man to hate, as Mark Geragos conceded in his closing arguments, but he won't be an easy man to kill. In the upcoming penalty phase of the trial of California v Peterson, I predict the jury will deliberate for a much shorter time, with the majority already satisfied that life without parole is a fitting punishment for the freedom-loving philanderer who gambled his future on the vicissitudes of the San Francisco Bay and, like many soggy sailors, lived to regret it.

NOVEMBER 20 2004
THE PETITION FOR REVIEW

What is probably one of the last in a long line of lame legal briefs filed by Mark Geragos on behalf of his soon to be ex-client, Scott Peterson, far be it for me, the proverbial "mouse that roared," to shirk my opportunity to fisk the *Petition for Review* filed in the Supreme Court of California (and summarily denied), asking for an immediate stay of the Penalty Trial. I liken the gravity of a petition submitted to the Supreme Court of a state to a final exam or a performance at Severance Hall: something I would not fathom approaching without arduous rehearsals, research, impeccable references and multiple edits. As expected, however, Geragos improvises, fabricates, exaggerates, and regurgitates his former inadequate and unsupported arguments for venue changes, and skates across the thin ice of indolence and incompetence with his trademark insolence.

The jury should never have been released from sequestration...[the] atmosphere of adulation has created a level of prejudice that now makes it impossible for them to fairly and impartially determine whether Mr. Peterson should live or die.[74]

...we can presume that any "lingering doubt" one or more of the jurors might have had about Mr. Peterson's guilt, a doubt which defense counsel could invoke at the penalty phase trial, was extinguished by the community's congratulatory responses to the verdicts.[75]

A new penalty jury must be empaneled, but it cannot be selected from San Mateo County. No jury drawn from this county can fairly decide Mr. Peterson's penalty at this point...the only way Mr. Peterson's penalty trial can be conducted...is to empanel the new jury in a new venue, a county sufficiently large enough to dilute the massive adverse publicity and public sentiment that has surrounded this case since its inception.[76]

As an ardent follower of this case and a student of history, I don't believe that continuing to sequester the jury between the guilt and penalty phases would have any bearing on the jury's ultimate decision. But don't take my word for it; let us look for substantiating case law or legal evidence to support Geragos's assertions. (Imagine the sound of my sorting through 59 pieces of paper.) Just as I suspected – no documentation, no professional survey results, no amateur survey results obtained by college students, no statistics, no case citations, no examples, whatsoever, to demonstrate that *Peterson's penalty phase was* compromised by allowing the jurors to return home after the verdict. Similarly, Geragos presents no supporting statistical evidence that Peterson would obtain his constitutionally protected rights to a "fair and impartial jury" in Orange or L.A. Counties, either. Why not? Obviously because, as in his previous motion to change the venue from San Mateo County to L.A. County, Geragos could not prove a significant statistical difference among any of the counties in California, large or small. If he could have, you can bet your lunch he would have included a survey demonstrating those results. Geragos's petition, like his case-in-chief, is based on hearsay, illusion, wishful thinking, and smoke.

With regard to any "lingering doubt" Geragos had hoped to produce during the penalty phase, what evidence, witnesses, or exonerating information can he present that were omitted from the trial? Are we (or the jury) to believe that Peterson's golf score, his Cub Scout badges, his ability to tie his shoes at age three, or his clean driving record are elements of doubt to his capacity to commit murder, despite five months of testimony, 40,000 pages of discovery, hundreds of pieces of evidence, and Peterson's cold-blooded behavior to the contrary?

---

[74] November 24, 2004, Scott Lee Peterson vs. Superior Court of San Mateo County, *Petition for Review*, p. 5.
[75] Ibid, p. 5.
[76] Ibid, p. 6.

We now have...actual evidence of the intrusion of community opinion on the deliberative process of the jury even before the guilt verdicts were reached. A juror who was dismissed one court day before the verdict was delivered [former juror #5 – the foreman] told the judge that he felt threatened and inhibited in the jury room because he had a point of view about the case that was different from the other jurors...[77]

Mr. Peterson submits that where a case has received the degree of publicity this one has, a trial must be held in the most populous venue available at the defendant's request, thereby providing the greatest chance the negative press will be diluted. Although there is of course no guarantee that changing venue to such county will provide an impartial jury pool, by doing so we can at least be certain that the judicial system has done everything it can, venue-wise, to ensure the defendant receives a fair trial guaranteed to him by the Constitution.[78]

Naturally, Geragos selects from the record excerpts of Jackson's statements out of context for his objectives and again fails to demonstrate how Jackson's dismissal from the jury will affect the penalty phase of the trial. In typical arrogant fashion, he continues *to request special* treatment, extenuating judicial privileges, and unprecedented legal maneuvering for his fertilizer salesman client who, without Geragos's shameless pandering to the press, would probably not be a household word in California. As I shuffle through the stack of pages again, I still do not see any supporting documentation that shows that a new jury in L.A. County is less tainted "venue-wise" than the current jury in San Mateo County. Where's the beef, Geragos?

...once the jury was released from sequestration the probability that Mr. Peterson's right to a fair penalty trial would be impaired was far beyond mere "risk." It was certainty.

The previous foreperson...asked to be removed from the jury because of "an enormous amount of hostility" focused at him. The juror stated that comments had been made to him personally that made him believe his safety might be at issue...Juror Number 6, who had replaced the second Juror Number 5 as foreman...told the judge that he didn't know why Number 5 felt as he did, other than the fact that he "wants to talk a lot more than other people, and he tends to take a long time." The Court made no other inquiries of any other jurors and failed to further pursue the matter with Juror Number 5.[79]

---

[77] November 24, 2004, Scott Lee Peterson vs. Superior Court of San Mateo County, *Petition for Review*, pp. 7-8.

[78] Ibid, p, 10.

[79] November 24, 2004, Scott Lee Peterson vs. Superior Court of San Mateo County, *Petition for Review*, pp. 22- 23, footnote 7.

Since none of the above banter has been shown to have any impact on the existence of a fair and impartial jury in L.A. County, I can only surmise that Geragos includes this information in his petition in order for it to be part of the record for appeal. It reads like a gossip column and has absolutely no probative value in obtaining an immediate stay of the penalty phase, or toward winning a change of venue. Similarly, Geragos documents in the footnotes his objections to the dismissals of both Jurors #5, Falconer and Jackson, and reiterates Falconer's unsubstantiated claims that he was threatened, his property was vandalized, and he was forced to leave the state due to his opinion that there was "reasonable doubt" of Peterson's guilt. The inclusion of yet more hearsay and specious allegations without a scintilla of corroborative documentation is signature Geragos strategy in all his high-profile cases. How the trial pundits and his peers consider this man a "brilliant" lawyer is beyond me.

As noted, Mr. Peterson also moved for a separate guilt and penalty phase juries, hoping that some of the adverse impact of the negative prejudging could be alleviated by not having a death-qualified jury determine his guilt or innocence.[80]

Peterson moved to have separate juries (to which he was not entitled), hoping for a more lenient, less prosecution-oriented panel to deliberate his guilt. If this motion had been granted, two panels of jurors would have been selected from the same "tainted" population, prolonging *voir dire* into the next decade, while Mr. Stone Cold Innocent sat in jail without bail. If Geragos legitimately found the jury pool to be impossibly prejudicial, he would have either A) used all his peremptive strikes and objected to the final panel for the record; or B) waived his client's right to a jury trial and moved to have the case tried before a judge. Since he did neither, the appeals court can only conclude that after "the big spin," he was satisfied with the extant jury.

Based on Geragos's wholly unsupported, carelessly prepared, and redundantly protracted *Petition for Review*, we amateur observers have realized that his celebrated strategies, superstar skills and distinguished, dog-eared playbook prove Geragos to be the most overrated player since the NFL's Brian Bosworth, who was described as "brash, arrogant, annoying and a total and complete bust as a professional football player." Bosworth went on to be an even worse actor after an injury curtailed his lackluster career with the Seattle Seahawks.

Recent scuttlebutt is circulating that Geragos plans on returning to the talking head circuit after he rolls up his circus tent in Redwood City, hoping for sudden, collective amnesia from his peers and the public. There will be some of us, however, who have long memories and copies of his motions.

---

[80] Ibid, p.29, footnote 10.

CHAPTER 12: THE PENALTY PHASE

December 4 – December 14, 2004

DECEMBER 4, 2004
THE SUBTLE REBUTTAL

Normally, the penalty phase in capital litigation is designed to present aggravating and mitigating factors either to support a sentence of death or outweigh the death penalty by demonstrating that the defendant deserves the jury's mercy. Since the case of California v Peterson has been anything but normal and the apparent lenience of mitigating information can range from the sublime to the ridiculous, it has become clear that the Peterson family's agenda is not merely to convince the jury to spare Scott's life, but also to present carefully scripted arguments that he was characteristically incapable of the crimes for which he was convicted. When Geragos signed on as the attorney of record back in May 2003, he made several statements to the effect that Peterson lacked the hereditary makeup to be a murderer, as if there were a scientifically proven genetic template for killers.

Let us evaluate the implications, subtle rebuttals, and occasional *faux pas* of the testimony from Peterson's family members that reveal a subliminal but persistent character exposé of Scott as a good little boy, devoted brother, favorite uncle, loving brother-in-law, perfect son, and industrious provider as a deliberately paradoxical contrast to the portrait of a callous, calculating, deceitful and careful murderer the prosecution painted in vivid colors during the trial.

Janey Peterson

> *I was looking at the houses and I was like, we need to turn around. I need to go change. I'm not dressed appropriately. But when we got to the house and, you know, it was a ranch-style house and when we went in and I met Jackie and Lee, they were just such a normal welcoming loving family and there was no, no pretentious arrogance at all.*

The words "pretentious" and "arrogance" were inserted to refute the prevailing criticism of Peterson as an arrogant creep with pretentious fantasies, exhibited in his relationship with law enforcement and his conversations with Amber Frey. Janey's theme is if some deemed Peterson arrogant, this is a misinterpretation or an anomaly. He is certainly not reflecting his parents' attitude! Unfortunately, for Janey and her coach, Geragos, most of us recall numerous occasions that belie this humble and unassuming demeanor.

> *So he actually just went down to Los Angeles or maybe Ventura County or something, took a class or something, got certified to install the vent himself, went back and installed it so he could get the restaurant opened.*

This story regarding Peterson's taking the initiative to obtain the credentials to install a vent in "The Shack" was intended to show his independence and contentiousness; instead, it proved to many of us that Peterson is capable of going to great lengths to achieve his objectives, such as buying a boat, acquiring a two-day fishing license with an ocean stamp, buying gear as props, and making homemade anchors, all while allegedly running Tradecorp's California office, communicating with his girlfriend, preparing for the holidays, and attending Laci's appointments. Janey would have been wiser showing Scott to be a disorganized underachiever who rarely completed projects. (I believe he possessed these defects as well, but that remains speculation.)

> *Q: Do you know Scott to also to kind of finance that habit of playing golf; to always do something golf-related, either working at a golf course or the golf repair business?*

> *A: Yes.*

That Scott worked at golf courses in order to play for free during his youth does not annul the fact that later, when he was 30, his parents financed his membership to Del Rio Country Club to the tune of $25,000. It would make more sense to the average observer if his parents supported his hobbies as a minor, and then expected him to pay his way as an adult.

> *He's gone fishing with the boys. He's golfed with them. Let them drive a golf cart.*

Subtle rebuttal interpretation: Look what a great dad he would have been! Scott would have enjoyed activities with his son, so he could not have murdered him.

> *The burden really fell on Scott to do a lot of that planning as far as, you know, we didn't know who most of their friends were up there. And he knew who they all were. And he tracked down all their addresses. And we probably spent a good two to three months preparing for that party.*

This story is in reference to the surprise 25th-anniversary party Peterson planned in Morro Bay for his parents that acts as another double-edged sword. He was a planner; he was capable of coordinating all the details of the event with little or no assistance from his siblings. The jury can conclude that he had the intelligence and tenacity to plan and execute a murder, as well.

> *He would often injure himself. And so one year we got him a big first aid kit for Christmas.*

"And I'm afraid, you know, men, we cut each other and we bleed," stammered Peterson to Ted Rowlands, as an explanation for the blood found on his truck after Laci "disappeared." We fail to see any preponderance of evidence that Peterson was a klutz. In fact, based on his graceful bearing, athletic prowess and the lack of serious injuries relayed in the anecdotes, the jury can conclude that Peterson is notably more coordinated and adroit than average.

I remember Laci first talking about [it]; we don't know if we are going to have kids. Then the next year would come along, and they would say probably going to have the kids after we're 30. I remember thinking I wish I had a tape recorder, you know, to play this back, you know, in five, ten years for her. And then another Thanksgiving or two later, she was taking her Folic Acid. They were trying to get pregnant. And it was just neat to watch them mature and grow as a couple.

Laci's medical records indicate she stopped using oral contraceptives in 2000, three years into the marriage. The first year of their marriage, Scott was still in college, and the next two years they ran The Shack, so that would coincide with their lifestyle at the time. The assertion Janey makes, however, is that Scott was a willing and dedicated participant in the reality of parenthood. It is much easier to play the occasional fun-loving uncle than to enlist in fulltime fatherhood with its attendant sacrifices of freedom and finances. Based on what we have learned about Peterson's (at best) superficial involvement in Laci's pregnancy, from the minor decorating of the nursery and accompanying her to doctor visits (yet unconfirmed), to his solicitation of an extramarital affair by the sixth month, most of us would hardly characterize him as being particularly enthusiastic about impending fatherhood.

John Peterson

He liked to emulate my father. He would wear the same khaki pants and golf shirt. Usually they were almost dressed the same color and everything. A little miniature dad. He was also mature and knew what he was going to do.

This "miniature dad" comment reminds me of Jerry Bledsoe's book, *Bitter Blood*, and the relationship between Fritz Klemmer and his famous physician father, whom he imitated and attempted to please with such ferocity, he pretended to attend medical school for years without his father being aware of the ruse. Ultimately, Fritz went on a murderous, suicidal rampage where nine people in the Newsome and Sharpe families were killed, including two little boys.

Q: As things -- as you got older, I assume you moved out of the house you said, what, 17, 18, something like that?

A: [age] 17.

Why did John move out at such a relatively young age? Things must not have been so perfect for him to leave the luxury of Rancho Santa Fe and fend for himself, especially if his parents respected and supported higher education, as was their history. Lee and Jackie, and Joe and Janey, met at a college campus. Why would John deviate from tradition?

Scott was the best man at my wedding. He gave a great stirring speech. Always a great speech giver. Always gracious host. Scott found out that there was a gap between my wedding and my honeymoon. We were just going to go to Vegas, but we weren't going until the next day. So he asked where we were going. I said we're going home. And before I knew it, he got called himself, got us a room at the Hyatt Islandia hotel in San Diego.

Here John reveals several of his little brother's interesting character traits. First, that Scott did not reciprocate the honor to his brother, John (or any of his other brothers), to be the best man at his wedding. Second, that Scott was a grandstander and showoff, stealing the spotlight from his brother wherever possible. Third, that Peterson made grandiose gestures in the guise of generosity that some could interpret as insulting. I admit that I am a little jaded about Peterson and may see tactless upstaging where others don't.

Q: Was it sort of like Scott to make sure that the gifts he gave were very personalized?

A: Definitely. I think he put a lot of thought into everything he did, and lot of thought into everyone he knew.

I doubt that the defense intended to remind us of the star theater Scott bought for Amber for Christmas or that he was an expert manipulator; but that's exactly what comes to mind.

I think my dad told us at an early age that anything that's given to you is not as valuable as something you earn, and taught us to work hard for, and we did. And Scott always had two or three jobs as a teenager. He always worked hard for everything he got.

Perhaps this was the message John received from Lee, but it was a mixed one at best. Meanwhile, his parents bequeathed Scott a free semester at Arizona State, a company to operate and sell, a generous down payment on his house, a country club membership, an assumption of his substantial debt, and a million-dollar defense team.

Joe Peterson

Scott took up fishing at the age of 5. He always loved being around the water. He wanted to do too much. I think he wanted more. He wanted to be his own man, be his own boss. He had ambitions about doing things on his own.

Joe's story attempts to describe Scott as independent and ambitious but also serves to make his brother appear ungrateful, anti-social, a poor team player, aloof, and disloyal.

> *They [my kids] were just enthralled with him. They would ride in his truck, use his fishing gear, wear his hats. They were so close -- they are so close.*

Note the quick correction from past to present tense. I find the use of the word "enthralled" to be rather telling. Apparently, Scott possessed some kind of mesmerizing charm, typical of narcissists, and managed to bamboozle virtually everyone who had only peripheral contact with him. So far, there have been no witnesses who were intimately involved with him as an adult to testify to his ordinary temperament. The only people capable of that are dead or had less flattering impressions to report, such as Eric Olsen, Shawn Sibley, and Amber Frey.

> *I know him better than anyone, at least as well as my parents. No way [could he be guilty of this.] Not my brother. Absolutely not. They [my kids] can't believe something like this can happen. They ask about how their uncle can be locked up. They ask why would somebody think he could do this.*

Why would *somebody* think he could do this? How about most reasonable people, an entire police force, every district attorney in Stanislaus County, at least two Superior Court judges, Laci's family, and a jury of his peers? I can appreciate the shock and disbelief with which the Peterson family reacted to the suspicions leveled at Scott and his arrest and eventual conviction, but to suggest that there is no evidence to support any of that is ingenuous.

DECEMBER 5, 2004
WHAT'S WRONG WITH THIS PICTURE?

There is an adage my father is fond of using that warns, "A little knowledge is a dangerous thing." With that caveat in mind, I will once again risk absurdity and offense by analyzing Lee Peterson's testimony about his relationship with his son, Scott, and speculate, based on my research and understanding of the narcissistic personality disorder, why a man like Scott Peterson has, to some extent, his father to blame for his future in prison.

> *Q: When Scott was a young baby what are your memories of being around that house, being around that apartment I should say?*

> *A: Well, I remember Jackie bathing him in the kitchen sink and when she'd get him all dried off and he was all nice and shiny she would take him and dance, she would dance around the kitchen and the living room to entertain us and Scott would have his huge smile on his face. He loved the motion, I guess.*

> *Q: How was he as a baby?*

A: He was -- he was perfect. He woke up smiling, he went to bed smiling. Great disposition.

Earlier in his testimony, Lee recalls that Scott contracted pneumonia as an infant and they were terrified of losing him. Perhaps that crisis, along with other compensatory behaviors motivated by guilt, formed the foundation of what was to become his parents' career of overprotecting, domineering and doting on their "perfect baby." According to child psychologists, spoiling and idealizing a child tend to dehumanize and objectify him. The parents project their frustrated dreams and hopes onto the child in the subconscious desire that the child can transform their failures (or previous parenting mistakes) to successes. The child learns to feel an unrealistic sense of power, supernatural abilities, and unconditional acceptance, as well as entitled to special treatment throughout his life. The parents' idolization of the child destroys personal boundaries, and the child does not learn to have a separate existence. This may result in what psychologists term a "schizoid, split, fragmented self." The "kid" is not allowed to make mistakes. The "kid" is not allowed to be human, flawed, embarrassing, unruly, irreverent, disrespectful or disloyal. The "kid" becomes an empty husk, a puppet, and a figurative extension of his parents.

Q: Once you started the crating business did he come to work with you, did he come as a child, did he come visit?

A: Yeah, after Jackie came aboard full time we had an area for him to play in where all his toys were, it was kind of gated off by one of these -- they're like accordion things that spread out, you know, to keep him in. He was there.

That poor little boy was penned like a veal calf! As a mother of children who were once toddlers, I feel genuine sympathy for him. Why didn't his parents at least put him in preschool or into an organized play group some of the time? He grew up without little playmates or siblings close to his age (the six years between him and John is giant gap between young children) without learning to cooperate, share, accept rejection or compromise, and many other important lessons developing children face. I suspect this was the result of a combination of overprotective fear of germ-infested daycare centers, and penny-pinching. No wonder Scott developed such a rich fantasy life and took up solitary sports like golf and fishing.

Q: Did you get to spend a lot of time with him when he was young or were you too busy working, how would you try and do that?

A: No, I spent a lot of time with him. I was home every night by then and of course weekends we did a lot of stuff in the backyard. He would work with me in the backyard if I had gardening to do. He wanted to be right there helping out.

How did Lee know Scott "wanted to be right there helping out"? What choice did he give him? It sounds to me as if Lee were compensating for not spending time with his first three children and that this was about his need to reconcile with his past rather than about Scott's needs. What Scott needed were playmates, scraped knees and mud pies, not being a "mini-Lee."

> *Q: Did you take vacations together?*

> *A: Yes.*

> *Q: Where all would you go?*

> *A: Catalina Island, Santa Barbara, Monterey, Carmel.*

Gorgeous Pacific coastal scenery was wasted on that child. Scott would have been happier in a big, old sandbox with a few children from the neighborhood with whom he could form friendships and clubs and wrestle and occasionally fight. Lee reminds me of Patsy Ramsey's dragging her little girl to beauty pageants, usurping her right to an ordinary childhood because of her personal ambition.

> *A: He was a good student. He got very good grades.*

> *Q: What did the teachers say about him?*

> *A: We went to all the parent-teacher meetings and they were all unanimously, unanimously they liked Scott. They said he was a good influence, he got good grades, never gave, gave them a problem. We never heard a word from the teachers, except he was a good kid. I mean, never went to the principal, never had a phone call from a teacher.*

> *Q: Never got in any trouble?*

> *A: Never.*

This is either a lie, revisionist history, or something was seriously odd about Scott. Every one of my siblings, every one of my children, and every child I know had a disciplinary problem in school at least once. I had a less than stellar reputation in grade school. What child doesn't spend at least one lunch hour in detention or earn one bad grade? It is apparent that the "disconnect" had taken place in Scott's psyche by age six, and he had learned to stifle his impulses completely. Imagine the suppressed, simmering frustration for the next two decades, like a human Krakatoa.

> *Q: When he was playing golf, when he continued to play golf, was this something he worked at everyday?*

297

A: Everyday. There were two summers where he would get up and he'd be at the golf course just at the sun came up and start practicing and then later in the day he'd pick up because he work at this golf course, you know, picking up the balls, washing them and putting them back in the baskets and I think he traded that labor for golf lessons with them.

Q: So he essentially paid for his own golf lessons by working at the course?

A: Some of it, yeah.

Q: Would you ever play with him?

A: Everyday almost.

Q: What was that like, the two of you?

A: It was wonderful. By that time the business was going well and I had a good manager and I would come home about 3:00, go to the golf course. Scott's school was right across the street. He would run across the street and I'd have some snacks for him. And we'd play nine holes and we'd practice or do both. And it was really, really very nice. It was just a wonderful bonding experience.

Bonding experience? Superglue comes to mind. The school bell rings; there's dad to take Scott to the golf course. Never mind if he wanted to hang out with his friends; if he had any besides Aaron, another overprotected child. Never mind if he wanted to go play video games or drink milkshakes or play volleyball on the beach. I can appreciate that Scott showed an aptitude for golf, and his father was encouraging that talent, but to commandeer this boy's leisure time was tantamount to kidnapping.

Q: What happened, what sort of happened, in your opinion?

A: Well, I think when he got to Arizona State he realized the depth of the ability there. He was with Phil Mickelson again and another Swedish fellow who's playing the tour now and these two guys were just standouts. They were, you know, unbelievably good. And I think Scott said, gee, I don't think I'll ever be that good. I'm not sure that was his thought but --

Q: Did you ever see him as a very competitive person?

A: Not terribly. I'd say talented, but not really driven. He was driven in the sense that he wanted to practice and do well, but he didn't have a real, I don't know what you call it. He lost several match -- matches because he didn't finish the job off. I think -- I think he didn't want to hurt the other guy's feelings or something I swear or something.

298

Yeah, we he was very serious about a career in golf and through high school. Other than picking up the balls at the range at the course where we live near. We told him your job is to get good grades and practice your golf and become a professional golfer. If that's what you want, you need to put the time in and basically that's your job.

Whose dream was it to be in the PGA, Lee - yours or Scott's? I sent my daughters to piano lessons, hoping one of them would be a concert pianist, but when they lost interest, I didn't force the issue. You can't expect your child to materialize your dreams; he is his own person, and the healthy parent accepts that his child may not subscribe to the same goals. I find Lee's excuse for Scott's shortcomings amusing: he wasn't competitive enough. The truth is more likely that when Scott realized he couldn't be the best, he forfeited out of ego, not because he was emotionally altruistic. If he sensed failure, he quit while he was ahead. This plays into the murder motive, since he may have decided that eliminating Laci and the baby was preferable to admitting failure in his "perfect marriage."

And then grandpa bought him a -- when he was still in a crib, it was a helicopter on a rod. It would go round and round and Scott would sit there and watch that for hours.

None of my babies ever watched anything, a mobile, toy, sparkling lights, television, animals or fish, for more than a few minutes, much less "for hours." I know of babies who sleep a lot (not mine), and those who are subdued by swings and rides in the car, but not something moving in a circular pattern endlessly overhead. Either this is fiction, or Scooter was a strange baby who grew into an even stranger kid.

Q: Was he loud, loud boisterous personality?

A: No, not around me anyway.

Q: What was his personality like?

A: He was sunny, but he was -- sunny, motivated. He always took care of business. Always had somewhere to go, always had a direction. You wouldn't catch him laying around in bed. He would be up. He used to wake us up with a bugle when he was in his early teen years. Bugle, he'd stand up, play revelry, get us out of bed.

Apparently, that "sunny personality" included a little passive-aggressive streak. It would never have occurred to me (much less to my children) to awaken my parents with a bugle, at least not more than once! This rude scenario, designed to demonstrate Scott's alleged discipline, really shows how indulgent his parents were, another common symptom of the narcissist's nurturing. From literature on child development, experts believe that overindulgent parents are a greater

299

detriment to their children (and society in general) than the overly strict type; not that either extreme is necessarily healthy, but most of us can cite examples of liberal, permissive parenting producing more than its share of social parasites, serial predators, and monsters.

> *Q: How did Scott accept the fact that he had a brother and sister, half brother, half sister he didn't know about?*

> *A: I think like the rest of us, he was, we had a bigger family now and they were such nice folks that it was just easy to take them into our family. And we see a lot of Anne or we saw a lot of Anne...and Don lives back east, we don't see much of him, although, he has traveled out here a couple times. We've been there a couple times. We're well acquainted.*

Lee should have prefaced his answer with "Once upon a time..." since that cozy little reunion smacks of fairy-tale validity. A more realistic reaction would comprise shock, embarrassment, shame, dismay, fear, unresolved sibling rivalry, and a myriad of probably unanswered questions. It became the proverbial "elephant in the middle of the room" that was tiptoed around, minimized, avoided or denied altogether. Nonetheless, knowing about Mom's previous children given up for adoption may have bolstered Scott's self-image as the special, planned, loved and wanted child, and the only legitimate heir to the throne.

> *Q: Let's talk about that for just a minute. When you say you decided you were going to start another crating company up in San Luis Obispo? What made you decide to do that?*

> *A: I think I missed Scott a lot and then I guess I just wanted another base of income, so I asked Scott if he wanted to go in with me.*

> *Q: And what did you two together to go in, what did you do?*

> *A: We each put $3,500 in and bought some tools and started making sales calls.*

> *Q: Business successful?*

> *A: Yeah.*

It does seem as though Lee has the golden touch, but following your adult son to college and then solidifying his continued affection with the enticement of future wealth reminds me of Sante Kimes following her son, Kenny, to several colleges, and refusing to cut the apron strings. Mother and son went on to con and kill several people, and testify in each other's murder trials. Lee clung to his symbiotic relationship with Scott long after even possessive parents reluctantly kick the bird out of the nest and let him fly on his own.

DECEMBER 6, 2004
"PETER-SPEAK"

In this analysis, we will review some of Lee Peterson's and his daughter, Susan's, testimony in the penalty phase of the trial for syntax, common expressions, oddities, and what I will dub "Peter-speak," and interpret the real meaning of their subtle rebuttal and sometimes obscure language, similar to the language of denial used by severely dysfunctional families.

> *Q: They [Scott and Laci] actually were dating and were married for a time period and lived in San Luis; is that right?*
>
> *A: Yes.*
>
> *Q: And you were there during that time period? Were you with them much, did you get a chance to see them often?*
>
> *A: Yeah, we saw them a lot. We saw them, they would come over and wash their clothes at our house because their apartment didn't have a washer. We'd have dinner at our house or go out. A lot of times we'd meet in San Luis Obispo for breakfast. Laci would come over. I know of at least twice she planted flower gardens for us. She wanted to try out some new flowers or new design and she would show up with her flats of flowers and go to work redecorating our yard.*

Picturing Laci planting flowers at her in-laws' house connotes a bittersweet image; and, what is more disheartening is Lee's apparent obliviousness as to how his stories are a tragic reminder of Laci's graciousness and generosity. I would probably resent my in-laws following my new husband around like a puppy and would find their looming presence somewhat intrusive. I speculate that Laci knew the Petersons wouldn't follow the newlyweds to Modesto, since it was her hometown and beneath the aristocratic standards of their ilk. Perhaps one of her reasons for wanting to move from exquisite San Luis Obispo was to get away from Scott's parents.

> *Q: Once they moved to Modesto did you get to see him very often?*
>
> *A: Not very often. We would probably visit two or three times a year. Scott and Laci always came down for Thanksgiving. Usually Easter and then we'd have a few days in Carmel before Christmas. That was our Christmas together. And a couple times they might run down during the year to see us. So it wasn't anywhere near the contact we had when we lived in Morrow Bay, but, you know, I'd say as much as we could we saw them.*

301

Evidently, that strategy worked. Laci was finally out from under her in-laws' constant inspection and free to create her home without their advice, recreational preferences (she didn't golf or fish), and her mother-in-law's criticism. I imagine Lee suffered from severe withdrawal like Puff the Magic Dragon pining for Jackie Paper. Seeing Scott only six times a year was a far cry from their daily golf games and business partnerships.

Q: Jackie, as far as her personality, you've known her for a lot of years, how would you describe how she reacts to adversity?

A: With stoicism, she's very stoic, very cheerful.

Q: Does she cry a lot?

A: Cry a lot?

Q: Yeah?

A: Never. Well, I shouldn't say never, but she, she doesn't indulge in self-pity, she accepts her circumstances and just goes on and tries to make things pleasant for people around her. She has tons of friends she corresponds with and calls and she just -- she's very high-spirited. She has a great heart.

To liken crying to "self-pity" reveals the Petersons' scorn for showing weakness. They consider sadness or anger, which often instigate tears, to be contemptible rather than natural responses to feelings. To stifle one's feelings of loss, grief, rage or ecstasy requires years of what people in recovery call "stuffing." Stuff those feelings down! Pretty soon, you have stuffed your real feelings down so much, you lose touch with them altogether.

Q: How old was Scott there?

A: I'd say nine again. This is -- I think it's in -- I think it's in France, actually. We were having dinner at a very nice place in Monte Carlo.

I have never been to Monte Carlo, and I would guess most of the jurors have never been to Monte Carlo, either. To boast that your nine-year-old son and you were having dinner at a "very nice place" on the French Riviera is totally inappropriate in the penalty phase of a murder trial. We are not impressed. In fact, some of us are perplexed.

Q: So even after they moved to Modesto, you were still seeing Scott a number of times per year?

A: Yeah. Probably average out to once a month, maybe.

Q: Ten or twelve times a year?

A: Yeah.

This is confusing. Earlier, Lee said that they only saw Scott a few times a year, and suddenly their visits have increased to once a month. Which is it? Did Scott inherit his inability to keep his stories straight from his father? I believe the defense was trying to show that Lee had a close relationship with his son; but that backfires again when we remember that Scott did not tell his dad about the new boat he bought or that he was fishing that afternoon of December 24, although we know from phone records that he called him twice.

Q: When you saw Scott in jail, what was he like? What was his attitude?

A: He always, just he amazed me. He was upbeat. He was -- I think he was trying to protect us from worrying too much about him. He tried to keep our spirits up. We were doing likewise. But it was always a positive thing, strange as that may sound. Just to -- just to be in close proximity to him, and then -- and then realize he was -- he wasn't, you know, totally devastated. He was upbeat. Like I said, I think mainly for our benefit, but he was.

Q: Obviously you are aware of why we're here. What effect would having your son put to death have on you?

A: I don't know. I don't even want to entertain that thought. I just can't imagine anything worse.

There's that "amaze" word again; however, I *would* be amazed if Scott is upbeat in jail. Lee describes an *amazing* demeanor for an innocent man falsely accused and then convicted of a crime he did not commit. Hopping mad would be a more appropriate reaction. As far as Scott's being put to death the worst thing Lee can imagine, as his father he is entitled to that response. That he never mentions Laci and his grandson's murder or how he felt when their remains were discovered, regardless of his belief that Scott is innocent, speaks volumes to the sincerity of his affection and respect for her. Note also that Scott has inherited his mother's ability to remain cheerful and stoic amid horrendous circumstances; it is probably a skill he honed from childhood.

Susan Peterson (Caudillo)

You know, I never, ever, ever resented Scott. I was happy that he was our baby brother. And, you know, he may have lived in a nicer house or bigger house than we did, and maybe went on more vacations than we did. But we were all loved equally. And that's what was really important.

Methinks the woman doth protest too much. If Susan didn't resent the bigger house, the comparative luxury Scott enjoyed, or his favored son status, she wouldn't have mentioned those issues at all. I also believe she held resentments against Jackie as the new wife, a situation that prevented any possible future reconciliation between her mother and Lee, about which most children from divorce fantasize. She may have embraced the family coping mechanism of "stuffing" those feelings and presenting a cheerful game face when *she visited her dad's new home* and hodgepodge family. I also suspect that Lee's children were not aware of Jackie's past until Don Chapman and Anne Bird showed up years later.

But in his adult years, he has made me proud of everything that he had accomplished.

His, you know, taking responsibility for his actions. He didn't want to worry me and have me come to the scene of the accident. And he took care of it. And he was capable of taking care of the problem.

In Peter-speak, taking responsibility for a car accident demonstrates that Scott would take responsibility for Laci's disappearance, if he were involved. Never mind that there would be far more serious consequences for the latter. The implication is that Scott had a moral compass and was not a sociopath, yet his behavior after Laci's "disappearance" sharply conflicts with that character endorsement, even if we believed he was innocent of her murder.

Q: What effect has Scott's arrest and being jailed have on your family?

A: That's one of the worse days of my life was April 18th. I just couldn't hear really the words when Jackie called me and told me that he was arrested. I didn't want to believe it. I didn't think that it could ever have happened. I broke down. We had to tell our kids that Uncle Scott was arrested and they -- they broke down. It was -- it was a horrible, horrible day.

"I didn't want to believe it. I didn't think it could ever have happened." This is a powerful denial system in place. Very few people who were aware of the discovery of Laci and Connor's remains on the East Bay shoreline were surprised when Scott was arrested. Considering all that Jackie, John, and probably Lee were doing to assist Scott in his escape from possible arrest by providing him cash, identification, credit cards, transportation and moral support, all evidence presented in trial, Susan's reaction is ludicrous and light years beyond the suspension of disbelief. The intrinsic dishonesty among Lee, Susan and Janey is so transparent, instead of their testimony humanizing Scott, it has served to dehumanize his family.

DECEMBER 12, 2004
DENY, DENY, DENY!

From Jackie Peterson's testimony in the penalty phase of her son's murder trial, I have excerpted parts of her story that I believe shed a bit of light on her attitudes about women, childrearing, work, and her son, and what appears to be deep-seated, unresolved insecurity of her place in the world.

> *And my brothers, each as they came out two years out apart, took care of her. And when I came home it was like, you're the girl, now we have somebody to do everything.*

I sense a certain justifiable resentment of being the only female in the family who, after growing up in an orphanage, assumed the entire gamut of domestic responsibilities of her invalid mother's home. Jackie's childhood was bleak by any standard, yet her feelings of abandonment, deprivation and despair are minimized in retrospect, demonstrating a powerful level of denial constructed from a very early age as a coping mechanism. Similarly, the sudden poverty of her youth might have motivated her to restore her social standing as an adult, no matter what the sacrifice. We can hardly blame her for that; however, more relevant are the emotional and psychological barriers that were in place for most of her life. Her well-defended psyche manifests in her "stoicism" and icy detachment.

> *Yes, my -- in those days my boss came and stood by my desk and said you have to leave. And I said why. She said because you're pregnant. And I -- I thought nobody knew. So I was about six months pregnant. It was just what you didn't -- if you weren't married, it wasn't acceptable.*

Jackie's encounter with discrimination as an unmarried pregnant woman in the workforce was unfortunate but relatively common in the 60s. After suffering the consequences of another abandonment, losing a job, and having to give up her firstborn, Don, for adoption, such a harsh lesson should serve as a learning experience. Yet, within a few months, she is romantically involved with her brother's best friend and discovers she is pregnant again. One unplanned pregnancy at age 19 suggests a minor scandal, but two within two years constitutes recklessness – or an agenda.

> *[Re: Anne's father] I was going to tell him that I was pregnant and I didn't because I didn't want to -- I knew he would have married me and I didn't want to marry someone that was in love with someone else.*

Maybe the truth is that Jackie was terrified and convinced of her lover's rejection and headed that disaster off at the pass by barring him knowledge and arranging her second baby's adoption with the same doctor who delivered Don. At this point, being raised in the Catholic Church (with its prohibition of birth control), many women would have taken a vow of celibacy for a period of time in

305

order to process the stages of mourning necessary to recover physically and emotionally from two pregnancies that resulted in adoptions. However, Jackie circumvents this critical passage and repeats the same mistake with a third, unidentified boyfriend whom she may have erroneously assumed would "make an honest woman of her," which is why she kept the baby, John. I deem three unplanned pregnancies in three years beyond defective judgment or bad luck: this behavior defines a pattern of entrapment.

> *Q: And along came John who the jury's heard from and he was born in 1966; is that right?*
>
> *A: Yes.*
>
> *Q: And by that time you were more self-sufficient?*
>
> *A: Yes. Well, not that. I think I wanted a family and I was trying to make a family and I finally had my -- I was a single mom and –*
>
> *Q: You raised –*
>
> *A: I enjoyed my life.*
>
> *Q: Did you raise John, at least for the couple of years as a single mom?*
>
> *A: Yes, until he was four and I met my husband.*

Apparently, three's the charm, since Jackie managed to avoid a fourth pregnancy until she met and married Lee Peterson. Although they conceived Scott within a few months of their marriage, at least this time, she finally had a gold ring on her finger *in the delivery* room, which in 1972, and with her previous track record, was a monumental victory.

> *[Prior to meeting Lee] I went to work for Kelly Girls and I took jobs when people were off work or injured for a while and I moved around in different companies, learned a lot of different things. And I was always employable.*

Jackie's tendency to seek geographical cures and temporary employment stints is a common tactic of people with personality disorders or addictions. This strategy prevents intimacy, commitment, and exposure of personal history that is shameful or unsavory.

> *[Regarding Scott as a crossing guard] There would be a car three blocks away and he wouldn't let anybody cross, he was so serious and so business like. And all the kids were waiting and this mother just snatched her kid and said, oh, he always takes too long!*

It's amusing to have young Scott portrayed as a little control freak, with his Day-Glo sash and stop sign, by his controlling mother who lurked in the background observing his conduct. We have learned that she and her husband kept him confined as a toddler and brought him to work as a "mascot"; thus, we already know that Scott was a strange child from lack of socialization with his peers.

> *Scott was so attached to it [the lab pup he found] that they told him that he could have the dog and they knew it had a good home so he taught him to swim and he played with him. He took full responsibility for walking him and feeding him, carrying for him.*

I don't think you need to teach a Labrador retriever how to swim; nonetheless, Jackie continues to bestow upon Scott exceptional abilities he does not possess. The inclusion of this story, intended to show Scott as a nurturing, responsible boy, demonstrates that what Scott wanted, Scott got, and Mom and Dad made sure of that.

> *[In reference to the adopted grandmother for grandparents' day at school] And he said, no, I adopted this old lady at the old folks home and I've been visiting her for months and she said she'd come to lunch with me as my grandparent so that's when I wanted to go to the school and see what he was doing because I realized -- I knew he was in community service, but I didn't know what he was doing.*

Scott's exact age in this fuzzy anecdote is unclear, but it appears that at least Jackie had loosed her grip on her son; but the protective baton was passed to Lee, who eventually hijacked Scott's extracurricular activities. In an ironic twist of fate, Scott's first opportunity for emancipation from his omnipresent parents is his current incarceration. It wouldn't completely surprise me if his father commits a felony some day so he can join his son in prison.

> *He said I'm 20 years old. I've been living off you long enough. I want to support myself and be on my own. And, actually, we were hurt. We wondered what we'd done wrong because we loved having him around. It was fun having him around.*

Most parents would rejoice at hearing their child declare his independence. They would congratulate themselves on a job well done for raising a self-sufficient adult who desired to leave home and fend for himself. Not the Petersons. They are hurt that their baby is abandoning them, since he had obviously become (and still is) their primary focus in life. It would be devastating for any parent to see his child go to prison or condemned to death, but for Scott's parents this punishment is utterly eviscerating. No wonder they were eager to hire a high-profile defense team and invest considerable resources to prevent that outcome. It wasn't only because they thought he was innocent, but that they could not envision a meaningful life without him. With that insight in mind, Jackie's final remarks take on a different, less offensive meaning:

And it would be a whole family wiped off the whole face of the earth. It would be like Laci never existed because she was a woman with him, she grew with him from 18 to 28. And it was a family member of ours and we would lose a whole family, both Sharon and I would lose a whole family. You know, it would be like they never existed. That it would be so unreasonable. Such a waste.

In "Peter-speak" this statement really means, "It would be like *we* never existed. We would lose a whole family. It would be like Scott never existed, and that is unreasonable and a waste because look at all we did for him. Look at all he means to us. He is our life." Jackie's pleas have nothing do with justice for Laci and Connor, her concern for their murders, or what their murder represents to her. Clearly, they were no great loss; she has already written them off emotionally and psychologically like she did her father, her mother, her brothers, her former lovers, and her first two children. Scott alone embodied the fulfillment of her ambitions and dreams, and her *raison d'être*.

DECEMBER 14, 2004
IF WE COULD READ YOUR MINDS

In the early days of Laci Peterson's "disappearance," media coverage of the story grew from the local newspaper (*The Bee*) and occasional blurbs on CNN or Fox News to global involvement within weeks. Despite the substantial number of journalists and reporters covering the case, it was obvious that most of them relied on limited and erroneous information trickling from *The Bee*; thus, almost all of the first months' worth of news was cookie-cutter rehash with little or no investigative journalism. The only versions of Bob Woodward to be found were on Internet crime forums, Web logs, or among tabloid reporters who interviewed friends, and patronized local establishments to uncover peripheral and sometimes salacious material.

After the jury handed down the death penalty verdict to Scott Peterson yesterday afternoon, several of the jurors conducted a news conference where they described the deliberation process and their views of the trial in response to questions from media personnel. Last night on Fox News, MSNBC, CNN, and Court TV, the usual cadre of legal pundits opined on the death penalty and their impressions of the jury. This morning a number of news outlets published stories about the jurors' remarks and, despite the short lag between listening to the jurors and meeting their deadlines, the writers' articles are replete with misquotes, omitted context, deliberate misinterpretation, careless errors, and insidious editorial bias. Here are a few examples:

***San Francisco Chronicle*, Headline**: *Autopsy photos a reminder of brutal murders*

Cardosi [Juror #5 Foreperson] wanted to study the autopsy photos of Laci Peterson and her unborn son and the aerial shots of the Richmond shoreline, where their remains were found in April 2003. (Walsh)

Steve Cardosi did not ask for autopsy photos or aerial shots. In fact, he corrected one of the media representatives who questioned him about that at the news conference. Cardosi asked for photos of Laci and Connor's remains on the east shore and somberly explained his reasons for that. You would think Ms. Walsh would check her facts. She wasn't alone. The "autopsy photo" request was misreported at least a dozen times in today's online stories.

New York Daily News:

Exhausted from their six-month ordeal, jurors said they were struck by how cold Peterson appeared in the courtroom and said the only emotion they detected in him was anger. (Staff)

The only juror who expressed this opinion was Steve Cardosi.

Outside, a loud cheer went up after the jury's decision was announced. But unlike after Peterson's conviction, which sparked some dancing in the streets, this time the joy was short-lived.

According to people outside the courthouse, there was no loud cheer after the penalty verdict from the relatively small crowd, compared to November 12. In the *Daily News*, it's stylish to portray the crowd as a bloodthirsty lynch mob. To accurately describe them as subdued lacks the drama these writers feel compelled to infuse in an already overly theatrical event.

So yesterday, Cardosi asked to see the grisly autopsy photos of the victims and the photo taken of Laci at a Christmas party while her husband was with his mistress, Fresno masseuse Amber Frey.

This is the misstatement *du jour*, similar to the massive misreporting of the statement Diane Jackson gave to police about the three dark-skinned men in front of Peterson's house and on the driveway the morning of December 24, who were actually (and it was in a court document if anyone bothered to read it) across the street near the Medina house.

The New York Post:

Although double-crossed, Scott's one-time lover, Amber Frey, had tried to save her married boyfriend from a death sentence by saying she would be opposed to seeing him executed. (Breuer)

When did Amber Frey say this and to whom? Has hearsay from her garrulous and omnipresent father now become fact? Perhaps Howard Breuer should apply for a position with Geragos & Geragos.

The Modesto Bee:

> *Cardosi, a Half Moon Bay resident who is a firefighter and paramedic, said defense attorneys Geragos and Pat Harris relied on "smoke and mirrors." Geragos caught much criticism from legal analysts for promising too much in his opening statement June 2 and delivering too little during the trial.*

This is worse than a quote out of context; it's not even Cardosi's quote. This misstatement originated when, during the press conference, true-crime author Aphrodite Jones asked the jurors, "We sat through the trial with all of you. Was there ever a turning point? I think the smoke and mirrors of Mark Geragos was enthralling to all of us. Then, after Justin was let go, things seemed to be going Scott Peterson's way."

Steve Cardosi's response to that was rather poetic: "As far as smoke and mirrors, if there are enough mirrors, pretty soon you see your own reflection."

> *"It's easy to pick on Geragos," said Robert Talbot, a University of San Francisco law professor. But, he called Geragos's effort "marvelous" and his penalty-phase summation "excellent. I'm surprised that none of the jurors bought them."*

I'm not.

Richard Cole on *Larry King Live*

> *That immediately after the verdict was read, Mark Geragos leaned over and said something to Scott Peterson. Obviously, we don't have any idea what it was, and Scott smiled a little ruefully. And that was cited later during the jury news conference by juror 7, who as we all know now, is Richelle Nice of East Palo Alto. And she said that was one of the things that lead her to conclude the death penalty was appropriate was the lack of emotion and the way he didn't react the way she felt a man normally should under the circumstances. I thought it was a very illuminating piece in how this jury was thinking and how they perceived Scott.*

Cole, a stalwart Peterson apologist, persists in his attempts to undermine the prosecution, the Modesto police, Karen Servas, the Rocha family, and now the jurors. What Cole hopes to achieve from his toxic tirades remains a mystery, unless his target audience is really Mark Geragos, and he entertains ambitions to parlay his fallacious ignominy into a public relations position with Geragos's firm. Only time will tell.

San Jose Mercury-News **Headline: Callous behavior a key factor, jurors say**

While Peterson's "callous" (and arrogant, perverse, obtuse, self-centered, and often reckless) behavior was contemptible and did not endear him to the jurors, it was not the "key factor" in his conviction or sentence. The implication that Peterson was condemned because he acted like a 14-karat jerk is shortchanging the jurors' thoughtful consideration of a six-month presentation of facts in this trial and the substantive evidence that affected their verdicts, such as the computer research, the secret boat, the "lost wife" story, his purchases and preparations for his "fishing trip," the location where Laci and Connor washed ashore; his repeated, inexplicable deceptions to his mother, Laci's family and the police, and his lies to the media. Legally, the jury can regard his lies as demonstrative of his guilt.

The Reporter: (Vacaville, CA)

> *Longtime Fairfield criminal defense attorney Leonard Oldwin said he didn't agree with the jury's death penalty decision, but it wasn't a surprise.*
>
> *"I expected it. It was a death-qualified jury, and people seem to enjoy vengeance," Oldwin said. "Our society today does not surprise me anymore."*

Of the array of emotions the jurors expressed last night, the sense of "vengeance" was not among them. To ascribe a vigilante mentality to these jurors is nothing more than a petulant fantasy. However, it's what we have come expect from outspoken criminal defense attorneys; they seem to orbit their own galaxies.

CHAPTER 13: THE UNDERWATER SEARCH FOR LACI PETERSON

THE REST OF THE STORY

It was January 6, 2003, almost two weeks after Laci Peterson's disappearance. Early in the morning, Scott Peterson rented a red Honda and drove to the Berkeley Marina to observe the San Mateo County diving team. When, after a few minutes, he was confident that they were looking in the wrong location, he returned to Modesto. That night, he exchanged several phone calls with Amber Frey wherein she confronted him about his missing wife.

Sergeant Tim Helton of the Modesto Police Department, assigned with the tactical patrol unit responsible for organizing the ground searches, contacted Gene Ralston, a renowned expert in underwater search and rescue operations, to enlist his assistance in the search for Laci Peterson in the San Francisco Bay and in selected local fresh waterways. By this time, Detective Craig Grogan had already compiled his list of 41 reasons why searches would primarily focus on the Bay and instructed Sergeant Ronald Cloward to employ whatever resources and expertise available to facilitate this objective. Ron Cloward spoke to Ralston later in the day to confirm his availability and that of his specialized side scan sonar equipment. The price was right: the Ralstons freely volunteered their services and asked only for reimbursement of their expenses.

Gene Ralston was born in Payette, Idaho, a small town near the Oregon border where the average temperature in August is only 74 degrees. Ralston studied Biology at Idaho College and earned his masters degree in Zoology at the University of Nevada in Reno. Between 1970-78, he was employed as a water quality specialist for the Idaho Department of Environment, and in 1978, he co-founded with his wife, Sandra, their company, Ralston & Associates, a biology and environmental consulting firm. Ralston's scientific projects led to a sideline in hydrographic surveying where the physical properties of rivers, reservoirs and other bodies of water are measured for mapping nautical charts.

Various types of equipment are used in hydrographic surveys, including a device called "side scan sonar." In 1999, Ralston began to implement and customize this technology to search for drowning victims.

The side scan sonar system's transducer is housed in a towfish, which is towed through the water 10 to 20 feet above the bottom. The reflected acoustic returns are processed into an image similar to an aerial photograph, which is viewed real-time on a computer monitor in the towing vessel. Typically, the side scan sonar searches a swath 60 to 120 feet wide at about two miles per hour, although other ranges can be used depending upon the size of the object being sought. ~ Ralston & Associates' Web site

Several teams in the underwater investigation in the Laci Peterson case used side scan sonar. In fact, sonar located a suspicious object near the old Berkeley Pier on January 10, and volunteer divers from four surrounding counties eventually discovered it to be an old ship anchor in the cloudy depth of about 27 feet. After the rumors of a body being found blazed like a wildfire through the media and press, this was a pretty embarrassing event for the 90 people involved in the operation.

Despite reports to the contrary, the Modesto police were not the first to leak information in January about the "find." A few overzealous volunteer search and rescue divers who were in the Berkeley marina area on a training exercise told the gathering media that they were "100 percent sure" they had found a body, although an expert who viewed the sonar image before they dove on it told them it was definitely *not* a body.

The Ralstons arrived in Modesto on January 13, the same day Peterson terminated his lease for the Tradecorp warehouse and office suite where the European-based company sold and housed fertilizer products. Within a few days, Tradecorp mysteriously and suddenly curtailed its business presence in California. The evening of January 13, Peterson received a confrontational phone call from Sharon Rocha, who interrogated him about his activities after she last spoke to Laci at 8:30 pm on December 23.

The Ralstons met in what was called the "war room" at the Modesto police station with about a dozen personnel involved in the search. Their initial task was to search beneath four bridges in fresh water lakes and reservoirs in the area. One of the investigator's theories was that Laci's body was deposited from a bridge into deep water.

Lake Tulloch in Tuolumne County was the first waterway the Ralstons searched. The road crossing the bridge leads to a golf course with which Peterson was familiar. A water dog, trained to find human remains in water, had alerted under the bridge before they arrived. They found a suspicious object with sonar that appeared to be the size of a large, filled garbage bag, similar to a leaf bag. When the divers recovered the bag, they opened it to find animal remains that resembled a butchered deer. This story was testified to, with derisive remarks by Geragos, at Peterson's trial. Ordinarily, a well-trained dog will not alert to animal remains. This was just one of many mistakes various dogs would make in the Peterson investigation.

From there, the Ralstons headed north to a bridge spanning New Melones Lake where, purportedly, other water dogs had alerted. They found what appeared to be another large plastic bag with something in it that was buoyant but anchored to the bottom. Unfortunately, it was more than 300 feet deep, which precluded a dive on the object with the on-hand equipment. That night, Ralston reviewed some images from a previous search he had conducted for the FBI near the same bridge over New Melones for an alleged Russian Mafia victim. The Russian Mafia in California was known for using concrete and chicken wire to sink its assassination victims. He found a similar image to those of that day's search in his files and discounted the new discovery's being Laci. Their find was reported to the FBI, and whatever further investigation resulted did not involve the Ralstons or the Modesto police.

Ralston's first search of the San Francisco Bay occurred on January 18th, the day Peterson announced he was going to Los Angeles to open a search center and right around the time that the Modesto police informed the Rochas about Peterson's affair with Amber Frey. While in the area, the Ralstons recovered a drowning victim in the Millerton Reservoir in San Joaquin and hit the San Luis Reservoir for a day. When Ralston arrived at the Bay, he asked the detectives, "Where do you want us to search?" The Bay, a nearly 500-square-mile estuary, was a huge area to cover. Cloward decided to have them start at the Berkeley marina, moving north toward the buoy on the west end of Brooks Island near the end of the jetty. A random search proved futile.

By then, the police had discovered the red paint scratches on Peterson's boat and determined he may have bumped or tied off to an even-numbered channel marker during his "fishing trip." (Even-numbered channel markers or buoys are painted red; odd-numbered are painted green.) Ralston made a few passes around channel marker four (which is not a buoy), and later, when reviewing the images from the sonar, he noticed an object near the channel marker that had two bright, reflective spots on one end. Next to the block-like shadows was an object that was determined by the sonar scale to be 65 inches long. He reported the results of his image review to Cloward, who sent other teams back to look for the objects. It

314

wasn't until Ralston returned in March and placed a marker near the object to guide the divers that they found and recovered two solid concrete anchors with thin, metal straps that had corroded and opened. If the anchors were tied to anything at one time, they had been released.

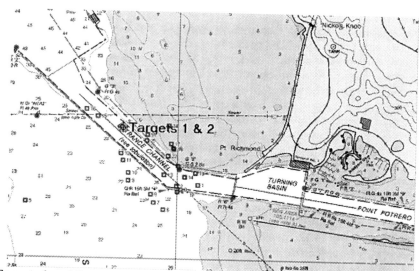

Targets 1 and 2

When the Ralstons returned to the Bay in March, they were given a list of GPS coordinates where water dogs had alerted in the area of the Richmond entrance channel, west of channel marker four and south of channel marker three. Some of the information used to narrow down the search areas of the Bay included culled results of Peterson's online research that indicated he had clicked on maps of deep water in the channel - more than one of the maps admitted into evidence showed the exact spot where he put Laci - and on areas where water dogs alerted to the possibility of a submerged human body. At least four different dogs were used in separate runs, deployed one dog at a time, in order for them to be "blind," or not influenced by another dog or handler. Ralston established a grid of parallel lines covering an area due west of Point Richmond.

The anchors discovered in the water at marker four, 12-inch square concrete blocks that appeared to have been cured in a box, were markedly different from the one found on Peterson's boat. Possibly because of their lack of evidentiary value or for other mysterious reasons to which we are not privy, the anchors were tossed back into the Bay.

At least one Modesto police officer was almost always on board Ralston's boat, the *Sandy Jean*, during the searches, to assist as well as to keep an official record (logs and charts of which were admitted into evidence) and to provide "secure" communications. Occasionally, the media intercepted the "secure"

315

communications, and a story would run in the press that Ridenour or Wasden would later refute.

From witness testimony at trial (i.e., Cloward, Armendariz, Grogan), it is evident that a significant number of the subsequent searches from May to September 2003 were focused on retrieving the two square anchors and any Peterson may have used. The search teams were definitely often looking in the wrong places, and it is entirely possible that by then, the anchors were buried in silt. The difficulty in finding an eight- or 12-inch block (or skull), or any object of that shape in the Bay, is that a lot of things look like rocks or blocks on sonar, and the weather and water conditions have to be suitable for searching and diving. It cannot be overstated that the Bay is a volatile body of water, somewhat like a combination shallow lake and small ocean: stirred up by wind, current changes, sudden storms, and tidal action. These treacherous conditions played havoc with the equipment, the divers, and the stability of the remote-operated viewer (ROV) used to transmit high-resolution images to the search teams.

Sonar resolution varies with the frequency used, depending on the application. Frequency is directly proportionate to resolution, but inversely proportionate to range; therefore, if you were searching for the *Edmund Fitzgerald*, you would use a much lower frequency, such as 1 kHz with a range of several kilometers. If you were searching for a toaster, you would need at least a 600 kHz frequency and decrease your range to 20 meters or less. Higher-resolution sonar is also more sensitive to water conditions and motion. The quality of sonar equipment varies as well, where the consistent "Cadillac" of technology is produced by Marine Sonic Systems.

The FBI, one of many law enforcement organizations involved in the search, has a Marine Sonic System, but it did not bring sonar to the Bay, because its operators had not been properly trained in its use at the time. The FBI provided divers, boats, and other expertise, particularly in the realm of potential fraud, money laundering, and import and export activities. Tradecorp's sudden disappearance from California may have been precipitated by federal inquiries, or the principals merely wanted to sever their relationship with Peterson because of the scandalous nature of the circumstances.

Late in the day on March 12, Ralston spotted a suspicious oblong object in the channel that was later designated "Target 2." The first image of Target 2 was exactly what Ralston was expecting Laci's body to look like if it were wrapped like a "package." Ron Cloward and other detectives were also expecting the body to be wrapped in tarp or plastic and submerged with weights. Because of rough weather and water conditions, the team decided to return the next day to take a closer look. On March 13, Ron Cloward was on board the *Sandy Jean* when Ralston lowered the towfish to the 40-foot depth near the middle of the Richmond entrance channel to relocate Target 2. There was always the risk that passing ships could dislodge or catch an object on the soft, dredged bottom and move it miles away. In addition, the shipping channel axis is 132/312, synchronous to the tidal current direction. The stronger ebb (outbound) tide could carry an object directly down the channel into the channel formed by the jetty extending west from Brooks Island. The current would then carry it east to the Point Portrero turn, then straight to the East Bay coastline. In other words, any object not sufficiently dense, weighted down, or snagged by a ship's propeller would eventually surface and wash ashore at Richmond or Pt. Isabel.

Ralston guided the towfish in the area where he had spotted Target 2 the day before and came across another object that also resembled a body, but more so. They designated this new find as "Target 1." The ROV was lowered and images of a head, neck, shoulders and most of the back of a prone person were outlined on the amber screen. Cloward had to film the video using his video camera pointed at the monitor, because one of the crew had brought the wrong cable to link the camera directly to the ROV. On the screen, they could see the body was covered in crabs, with no visible clothing on the torso, but streams of light-colored fabric floated vertically like noodles above the lower portion. When Laci's body washed ashore a month later, her cream-colored pants would be found in shreds.

Once again, as if by cruel cosmic intervention, the wicked Bay kicked up more turbulent conditions, and the divers were unable to pursue a recovery that afternoon. Target 2 was never relocated by the ROV, and the consensus between Ralston and the investigators was that it was evidence from the murder that

Peterson had wrapped in a tarp and sunk along with Laci the night he (theoretically) launched from Richmond Point to reach the deep water of the channel and returned to Modesto before 5 am. Because of this sighting, we now know Peterson took two trips to the Bay, since it would have been logistically impossible for him to have launched from the Berkeley Marina at 1:00 pm on December 24, motored to the entrance channel four miles away, and be back in time to make a cell phone call relayed from a tower in Berkeley at 2:15 pm.

A few questions come to mind:

- Why didn't the rescue team recover Laci's body? What happened to Targets 1 and 2 when the team returned in late March?
- Why didn't the prosecutors introduce the sonar images into evidence in the trial?
- Why didn't prosecutors propose a two-trip theory when it had cell phone records proving Peterson made no calls between 8:37 pm on December 23 and 10:08 am December 24 when he checked his voicemail, along with sonar images from the Richmond entrance channel showing Laci intact?

Geragos had not likely seen the sonar or ROV images in the 40,000 pages of discovery material he received early in the case, when he perpetrated the satanic cult theory and leaked the conditions of Laci's body as having been intentionally dismembered. It's obvious why he did not float that theory a year later in court, since he knew that the People could refute that fiction with some stunning evidence. That may also be why he didn't introduce testimony about the lost anchors to embarrass the Modesto police, although police incompetence and corruption were subjects near and dear to his defense.

On March 14, the day after Ralston sighted Target 1, that most on board believed was very possibly Laci's body in 40 feet of water in the middle of the Richmond entrance channel, the team returned to the area to attempt to relocate Targets 1 and 2 in order for divers to recover the finds. A number of natural and unnatural snafus thwarted its efforts. After repeated attempts with positioning, the ROV could not locate either object because of heavy currents and poor visibility. The divers went down into the black, cloudy depth and crawled around on their hands and knees, blindly groping in the mud for any solid object.

One of the divers even argued that what they had seen on the ROV video could have been a dead seal; however, a seal (with so much body fat) would have been floating, and seals don't have a clear outline of a human neck and shoulders, nor do they wear clothing. One of the detectives speculated that the noodle-like streamers were actually vegetation, but no such botanical organism grows at the bottom of the Bay, and certainly not on remains.

The operation was temporarily suspended that afternoon, and the Ralstons went back to Modesto to meet with several detectives to discuss what they had found and to formulate a recovery plan. At least 10 people were in the meeting, and Cloward shared the plan with about 15 others who were involved in the searches. They mentioned the film of the monitor taken with the video camera that showed some horizontal bars across the center portion, but the shredded pants could be seen quite clearly. During the meeting, Ralston opined that if Targets 1 and 2 were both bodies, one of them was not Laci. A detective suggested that Target 2 was Connor, but Ralston argued that the "package" was too large to be a baby. Toward the end of the meeting, Sharon Rocha arrived unaware of the potential find. She met Ralston and his wife and asked to see their boat and equipment that was in the police department's parking compound.

Ralston returned to the Bay on March 16, 17, 18 and 19, and on each trip he was frustrated by bad weather, rough, churning water and technical challenges maintaining the temperamental ROV in line. Sonar images during this period showed that both targets were still there. Incidentally, when Ralston first found Target 1, he contacted a team of commercial divers he knew from Tracy, California (yes, that Tracy) that was more experienced in demanding, unpredictable water conditions. Because of other commitments, the replacement divers were unavailable for 10 days. By the time they arrived at the Bay on March 25, both targets had disappeared. Even the surface of the muddy bay floor had changed.

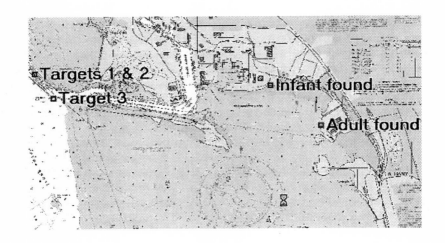

To the investigators on the case, the sonar images of Target 1 were very controversial. Ralston was told to send copies of the images to two other "experts," including a representative of Marine Sonic, who were skeptical that the image was of a human body and demanded to see the video of the ROV for confirmation; yet, these "second and third opinions" were never shown the video. The ROV has a limited view, and the video screen was filled with about two-thirds of the subject's back. They were able to carefully rotate the ROV to display the back of her head, her neck and shoulders, but did not see any anchors because the field of view was so small and was taken up by the body. Additional anchors (besides Target 3) never showed up on the sonar, but that was also the case with four homicide victims Ralston recovered in New Melones who were weighted down with several 45-pound barbells. Nonetheless, when Laci's remains were found with the shredded pants and marine damage, Ralston and Cloward agreed that the body they spotted in March matched too closely to be a coincidence.

How did Targets 1 and 2 move from the shipping channel, and what path did Laci, and eventually Connor, take to end up on the rocky east shore, only a mile from Brooks Island? Large ships that pass through the area where she was originally sighted have as little as three or four feet of clearance from the bottom. It was likely that any number of large-hulled ships or tankers could have passed directly over her, stirring up the area to cause one or more weighted (and decomposing) appendages to disarticulate. Based on further investigation, not all of the weights came off at the same time. Losing one or two weights could have enabled the currents and tidal action to move her along the bottom, assisted by other ship traffic creating wakes and propulsion.

In fact, Ralston found a seven-inch-wide drag mark on the sea bottom just east of the Point Portrero turn (the elbow at the east end of the shipping channel), several hundred feet from the bend, that made a very sharp turn almost coming back upon itself. Nothing could have made a groove like that except something being moved by the tide. The tide changes direction every six hours and had reversed the object's direction back into the shipping channel. The drag mark could be plotted in a straight line directly to where Laci was ultimately found. The sonar software is capable of measuring the size (width and height) of an object that, in this case, matched the eight-by-seven-inch tapered anchor found on Peterson's boat, and many images of this drag mark were recorded. Ralston covered the area between the channel and the Point Portrero turn as many times as weather and manpower permitted.

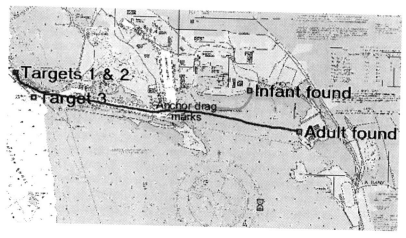

Meanwhile, Dr. Ralph Cheng was consulted, without knowledge of the sonar sighting in March, to determine, based on where Laci and Connor were found, where their bodies were originally submerged. Cheng had devised a mathematical model of the San Francisco Bay using "Lagrangian particle" movement. A particle is said to be Lagrangian when it moves as though it is an element of fluid. Cheng's original Power Point presentation (prior to the recovery of the bodies in April) predicted that if Laci's body had been sunk near Brooks Island, she would have surfaced near Angel Island, several miles southwest of where she was found. Needless to say, both of his conclusions before and after the bodies were found were erroneous.

A human body does not move as an element of fluid. If a significant portion of the remains is above water, the wind will also affect where it eventually travels, and depending upon the length of time she was floating, she could have zigzagged in response to the tide changes. Other experts disagreed with Cheng as well and surmised that comparing the point in the channel where Target 1 was found to the points on the east shore where Laci and Connor ended up is similar to the angle from the Golden Gate Bridge to the point on the south Berkeley shore where several jumpers' bodies were recovered. With the known water patterns, it could have been scientifically extrapolated that Target 1 would have landed where Laci's body was recovered.

Cheng appeared credible and professional in court, but to conclude with any certainty that Laci's body was sunk southwest of Brooks Island in shallow water was easily refuted by mathematics and physics. Unless you know within one hour when a body comes to the surface, Cheng's model is useless. In fact, running the model 24 to 48 times with different hours and days would yield widely different results. The first thing Cheng asked the detectives was, "When did she surface?" Someone guessed a time and they built their strategy upon insufficient data, not unlike ace defense witness, Dr. March, determining Connor's conception date based on the date of a positive pregnancy test. Fortunately for the prosecution, nobody on the jury was a hydrologist, marine biologist, or scuba diver.

I speculate that the prosecution did not have enough facts to support a two-trip theory and had to place Laci closer to Brooks Island in order for a one-trip scenario to work within the timeline, and because Peterson admitted to trolling in the shallows along the island on December 24. Cheng's model wasn't completely off, because where the baby and Laci probably separated was close to where he testified to her original location. The DAs and Geragos knew better, but neither side was willing to produce the sonar images for quite different reasons.

Although Target 1 was found about four miles from Pt. Isabel, the distance is not that far, considering the current can move at two to four knots, and in a month could easily move a body with a remaining weight or two along the east end of the channel (where the drag mark was located in 35 feet of water), at which point Laci's body surfaced, separating from the baby due to a decrease in hydrostatic pressure and maceration of the fundus, and buoy the last two miles to shore. Pressure increases one atmosphere every 33 feet of depth. There would have been two positive atmospheres of pressure at 40 feet (the depth of the shipping channel). That would compress the gases of a body to less than one half of what the volume would be at the surface. This phenomenon helped to keep the body submerged along with the probable weights attached. Conversely, as an object rises to the surface, the gases expand to twice the volume. If the body were fragile and could not contain the gases, it would burst. Based on the drag marks, the body appeared to have been caught in the turn for some time. With each passing ship, the last anchors (and appendages) finally dislodged, while outbound ships, which tend to bring the power up once they have made the turn, further agitated the waters.

There was a strong southwest wind the night before Connor's body was found. Since he was in much better condition, he floated higher and was more vulnerable to the wind and wave movement that carried him a mile north to the marsh in Richmond. The ebb current would have carried Laci's remains, floating lower in the water, more easterly. According to a story from an April 16 edition of KRON, a possible sighting of Laci was reported on April 12:

"We've had calls from passersby," says sergeant Danny Lopez. "They had seen a body floating last Sunday [April 12]. Between our boat going on the scene within 20 minutes and commencing the search, we searched for two hours and we were unable to locate the person."

Then there was this infamous (and erroneous) story:

Excerpts from the Oakland Tribune, April 27, 2003:

"Cops' big secret in Laci's death Sonar experts located body in Bay in March" by William Brand
...investigators say they had found her watery grave through side- scan sonar that penetrated the inky darkness in a Chevron shipping channel.

Modesto Police Chief Roy Wasden confirmed investigators believe they found the body as early as mid-March, but could not retrieve it. "The scan sonar that penetrated the inky darkness inside a Chevron shipping waves came up and we couldn't go down. I can't tell you the frustration we felt," Wasden said.

"This sonar is the best way to see stuff underwater," Ralston said. "In San Francisco Bay, because of all the silt, you've got zero visibility on the bottom.
At the range we're looking at, I've seen things as small as a half-gallon can, a small coffee can. The bottom varies; there are some rocky areas and lots of smooth, mud bottom. Some places the floor is reticulated -- like the surface of the moon -- there are little pockmarks."

Ralston said he's prepared to help again. "We're optimistic we'll be able to find the rest," he said. "I only hope we can get there before the killer hires someone to go out. You know, money talks."

Ralston's comment was extemporaneous and regrettable. At the time of the find, he felt that if someone from the Peterson camp believed that the searchers had found Laci, he had the means to hire someone to recover the body and move it to prevent her discovery. That possibility was not unreasonable, since under ideal circumstances (flat high tide and no current), a hired crew could have successfully achieved this mission. However, in retrospect, the actual weather and water conditions were so challenging in March, and with the constant presence of searchers during tolerable periods, it is very unlikely that anyone ("real killers," mercenary divers, or legitimate personnel) could have recovered the body

Reviewing the scant portion of the trial record that relates to the sonar results and the dog evidence, based on what we now know about the targets sighted in March, it is interesting to observe how both Distaso and Geragos deliberately circumvented this information. The Peterson case was subjected to an avalanche of amateur speculation before, during, and after the trial; thus, it may be a refreshing and novel concept to include some professional speculation from people who were actually involved in the investigation, as opposed to that of uninformed media pundits, rampant hearsay and specious allegations from "sources close to the defense," and the worthless opinions of a dismissed juror who spent a total of 13 days at the trial.

Tenuous Testimony

Ronald Cloward:

Distaso mentions in one of his questions to Ron Cloward that the investigators did not have a National Oceanic and Atmospheric Administration chart of the Bay. In fact, there was one on the wall of the "war room" as early as January 2003. The NOAA chart should have been admitted as an exhibit, enlarged to an eight-by-10-foot poster. By not taking the jury to the Bay or giving it any more geographical data than the minimum necessary to promote a one-trip theory, the prosecution (and the defense by tacit agreement) removed the Richmond entrance channel from the equation.

In reviewing Ron Cloward's testimony, I noticed that the chronological presentation of the searches skips over the March sightings, as noted in the following excerpts from Geragos's cross-examination (emphasis in italics mine):

Q: And that's listed on your sheet here as well, where there is a notation that the Ralstons were there?

A. On January 24th, correct.

Q. Okay. Now, on that search, what the -- what was happening was [this] diagram up there. This diagram appears to look like the surface of the water out there with the boat, and then the sea floor. And is that a fairly accurate representation of what was going on there with the Ralstons?

A. That's what their equipment would essentially do, yes.

Q. Okay. Now, on the 24th of January when you did the search with the Ralstons, it looks like the search extended to the Bay, in the San Francisco North Bay, and that the target area of the search included the *Richmond Turning Basin,* Brooks Island area, and the Berkeley Marina; is that correct?

A. Is that Detective Owens's report?

Q. Yeah.

A. I'm going to probably have to *defer you then to Detective Owens,* because I really don't feel comfortable testifying what he -- testifying what he said we searched that day.

Q. Were you out there that day?

A. Yes, I was.

Q. Is it a fair statement that you covered quite a bit of ground that day?

A. We covered quite a bit of ground every day.

Q. Now, the 24th when you were out there, the -- specifically what kind of a search were you doing then, do you remember?

A. We had the Ralstons. We had the Ralstons out there. We were doing side scan sonar. But, again, *I would have to look at Detective Owens' report* to see exactly what other equipment. And I would feel more comfortable if you asked him.

Q. I'd be happy to do that. But your memory is that, as you were out there covering quite a bit of territory, that includes the marina, Brooks Island, and in the Bay, correct?

A. I believe so. But, again, I would have to *refer you to him.*

Q. And is it a fair statement you didn't find anything?

A. No, there wasn't anything we found that day, *as far as the investigation of the search.*

Q. March 2nd -- what was your last day, by the way, that you had indicated?

THE COURT: I think he said March 29th.

MR. GERAGOS: Is it March 29th?

THE WITNESS: March 29th was the last day I was out there, yes.

MR. GERAGOS: Okay. And how many more searches between March 2nd and the 29th did you request?

A. One, two, three, four, five, six, seven, eight.

Q. And if I could just run through them. Out of those searches you had side sonars, [sic] correct?

A. Correct.

Q. You had boat -- you had boats out there, correct?

A. Correct.

Q. You had both platform boats and other style boats, correct?

A. Correct.

Q. You had dogs out there, correct?

A. Correct.

Q. And divers; is that correct?

A. Yes.

Q. Okay. And the searches up until the 29th, as you indicated that you were in charge of, all met with negative results for producing *anything of any evidentiary value*; is that correct?

A. Correct.

Q. The -- just so that I understand, the platform boat, was that used specifically so that you could use that ROV device?

A. Yes.

Q. And why was that -- why did you need a platform boat?

A. Well, it's -- Tuolumne County works off of their platform boat with that equipment, and the ROV is very easy to operate off of it as well, but it's not designed for the San Francisco Bay, as we found out.

MR. GERAGOS: May I have just one moment, your Honor?

THE COURT: Yes. (Pause in proceedings)

MR. GERAGOS: Q. I'm sorry, I didn't mean to jump around, but there was one area I just didn't ask you about. Goes back to your -- to the daily log reports, which looks like page four of six on 12/30 of 2000 and 2. Read the yellow highlighted areas.

A. (Witness reading) Okay.

Q. Okay. On the 30th, when we had spoken before, you were actively looking for or *following up any leads as to this van*; is that correct?

A: Yes.

Typical of Geragos's cross-examination, he asks a series of reiterative or unrelated questions to confuse the witness and bore the jury, and then abruptly changes the subject from platform boats (irrelevant) to leads about the vans in the

325

neighborhood. His phrasing of "producing anything of evidentiary value" is interesting. Notice he didn't directly ask Cloward if the searchers found anything during the March period, but rather states for the witness that what was sighted did not produce anything of evidentiary value. Cloward could have responded truthfully with a "no."

Armendariz:

A: [Re: May 16 and onward what agencies were involved] And it's page six of seven, drawn up by Detective Hendee. And he lists the various agencies that were involved, which were consisting of, but were not limited to, the U.S. Coast Guard, San Mateo Sheriff's Team, San Luis Obispo Sheriff's Department, Berkeley PD, Contra Costa Sheriff's Department, San Francisco Police Department, Richmond Police Department, East Bay Regional Park Police Department.

There is no mention of the Ralstons, although they were involved. There appeared to be a deliberate omission of the Ralstons' activities after March, bolstered by misreported media stories that intimated that the Ralstons had had a falling out with the Modesto police. This was not true. In fact, the Ralstons received an award at a ceremony conducted by the Modesto Police Department on May 16 and continued to search in the area of the anchor drag marks in May. Ralston discussed the idea of back tracking from the channel as the starting point and working inward to search for the missing objects, and Chief Wasden gave him *carte blanche*. However, those actually in charge of the investigation insisted that the searches focus on the shallow waters southwest of Brooks Island.

Hendee:

Cross-examination from Geragos:

Q: [did Marine Technologies offer to] give a second opinion on what Ralston had found, correct? Or what Ralston had already done in terms of the side scan images?
A: That was not the reason for contacting him at that point.
Q: Hadn't you previously said that they were aware, or that you were aware of that company offering to give - Sonic Tech offering to give a second opinion on some of these images?
A: I was under the impression they were willing at first to come and help us out in the search. When I called the company, then I spoke to the VP who said, well, he was under the impression that they might be willing to review images for us.

It appears from this line of questioning that Geragos was aware of the images that were sent to John DeMille (from Marine Sonic) and another "expert" to review. He fails to follow up with any questions about the "anchors overboard!" debacle or the inability for the teams to recover Targets 1 and 2, reports of which were included in the discovery. Perhaps he chose to let sleeping dogs lie.

Doggie Theory Voodoo

According to the professional opinion of someone involved in search and rescue for over 20 years, the only dog evidence admitted to trial was dubious at best. Laci was never at the Berkeley Marina; if Trimble was actually following Laci's scent, it was residual from Peterson's jacket or the boat cover he probably shook off on the pier and crumpled up in his usual fastidious manner, and shoved in the hollow between the bench seats when he went to park the truck. What else is the dog going to do when it gets to the end of the pier with nothing but water ahead? Stop, turn around, and look at its handler in frustration. Ms. Anderson, in good faith, may have misinterpreted this gesture as an alert.

Since admitting any dog-related evidence, according to California code, requires corroboration by other facts, the water dog hits (graphically represented by red squares on the chart in Part II) should have been admissible, since the sonar "finds" as well as the ROV video confirmation were sufficient corroboration. However, the prosecution decided not to argue the water dog results in either of the two 402 hearings on the canine matters.

Frequently Asked Questions: An Interview with Gene Ralston

Q: What were the "discrete deposits" Dr. Peterson described (in the preliminary hearing) on Laci's tattered clothing?

A: Concretions can form underwater with no exposure to the air. Magnesium nodules are mined as a source of almost pure magnesium. Quite often, concretions or deposits form as the result of biological activity and respiration (expelling CO_2), which causes a localized chemical imbalance causing a precipitate to form. It happens more often in salt water due to the higher concentration of minerals. If an object were subject to alternate wetting and drying, the deposits would be uniform over the surface exposed and not in discrete stones.

Q: Were divers searching for the anchors after the preliminary hearing?

A: Contra Costa County asked a commercial dive operation to assist in searching for the anchors. There were also various "training runs" in areas where the former underwater investigation had taken place, ostensibly to search for evidence.

Q: From where did Scott Peterson launch to get to the Richmond entrance channel, and how long would it take to get there? (Estimate a three-hour round-trip from Modesto.)

A: One of two possible venues: Richmond Yacht Harbor or Brickyard Cove. The Harbor has a secluded ramp next to the fuel dock. From there, he could motor to the channel in less than 20 minutes, dump the body and the package of evidence, and return to the ramp. Total mission time: four hours.

Q: How did he dispose of the body from the boat?

A: He could have rolled her over the bow with a tarp under her to catch any leakage.

Q: How do you think he killed her? (Obviously not in a bloody way.)

A: Most likely he suffocated her with a pillow and rolled up any blankets, towels, pillow case, rug, clothing or other material in a tarp or plastic (Target 2).

327

He may have used the blue tarp found in January in the water near Caesar Chavez Park to wrap her in to take her to the Bay. During the process of tying the weights to her just before dropping her, the blue tarp blew off and floated away in the darkness. That is why he had to go back during the daylight to look for it. Cadaver dogs alerted on the tarp and continued to be attracted to it, even after it was stowed in a compartment on board the police boat.

Q: What happened to the tarp they pulled out of the water in early January?

A: It probably was related, but why it was not introduced we may never know.

Q: Is there any way Peterson could have done this in one trip from Berkeley at 1:00 pm to 2:15 pm?

A: No. He would not have been so stupid as to take her to the Bay in broad daylight. The second trip was to look for the tarp he lost during the night and to make sure nothing had surfaced.

Q: What is the story on the chicken wire, and why was it an issue?

A: Early in the investigation, detectives found chicken wire in Peterson's truck, and they thought he might have used it in sinking the body, similar to the Russian Mafia. That theory complicated the work, because it required examining any object that looked like it might be "packaged" that way. Instead of just looking for the typical image of a drowned person having a torso, arms and legs, anything that size (60 inches) or a "fat cigar" shape was suspect.

Q: Why, knowing about the drag marks (that someone thought were made by a sailboat keel), did searchers not look along that path, after the bodies surfaced, for the rest of the anchors and remains?

A: There was a lot of pressure from certain detectives to continue searching in the area Dr. Cheng plotted after the fact.

If there was any "tunnel vision" by cops in this case, it existed with regard to the underwater search, and not with the justifiable focus on Peterson.

CHAPTER 14: THE SENTENCING

FEBRUARY 25, 2005
SENTENCING DELAYED – AGAIN

In San Mateo County court today, Judge Al Delucchi granted the Peterson defense yet another postponement of the formal sentencing to March 16, which was originally scheduled for February 25 (today), then pushed back to March 11. Delucchi warned the defense that he would grant no more delays, and that he was sealing until March 9 the defense 120-plus-page motion filed today until the People have an opportunity to respond. According to news reports (that we have learned to take with a shaker of salt), one of the arguments in Geragos's motion accuses prosecutors of not adhering to discovery rules in the trial. Additionally, the defense team is asking for a new trial, or that the verdict be set aside, among undoubtedly other futile requests, considering its length.

Never without his supply of slimy red herrings, Geragos's favorite lackey, Michael Cardoza, told KTVU reporters that the defense was in possession of an audio tape from a phone call exchange between two brothers, one in jail (supposedly a state facility, but it's not specified), and one on the outside, that would exonerate Peterson. Amazing! (ding) In the motion, Geragos accuses the People of failing to disclose in discovery the alleged tape. How the prosecutors came by this evidence (if it exists) remains to be revealed.

One of the brothers had heard that people had burglarized Laci and Scott's house [and] that Laci had surprised them and that there were words between the burglars and Laci and then it went from there.

There was no burglary at the Peterson house prior to Laci's disappearance. The only burglary I know of is when Kim McGregor broke in and had a little party. As usual, the defense is perpetrating fiction for publicity and attention, and this story will prove to have no more exculpatory value than the dark-skinned men in the tan van, the satanic cult, a Croton watch pawn shop ticket, a homeless convoy to the Albany Bulb, or any of Geragos's other proffered poppycock.

During Court TV's broadcast regarding the hearing today, Kimberly Guilfoyle-Newsom asked prosecutor Dave Harris when was the "turning point" in the trial? Dave Harris's response reflects the crux of my analysis:

It's almost like there was two trials. There was a trial in the courtroom, and there was a trial outside of the courtroom. The turning point might have come for the trial outside of the courtroom. But, inside we had a plan, we followed that plan, and I don't think there was anything that just made, as the jurors have said afterwards in some of their statements; it was all of the pieces. So right from the beginning to the very end it was all of the pieces that made that for them. There wasn't a single turning point where they all of a sudden went "okay I'm changing my mind today."

The media still don't get it. During the trial they were so caught up in their spin, titillation, gossip, personal agendas, commercial interests, competition for

329

ratings, and other irrelevant agendas that they forgot to watch the trial. It was as though a bunch of high school friends met at the football game and watched a few plays and the halftime show, but socialized through the rest of it, only to glance at the final score on the way out of the stadium. It was a long and sometimes boring trial, however, from my vantage point, there were two trials taking place: the sensationalized media accounts that bore little resemblance to actual events, and the real trial.

The reality is that Peterson will be in San Quentin in time to celebrate Easter and the two-year anniversary of the discovery of Laci and Connor's remains on the east shore of the San Francisco Bay. I only hope the irony is not entirely lost on him.

MARCH 14, 2005
THREE SIDES OF THE STORY

Today, the San Mateo County Superior Court press information site finally published the defense's *Motion for New Trial* and the People's *Opposition to Motion for New Trial* in the continuous saga of the case of California v Peterson. The motions are available on other Web sites, so rather than excerpting major portions for analysis, I will summarize the points and authorities presenting the defense side, the prosecutor side, and my side.

Peterson moves for a new trial on the following grounds, most of the points of which already exist in motions that were denied in previous hearings.

- Newly discovered evidence not disclosed by the prosecution in discovery.
- Denial of a second change of venue and separate juries for the guilt and penalty phases.
- The Court erred removing the first two jurors (Falconer and Jackson) and not declaring a mistrial
- Misdirection of the jury on legal issues – specifically, the jury instructions to deliberate second-degree murder and not include manslaughter, and instructing on "flight" as consciousness of guilt.
- Receipt by the jury of evidence out of court. (The boat "experiment")
- Denying the defense's boat demonstration video.
- Erroneous admission of wiretap evidence.
- Erroneous admission of phone calls between defendant and Amber Frey.
- Erroneous admission of dog evidence.
- Erroneous admission of defendant's purchase of "adult programming."
- Insufficient evidence to support the jury's verdict of guilt.

Does this feel like déjà vu all over again? It should. The Court has already ruled on nine of the 11 grounds reiterated in Geragos's motion in various 402 (evidentiary) hearings, *in camera* hearings, and public hearings. That doesn't stop him from forcing the People and the Court to suffer yet another tedious reading exercise searching for any new arguments, case law, relevant empirical support, or enlightenment. At the risk of further redundancy, I will attempt to limit my analysis to fresh material from each side.

Newly Discovered Evidence

An alleged conversation between Adam and Shawn Tenbrink about the burglary at the Medina house was not newly discovered, nor was it evidence. According to the defense, the prosecution produced a letter some time in the fall of 2004 from Adam Tenbrink. After further investigation, the defense learned that a recorded phone call existed between Adam and his brother regarding Steven Todd's mention of Laci Peterson witnessing his and Pearce's burglary of the Medina house. The defense contends this "evidence" justifies a new trial because it is "newly discovered," not cumulative to evidence already presented, and could not have been discovered earlier using "reasonable diligence."

I guess it depends on your definition of "reasonable diligence." According to the People:

The evidence was not newly discovered. As set forth above, it was provided to the defense five months prior to the preliminary hearing and over one year before opening statements. Even if we were to assume for the sake of argument that the prosecution had a duty to point out everything that might be beneficial to the defense (which the prosecution does not concede), the defendant has failed, because he cannot show the "materiality" of the statement.

We know from testimony that did occur in the trial that Karen Servas had returned the dog to the yard at 10:18 am, before the Medinas left for their holiday trip at 10:30 am. Therefore, unless there was evidence to show that Laci walked across the street during the burglary (which actually took place in the early morning hours of December 26), this triple hearsay is without probative or exonerating merit.

Denial of a Second Change of Venue

Geragos attempts an encore performance of "Change of Venue - The Thing That Would Not Die!" When the curtain opens, he finds the auditorium empty. Everyone has gone home. After obtaining his first change of venue from Stanislaus County to San Mateo County, Geragos moved to change the venue to L.A. County halfway through voir dire. When the motion was denied, he dusted off the flag and raised it again in his motion to set aside the verdict in November. When nobody saluted, he took it to the court of appeals. Rebuffed for the third time, he took it to the Supreme Court. Smacked down yet again, he recycles the faded, tattered banner for his final curtain call. This is a perfect example of insanity: doing the same thing over and over and expecting a different result. The greater insanity is that somebody is actually paying for this. Apparently, this perennial motion has the half-life of a nuclear isotope.

Improper Juror Dismissals

The defense argues that the removal of Falconer and Jackson (both jurors #5) "was an abuse of discretion." With regard to the judge's use of the word, "cancer" to describe the toxic effect of the dismissed jurors, Geragos quips, "Metaphor is no substitute for legal grounds," as he waxes poetic with colorful language such as "surgical zeal." Then, in a dialogue between him and Delucchi, Geragos has the incredible gall to say, "Look, we're letting hearsay trump testimony?"

You may recall that in cross-examination Geragos conducted during the trial (touted as "brilliant" by his legal peers), he elicited hearsay as a substitute for his client's testimony and to impeach the Modesto police. Virtually his entire case-in-chief was constructed from a flimsy frame of innuendo, illusion, assumption, and conjecture. Hearsay would have been an improvement.

In the People's rebuttal to the juror removals, David Harris characterizes the defense's complaints as "taking liberty with the facts," "creating a claim out of whole cloth," selectively quoting the transcripts, taking remarks out of context, and hatching a "mysterious conspiracy." In the prism of a potential issue for appeal, the juror dismissals will be moot because the appellate court will defer to the trial judge. Besides, three other jurors corroborated Falconer's misconduct, and Jackson refused to continue deliberating, which legally disqualified him.

MARCH 16, 2005
HOW DO YOU KILL A DEAD MAN?

> *The evil of this world is committed by the spiritual fat cats...the self-righteous who think they are without sin because they are unwilling to suffer the discomfort of significant self-examination. It is out of their failure to put themselves on trial that their evil arises. They are...remarkably greedy people.* ~ Scott Peck

In the formal sentencing hearing held today, the victims' family members gave impact statements directed at the convicted murderer, their son-in-law. Among the unflattering words used to describe Peterson included empty shell, soulless, hateful, delusional, cowardly, selfish, arrogant, and stupid; all appropriate and fitting and reflect the core evil of Scott Peterson's pathology. True to form, he waived his opportunity to speak to those present, words that he knew would instantly appear in publications around the globe. The investigation and ultimate trial were an inconvenience, a "waste of time," a farce to Peterson, because he is and will remain incapable of admitting his crimes. This isn't an intellectual incapacity, but a completely conscious absence of guilt.

> *Those who have crossed over the line are characterized by their absolute refusal to tolerate the sense of their own sinfulness.*

Peterson's indifference is the antipathy of love. The depraved nature of his glib affect confounds us with its perversity. His roles of tempter, thief, deceiver, and destroyer created chaos and immeasurable loss, yet he hides behind his image of perfection and innocence as his parents lash out at his accusers with sputtering fury. In order to escape their guilt, their behavior only serves to demonstrate a spiritual void.

Although Laci's family must yield to the cruel reality that they will never see her or her unborn baby in this lifetime, they emerge victorious in love. Without the ability to love, Peterson is already as good as dead.

DAY OF RECKONING

Image carved from brittle shale,
You look across the bay at the stone fortress of shame and secrets
where thousands before you,
from narrow lives of neglect and scarcity,
surrendered their search for meaning in fear and blood,
their once pounding, flashing thoughts replaced by
gray smears of random memories,
enclosed in the echoing walls of their living death.

In the yard muscled inmates suspend from chin up bars
as though to suspend time and prolong the sun
before being shut back in black boxes.
Many would have leaped through flames
to save the life you threw away;
thrilled to brush off the charred edges and cherish it
like a perfect pearl.

Savoring salty breezes along the Pacific coastal highway
you let luscious slices of tenderloin melt in your mouth,
chased with heady red wine,
and the crisp smoke of fine cigars.
The smell of spring grass on the rolling hills of Morro Bay,
the impossible brightness of the morning sun on the mountain snow,
the soft, tiny fingers of a baby boy
and the warm, loving gaze of a brown-eyed girl,
replaced by the muffled thud of your black heart,
its hollow, rotted pit a stone thrown into the bay.

Loretta Dillon
March 16, 2005

ACKNOWLEDGMENTS

This book would not have been possible without the assistance, resources and generosity of many individuals, but especially Gene Ralston, Paula Gustafson, Robin C., Harriet Van Epps, Dianne Patrizzi, Lynda and Natalie, Karen, Rose, Cindy W., John F., Mary B., Donna G., Kate, Cassie, and Jim Cypher.

REFERENCES

- *California Criminal Law Procedure and Practice*, Sixth and Seventh Editions, Continuing Education of the Bar, Oakland California, 2003, 2004.

- Peck, M. Scott, *People of the Lie*, New York, Simon & Schuster, 1983.

- McGinniss, Joe, *Fatal Vision*, New York, Putnam, 1983.

- Vaknin, Samuel, *Malignant Self Love – Narcissism Revisited*, Narcissus Publishers, 2005 (Formerly an E-book, copyright 2000.)

- Lasch, Christopher, *Culture of Narcissism: American Life in an Age of Diminishing Expectations*, W.W. Norton & Co., 1991.

- Douglas, John, *The Anatomy of Motive*, Pocket, 2000.

- Bledsoe, Jerry, *Bitter Blood*, Dutton Adult, 1988.

- Staff, West (Editor), *California Penal Code 2004*, West Group, Annotated edition, 2003.

Printed in the United States
66942LVS00006B/56